THE BAHAMAS FLY-FISHING GUIDE

THE BAHAMAS FLY-FISHING GUIDE

Stephen Vletas and Kim Vletas

THE LYONS PRESS

10   9   8   7   6   5   4   3   2   1

Printed in Canada

Library of Congress Cataloging-in-Publication Data

Vletas, Stephen.
    The Bahamas fly-fishing guide / Stephen Vletas and Kim Vletas.
        p.   cm.
    Includes index.
    ISBN 1–55821–961–7 (pbk.)
    1. Fly fishing—Bahamas Guidebooks.   2. Bahamas Guidebooks.
I. Vletas, Kim.   II. Title.
SH578.B3V59   1999
799.1'66463—dc21   99–37556
                                                                           CIP

Contents

Acknowledgments

Most of the research that went into this project could not have been accomplished without the tremendous support of the people on the Out Islands—lodge owners, operators, and their staffs, fishing guides, taxi drivers, restaurant and service personnel, and everyone else who took the time to make us feel welcome over the years. They are the reason we were able to complete this book. In particular, our many friends on Andros and Abaco are responsible for us thinking of the Bahamas as our second home. Guides such as Charlie Neymour (who was our first guide in 1988), Andy Smith, Simon Bain, Barry Neymour, and O'Donald Macintosh have been great fishing companions over the years, and have been instrumental in our ongoing efforts to explore and better understand the fisheries. Thanks to everyone at Tranquility Hill Lodge, including Ivan and Dwain Neymour and Ray Mackey and Jannis Neymour, for creating the welcoming feeling anglers always remember, and want to return to.

We are also grateful to the many traveling anglers who took the time to relate their experiences to us. We appreciate the information, the stories, and the friendships that developed out of these conversations.

The Bahamas Ministry of Tourism provided assistance at all stages of this book. In particular, Sheena Newton pointed us in the right direction within the ministry. Lynville Johnson was a great source of guidance and information, and instrumental in helping us obtain original maps of all the islands. Nalini Bethel, Craig Woods, Benjamin Pratt, Earl Miller, and Kristal Bethel were all helpful in answering numerous questions. A special thanks goes to Judy Miller at Bahamasair for helping us with travel arrangements, which we often requested at the last minute. Donna McQueen on Andros, Rena Mae Symonette on Grand Bahama, and other tourism representatives provided additional assistance particular to their islands.

On the publishing side, we consider ourselves extremely fortunate to have worked with the people at Lyons Press, people who share our love of fly-fishing. Nick Lyons's encouragement and inspiration were invaluable in keeping us going when the project bogged down a couple of times. Tony Lyons supported the project from the beginning and gave us the green light to make it happen. We also extend thanks to Jay Cassell for his excellent editorial insights, and hard work in putting this manuscript into such great shape.

We are grateful to Angela Burton, and her extraordinary design skills, for taking raw maps and turning them into the distinctive and informative maps included in the book.

Many of the photos in this book came from our friend Brian O'Keefe, whose work always reminds us of the fact that fish never live in ugly places.

To our founding partners in Westbank Anglers, Reynolds and Bettie Pomeroy, for helping us turn fly-fishing into a way of life, and for making sure the business stays in one piece while we pursue our passion for travel. Also to our managing partners in each of the Westbank Anglers city locations: Cathie and David Coleman in Dallas, Andy Packmore and Debbie Thompson in Houston, and Chris Lemons and John Monroe in Charlotte. Also, to Mike Michalak at The Fly Shop, who set up our first trip to The Bahamas.

And to our families who supported us in our choice of a nontraditional career, and who never asked us when we were going to get real jobs.

Introduction

The idea for this book came from a traveling angler whom we ran into a number of years ago, while sitting at the bar in a fishing lodge on Andros. "Why isn't there more information on fly fishing in the Bahamas, a guide book or something?" he asked. It was a good question, one that has been repeated to us many times over the years by people gathering information for trips to saltwater destinations.

The light finally clicked on and we decided to write this book, with the following goals in mind. Number one, the book is designed to help anglers who have already arranged trips. Once you reach your destination you can use the maps to find lodges, restaurants, and fishing access points. You can use our tide suggestions to pick the best fishing times during a day. You can use our suggestions to pick a fishing guide, a restaurant, dive shop, or car rental agency, or to extend your vacation and stay at one of the locations we recommend.

Number two, the book is designed to assist anglers in the planning of a future trip. The information in this book will help you select the destination that is right for *you*, based on goals you set for your trip. Are you planning a hard-core fishing trip? Will non-anglers join your group? Are you looking for simple accommodations or a luxurious resort with a variety of amenities? Hopefully, the accuracy of the information will point you in the right direction, and help you set realistic expectations for your trip.

Ric Fogel

Authors Kim and Stephen Vletas

Number three, we want to make it easy for you to book your vacation, either by using a professional travel consultant, or by arranging the details yourself.

And for those of you who might be wavering, who may be thinking about going to the Bahamas for the first time; or, if you've been to the Bahamas before, and are looking for a different place there, we hope the book will be an enticement. We hope that somewhere we've written something that touches you, that makes you think, yep, I've got to go there. I've got to see that. I've got to try that. If we accomplish that, then we've achieved our goal, which is to give anglers something that can change their lives, like the Bahamas has changed ours.

Angling travel is by no means just about catching fish. As Yvon Chouinard of Patagonia has said about mountain climbing, "it is the process itself, the opportunity for striving, and becoming a better person." We know from experience that the planning and preparation process of a trip can be just as much fun as the trip, and in most cases, this process lasts longer than the trip itself.

So, whether you're a serious angler headed to the Bahamas for your tenth time, or planning a honeymoon trip where you may only fish for a few hours in a week, this book was written for you.

How to Use This Guide

O ne of the goals of this book is to make it as easy as possible for anglers to gather the information they need to plan a trip to the Bahamas. We recommend reading, or at least skimming through, the first three chapters before going on to the island chapters. They will give you an overall perspective of the Bahamas, one that will enable you to better evaluate the specific information in the island chapters.

Each island chapter is then broken down into the following sections:

Island Introduction—This section is an overview of the island, describing its location and geography, population, atmosphere and culture, adventure activity highlights, and travel tips specific to the island.

Around the Island—This section is a detailed tour of the island, with maps for reference. The tour is for boaters and land-based travelers. Specific information covers the structure of the fishery, fishing access points, boating routes and marinas, ferries and bridges, highways and roads, towns and settlements, lodges, restaurants, and sightseeing opportunities.

Fishing Highlights—Everything you need to know for a general understanding of the game-fish species, habitat, tides and food sources, including best tides for fishing, and specific tidal characteristics. The top game-fish species—bonefish, permit, tarpon, sharks, barracuda, and others—are discussed individually. We also discuss the best months to fish for each species, along with our favorite tackle and flies.

Optional Activities—If you're not fishing every day, you'll want to know what else there is to do. Diving, snorkeling, sea kayaking, windsurfing, sailing, ecotours, camping, wildlife observation, bicycling, golf, tennis, shopping, and other activities are available on the various islands.

Lodging and Services—This section is broken down into Featured Lodges, Additional Accommodations, and Services. This is where you will find specific descriptions of lodges, accommodations, food, service, amenities, suitability for anglers and/or nonanglers, vacation packages, and general pricing information.

Featured Lodges are our top recommendations on each island. What criteria did we use to make these recommendations? We combined our personal experiences with thousands of reports from fellow travelers, but these recommendations are subjective. The best way to put it is to say that these are places we would want to visit again soon.

These resorts and lodges range from properties with elegant accommodations and superior service, to simple, rustic destinations where a cold Kalik and a comfortable bed are all you need to enjoy your fishing vacation. They also cover the pricing spectrum from very expensive to great value.

The Additional Accommodations section contains locations that are suitable, or not, depending on the type of vacation you want. We've had good experiences at many of them.

The Services section contains information on marinas, booking optional activities, car rentals, taxi services, restaurants, grocery stores, banks, clinics, and more.

New Developments—New or proposed resorts, lodges, and fishing grounds are being developed all the time. New guides and outfitters are promoting themselves every day. We assess these developments based on our experience and reports from fellow anglers.

A word on pricing: While we are reluctant to provide specific pricing for lodges, guides, and other services—as much depends on packages, time of season, options chosen, and so on—we did want to include a general guideline for anglers to begin their trip planning in the right direction. Our guidelines are as follows: $ indicates inexpensive pricing, $160 to $225* per day; $$ indicates moderate pricing, $225 to $380* per day; $$$ indicates expensive pricing, $380 to 475* per day, $$$$ indicates very expensive pricing, $475* and up per day.

Please be aware that all prices throughout the Bahamas are subject to change without notice: In fact, they change regularly on a seasonal basis. We believe traveling anglers will be best served by requesting specific lodge and activity pricing for specific dates of travel. This is the only way to obtain accurate prices for the trip you want. The same is true for air travel. Current pricing is available directly from lodges, guides and airlines, or through a professional travel consultant.

Generally, the winter season runs from mid-December through April. The summer season is the rest of the year. Winter rates are normally the most expensive, with bargains sometimes available in summer and fall. Different lodges have different policies about charging for maid service, air-conditioning, and service, and these policies change often. Meals can be included or not included. Optional activities can be included or not.

Rates at bonefishing lodges are usually consistent throughout a given season. The bonefishing season runs from October through May, with some lodges open in June and July. Most bonefishing lodges work on a package plan per person (double basis) that includes accommodations, meals, guided fishing, and Bahamian taxes. If you are traveling solo, you will pay the entire guided fishing expense yourself, which means your rate will be significantly higher than the double rate. Your reward is that your guide will devote his full attention to you, and all the fishing time on the deck will be yours.

---

*These pricing guidelines are based on double occupancy rates per person and include accommodations, all meals, and guided fishing. Other expenses may also be included, such as Bahamian taxes and airport transfers.

1

The Bahamas—An Overview

Fly-fishing is a way of life. The experience goes well beyond casting a fly, hooking a fish, landing, and releasing it. The total experience includes relaxation, beautiful settings, camaraderie, good food and drink, and a diversity of angling challenges. That's why fly anglers spend so much time and money traveling to different locales. We're all looking for that *experience* . . . the one that will lighten our souls forever.

The islands of the Bahamas are an idyllic source of fishing opportunities for those pursuing that experience. Fishing has long been an integral part of the Bahamian lifestyle and culture, in no small part due to its physical makeup and geography. The Spaniards called the region "Baja Mar," the Shallow Sea, and it is one of the most magnificent saltwater fisheries in the world.

Practically speaking, the fishing opportunities are divided into two distinct types. The most popular is the shallow water flats fishery. The blue-water, or offshore, fishery has been recognized as sen-

Fishing for bonefish on a tranquil Long Island flat.

Brian O'Keefe

1

sational by conventional anglers for years, and is now becoming more popular with fly anglers.

Flats species consist of the big three: bonefish, tarpon, and permit; plus barracuda, lemon and blacktip sharks, jack crevalle, mutton snapper, and mangrove snapper. Fishing over inshore reefs, cubera snappers, grouper, a variety of jacks, barracuda, numerous species of sharks, sierra and king mackerel, and amberjack become the most abundant game fish.

Many of the best flats regions have been well known for years, while others have become famous recently. Bimini maintains a tradition of great flats fishing for big bonefish. Look in the International Game Fish Association (IGFA) record books and you'll see that Bimini is well represented. On the East End of Grand Bahama, Deepwater Cay has established itself as one of the premiere bonefishing lodges in the world. The North and Middle Bights of Andros have been visited by the rich and famous since the 1930s. The Bang Bang Club, on Pot Cay in the North Bight, was one of the first bonefishing clubs. On Abaco, Nettie Symonette, owner of Different of Abaco Bonefishing Lodge, recently created a road and channel access to the Marls, one of the most extensive mangrove flats in the world. Club Peace & Plenty, a tradition on Great Exuma, has expanded in recent years, and now offers traveling anglers access to areas that have rarely been fished.

In spite of numerous well-known locations, many flats regions and fisheries in the Bahamas are relatively unknown or unexplored. One example is the Andros tarpon fishery, which is one of the best in the world; few anglers have fished it.

Another example is the permit fishery that extends from Chub Cay in the Berry Islands to north Andros and the Joulter's Cays, then on around past Red Bay to Williams Island. While few areas in the Bahamas have any concentrations of permit, this region has concentrations of *huge* permit. Then you have Crooked Island and Acklins Island, which together compose one of the hottest new flats and offshore fisheries in the world. We expect to see a gold rush of anglers fishing this region in the near future.

Bahamian blue-water species include blue and white marlin, sailfish, a variety of tuna, wahoo, and dolphin. Some of the more fished areas are Walker's Cay on north Abaco, Bimini, Nassau, and Fresh Creek on Andros, where the Tongue of the Ocean sweeps in against the flats and plummets to depths of six thousand feet. U.S. Naval buoys off the eastern shore of Andros are phenomenal dolphin and Allison tuna magnets.

Renowned billfish tournaments are a tradition. They include the Hemingway Championships out of Bimini, the Bahamas Billfish Championship Series, plus others out of Walker's Cay, Green Turtle Cay, Treasure Cay, Marsh Harbor, and George Town. The Bahamas Wahoo Championship Series is held throughout the islands, generating a spirit of lively competition throughout the winter months.

A quality that is foremost in our minds about the Bahamas is its tranquillity and charm, especially on the Out Islands. The fact is, there are really two Bahamas. One is the high-profile resort setting of Freeport and Nassau. The other consists of all the Out Islands, or Family Islands, where the residents are friendly and welcoming, and things rarely change.

Out Island residents make a habit of welcoming guests. Anything you need, no problem, mon. The simple truth is you don't need much—a comfortable room, good food, a cold Kalik, a place to hang out with friends and maybe tie some flies or rig

View of pool area at the old part of the Atlantis Hotel in Nassau.

some leaders. This is our favorite place in the world to relax and just live day to day. "Eat, fish, drink, sleep, eat, fish, drink, sleep," becomes the hypnotic mantra.

A phrase we often use is "how bad can it be in a place like this?" The settings of the Bahamas are sometimes stunning and dramatic, though more often the beauty is simple, subtle and soothing. Clear turquoise water, white sand beaches, lush mangrove cays, cool pine forests, the sound of the surf as it pours over a reef, along with the abundant bird and sea life, these are your constant companions.

While the people are laid-back, they also possess an old-fashioned sense of purpose. As tourism moves into the mainstream, new energy and enthusiasm are being focused on developing marinas and resorts. In spite of this, the way of life remains unchanged on the Out Islands. Work hard, honor your family, have pride in yourself, and be friendly, seems to be the motto. This way of life has persisted for generations. It is the essence of harmony that can seep into your soul and, along with the fishing, it can keep you coming back and back.

Andros guide and lodge owner Charlie Smith. Charlie's Haven is across the street from this shack.

A BRIEF HISTORY

Everyone knows Columbus sailed the ocean blue in 1492, but exactly where he landed first in the Bahamas is a matter of debate. Most people believe he landed on Guanahani, where a native culture had existed for years. Columbus then renamed the island San Salvador, which is Castilian for Holy Savior. The name the Spaniards gave the present-day Bahamian Islands, Baja Mar, Shallow Sea, is somewhat misleading. The islands are actually mountain plateaus that emerged from the Atlantic Ocean hundreds of thousands of years ago. These plateaus fostered an expanse of sea-strewn coral, which comprises the limestone base of the islands today.

The Lukku-Cairi, or island people, as they called themselves, were the first settlers. It is believed they wandered in boats from South America, through the Caribbean, to the Bahamas around the ninth century A.D. Historically, they are known as Arawaks, but they are usually referred to as Lucayans, a Spanish distortion of their name. Columbus mistakenly referred to the Lucayans as Indians because he believed he had landed in the East Indies when he walked ashore in the Bahamas.

The Spanish conquistadors followed Columbus in 1500 in search of gold and other riches. They initiated the first slave labor, kidnapping most of the Lucayans to work the gold mines and pearl beds of Cuba and other nearby islands. Enslavement and disease soon wiped out the Lucayans. And once slave labor was no longer available, the Spaniards sailed away, having never settled the islands, though they ruled them for more than a century.

Bahamian history moved into a new era in 1647 when Eleutheran Adventurers arrived from Bermuda. In pursuit of religious freedom, they formed the first British colony on the island of Eleuthera, and were soon followed by other English settlers. A prosperous agricultural economy developed on the island; it is still maintained today.

The geography of the islands attracted many well-known pirates, including Edward Teach, Henry Morgan, and Anne Bonney. Their primary operating method was to lure unsuspecting ships into the treacherous shallow waters, then attack and loot whatever treasure was on board.

Britain claimed the islands in 1670, but remained powerless against the pirate predators for almost fifty years. By 1700, lawless chaos reigned in Nassau. Edward Teach, the notorious Blackbeard, took Fort Nassau as his residence and harassed the British Royal Navy for years.

The British government actually contributed to the islands' pirating ways by sanctioning privateers. Privateers were essentially pirates who carried a license, a Letter of Marquee, which allowed them to loot and plunder legally. For the most part, these marauders were beneficial to British interests as they preyed on merchant ships of Britain's Spanish, French, and Portuguese enemies. When the opportunity arose, however, many privateers looted indiscriminately, often attacking the Crown's own ships.

In 1718, the British decided to put the pirates out of business forever. They appointed the successful privateer, Woodes Rogers, as Royal Governor of the colony. Rogers began his campaign by offering royal pardons to pirates who would cease their illegal activities. To make a point, however, Rogers did not offer these pardons to everyone. Instead, he pursued them to the death.

Among those pursued were Blackbeard, Roger Vane, and eight other notorious compatriots. Blackbeard and Vane escaped the initial attacks, Vane by burning a ship to cover his getaway.

Blackbeard was eventually killed off the coast of Virginia in June 1718. An outlaw to the end, he ignored the warnings of his allies and allowed the British ship,

Pearl, to trap his vessel near a sandbar. Blackbeard chose to fight rather than surrender. In the brutal hand-to-hand fight that followed, it is said that Blackbeard suffered five pistol ball and twenty cutlass wounds before succumbing.

Roger Vane was apprehended after his ship ran aground. He was then taken to Kingston, Jamaica, where he was tried, convicted, and hanged. The other eight pirates were hanged in Nassau from gallows standing on what is now the British Colonial Hotel's west beach. Having cleaned up the port city, Woodes Rogers moved into Fort Nassau and lived there until his death a few years later from mysterious causes.

Rogers' victory allowed the Bahamas to emerge as a recognized British colony, though privateering continued when it suited the Crown. Many Spanish ships loaded with treasure stolen from South and Central America were in turn plundered as they came through the islands on their way to Europe. Much of the treasure was lost and has not been recovered to this day.

The art of plundering was not left solely to pirates and privateers. Many people of the Abacos made their living by looting ships unfortunate enough to be wrecked off the islands, either by storm or by help from unscrupulous islanders swinging lanterns off the treacherous sandbars and reefs. This lucrative industry did not stop until the first lighthouse was built in 1836.

During the Revolutionary War, Spain sided with America and briefly regained control of the Bahamas in May 1782. A year later, under the Treaty of Versailles, the Bahamas once again became a British colony.

After Britain's defeat in the Revolutionary War, Southern Loyalists immigrated to the islands with their slaves to grow cotton under the protection of the British Crown. In 1838 the Crown abolished slavery, which put most cotton plantations out of business and caused a general decline in agriculture.

Turbulent times in America meant prosperity for the islands. During the Civil War years, the North established a naval blockade in an attempt to cripple the Confederacy. Bahamians amassed great wealth running Confederate cotton to English mills then sending military equipment back to the Confederates.

Tough times hit the Bahamas after the Civil War, and lasted until the Roaring Twenties and Prohibition, when rumrunners used the Bahamas as a base of operations. Cash again flowed into the islands, bringing prosperity to many residents. After the repeal of Prohibition, the economy stagnated.

The arrival of rich Americans on luxury yachts was a bright spot in the hard times of the 1930s. Families like the Mellons spent weeks and even months at various islands, contributing jobs and currency to the local economies. The Middle Bight area of Andros Island was a consistent beneficiary. The Mellons hired local guides from Moxey Town to take them bonefishing, which began a tradition of famous bonefishing guides in the Moxey family.

Still, it was not until World War II, when the United States and Great Britain used the islands for air and sea bases in the Atlantic, that general prosperity reemerged.

In the 1950s tourism was recognized as an industry, which changed priorities in the islands forever. The Hawksbill Creek Agreement, in 1955, laid the groundwork for the creation of Freeport/Lucaya to become the second largest city in the country.

When Cuba was closed to U.S. tourism after the Castro revolution in 1959, the Bahamas again benefited from nearby trouble. More and more Americans began traveling to the islands to enjoy the tropical atmosphere.

Great Britain granted the islands self-government in 1964, and changed the Bahamas status from colony to commonwealth in 1969. In 1973, the Commonwealth of the Bahamas became independent within the Commonwealth of Nations, but retained Queen Elizabeth II as constitutional head of state.

In 1992 the opposition Free National Movement won the general election, which ended twenty-five years of rule by the Progressive Liberal Party. In 1997, Prime Minister Hubert Ingraham and the FNM won a second term.

Prime Minister Ingraham's government has brought about many positive changes throughout the islands. The country encourages foreign investment, which has stimulated growth and improved tourism services in Nassau and Freeport. The formation of local government districts has focused attention on improving the quality of life in the Out Islands. New roads, plus better power and telephone service to the Out Islands, has raised the standard of living throughout the Bahamas.

CULTURAL NOTES

The roughly 275,000 people who live in the Bahamas are predominantly of West African descent, brought to the islands as slaves to work the cotton plantations. The majority of white residents of the Bahamas are descended from the Eleutheran Adventurers, or Loyalists, who emigrated from the southern United States.

Religion is an integral part of Bahamian life. Even the tiniest village has a church, which often is the center of community interaction. Music is another spiritual part of Bahamian life. African rhythms, Caribbean Calypso, and English folk songs meld into the unique Bahamian musical medium, the Goombay beat. The fast-tempoed *goombahhh* drumbeat can be traced back to the days of slavery and is used both for storytelling and dancing.

Junkanoo is a national festival in the Bahamas, the only place where it holds such an honor. The origin of the word Junkanoo is obscure. Some say it comes from the French "L'inconnu" (meaning the unknown), in reference to the masks worn by the paraders. Others contend the name derived from "John Canoe," the name of an African tribal chief who demanded the right to celebrate with his enslaved people.

It is believed that this festival began during the sixteenth or seventeenth century. Slaves were given a special holiday at Christmas when they could leave the plantations to be with their families. They spent the holiday celebrating with African dance, music, and costumes.

Today you can go down to Bay Street in Nassau during the early morning hours of Boxing Day, the day after Christmas, and you'll be bombarded with a cornucopia of color and sound. If you miss the Christmas celebration, Junkanoo parades are also held in conjunction with other special holidays such as Independence Day (July 10).

To find out more about Bahamian culture, contact the People-to-

One of the oldest churches on Long Island, in Clarence Town.

People program center at 242/326-5371 or 242/328-7810. This year-round Ministry of Tourism program gives visitors a genuine and informal view of Bahamian hospitality and culture.

BAHAMAS NATIONAL TRUST (BNT)

BNT is a nonprofit organization responsible for the preservation of Bahamian places of historic interest and natural beauty. The patron is HRH the Duke of Edinburgh.

The BNT, now over forty years old, administers more than 320,000 acres in twelve national parks and protected areas. One of BNT's most noteworthy accomplishments was the saving of the nearly extinct West Indian flamingo, which is the national bird of the Bahamas. Thanks to BNT efforts there are nearly 60,000 flamingos on Great Inagua. Ongoing projects include work to prevent the extinction of the Bahama parrot and the green turtle.

BNT maintains close relationships with important scientific organizations throughout the world, all with an eye on protecting the Bahamas' invaluable marine environment, which includes some of the most magnificent living reefs in the world. For anglers, this effort is a key reason the fisheries of the Bahamas remain in such pristine condition.

Donations, membership dues, a small annual government grant, and an endowment fund sustain BNT. Dues and fees paid by U.S. citizens in U.S. dollars to the Environmental Systems Protection Fund are tax deductible. Membership applications and additional information are available from the Bahamas National Trust, P.O. Box N-4105, Nassau, Bahamas; telephone: 242/393-1317 or 242/393-2848.

FOOD AND DRINK

Although most types of international food are available in the Bahamas, it would be a mistake to miss an opportunity to sample the local cuisine. No matter where you are, it's easy to find restaurants or lodges serving Bahamian specialties at reasonable prices.

Seafood is the staple of the Bahamas, and conch (pronounced konk) is a specialty. The firm, white, peach-fringed meat comes from a large ocean mollusk. Fresh uncooked conch is often served ceviche-style, cut into small pieces and marinated with lime juice and spices. Most commonly, conch is fried. Conch fritters, served with a rich sauce for dipping, and washed down with a cold Kalik beer, is our favorite apres fishing tradition. Conch is also steamed, used in soups, salads, and stews, or made into chowder.

The Bahamian rock lobster is a spiny variety without claws that is served broiled, minced, or used in salads. The lobster season runs from August 1 to March 31. Other delicacies include boiled or baked land crabs, which are usually caught on the back roads after dark or after a heavy rain.

Fresh fish also plays a major role in Bahamian cooking. A popular brunch is boiled fish served with grits. Stewed fish, made with celery, onions, tomatoes, and various spices, is another local specialty. Pigeon peas and rice, seasoned with spices, tomatoes, onions, and bacon, accompany many dishes. Andros Island has a population of wild boar, as do several other islands, so locals there eat a lot of pork. If you get the chance we highly recommend a meal of pork with peas and rice, or black beans and rice, accompanied by warm Johnny Cake bread.

Brian O'Keefe

*Conch and Kalik: An
island ritual!*

Peas figure prominently in an array of fragrant Bahamian soups. Pea soup with dumplings and salt beef is one of our favorites. A unique soup is called "the souse." The ingredients are water, onions, lime juice, celery, peppers, and meat. No thickeners are added. The meat added to the souse is often oxtail or pigs feet, giving the souse a delicious flavor that is new to most visitors. Remember that the cuisine of the Bahamas is rarely bland. If spicy food is a problem, be sure to mention this before ordering any local dishes.

For dessert our favorite island choice is Key lime pie. Chef Iyke Moore on Andros Island makes the best we've tasted anywhere.

Blended drinks are an art form in the Bahamas. Bartenders take pride in their own special recipes of rums and fruit juices. Be careful with these concoctions, as they usually possess a serious kick.

Kalik, the beer of the Bahamas, is light and wheaty. We don't drink any other beer while we're in the islands, though many imports are available.

The Bahamian refresher of choice is coconut water (not the heavier fattier coconut milk) blended with sweet milk and gin. Some of our guides spend hours on the flats singing the famous "Gin and Coconut Water" song to hold them over until we return to the lodge for the real thing.

GEOGRAPHY AND CLIMATE

The Bahamas are strategically located in the Western Hemisphere, at the crossroads of the Americas. The northernmost islands are only fifty miles from Florida, and the coral archipelago stretches south to the Caribbean Sea. Located along the Tropic of Cancer, the Bahamas are warmed by the waters of the Gulf Stream and cooled by southerly trade winds. Also called the Isles of June, the Bahamas tropical climate is one of the most pleasant in the world. The average year-round temperature is 77°F, with daily maximum and minimum temperatures differing by about 12°.

There are two distinct weather seasons in the Bahamas, winter and summer. Winter weather patterns generally begin in November, but can be postponed to as late as January. Winter begins with the first cold front, or norther, generated when normal easterly flows of water-tempered air are disturbed by continental high-pressure air. Cold fronts occur throughout winter, and usually begin with the wind veering to the south or southwest. Once the cold front arrives, winds usually shift quickly to the northwest, then north, and blow themselves out from the northeast. These winter cold fronts usually take two to four days to blow through, and winds range from twenty to thirty-five knots. In general, the more severe the weather in the United States, the colder and windier it becomes in the Bahamas. Once a cold front reaches Florida, it is only twelve hours away from the northern Bahamas.

The summer weather pattern usually begins by May, or after the last cold front. This pattern is governed by easterly flows of maritime air. Winds tend to blow from the eastern side of the compass, with southeast being predominant. Summer winds are usually light, in the five- to ten-knot range, and calm evenings are common. Cotton ball cumulus clouds mushroom most afternoons, and can turn into thunder and lightning storms. Heavy afternoon rains account for the bulk of rainfall throughout the islands, with June producing more rainfall than any other month. The main hurricane season is August and September, with July and October as shoulder hurricane months. Weather forecasts are available on the Internet at www.bahamas-on-line.com/bhw.html or at www.weather.com

ADVENTURE ACTIVITIES

This topic brings us back to our query, "how bad can it be in a place like this?" If you did nothing in the Bahamas except relax, eat, drink, and sleep, you would probably have a great vacation. If you never fished a minute, there would be plenty of activities to keep you busy.

If you like resorts, Nassau's Cable Beach and Paradise Island will make most people happy. The Atlantis Resort on Paradise Island is spectacular, combining a Las Vegas–style casino and show-room with a playground of water sports, a massive saltwater aquarium, and elegant guest accommodations. Nightclubs, world-class restaurants, tempting beaches, golf, tennis, and duty-free shopping are all available.

Visiting the aquarium at Atlantis is something we highly recommend, even if you just have a few hours to spend in Nassau. Bonefish, permit, tarpon, mutton and other snappers, sharks, barracuda, jacks, and a variety of exotic saltwater fish can be viewed from above or below the water's surface. From an angler's perspective, watching these gamefish is fascinating. We credit our recent jump in permit fishing success to observations made at this aquarium.

Boogey boarding on the beach at the Pink Sands Hotel, Harbour Island.

Freeport/Port Lucaya on Grand Bahama is considered the Bahamas' second city. The streets are clean, beautifully landscaped, and traffic is rarely congested. If you enjoy nightlife, this is our favorite place in the islands. Casinos, duty-free shopping, diving, snorkeling, golf, tennis, water sports and white sand beaches will keep non-anglers appeased.

There are a variety of deluxe accommodations, from hotels to condominiums, and many excellent restaurant choices. A new mega-resort and casino, the Lucayan Resort, features international convention facilities and the Bahama Reef golf course. Pelican Bay Bonefishing makes Freeport the best of all worlds. Located in the Port Lucaya Marina, Pelican Bay offers a quality fishing program on the northwest end of the island.

Forget the gambling, shopping, and lots of people, but keep all the other options, and you have Treasure Cay, Abaco. You can rent a house or condo on a secluded beach and fish the incoming tide on the leeward side of your favorite cay.

Wander around the Out Islands at your leisure. Take the mail boat along with the locals to one of the many remote ports. Travel is inexpensive, and you can get on and off wherever you choose. Be sure to take a casual attitude, though, because the mail boat schedule is subject to frequent changes.

How about *adventure* travel, the new buzz in the travel industry? Ecotourism is thriving in the Bahamas. Sea kayak through the Exuma Cays Land and Sea Park. Dive and snorkel over vivid living reefs, or explore underwater caverns and blue holes. Fish in places rarely visited. Camp out on cays without names, cooking fish freshly caught from the sea. Visit the national parks and bird sanctuaries, examine more than forty species of wild orchids, or dive along the six-thousand-foot wall of the Tongue of the Ocean.

Looking for a romantic getaway? The problem you'll have is deciding which intimate remote beachfront resort to choose. Some of our favorites include the Pink Sands Hotel on Harbour Island, Fernandez Bay Village on Cat Island, Cape Santa Maria Resort on Long Island, and the Bluff House on Green Turtle Cay, Abaco.

If photography is your pleasure, you'll have a hard time conserving film. Only your imagination will limit your activities in the Bahamas. Kim's favorite film for slides is Fuji Velvia or Sensia. Make sure to take a polarizing filter to bring out the blues and greens, and to get a clear shot of your bonefish swimming away after a gentle release.

Swimming pool at the Coral Sands Hotel, Harbour Island.

TRAVEL TIPS

The English language, friendly people, stable currency, and the acceptance of U.S. dollars combine to make travel to the Bahamas convenient and carefree. The Bahamian dollar is one-to-one with the U.S. dollar.

Bahamasair, American Eagle, US Airways, Delta, Comair, Continental, TWA, Laker Airways, and numerous smaller air carriers and charter companies offer flights daily from the United States. Air Canada, British Airways, Air Jamaica and others offer additional international service. We usually travel to the Bahamas through Atlanta, Orlando, West Palm Beach, or Ft. Lauderdale.

Nassau is the air hub for Bahamasair, with most flights from the states landing here, then funneling travelers on to the Out Islands. Smaller commercial carriers such as Gulfstream, Air Sunshine, Island Express, Lynx Air, plus numerous charter companies offer direct flights from Florida to many of the Out Islands. Clearing customs in Nassau or Freeport is relatively convenient at all hours, seven days a week. If you need to clear customs on one of the Out Islands outside of regular business hours, or on weekends, you need to arrange for customs officials to be present, and you will have to pay for this service.

Be aware that all services such as banks, customs ports, rental agencies, and fuel stations do not necessarily operate on American schedules, especially on the Out Islands. Normal banking hours in Nassau and Freeport are 9:30 A.M. to 3:00 P.M., with some banks open until 5:00 P.M. on Fridays. There are a few ATMs in Nassau and Freeport, but don't count on this convenience on any of the Out Islands. If you need to get some cash, rent a car, or buy a stamp, make sure you know the hours of operation for the services you need.

The same is true for hospitals and clinics. The quality of the government-run clinics is good, but you have to consider your location. If you're visiting a remote fishing or diving camp, how long will it take to reach a medical facility? It is your responsibility to know these things, especially if you have a preexisting condition.

Use common sense in how you pack, and in the type of luggage you use. Soft luggage is preferable to hard luggage, especially if you will be traveling in a small aircraft or by boat. Make sure your luggage is clearly marked for easy identification. Some anglers we know use bright orange or yellow tape on their luggage for this purpose. Pack so you can carry your own belongings. Be aware of where your luggage is

Bahamasair: your passport to fly-fishing paradise.

at all times, and double-check the transfer of your luggage whenever possible. Definitely take carry-on gear that never leaves your sight, so you can fish and/or brush your teeth no matter what happens to checked luggage.

We always carry on multipiece fly rods, several reels, flies, leaders, guide lanyards with tools, plus basic clothing, polarized sunglasses, insect repellent, sunscreen, prescription medicines, toiletries, and other essentials. If you travel with two-piece rods, we suggest you pack them in protective rod cases and check them, since all airlines, and especially smaller carriers, have become more restrictive in what they allow travelers to carry on. Anglers should use a travel checklist in preparing for any trip. Specific lists are available for specific destinations from professional booking agents, or you can use our list for all Bahamian travel located in Chapter Three of this book. Kim has added a number of items to our list especially for women, items rarely found on other lists.

CLOTHING

Casual summer clothing can be worn during the day any time of the year. We recommend comfortable and functional outdoor clothing from companies like Patagonia, Ex Officio, Royal Robbins, and others. These companies produce fashionable sportswear and fishing clothing that is attractive, lightweight, cool, easy-to-pack, and relatively maintenance-free. This type of clothing is easy to wash at night, and it will be dry by morning. A light jacket or sweater is recommended for cooler evenings and during cold fronts, especially from December to February. Raingear is essential, especially on the Out Islands. There are a number of upscale restaurants in Nassau and Freeport that require appropriate evening attire, which in some cases means a jacket for men.

While the Bahamas is a laid-back country, it is also relatively conservative, with a firm religious foundation. So how does this relate to clothing? It is inappropriate to walk through the streets of Nassau or Freeport in swim trunks or bikinis. The same is true for restaurants, shops, and casinos. This guideline especially applies to the Out Islands.

CUSTOMS REGULATIONS AND TAXES

It's best for U.S. citizens to have a passport for entry into the Bahamas, though an original birth certificate and valid photo ID are acceptable. British subjects and Canadian citizens may enter the Bahamas without passports for stays of up to three weeks. Stays of longer than that require a passport.

Upon entering the Bahamas, you must fill out and sign an immigration form. This form is usually supplied on board the commercial aircraft flying you into the Bahamas. If not, you can get the forms at the customs location upon arrival. You need to keep part of the form with your passport, and hand it back in when checking in for departure. An oral baggage declaration is required. This is usually a routine procedure, though customs officials can ask to inspect your luggage.

Each adult visitor is allowed fifty cigars (not Cuban if you are a U.S. citizen), two hundred cigarettes or one pound of tobacco, one quart of spirits, and a variety of personal effects, including radio/Walkman, bicycle, cameras, fishing gear, and so on. Upon departure, all visitors are required to pay a $15 departure tax (plus $3 security fee leaving Freeport), though children six years and under are exempt. This tax is normally paid at your commercial airline ticket counter when you check in. If you are flying back to the United States on a charter aircraft, this fee may or may not be included

Taxi Driver Doy Leadon waits for a fare at the Andros Town airport.

in your rate. Charter flight passengers are also subject to U.S. entry and/or departure fees. It is your responsibility to check on these fees and know what you owe.

Departures to the U.S. from Nassau and Freeport must go through U.S. Customs preclearance. U.S. visitors may take home $600 worth of duty-free merchandise. The next $1,000 is taxed at 10 percent. Gifts valued up to $50 may be mailed home duty-free. One liter of wine, liqueur, or liquor may be taken duty-free.

DRIVING

British rules apply! This means you drive on the left. Be especially careful at those roundabouts, and keep left. You can use your regular driver's license for up to three months, and you can also apply for an international driver's license. Pedestrians need to remember to look right before crossing streets. To be on the safe side, look everywhere.

ELECTRICITY

AC, 120 volts. We use all of our American appliances throughout the islands without a problem.

FISHING AND DIVING

The Bahamas is an environmentally friendly country. To protect the marine environment, spearfishing using scuba gear is illegal, and possession of spear guns in the islands of the Bahamas is illegal. Cruising boats must clear customs at the nearest port of entry before beginning any diving or fishing activities. A permit is required for visiting vessels to engage in sport fishing. The cost of a permit is $20 per trip or $150 per year for vessels on which not more than six reels will be used. Areas within national parks such as the Exuma Cays Land and Sea Park have strict rules against the taking of any natural resources. The Bahamas National Trust administers these parks. It is your responsibility to know where you are and what the laws are. For updated regulations you can visit the Ministry of Tourism's official Internet site at www.bahamas.com.

The International Bazaar entrance in Freeport.

SHOPPING

Nassau and Freeport are the shopping Meccas, though a number of colorful shops are sprinkled through the Out Island. Bay Street is Nassau's shopping haven, with designer stores from all over the world presenting their wares in enticing fashion. A huge straw market is part of the Bay Street frenzy, which really becomes wild when one of the giant cruise ships unloads a thousand passengers at one time.

In Freeport, the International Bazaar and Port Lucaya Marketplace are the main attractions. Both combine name-brand stores with local merchants and straw markets.

The better resorts and hotels have specialty boutiques and shops for gifts and tourist necessities. The real draws in the Bahamas are duty-free shopping and bargain prices on many luxury items such as fine perfumes and watches. Be aware that many stores are closed on Sunday.

SPRING BREAK SEASON

Spring break season normally runs from February 28 to mid-April. Plan ahead for any trip to the Bahamas during this period, as airline reservations can be extremely tight. Spring breakers normally stay in the bigger resorts on Nassau and in Freeport, so you may want to avoid these areas if you're looking for peace and quiet. The Out Islands remain tranquil, but you've got to make flight reservations as far in advance as possible.

TAXES AND TIPPING

This can be confusing, but here are the basics. A 10 percent government tax is added to all accommodations, and/or all room/meal packages. There is no tax charged on guided fishing rates. Many resorts will charge an additional energy tax and a maid service fee. Some resorts will add on a 15 percent service/gratuity charge. Take the time to ask what charges will be added on so you won't be unpleasantly surprised.

Tipping customs are the same as in the United States. Tip according to the quality of service you receive. Bellboys and porters usually receive $1 per bag, while other servers such as waiters and taxi drivers receive 15 percent. A professional flats fly-fishing guide normally receives $40 to $50 per day ($20 to $25 per angler based on two anglers per guide), and more if the guide is exceptional. Offshore boats with a captain and mate generally receive $60 to $80 per day given to the captain, and more if the experience was exceptional.

TIME ZONE

Eastern Standard Time is used throughout the islands of the Bahamas. From the first Sunday in April to the last Sunday in October, Eastern Daylight Time is followed, in accordance with U.S. daylight saving time.

OUT ISLAND AIRLINES

Commercial Airlines
Bahamasair—800/222-4262 or 305/593-1910, Fax 305/593-6246
Air Sunshine—800/327-8900 or 800/435-8900, Fax 954/359-8211
American Eagle—800/433-7300 or 787/749-1747
Continental/Gulfstream—800/231-0856 or 305/871-0727
Island Air Charters—800/444-9904 or 954/359-9942, Fax 954/760-9157
Lynx Air—888/596-9247 or 242/352-5778 or 954/491-7576, Fax 954/491-8361
US Airways Express—800/622-1015

Resort Charters
Deep Water Cay Club, Grand Bahama—954/359-0488, Fax 954/359-9488
Fernandez Bay Village, Cat Island—800/940-1905 or 954/474-4821,
    Fax 954/474-4864
Great Harbour Cay, Berry Islands—800/343-7256 or 954/921-9084,
    Fax 954/921-1044
Greenwood Beach Resort, Cat Island—242/342-3053
Hawk's Nest Club, Cat Island—242/357-7257
Riding Rock Inn, San Salvador—800/272-1492 or 954/359-8353, Fax 954/359-8254
Small Hope Bay Lodge, Andros—800/223-6961, Fax 242/368-2015
Stella Maris Resort, Long Island—800/426-0466 or 954/359-8236, Fax 954/359-8238

OUT ISLAND MAIL BOATS

Interisland mail boats run weekly to and from all major islands. The mail boats provide a leisurely way to cruise through the islands. One-way passage to just about anywhere costs around $35. Remember that these mail boats run on Bahamas time, which will not always coincide with your watch, or with the published timetables.

The following are the mail boat routes to/from Nassau:

MAIL BOAT NAME	Scheduled Stops
ABILIN	Long Island: Clarence Town.
BAHAMAS DAY BREAK II	Eleuthera: Rock Sound, Davis Harbour, South Eleuthera, Spanish Wells, Harbour Island, The Bluff.
BIMINI MACK	Cat Cay & Bimini
CAPT. MOXEY	South Andros: Kemp's Bay, Bluff, Long Bay Cays, Driggs Hill.
CHAMPION II	Abaco: Sandy Point, Moore's Island, Bullock's Harbour.
CURRENT PRIDE	Eleuthera: Current Island, Upper & Lower Bouge.
DEBORAH K II	Abaco: Marsh Harbour, Treasure Cay, Green Turtle Cay.
ELEUTHERA EXPRESS	Eleuthera: Governor's Harbour
EMMITT & CEPHAS	Ragged Island only.
GRAND MASTER	Exuma: George Town
HARLEY & CHARLEY	Eleuthera: Governor's Harbour, Hatchet Bay.
LADY D	Central Andros: Fresh Creek, Stafford Creek, Blanket Sound, Staniard Creek, Behring Point.
LADY FRANCIS	San Salvador: United States, Rum Cay, Cockburn Town; Exuma Cays: Staniel Cay, Black Point, Farmer's Cay, Barraterre.
LADY GLORIA	Andros: Mangrove Cay, Cargill Creek, Bowen Sound.
LADY MATHILDA	Mayaguana/Acklins: Abraham's Bay; Inagua/Crooked Island: Matthew Town.
LISA J II	North Andros: Nicholl's Town, Mastic Point, Morgan's Bluff.
MANGROVE CAY EXPRESS	Andros: Mangrove Cay, Lisbon Creek.
MARCELLA III	Grand Bahama: Freeport, High Rock, Eight Mile Rock, West End.
MIA DEAN	North Long Island: Salt Pond, Deadman's Cay, Seymour's.
NORTH CAT ISLAND SPECIAL NORTH & SOUTH	Authur's Town, Bennet's Harbour, Bluff, Bight.
SEA HAULER	South Cat Island: Smith Bay, Bight, Old Bight.
SPANISH ROSE	Spanish Wells only.

Check with the Dockmaster's office in Nassau for specific schedules, then be sure to reconfirm times the day of departure. Call 242/393-1064.

QUESTIONS THAT PEOPLE FREQUENTLY ASK US

1. *How far in advance should I book my trip?* Book as far in advance as you possibly can. Booking a year in advance is not too far for the better bonefishing lodges, and at least six months is recommended. Remember that April and May are the most popular bonefishing months. Also, if you plan on using frequent flier miles, booking six months ahead is minimum.

2. *How is the drinking water?* You can drink the water from the tap at the major resorts in Nassau and Freeport. Otherwise, each island is different and you should use caution. Andros Island has more fresh water that any Bahamian island, yet we always drink bottled water on Andros. We recommend drinking bottled water at all times, if for nothing else but the taste. As a doctor friend of our says, "Anytime you change your water, your system can get upset. Why take a chance on ruining your vacation?" Bottled drinking water is available on all the Out Islands.

3. *Are groceries and liquor available on the Out Islands?* This depends on the island, but all the islands rely on supply boats or aircraft. The smaller the settlement or the more remote a location, the less often it is resupplied. This includes some of the established fishing lodges. It is not uncommon for fresh fruit, produce, milk, or red meat to run low, or run out. At times, bottled water can run out. Red meat, milk, and eggs are also expensive items in general.

Our motto is simple: "When in doubt, stock up." If we're staying in a rented house, cottage, or whatever, we stock up right away, or as soon as we can, based on available supplies. We also establish a rapport with the local grocery people to find out the resupply days. It pays to be at the store when the boat arrives.

You need to find out ahead of time if liquor is available at local stores, so you can take your own if necessary. If you like particular brands of wine or liquor, we recommend that you take them with you. Kalik, the beer of the Bahamas, is available almost everywhere.

4. *How do payments work on the Out Islands? Are credit cards and traveler's checks okay?* Cash is always accepted and preferred. U.S. dollars are one-to-one with the Bahamian dollar, and both are accepted everywhere. Travelers' checks, credit cards and personal checks, when accepted, will often be charged a service fee of 2 percent to 5 percent per use. Many Out Island establishments do not accept credit cards, traveler's checks, or personal checks, period. Also, change may not be available for large bills, so be sure to have plenty of small bills. It is your responsibility to know what forms of payment are accepted at each location you visit. We recommend the use of a professional travel agent to make sure that none of these little details slip by. If you are booking on your own, make sure you know all payment and cancellation policies.

5. *Is medical care available?* Yes, but depending on where you are, it might take hours to reach a clinic or a doctor. National health care clinics in the Bahamas are good. In addition to larger facilities in Freeport and Nassau, the Ministry of Health operates more than one hundred clinics throughout the Out Islands. As in the U.S., the larger clinics offer more services than the smaller, remote clinics. When additional care is needed, patients are flown to Princess Margaret Hospital in Nassau. For very serious accidents and illnesses, Air Ambulance services can be called to evacuate people to West Palm Beach, Ft. Lauderdale, or Miami. You will be billed for this service, and rates are extremely high.

Prescription drugs are available in the larger towns and settlements, but supplies can be limited. You should take all necessary prescription medicines with you in your carry-on luggage.

You should always travel with your health insurance card or information. We recommend the purchase of trip cancellation insurance, which can also include trip health insurance. It is your responsibility to know what care is or is not available at any destination you visit.

6. *What about boat, car, golf cart, and other rentals?* All types of rentals are available in Nassau and Freeport. Limited rentals are available on the Out Islands. We recommend booking your rentals ahead of time, along with the rest of your trip. Booking rentals ahead of time is essential during the prime months, especially in places like

Treasure Cay or Elbow Cay, where boats, cars, and golf carts are limited in numbers. Car rentals are generally expensive, between $60 and $80 per day, though deals are available for rentals of a week or more.

7. *Should I bring my own fishing gear?* You should always take your own fly-fishing gear. Very few lodges or guides have equipment for clients to use, though the better guides will have backup gear if something happens to yours. Some lodges do have rental fly-fishing equipment. You should check on this in advance of your trip. Conventional fishing gear is more readily available, though we recommend taking your own if you have it. Most offshore fishing boats provide conventional fishing gear and lures. There is always an additional charge for bait.

8. *Should I take my own snorkeling and diving gear?* The better dive operations will have complete diving and snorkeling gear. You should confirm this before your trip and reserve this gear in advance however. We always take our own masks, snorkels, and fins. This way we are sure the gear fits comfortably, and we have the flexibility to use it whenever we choose.

9. *How is the nightlife, including restaurants?* Nightlife rocks in Nassau and Freeport. Everywhere else it is fairly sedate, though special parties and events are held throughout the Out Islands, most commonly on Friday and Saturday nights. As for restaurants, we suggest making reservations, or at least confirming hours of operation, in all cases. The better Out Island restaurants fill up during prime months, and others may or may not open unless they have reservations.

10. *Will my cellular phone operate in the Bahamas?* If you must take your phone, you will need to register it with the Bahamas Telecommunications Corporation. You can call them at 242/394-4000 or contact them by fax at 242/394-3573. After registering your phone, it should work in Nassau and Freeport, but cell service is limited or unavailable on most of the Out Islands.

11. *What about bugs?* Yep, lots of bugs live in the Bahamas. The islands with a lot of freshwater lakes, like Andros, have the most "doctor flies." These big green-headed flies draw blood when they bite. They mostly live around mangroves, so you'll be most susceptible when you're out fishing. Wearing long pants will protect you, especially when wading, as these bugs mostly like to bite legs and feet. Around lodges and on the beaches, mosquitoes and no-see-ums will be out when the wind is down, and in the evening and early morning. Avon Skin So Soft works against the no-see-ums, while regular DEET-enhanced repellent works against the mosquitoes. If the bugs really like you, wear a long-sleeve shirt, pants, and shoes with socks when you go out to dinner.

12. *How do I get tide information for the Out Islands?* Visit this book's Web site at www.bahamasflyfishingguide.com. We have specific tide information for every island. If you would like to purchase your own tide software, call Bluewater Books & Charts at 800/942-2583.

Recommended Internet Sites for the Bahamas

www.bahamasflyfishingguide.com The accompanying site for this book, which is updated on a continuous basis. News, new lodges, tide information and more. We encourage you to email us through this site with fishing reports and updates of your own.

www.bahamas.com The official site for the Bahamas Ministry of Tourism. This is a reliable means for obtaining additional updated information.

www.bahama-out-islands.com The official site for the Bahama Out Islands Promotion Board.

www.bahamasvg.com The Bahamas Vacation Guide is a good source of different information on resorts and services not necessarily found on other sites.

❦

Disclaimer: We are not promoting or endorsing any air or water carriers, just listing some of the ones we, our clients and friends have used. Select your carriers and methods of transportation at your own risk. We recommend that all travelers use a qualified professional travel agent. We also recommend the purchase of trip cancellation insurance, especially if you end up booking your own trip. If you book your own trip, and don't know how to obtain trip cancellation insurance forms, call 800/922-3474, and the forms will be mailed to you.

All boating references are for descriptive purposes only and are not intended for navigational purposes. Boating navigation throughout the Bahamas requires specific knowledge and experience, and the use of accepted navigational maps and charts. It is your responsibility to make all the preparations necessary for a safe boating trip.

2

Tips, Tactics, and Tackle

We have spent considerable time the past ten years pursuing our saltwater fly-fishing passion. Much of this time has been spent in the Bahamas, exploring, hosting groups of clients, working with lodges to improve services, and training guides on many of the islands.

Many hours have been spent talking with anglers over apres-fishing Kaliks or at dinner tables throughout the islands. As fly fishers, we all want to learn, to improve our skills, to gain an edge for that next day on the water. The following topics are the ones that have been brought up to us most through the years. We hope some of these ideas will be useful the next time you venture onto the flats.

FLATS FLY-FISHING FROM A POLED SKIFF

Wading is one thing, but everything is different when you're in a boat. That's true in a drift boat on a river, or in a flats boat on the salt. When it's your turn on the bow, make sure you and your guide are in sync. Guides will focus your attention on incoming fish by using clock positions and distances to the target. Good guides will add in clock directions for which way the fish is moving. Point your rod at a clock position, then ask your guide to direct you from there. The guide will say something like, "Go right, stop, a little more right, stop, forty feet, moving from eleven to twelve, cast now." Follow your guide's directions and you will catch fish even when you don't see them. If you have any questions about clock positions ask your guide right away. Fishing from a poled skiff is a team sport, and your team needs good communication.

Only strip off the amount of line you can cast accurately. Make a few casts so your guide can assess your ability, then have your guide call out the distances of each practice cast. This will help you get in tune with each other, and with true distances. Line handling is just as important as casting. Make some practice strips, varying between short, medium, and long strips, while working with your guide to understand what he means when he uses stripping instructions.

Make sure your fly line is stretched out, and in a position on the deck to avoid any obstructions when you shoot line or clear line. Pull at least a full rod's length of

Stephen with Andros guide Andy Smith, hooking a bonefish.

fly line out of the tiptop guide. Hold your tippet, just above the fly, in your noncasting hand. Now, assuming a nine-foot rod and nine-foot leader, you could make a simple roll cast and the distance would be about twenty-seven feet. Use this formula to help judge distances accurately.

You shouldn't need to false cast for anything under thirty feet. In general, make as few false casts as possible. Flats fish are usually on the move, and are often swimming toward you. You need to present your fly quickly and accurately, before the fish spooks off or changes directions. Your goal should be no more than one false cast for casts to fifty feet. For casts out to eighty feet, your goal should be no more than two false casts.

Once you make your presentation cast, you should follow your fly line to the water with your rod tip. This will help prevent slack from forming in your line, and will allow you to move your fly with your first strip. This is very important. The first strip needs to move your fly, as bonefish often eat a fly before the first strip. If it takes two or three strips to remove the slack, you won't be able to set the hook before the fish spits your fly.

Set the hook with your line hand first. Do this by making one long strip, as long as your reach allows, or until you feel a solid hookup. Don't trout set, which is setting by quickly raising your rod tip. Not only will you rarely hook a fish this way, but you will pull your fly completely out of the fish's feeding zone. If you miss the hook set with a line hand strip, the fly will still be in front of the fish, and chances are good the fish will eat the fly again.

If the fish doesn't eat your fly immediately after your presentation, let it sink to the fish's level, then begin a retrieve. The retrieve is used to attract the fish's attention. Learn to vary your retrieve based on the fish's behavior. More important, learn to *let the fish eat the fly.* Many people think they need to keep stripping once a fish charges their fly. This is a definite no! When the fish swims for the fly, *stop stripping.* Let the fish eat it. If the fish stops, make a long strip to set, because a fish will rarely stop unless it has eaten the fly.

When casting to moving fish, learn to lead the fish according to water depth and wind conditions. A longer lead is usually required in skinny water, or in low wind conditions. You can present your fly closer to a fish in deeper water or in windy conditions. In deeper water, however, you have to lead the fish enough so that your fly will sink to the proper depth by the time the fish arrives at that spot.

Watch your target carefully. Judge the swimming speed and wind direction. Don't wait too long to cast, especially when fish are swimming toward you. The farther you can cast the better chance you have of getting a second or third shot before a fish gets too close.

A good guide has a plan for the fishing day. This involves running time to the flats in various directions. If you have any special requests, make these known to your guide first thing in the morning, then rely on his judgment of what is possible according to the present conditions and your fishing skills.

WADING THE FLATS

Many of the basics discussed above apply to wade fishing, but here are some differences. You don't necessarily want to strip off as much line as you can cast accurately, especially if you can cast over sixty feet. We recommend stripping off fifty to sixty feet of line, then trailing it behind you in one long loop. This will allow you to break the water surface tension on the line and make a good cast quickly. You should still have at least a rod's length of line out of the tiptop guide, and be holding your tippet just above the fly in your noncasting hand.

In general, wading anglers can get closer to fish without spooking them than boat anglers can. To balance this out, however, wading anglers are often fishing to tailing fish. Bonefish in skinny water will usually be more spooky than fish in deeper water.

It is important to notice a fish's behavior. Is it cruising, stopping occasionally to feed, or is it feeding aggressively? This will tip you on how you should present your fly. We like to cast very close to aggressive fish, especially when their heads are buried and kicking up mud. Fish feeding sporadically need a longer lead. Cruising fish need the longest lead, and especially if they're bunched into large schools.

When we see a school of ten or more fish in skinny water, tails and fins breaking the surface, we often drop a fly twenty or more feet in front of them, then just let the fly sit. A small Yarn Crab is our favorite pattern for this tactic. As the fish reach the fly, we give the fly just the slightest twitch. This method works most of the time, even on the spookiest of fish on flats that are hammered by anglers. The mistake most anglers make is to strip too soon, or too long. A longer strip makes too much commotion. You just need a tiny twitch, and patience, patience, patience.

Another tactic we employ when wading is casting directly into the wind. By doing this you will be able to straighten out your backcast, then drive it forward with ease. You can crouch low and use a sidearm cast to avoid most of the wind, too. But most of all, the wind will be carrying any sounds or disturbances you make away from the fish. You'll be able to get close for good visuals on the hook set.

Stephen and Andros guide Charlie Neymour on a flat in the Middle Bight.

The last tip is on how to walk when you wade. Shuffling or sliding your feet is a good option when fishing on flats with a lot of stingrays, though there are not many of these in the Bahamas. If you shuffle, be careful to do it slowly and smoothly. You don't want to put up a wake that will alert nearby fish. Our favorite method, taught to us by some long-legged Bahamian guides years ago, is to walk like a heron. Pick your leg up slowly, completely out of the water, then point your toes and ease your foot back down to the bottom. Total silence is the goal here. No splashing. Stealth is key when stalking tailing bones.

MAKE USE OF YOUR FISHING PARTNER

This seems like common sense, but it amazes us how rarely this is practiced. At its best, flats fishing from a poled skiff is a team sport. When your partner is on the deck fishing, you should be the line tender. Stretch the line, coil it so it clears from weighted line to running line. Make sure there are no obstacles near the line—shoes, bags, clothes, and anything else that could catch the line should be out of the way.

Once your partner makes a cast and starts stripping in line, gather the slack in an orderly manner, coiling it on the deck again. This is especially important in windy conditions. If a fisherman is stripping line, and the wind is blowing the line in the water, or under the boat, recasting will be difficult or maybe impossible. Be alert for the fisherman's recast. Be ready to let go of the line. Watch your feet. Don't step on the line.

You can help with clearing the line when your partner hooks up. Not only will this sort of teamwork produce better results, but it keeps both people involved, and is a lot more fun.

HUNTING FOR SPECIFIC FISH— BIG BONES, PERMIT, TARPON

The hunt for big bonefish often means sacrificing numbers of fish and fishing in deeper water where it is more difficult to see. While it is certainly possible to catch big bones on a variety of flats, your chances will increase dramatically if you make a special effort.

You have to be mentally prepared for this type of fishing. You have to be willing to catch nothing. You have to put in your days, and fish the islands with the most big fish. If we could only fish one island for big bonefish, Andros would be the easy choice. If we had to pick one fly that would also be easy, a #2 Clouser Minnow in a Gold Shiner or Gotcha color.

Part of being mentally prepared is understanding that fishing for big bones is just like fishing for permit. Big bones look at flies, and treat flies, with the same disdain as permit. Opportunities are what you're looking for. Cashing in on those opportunities is what we all hope to do.

If you're on a permit quest there are only a few places in the Bahamas worth your time, though permit are available throughout the islands. Our favorite place for permit is north Andros, from the Joulter's Cays to Red Bay, then down along the west coast to

Williams Island. This is vast, relatively unexplored territory loaded with big permit. That's the good news. The bad news is that they're as hard to catch as anywhere else in the world. More good news is that you can often find permit feeding on rays in these areas. When you get an opportunity to cast to a permit on a ray, get it all together and make the cast. If you do, you'll have the optimum chance of getting the fish to eat.

Getting a tarpon to eat in the Bahamas isn't much of a problem, but setting the hook is just as difficult as anywhere else. If you've never been tarpon fishing before, you have to be realistic about your ability. Going tarpon fishing is one thing, catching tarpon is another. Try to keep your expectations on a

Brian O'Keefe

A bonefish this large will put a smile on anyone's face.

level and realistic plane, and pick locations that will give you the most opportunities. The west coast of Andros holds the largest tarpon populations in the islands, though few guides have the experience to put anglers onto these fish consistently. Guides on the other Bahamian islands have even less experience and knowledge about tarpon. Factor this into any desire you might have to go tarpon fishing in the Bahamas.

SPOTTING FISH

Spotting fish involves intense concentration and training, not great eyesight, as glasses give most people equal physical vision. Adopt a consistent scanning pattern. Start in close, twenty to fifty feet, then scan outward looking for obvious signs of movement, mud or nervous water. Nervous water is a ripple-type pattern on the surface that is different from the natural surface conditions. After scanning outward, return to the closer zone and do it again. Your scanning range should be between 10 and 2 on the clock, with occasional glances out to 9 and 3.

If you can reduce the zone you have to scan, your chances of seeing fish farther out will increase. You do this by understanding the path bonefish will take across flats or along shorelines. At times sun angles and surface glare will limit your vision areas. A good guide will set you up so you can see the best areas clearly.

Learn the clock directions until you can react instinctively to your guide's instructions. If you have to think about 2 o'clock before you look or before you cast, you've given the fish more of an advantage than they already have. Learn to judge distances by using your rod. Most rods are nine feet long, so let's round that off to about ten. Three rod lengths is close to thirty feet. If you know the clock, and know your distances, you'll be able to look very close to where your guide has called out a fish. The sooner you see the correct area, the better chance you have of seeing the fish.

It is certainly common for anglers to catch fish they never see by following their guide's instructions, but when you see the fish yourself, your hookup percentage will improve dramatically.

SIGHT HOOKING

This is closely related to spotting fish, and is just as important as sight casting. There is no simple way to teach this. This is a skill you develop after spending some time on the water. There are, however, signs you can look for to get started.

We talked before about "letting" the fish eat your fly. This is critical. You spot the fish, make your cast, start stripping, then watch the fish charge your fly. Stop stripping. Let the fish eat the fly. How do you know when he's got it? When the fish stops, he probably has the fly. Set the hook with a long strip. This is like sight nymphing in a river. You can't see the nymph, but you see the fish move to where the fly should be. You set the hook. You need to have faith. When the fish stops, long strip.

Maybe you can't see the whole fish, but you can see the head and gills. When you see the gills flare, this means the fish has sucked in your fly. Long strip. If the fish tilts downward, long strip. If you see the mouth open, long strip. One day you'll see it all perfectly, everything, the fly disappearing into the mouth, and you'll make a long strip and feel the weight of the fish and it'll be an exhilarating experience.

Or maybe you've seen it many times already. Whatever the case, sight hooking is the ultimate bonefishing experience. When you see the fish eat your fly, chances are he's yours.

Ric Fogel

Kim with a good-sized tarpon she took in Andros.

HANDLING SALTWATER GAME FISH

Saltwater fish are tougher and hardier than freshwater fish, but you still have to handle them with care, and as little as possible. Bonefish, permit, and tarpon all have a protective slime or film that acts as a cloaking device. This slime protects fish from infections and diseases, and contains their scent. When the slime is removed by excessive handling, this scent is radiated across the flat. Every shark in the vicinity can then zero in on this fish. Insect repellent and suntan lotion can also burn these fish like acid. Make sure to wash these lotions off your hands before handling fish.

Tarpon are big beautiful monsters, but they have delicate internal organs that can be harmed if you pull them up out of the water. There are ways you can do this, but you have to be careful. Treat all game fish as gently as you can so they can live to fight another day.

GUIDED TRIPS VS. DO-IT-YOURSELF

We almost always fish with a guide. Why? We want to give ourselves the best chance to catch fish every day. Even though we fish in salt water many days each year, every day is precious. If you only have six or seven days a year for flats fishing, you need to make the most of them. The only way to do that is to fish with a good guide.

That said, we understand some people like to do it on their own. That does not preclude fishing with a guide. You can use a guide as a fish finder and boat handler, then do everything else yourself.

Okay, you also want to find the fish yourself, or you want to save money. The first thing you need to do is pick a location that is conducive to fishing on your own. Carefully research the tides, based on the time of day of the tides, for your proposed destination. If you wade fish, you will only be able to fish one set of tides per day in some locations. If you hit high tides during the morning, or at midday, you'll have a tough trip due to your limited access. The best locations will be those that allow you to fish different stages of tides by moving from one area of an island to another, in a short period of time.

Anglers cruising the Bahamas in their own sailboat or motor yacht will have a better chance for fishing success on their own than will land-based anglers. With the use of a dinghy, access to many of the best flats, cays, cuts, and creeks is possible. Please see the "Around the Island" sections of each island chapter for the best fishing options for boaters and do-it-yourselfers.

TACKLE RECOMMENDATIONS

Saltwater game fish tend to be tackle busters. It doesn't make sense to spend a good chunk of money on a trip, then skimp on your rod, reel, line, and flies. Buy the absolute best equipment you can afford. That includes a comprehensive selection of flies; better to have too many flies than not enough.

Most Bahamian lodges and guides do not have fly-fishing tackle or flies available for client use. Where fly tackle is available, it is often in poor condition. If you plan to use lodge or guide equipment, be sure to confirm the type of equipment that is available, and the condition it is in. Also confirm the type of flies that might be available.

We are working with the Bahamian government, and with individual lodges and guides, to have top-quality equipment available in the future. In the meantime, we urge you to take all of your own fly-fishing equipment, flies, and accessories. If you do not want to purchase new equipment, ask your favorite fly-fishing professional to rent you the necessary gear.

We recommend medium-fast to fast-action fly rods from Sage, Scott, Winston, Thomas & Thomas, Loomis, Powell, and Orvis. There are numerous other good brands available, but these have proven themselves most reliable to us, and to our angling friends and clients, over the years. Several manufacturers, including Sage, Scott, and Winston, also produce medium-action rods that generate plenty of line speed for accurate casts in windy conditions. While we enjoy fishing with these slower rods at times, they require more patience to cast. If you have an aggressive casting style, these slower rods will not work as well for you.

If you only have one rod for flats fishing, and for bonefish in particular, we recommend a nine-foot 8-weight in a multipiece travel model. For women, Kim recommends light, crisp, rods with very little swing weight. Swing weight is how heavy a rod feels as you cast it. Does it drag through the air, or does it move through the air effortlessly? Swing weight is much more important than the actual weight of a rod, and it does not follow that the actual weight of a rod correlates to its swing weight. Kim's favorite rod is Sage's 890-3 RPLXi. She also recommends Winston's nine-foot 7-weight BL5 "Joan Wulff Favorite," and Scott's nine-foot 8-weight three-piece Eclipse.

You will need at least one backup rod anytime you travel to a remote location. If you want to cover the range of flats fishing, think in terms of an 8-weight, 10-weight, 12-weight triumvirate. The 10-weight will be ideal for sharks, barracuda, dorado, tarpon to 120 pounds, plus general

When fishing the Bahamas, think in terms of 8-, 10- and 12-weight rods. Here, Kim fishes with a 10-weight for tarpon.

Ric Fogel

inshore, reef, or creek fishing. The 12-weight will cover larger tarpon and many off-shore fishing situations.

Bonefish reels must have a reliable disc drag and a capacity for at least 200 yards of 20-pound backing. Green-colored micron is our favorite backing. Go with at least 250 yards of 30-pound backing on the 10-weight rig, and at least 300 yards of 30-pound backing on the 12-weight rig. Our favorite reels are the large arbor models from Abel, Tibor and Bauer. These reels are smooth, durable, and retrieve line faster than conventional models. Conventional fly reels with good disc drags from Billy Pate, Ross and Scientific Anglers have also proved reliable for us over the years.

Fly lines can get complicated if you let them, so keep things simple. Scientific Anglers Mastery Series floating lines in the Saltwater Taper, Bonefish Taper, and Tarpon Taper are consistently reliable. We also like to fish with the Flip Pallot Saltwater Line from Teeny. An extra spool for your 10-weight and 12-weight should be rigged with a Tarpon Taper intermediate sinking line, or a Teeny Saltwater 350. Once you accumulate lots of tackle, consult with your favorite fly-fishing professional for the best line and head systems for any given situation.

Terminal tackle is critical. Leader butt sections must be stiff to snap over into the wind with heavy flies. Tippets need to be abrasion-resistant around mangroves and coral. Climax, Umpqua, Scientific Anglers, and Rio make good tapered leaders for bonefish and other species, but we prefer to tie our own with Mason tippet material. A nine-foot 10-pound leader is standard for most bonefishing situations. When fishing for larger bones around mangroves or coral, go up to 12- or 15-pound tippet. We recommend that all saltwater anglers buy a good knot book and practice tying knots. Our favorite book is *Practical Fishing Knots,* by Mark Sosin and Lefty Kreh. If you prefer seeing knots tied on your television screen, we recommend the video tape, *The Art of Knot Tying,* by Chico Fernandez.

A key ingredient in selecting flies for the flats is the sink rate of each fly. You need to match the fly sink rate to the depth of the water combined with any tidal flows. The best cast in the world won't do you any good if the fly doesn't sink to a level where the fish can see it. In deeper water, lead eyes are helpful in getting flies down fast, and a sparsely tied offering will sink faster than a bushy one.

If we were tortured into deciding on a single favorite Andros bonefish fly, we'd have to say a #2 Clouser Minnow in a Gold Shiner or Gotcha color. The original Gotcha color includes a hot-pink head, pearlescent body, and tan craft fur wing. A #4 Clouser would be our favorite choice throughout the rest of the Bahamas, though colors would vary. For tailing bonefish on ocean flats our favorite fly is a #6 Tan Yarn Crab. In the spring and fall, when glass minnows and sand worms congregate in the outside bays and creeks, #4-6 White Rubber Band Worm patterns and White Slinky patterns are essential.

As a general bonefish selection, you should have the following flies: #2-6 Clouser Minnows (Gotcha, Gold Shiner, Silver Shiner), #2-6 Gotchas, #2-4 Bunny Gotchas, #4-6 Krystal Charlie's (Gold, White), #4-6 Horrors, #4 Bonefish Specials, #4-6 Tan Yarn Crabs, #4-6 Tan Mantis Shrimp, #4-6 Miheve's Flats Flies, #4 Orange Christmas Island Specials, #4-6 Tan/Orange Bonefish Puffs.

A tarpon fly selection is relatively simple. Our favorite fly is a #4/0 Shallow Water Cockroach. Your box should also include #4/0 Sea Bunnies in red/black and red/white, #3/0 Whistlers in orange/yellow and orange/black, #2/0 Clouser Minnows in white/chartreuse, and #2/0 Deceivers in green/white and blue/white.

Our favorite barracuda and shark fly is a #4/0 Orange Popovic's Banger. This may seem like a surprising choice, but fishing a topwater popper is the most exciting and effective way to catch both of these aggressive game fish. Additional shark and

Stephen and guide Andy Smith with a permit Stephen took in Joulter's Cay, Andros. There is no such thing as one "killer" permit fly.

barracuda flies should include: #1/0 Cuda Killers, #1/0 Candy Eels, #2/0 and #5/0 Deceivers in a variety of colors. Red/black is our favorite color combination.

We have caught permit on a variety of flies, and have several favorites, but there is no such thing as one single killer permit fly. If permit were human, they would need years of psychiatric treatment to function in the realm of normality. Yarn Crabs, Clousers, and Gotchas can all entice permit to eat. Add a couple of Del's Merkins and Epoxy Crabs to your box, then give it your best shot if a permit materializes.

A number of companies are now making high-quality functional warm-weather clothing. Patagonia and Ex Officio are our favorite brands. Ex Officio's Air Strip long-sleeve and short-sleeve shirts are like wearing air. Patagonia's Tropical Fishing shirts, shorts, and pants are best for anglers who prefer a soft cotton fabric. Whatever clothing you choose, it should be lightweight, offer sun protection, dry in minutes, and be maintenance-free. A cool hat that will protect ears and neck is also essential. Footwear should be suitable for wading hard coral bottoms. Simms makes exceptional Neoprene wading booties, while Patagonia's Marlwalker shoe is also a great choice.

The highest-quality polarized sunglasses are mandatory, and may be the most important piece of gear you own. The more fish you can see, the more fish you will catch, period. If you are willing to spend $300 and up for a rod or reel, you should be willing to spend up to $200 on a pair of polarized sunglasses. A number of companies manufacturer high-quality glass lenses. Our favorite brand is Action Optics by Smith, and our favorite all-around lens colors are photochromic amber and photochromic copper. Amber lenses cut blue light from the spectrum and increase contrast so your vision can penetrate the surface and let you see even the slightest movement. Side shields are also important to a glare-free field of vision, and to protect your eyes from the wind.

Sunscreen, bug dope (Kim's favorite is Off Skintastic), soft durable luggage, a boat bag, first-aid kit, prescription medicine, and other personal items are all necessary for a comfortable trip. Consult with your favorite fly-fishing professional to prepare for your specific destination. The following is the travel checklist we use when preparing for a trip. We do not necessarily take all of these items on every trip, but the list is the best way we know to get organized.

SALTWATER TRAVEL CHECKLIST

Passport
Copy of passport
Airline tickets
Vouchers/itinerary
Wallet/cash/traveler's checks
Destination phone numbers

Fly rods
Fly reels/spools
Neoprene reel protectors
Extra fly lines/extra backing
Leaders/tippet/wire spools
Flies/fly boxes
Pliers/hemostats/snips
Hook sharpener
Fly line dressing
Stripping basket
Leader stretcher
Chest pack/fanny pack
Guide lanyard
Wading booties/shoes
Wading socks
Snorkel/goggles/fins

Long pants
Shorts
Swimsuit
Long-sleeve shirts
Short-sleeve shirts
Sweater/windbreaker
Wide-brimmed hat
Updowner hat
Tennis shoes
Comfortable shoes
Underwear/socks

Rain gear/pants and jacket
Flaps/thongs/sandals
Sungloves
Polarized sunglasses
Extra sunglasses/glasses
Optical cloth/cleaner
Sunscreen 20+ SPF
Lip balm
Insect repellent/DEET
Avon Skin So Soft
Ziploc bags
Tupperware
Fishing towel/beach towel
Camera/film/batteries in
   a waterproof bag
Toiletry kit
First-aid supplies/itch balm
Band-Aids/alcohol
Aspirin/Advil/Motrin/Aleve
Caladryl/Benadryl
Prescription medicines
Dramamine or substitute
Travel flashlight
Travel alarm clock
Laundry bag
Boat carry-on bag
Water bottle
Travel iron/clothes line
Waterproof tape
Glue/moleskin
Reel lubricant
Knot book
Reading material
Notepad/pen

3

Travel Expectations
and Booking a Trip

No one should go to the Bahamas, or to any foreign destination, and expect it to be the United States. What we mean by that is, relax and enjoy the local culture. Engage the locals in conversation, ask them questions, and participate in their way of life. If you hold yourself apart, you will rarely have as much fun.

Traveling anglers need to acknowledge ahead of time that destination travel means encountering different ways of life and different cultures. Passing quick judgments on the differences, or comparing the quality of services to those in the United States, can set anglers up for disappointments. All this may sound obvious, but if it is, many anglers are not aware of it. Ninety-nine percent of the complaints we have heard over the years from traveling clients and friends were caused by unrealistic expectations.

The question then becomes, how does an angler gather the pertinent facts to choose a destination suitable to his or her wishes? The first part of the answer is that anglers have to establish a list of priorities for a particular trip. In defining those priorities, anglers need to set a budget, a time frame, and overall trip objectives. Is this a hard-core fishing trip, or will other vacation activities be included? What are the ability levels of the anglers going on the trip? What type of accommodations and services do you expect? Once you have your basic goals in mind, you can begin to ask additional questions that will give you the best chance for planning a successful vacation.

Let's begin with novice saltwater anglers. Bonefishing is the best way to get started for a number of reasons. First, bonefish are plentiful throughout the Bahamas. Beginning anglers need as many "shots" as possible. You can't get better if you don't get opportunities. Second, bonefish eagerly take flies. In spite of being finicky and spooky at times, bonefish are such voracious feeders that they often eat recklessly. We like to call aggressive bonefish suicidal, and as a beginning bonefisher you will want to see as many suicidal fish as possible. Third, bonefishing is pure fly-fishing, meaning that you stalk the fish, see them, and then sight cast to them. This visual experience is remarkable and extremely rewarding. Fourth, bonefish are fast and powerful.

Stephen displays a good-sized bonefish he took in the Middle Bight, Andros, with guide Simon Bain.

After you hook up, that first run is awesome. All you can do is let them go and hold on in amazement while your backing melts off your reel.

For a first blue-water angling trip, dorado (also called dolphin fish) are your best bet. Dorado are abundant throughout the Bahamas, and eagerly slam subsurface flies and topwater poppers. Catching them on top or just under is an exhilarating visual experience. The way they accelerate to take a fly is breathtaking. When they feel the hook they go ballistic, often jumping ten or more times during a fight. The bright yellow, orange, green, and blue colors of dorado often light up the ocean around buoys or flotsam. When dorado school around this sort of surface structure, you sightcast to them the way you would to bonefish. At other times you troll teasers offshore, not knowing if you'll bring up dorado, or wahoo, tuna, or billfish.

Once you decide on the primary species you want to pursue, you need to pick the best location for that species based on what type of trip you want. If this will be a hard-core fishing trip, you'll want the best guides, and you won't care as much about accommodations, meals, or optional activities. If you're a beginner, you'll want to see as many bonefish as possible, with size of fish being less important. If you're a veteran bonefisher, you might be looking for a fish over ten pounds, and you'll be willing to sacrifice numbers. Of course everyone wants to catch lots of **fish,** *and* big fish. It's fine to want that, and if it happens, great, but if you expect it, you might be disappointed.

Maybe you've decided to concentrate on bonefish, but want some variety as well. Most Bahamian flats destinations offer variety, with barracuda and sharks commonly available. In planning any trip, you'll want to know the best times to go, but this becomes trickier when you want to pursue multiple species. Pick the time that is best for your primary species, then try to overlap with good times for your secondary species.

Picking the best time to go to a particular destination to pursue a particular species is a matter of playing the odds. There are no guarantees that the wind, weather, or fish will go along even during the traditionally best times. However, by playing the odds, and by choosing the best tides and best guides, you'll have an excellent chance of having good fishing. Even if the weather turns horrible, if you're fishing with a great guide on a good tide, you will probably catch fish.

You will also need to decide on the length of your trip. Some anglers can only get away for a few days. Many people book four-night/three-day fishing packages all over the Bahamas. If this is all the time you have, go for it, but remember that shorter trips are more likely to be affected by weather. Generally, on a seven-day trip, you have a better chance of getting some good weather days. This is simply a matter of putting in your days.

Which brings up other types of trips you might choose. Maybe you'll decide that fishing, relaxing, and sightseeing are of equal importance. In that case, you will still want good guides, but you might also want deluxe accommodations, and maybe some optional activities such as diving, snorkeling, golf, tennis, or shopping.

Now comes the moment of truth, time to realistically assess your angling ability. If this will be your first bonefishing trip, it *doesn't matter* how good you are in fresh water or offshore. Consider yourself a beginner, and set your expectations at beginner level. You're going to prepare yourself the best you can, then go and fish the best you can. If you knock 'em dead, great, but if you don't, you can still have a blast, learn a lot, and be better next time.

There are a number of things you can do to prepare yourself for your first bone-fishing trip. First, practice casting in the wind. Do it on water, or on grass, but do it into the wind, across the wind, and down wind. Work on quickness in delivering the fly, and on accuracy. Quickness means you make a minimum number of false casts, then shoot your line. One false cast is best, two is okay, three is too many. Work on your accuracy out to fifty or sixty feet. If you can make a quick and accurate cast to fifty or sixty feet, you'll catch more fish than you know what to do with. If you can make a quick accurate cast thirty to forty feet, you'll catch enough fish to be de-lighted. Make sure you practice with a fly on (hook clipped off), and when the wind is ruffling your shirt.

If you think practicing your casting isn't worthwhile, or if you tell yourself you don't have time to practice, think about tennis or golf. Beginners in either sport, re-gardless of athletic ability, are not very good at first. Extensive practice is required in both sports to become competent. Fly-fishing is no different. If you spend a couple of thousand dollars on a bonefishing trip, and don't practice before you go, what results can you expect?

Besides practicing your casting, you'll need to assemble your gear. For many an-glers, preparing for a trip is half the fun. Playing with gear and flies is like playing with toys. Practice your knots, too. Know how to tie a perfection loop, blood knot, Albright knot, sur-geon's knot, improved clinch knot, and nonslip mono loop knot. Know-ing a nail knot and a Bimini twist will be helpful also.

We recommend the following books: *Practical Fishing Knots* by Mark Sosin and Lefty Kreh; *Bone-fishing with a Fly,* by Randall Kaufmann; *Fly-Fishing for Bone-fish,* by Dick Brown; *Fishing the*

Dolphin hooked at one of the naval buoys off Andros. For your first blue-water fishing trip, you can find no better gamefish.

Flats, by Mark Sosin and Lefty Kreh; *Fly-Fishing Is Salt Water,* by Lefty Kreh; *The Essence of Fly Casting,* by Mel Kreiger (book and video); *Saltwater Fly Patterns,* by Lefty Kreh; *Bonefish Flies,* by Dick Brown; *Fly-Fishing the Flats,* by Barry and Cathy Beck.

Videos: *The Art of Knot Tying,* by Chico Fernandez; *The Art of Advanced Fly Casting,* by Chico Fernandez; *Saltwater Fly Tying,* by Lefty Kreh.

CDs: *Tying Flies for Saltwater,* by Dick Stewart and Farrow Allen (an interactive CD with full motion video); *Florida East Coast and Bahamas,* by Saltwater Software (an amazing CD that will give you vital tide information throughout most of the Bahamas).

As we mentioned previously, fishing with a top-quality professional guide is the most important element in a successful fishing trip. We recommend booking guides in advance, through a professional travel consultant who has fished with that guide, or on your own based on the recommendations of a friend who has fished with that guide.

When choosing a guide, look for the following qualities: personality; experience; professionalism; ability to plan a day's fishing strategy; understanding of tides; understanding of different fish species; boat handling to get you into position to cast; ability to instruct casting and line handling.

Remember that even the best guides have off days sometimes. Anglers paying good money and spending precious time on a trip usually have a hard time with this, but it can happen. You need to get past this by talking to your guide about your concerns. Even top guides will have trouble finding fish on occasion, especially if you are looking for big

Stephen with guide Simon Bain on flat off Andros. When choosing a guide, look for personality, experience and professionalism.

bonefish, permit, or tarpon. If you have special goals or requests, ask your guide if he thinks there is a reasonable chance for success. If you really want to go tarpon fishing, but your guide says the weather is wrong, we suggest you trust your guide's judgement.

In assessing your ability, consider your skills in the following areas:

Vision—How well can you see fish in varying water conditions and depths? If you fish for a week you'll probably see better every day.

Casting—How far can you cast accurately in the wind? Practice, practice, practice, and then be realistic about your ability. Then practice some more.

Line handling—How well do you control your line? Do you vary your retrieve? Can you see the fish eat your fly? Do you set well with your line hand? You can learn these skills by listening to your guide, and by experimenting on your own.

Fish fighting—Do you have trouble clearing line when a fish takes off? Once the fish is on your reel, can you anticipate when he'll stop, or start running again? Do you know how much pressure you can put on a fish without breaking it off? Experience will improve your skills, as will listening to your guide.

Wind and weather—Can you deal with any weather condition? Count on conditions being challenging; then, if it's gorgeous, so much the better. Wind will make casting more difficult and clouds will make it hard to see. Relax and have fun anyway.

Tackle—Do you have reliable tackle? Is your rod fun and easy to cast? Does your reel have enough fresh backing? Are your leaders and tippets fresh? It does not pay, or make any sense, to cut corners with saltwater tackle. You can rely on a good fly shop or mail-order house to tie knots, rig tarpon and billfish leaders, and set up reels, but the more you know the better. And it's fun to learn!

Before booking your trip, you can gather information directly from lodges, hotels, guides, tourist bureaus, travel consultants, or on the Internet, and we encourage you to do so. But when it comes time to book your trip, we suggest using a qualified travel agent. Fly-fishing travel agencies charge the same price you would pay by booking a lodge or guide directly. There is no premium. We make these statements to dispel the misperception that booking directly with a lodge or guide will save you money. In most cases, booking directly will cost you time, and maybe money, in terms of aggravation and inconvenience. Also, if something goes wrong with your trip, trying to deal with a lodge or guide in a foreign country can be difficult at best. A professional travel agent will be on your side and will aid in solving any problems.

Fly-fishing travel is extremely specialized. You should not book travel with an agent who has not stayed and fished at your chosen destination. Good agents will be able to give you unbiased opinions about facilities, service, guide quality, fishing conditions, best tackle and flies, and best means of travel. The only downside to booking with an agent might be if that agent has exclusive agreements with certain lodges or guides. If you are concerned about this, ask the agent if they are the exclusive representatives for any destinations.

If you have done your homework, you will be able to supply your chosen travel agent with the necessary information to book the trip you want. The more accurate information you supply, the better job the agent can do. This might include the agent suggesting a different destination from the one you chose originally. Good agents make suggestions based on their experience, and their desire to match you with the location that best fits the information you provided.

Paradoxically, good agents, and quality professional lodges and guides, create some of their own problems. How? By spoiling anglers, especially beginning anglers, with great fishing experiences. For example, you go on your first trip and the weather is fabulous. The tides are perfect and you catch lots of fish. You've just enjoyed the ideal scenario. You'll compare this experience against all those to come, forever more. Big mistake. Evaluate each trip on its own merits, don't compare, and you'll be a lot happier.

The following is a recommended list of experienced travel agents who can book destinations throughout the Bahamas, and who have the specialized knowledge to suggest and sell the proper tackle, flies, clothing, and accessories. Our bias here is toward professional fly fishers who are travel agents, as opposed to just being travel agents.

Westbank Anglers
P.O. Box 523
Teton Village, WY 83025
Voice: 800/922-3474 or 307/733-6483
Fax: 307/733-9382
E-mail: wbajh@wyoming.com
Internet: www.westbank.com

The Fly Shop
4140 Churn Creek Rd.
Redding, CA 96002
Voice: 800/669-3474 or 530/222-3555
Fax: 916/222-3572
E-mail: mike@theflyshop.com
Internet: www.theflyshop.com

Kaufmann's Streamborn
P.O. Box 23032
Portland, OR 97281
Voice: 800/442-4359 or 503/639-6400
Fax: 503/684-7025
E-mail: kaufmanns@kman.com
Internet: www.kman.com

Bob Marriott's Flyfishing Store
2700 West Orangethorpe Ave.
Fullerton, CA 92633
Voice: 800/535-6633 or 714/525-1827
Fax: 800/367-2299
E-mail: bmfsinfo@bobmarriotts.com
Internet: www.bobmarriotts.com

4

Andros Island, Heartland of the Bahamas

Andros Island is our favorite Bahamian destination, and considered by many people to be the "Bonefishing Capital of the World." We would certainly endorse this title.

Located 150 miles southeast of Miami, and thirty-six miles west of Nassau, Andros is surrounded by the best saltwater flats habitat on the planet. The North, Middle, and South Bights are the heart of this famous fishery, but they are only the beginning. Andros sprawls over one hundred miles from the Joulters Cays on the northern end, to the Water Cays and Curly Cut Cays on the southern tip, and spans forty miles from the east coast to the West Side. Composed of serpentine channels and creeks, fresh- and saltwater lakes, verdant mangrove cays, and countless miles of sandy flats, Andros is blessed with more fertile fishing grounds than any other area in the Caribbean.

Roaming these flats are uncountable numbers of bonefish averaging three to six pounds. There are also abundant fish in the six- to nine-pound class, plus many unforgettable double-digit giants. If you're looking for *big* bonefish, Andros is *the* place to take your shot. Andros also offers year-round tarpon fishing, plus seasonal fishing for permit, barracuda, sharks, jacks, snappers, amberjack, grouper, billfish, wahoo, tuna, mackerel, and dolphin.

The local atmosphere on Andros is a blend of casual everyday life, Caribbean charm and friendliness, plus a pinch of superstition. Most people follow a simple routine. Nothing is hurried. No traffic. People go to work. Children dress in uniforms and go to school. People believe in local witch doctors, and in the spirit of the mythical Chickcharnie, a small birdlike being with huge eyes and a penchant for mischief. Potions are mixed and blended and taken for good health. People possess ambition and pride, but there is no demanding timetable set for progress.

The roughly eight thousand residents of Andros are concentrated on the eastern coast. The western coast is unsettled and relatively unexplored, as are many of the interior lakes. Andros is the Bahamas' most important farming region, and the largest source of fresh water. Farmland, plus pine and hardwood forests, cover the northern

Brian O'Keefe

Andros is blessed with more fertile fishing ground than any other area in the Caribbean.

part of the island. Hardwoods include mahogany, horseflesh (used in shipbuilding), and lignum vitae, also known as sailor's cure because its sap provided the most effective treatment for syphilis until the 1900s.

Bird life is more prolific on Andros than most other islands, and so is insect life. Due to the large amount of fresh water, mosquitoes, sand flies, and green-headed horse flies, known locally as "doctor flies," are abundant, especially when the wind is down.

Historically, Andros has always been a mysterious island. Spanish sailors visited in the sixteenth century and called the island "La Isla del Espiritu Santo," Island of the Holy Spirit. This name came from the Spanish belief that the Holy Spirit lives over water, and Andros presented itself to them more as water than land.

Andros's dense, lush interior—a combination of mangrove swamps, thorny underbrush, and thick forests—was seen as virtually impenetrable, and perhaps haunted. This inaccessibility and mystique was the draw for runaway slaves and Seminole Indians escaping from the Florida Everglades in the mid-nineteenth century. These refugees settled in Red Bay due to its peace and obscurity.

Logging, farming, fishing, and sponging has dominated the Andros economy over the past hundred years. Conservation efforts have put an end to logging, at least for the time being, while farming, commercial fishing and sponging are still important revenue sources. Tourism, which focuses on sportfishing, ecotours, and diving, is the fastest growing sector of the new economy.

The island residents are quickly adapting to this tourism-based economy. Young men are training to become professional fishing guides. New lodges are being built, old ones are being renovated. Taxi services have improved dramatically. Most important, the locals look forward to sharing their island with visitors, to revealing their secret treasures. This type of outgoing sincerity goes well beyond just good service, and leaves many visitors with a desire to return.

In spite of its size and proximity to Nassau, Andros is one of the least visited of the Out Islands. This is partly due to the overall lack of development, and until recently, the lack of promoted adventure activities.

Small Hope Bay Lodge has made a consistent and successful effort to promote Andros as a diving and snorkeling destination. The island has more dive sites than any other Bahamian location. The world's third largest barrier reef is just offshore, and the Tongue of the Ocean creates unparalleled wall diving.

Small Hope is an ideal place for families and couples looking for a relaxing remote location. Swim, windsurf, dive, snorkel, bike, hike, explore blue holes, and eat great food on your own schedule. Guided bonefishing and reef and offshore fishing can also be arranged.

A new resort, Point of View Villas, is five minutes away from Small Hope, just north of Fresh Creek. This deluxe resort features all the activities available at Small Hope in a more luxurious atmosphere, complete with air-conditioned villas, lighted tennis courts, swimming pool, fine dining room, and bar overlooking the ocean.

There are a number of possible new developments, such as marinas, resorts, and gated residential communities, which could dramatically change the tourism business. For now, however, Andros is still an intriguing remote location best suited to anglers and outdoor enthusiasts looking for a sense of adventure in a magical place.

The fastest and easiest way to reach Andros is by air. Several charter carriers make this convenient with nonstop service from Ft. Lauderdale. We usually fly into Nassau on Delta, though Bahamasair and other carriers offer the same service. Flying into Nassau allows us to make the best use of frequent flier tickets and other upgrades.

Bird life is more prolific in Andros than in most other islands.

Pool and restaurant at Point of View Villas.

From Nassau we usually fly Bahamasair to Andros Town or San Andros. Congo Air, which is operated by Bahamasair, flies into Mangrove Cay and Congo Town. We also use several air charter companies out of Nassau to reach Andros when we travel with groups of four or more. You need at least an hour and a half in Nassau to clear customs and walk to the domestic terminal for Out Island connections.

Check the connection time when you make reservations. If it shows less than an hour and a half, make different arrangements. You can either change your schedule to give you more than an hour, schedule a charter flight, or arrive in Nassau the day before your trip to Andros.

Arriving in Nassau the day before your flight to Andros, or to any of the Out Islands, is a good idea. This will give you time to relax, and Nassau is a lot of fun. We recommend staying at the Nassau Beach Hotel on Cable Beach; at the British Colonial Beach Hotel at Bay Street; at Compass Point near the airport; or on Paradise Island at the Atlantis Resort Hotel. It is a ten-minute, $12 taxi ride from the airport to the Cable Beach area. It is a thirty-minute (at least) $25 taxi ride to Paradise Island.

If you spend the night in Nassau, Bahamasair has an early morning flight that will get you to Andros in time for a full day of fishing.

For the adventurous traveler with time to spare, Andros can be reached from Nassau via several mail boats. Sailing or cruising in private vessels is another popular way to reach Andros from anywhere in the Bahamas. Call ahead to any port to confirm what facilities and supplies are available.

We suggest that you take everything you might need for convenience and safety with you, as supplies can be scarce on Andros. This would include a good first aid kit, sewing kit, and prescription medicines.

AROUND THE ISLAND

North Andros includes the area from the Joulter's Cays to Fresh Creek. This is the most populated area of the island, and the center of the island's farming industry. Most populated is a relative term, however, as the two largest towns, San Andros and Nicholl's Town, have a combined population of less than two thousand people. Adding in Morgan's Bluff, Lowe Sound, Red Bay, and Mastic Point moves the population to around three thousand.

The easiest way to access North Andros is to fly into San Andros on Bahamasair. Charter flights are also available from Florida and Nassau. Several reliable taxi drivers service this area. We highly recommend that you set up any fishing trip to North Andros in advance, and take special care in selecting your guide if you choose to go the independent route. Ask every question you can think of when talking to a guide or agent about this trip: Has the agent personally fished at this destination? If so, how recently? What are the accommodations and meals like? Are the rooms air-conditioned? What type of boat and motor does the guide use? How long has the guide been working in this area? Does the guide have fly-fishing equipment and flies available? Is the guide a good instructor? These are just the basic questions, questions you should ask when booking any trip, but it is even more important here.

The best place to stay is the Conch Sound Inn, located on the road between Nicholl's Town and Conch Sound, a ten-minute walk from the beach. Oversize rooms are clean and air-conditioned. The bar and restaurant serves good Bahamian food, and the staff is helpful and friendly.

Another lodging option is the Green Windows Inn, located on the main road in Nicholl's Town next door to the Texaco gas station. Basic rooms are located upstairs,

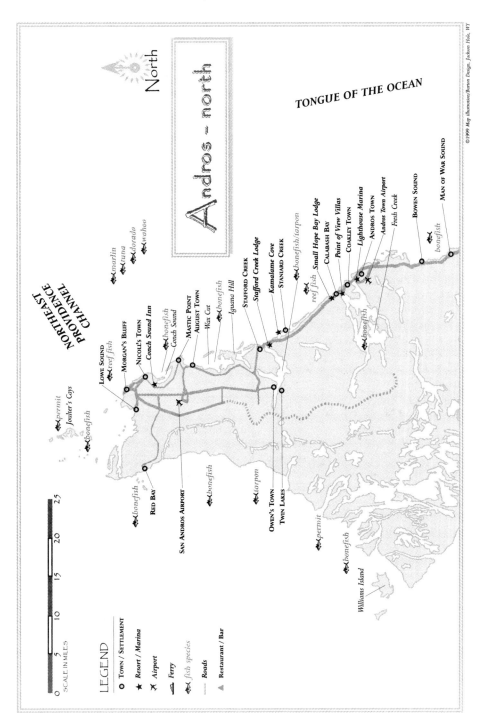

North

Andros ~ north

TONGUE OF THE OCEAN

NORTHEAST PROVIDENCE CHANNEL

LEGEND

SCALE IN MILES
0 5 10 15 20 25

○ Town / Settlement
★ Resort / Marina
✗ Airport
Ferry
fish species
▲ Restaurant / Bar

permit
Joulter's Cays
bonefish

bonefish
RED BAY
SAN ANDROS AIRPORT

bonefish

tarpon
OWEN'S TOWN
TWIN LAKES

permit

bonefish

Williams Island

LOWE SOUND
reef fish
MORGAN'S BLUFF
NICOLL'S TOWN
Conch Sound Inn
bonefish
Conch Sound
MASTIC POINT
AUGUST TOWN
Wax Cut
bonefish
Iguana Hill

STAFFORD CREEK
Stafford Creek Lodge
Kamalame Cove
STANIARD CREEK
bonefish/tarpon
reef fish Small Hope Bay Lodge
CALABASH BAY
Point of View Villas
COAKLEY TOWN
Lighthouse Marina
ANDROS TOWN
Andros Town Airport
Fresh Creek
bonefish

marlin
tuna
dorado
wahoo

BOWEN SOUND
bonefish
MAN OF WAR SOUND

over the restaurant and bar. We have seen this little motel promoted as the North Andros Bonefish Club, though that is an overstatement.

Morgan's Bluff, named after the infamous pirate, is only fifteen miles by boat from Chub Cay in the Berry Islands, and thirty-six miles from Nassau. For boating anglers, Morgan's Bluff offers easy access and good anchorages in the harbor proper. There is a restaurant and bar that, when open, serves good lunches and cold Kalik. Additional anchorages can be found on the tide at nearby Lowe Sound. Fuel, fresh water, ice, and groceries are usually available in Lowe Sound and Morgan's Bluff, though fruit and staples can run low. If you need a bigger market you'll have to make the trip to Nicholl's Town. We suggest taking a taxi, as it is too far to walk when carrying supplies.

The flats habitat from Morgan's Bluff and Lowe Sound to the Joulter's Cays, approximately eight miles as the crow flies, is a vast gourmet feeding area for bonefish and permit. This habitat is part of an extensive ecosystem that extends north across the Great Bahama Bank to Great Stirrup Cay in the Berry Islands, northwest to Bimini and the Gulf Stream, and west to Red Bay. Blue crabs, sea crabs, swimming shrimp, and gobies combine with mussels and clams to create a massive food supply for game fish. The blue crabs are especially numerous, and their scent in the water is a major draw for good numbers of large permit. These crabs are also responsible for the high concentration of big bonefish.

Running from Morgan's Bluff to the Joulter's can be a battering experience when the wind is up, though on a calm day it's spectacular. Lowe Sound is more protected, and provides quicker access to all the cays, including the Joulter's, but navigating is tricky and requires local knowledge. Arthur Russell, also known as "King Arthur," is the dean of guides in the area. He can be booked as an independent, though he is currently working with Prescott Smith out of Stafford Creek Lodge. Russell also rents a couple of rooms across from his dock.

The settlement of Lowe Sound is simple and idyllic, perched on the water's edge, which is piled high in many areas with conch shells. There is a good boat launch for flats skiffs next to a bar and snack stand; that stand serves the best fresh conch salad in the universe.

There is good wading for bonefish right in front of the settlement. You can see the Joulter's, along with many other inviting cays in the distance. Miles of flats stretching out from northern Andros become completely dry during low tide, creating wet sandy and grassy hillocks teeming with burrowing shrimp and scampering blue crabs.

There are flats here where you can be standing in ankle-deep water and see nothing but ankle-deep water 360 degrees around you. In other areas deep blue creeks cut through white sand flats that are only a hundred feet wide. Some of the best permit flats lie along the edges of the boating route to the Joulter's Cays anchorage, where water depths are six to ten feet. Others lie to the north where white sand turns to dark grass that runs to the horizon.

For boaters, the easiest Joulter's anchorage is at the southwestern tip of the cays, but there is also a good anchorage accessible on the tide at the northeastern tip in a beautiful creek adjacent to a crescent-shaped beach.

The eastern tides, similar to the ones in Fresh Creek and Nassau, influence the fishery most, but tide issues are complicated as you move west. This is the same phenomenon anglers experience farther south when fishing the Bights and moving toward the West Side.

Wind is also a major factor on the many open flats. Lees can be found from the prevailing winds around Pine Cay, Hog Cay and on the western side of Long, Candle, and the Joulter's Cays, but the vast area of central flats is completely exposed.

Kim on a flat on West Side of Andros.

Sand, coral, and mud are the main bottom types. Most are light in color, which makes spotting fish easier. Conversely, the complex bottom structure, with countless contours, potholes, and troughs, provides great cover for those ghostly bonefish. Water depth is especially critical in this region. Bonefish congregate in the deeper channels and troughs waiting for incoming tides to cover the flats so they can begin to forage. Once you discover these congregation points you can have some of the best bonefishing imaginable, casting to tailing fish for hours.

South of Nicholl's Town is Conch Sound, a large protected bay cut into the island. There are a number of pretty beaches here, plus some flats that are wadable at low tide. These flats are the easiest northern oceanside flats to access because they are not guarded by thick mangroves.

The best reef and offshore fishing begins near Mastic Point. Boaters can travel either inside or outside the reef on the way south. Trolling hookless teasers is a good way to raise a variety of fish. Be prepared with a fly rod, then have a boat mate yank the teaser away so you can substitute a fly. If you just want some meat for the galley, add hooks to the teasers. This is also a good area to fish with conventional gear for grouper.

South of Mastic Point is Mastic Bay, a huge expanse of flats and backcountry shoreline mangroves. The shorelines are rugged and often covered with soft mud, so fishing here is best done from a poled skiff or sea kayak.

Paw Paw Cay and the surrounding cays on the outside of the bay create sensational bonefish habitat. The hard sand and coral bottoms are ideal for wading. Fishing is best on a low incoming tide, and very good on the last part of the falling tide. On a high tide large schools of bonefish lay up on the leeward side of Paw Paw.

Continuing south past Rat Cay, the shoreline cuts back away from the reef toward the Saddle Back Cays. This diverse habitat consists of a series of shallow wadable flats and deeper channels. At low tide you can wade for several miles, but as the tide rises you shouldn't stray too far from your boat. Channels and cuts become waist deep in a hurry, and these oceanside flats are loaded with aggressive black tip and lemon sharks. If you are looking for big tailing bonefish, this is one of the best rarely fished areas on Andros.

Boaters cruising inside the reef in this area will need to stay on the outside of the Saddle Back Cays. Check your charts and be extremely careful. Exploring this area, and accessing the wadable flats is best accomplished by dinghy or flats skiff.

The entrance to London Creek is just south of Saddle Back Cays. Once inside, the creek slices back north then doglegs west for more than eight miles. A shallow draft flats boat or dinghy is the best way to explore this area, which offers consistently good bonefishing, even during stormy weather and winter cold fronts.

The shoreline around Stafford Creek is a series of white sand beaches, coral out-croppings, casuarina trees, and palm trees. Shallow wadable flats are located on either side of the creek mouth. Anglers can walk straight out from the settlement on the north side of the creek to stalk tailing bones on an incoming tide.

The entrance to Stafford Creek itself flows like a river, especially on the falling tide. The water is up to fifteen feet deep here. Two good anchorages are available, but there are no facilities. A jetty whirlpool, which can be extremely dangerous to boaters, is located at the far southern corner of the creek mouth. Just beyond the jetty pool the creek makes a hard left and passes under the highway bridge.

If you're standing on the bridge, the creek looks like a wild Rocky Mountain river. On an incoming tide, the clear green water rips through the narrows then settles into the wider expanse of the inner creek. Rock and coral banks topped with native pines rise to two hundred feet as the creek swells and turns west.

Just before the bend, on the southern shore, is the site of Stafford Creek Lodge. The lodge, owned and operated by Prescott and Samantha Smith, opened in October 1998. We consider this lodge a unique and appealing fishing destination. Catering to just six guest anglers at a time, the focus here is on great fishing and service. Large air-conditioned rooms overlook the water and dock, which is a perfect spot to practice your casting. The landscaping is fabulous, with native stone paths leading from the guest rooms to the lodge, the dock, the hot tub and gazebos.

Stafford Creek guides fish the Joulter's Cays from Lowe Sound, plus miles of creeks and outside ocean flats. The drive from the lodge to Lowe Sound takes about twenty minutes on the main highway. If you are interested in booking at Stafford Creek Lodge, you will need to make your reservations at least six months in advance, a year in advance for April and May.

Stafford Creek sprawls inland for over ten miles in a series of channels, flats, and connected lakes. When the wind is howling and most flats on the island are unfish-able, anglers can still enjoy a good day of bonefishing here, or in London Creek. Tarpon, permit, jacks, and snappers can be found in the creek throughout the year.

The few guides who know this area use the old logging roads for access to some of the inland lakes. These lakes hold landlocked tarpon, cubera snapper, jacks, and permit.

South of Stafford Creek, the Blanket Sound flats feature good wading on sand and coral bottoms. Boaters need to stay well off the shoreline all the way to Staniard Rock Passage. The golden sand banks that protect the northern entrance to Staniard Creek make it easy for wading anglers to see ocean-dark bonefish cruising out on a falling tide.

Ric Fogel

Stafford Creek Lodge.

The Staniard Creek area is lush and beautiful. Casuarinas and coconut palms hover over white sand beaches. An offshore breeze keeps most of the bugs down year round. The peaceful settlement is just off the main road on an island accessed by a bridge that was recently rebuilt.

Kamalame Cove, with its adjoining private cay, is on the northern end of Staniard Creek. Deluxe accommodations here cater to fly fishers and their nonangling companions. While there are areas to wade on your own, Kamalame guides fish from here all the way to the Joulter's.

The Staniard Creek Quality Inn is located on one of the three arms of the creek, just south of Kamalame. Clean rooms, some with air-conditioning, offer the budget-minded angler access to this area. During lower tidal periods it is possible to wade for bonefish right in front of the hotel. There are other good wading options to the north and south on bottoms that vary from hard sand to mushy grass.

The nine-mile coastline from Staniard Creek to Fresh Creek is a relatively straight southeasterly shot. The highway takes a more circuitous route and is in good condition, with driving time from Fresh Creek to Staniard Creek about twenty minutes. For boaters, the passage inside the reef is straightforward, though it's better to stay out near the reef as coral heads and sand banks rise near the surface on low tides.

This nine-mile stretch is rarely fished by flats anglers. Some guides from Small Hope Bay work this area, but they usually go south instead. The best fishing is on the outer flats that are difficult to reach from shore. A flats skiff or a dingy offers the best access to areas where we've seen countless bonefish over ten pounds, with the average fish being seven pounds.

Small Hope Bay is located on a protected beach north of Fresh Creek. Comfortable accommodations are on a serene stretch of white sand. The casual relaxing atmosphere is ideal for families or couples who want to combine superior diving with a variety of water sports and fishing.

The reef fishing along this stretch is outstanding. Permit, jack crevalle, mackerel, amberjack, barracuda, grouper, and a variety of sharks are all abundant. Trolling teasers is consistently effective. Fly fishers will have their best chances for success using chum to concentrate the reef fish into a feeding frenzy.

Point of View Villas is a new fourteen-suite resort just north of the Fresh Creek bridge. For now, this is the nicest lodging facility on Andros, and is well suited for nonanglers. The restaurant, open to the public, is our favorite place to eat in the area,

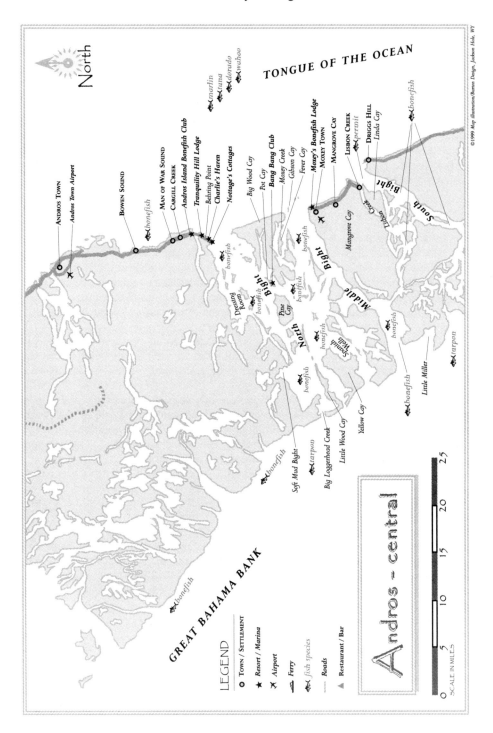

North

TONGUE OF THE OCEAN

marlin
tuna
owahoo

ANDROS TOWN
Andros Town Airport

BOWEN SOUND

bonefish

MAN OF WAR SOUND
CARGILL CREEK
Andros Island Bonefish Club
Tranquility Hill Lodge
Behring Point
Charlie's Haven
Nottage's Cottages

Big Wood Cay
Pot Cay
Bang Bang Club
Moxey Creek
Gibson Cay
Fever Cay

Moxey's Bonefish Lodge
MOXEY TOWN
MANGROVE CAY
LISBON CREEK
DRIGGS HILL
Linda Cay
permit
bonefish

South Bight

Lisbon Creek

Mangrove Cay

Middle Bight

North Bight

bonefish
bonefish
bonefish
bonefish
bonefish
bonefish

Dressing Room

Pine Cay

Stingrah Walk

Yellow Cay
Little Wood Cay
Big Loggerhead Creek
Soft Mud Bight

tarpon
tarpon

Little Miller

bonefish
bonefish

GREAT BAHAMA BANK

bonefish

LEGEND
⊙ TOWN / SETTLEMENT
★ Resort / Marina
✕ Airport
🐟 Ferry
🐟 fish species
----- Roads
▲ Restaurant / Bar

Andros - central

SCALE IN MILES
0   5   10   15   20   25

©1999 Map Illustration/Barros Design, Jackson Hole, WY

although nearby Hank's Place is hard to beat for large portions of Bahamian fare and classic local atmosphere.

The next section of the island, central Andros, runs from Fresh Creek/Andros Town to Moxey Town on Mangrove Cay. The highway is in relatively good shape, with only a few potholes, to where it ends at Behring Point. From there, you'll need a boat to reach Mangrove Cay.

Fresh Creek offers one of the best anchorages on Andros. Coakley Town sprawls along the north shore of the creek, and Andros Town occupies the south bank. The Andros Town Airport, a couple minutes' drive south of the settlement, is the airport used most often by anglers traveling to fish this area. Bahamasair operates two scheduled flights from Nassau every day.

A good place to stay in Fresh Creek is the Lighthouse Yacht Club and Marina on the south side of the creek. The spacious villa rooms feature air-conditioning, tile floors, private bath, and overlook the swimming pool and marina. A restaurant and bar are on the premises.

The marina offers boaters seventeen slips with water, electricity, and fuel. We have rarely seen a vacant slip here, so we suggest calling ahead for reservations.

Across the road from Lighthouse is the Androsia factory outlet for unique island-style clothing. Kim and many of our women angling friends are frequent shoppers here.

Lighthouse is within easy walking distance of other local restaurants that include Hank's Place, Skinny's, and the Chickcharnie Hotel. Delicious Bahamian dishes, including lobster feasts, are served for around $10 per person.

Papa Gay's Chickcharnie Hotel, located across the creek from Lighthouse, is a pastel-colored three-story structure that sits right on the water's edge. Rooms are comfortable and priced to meet the demands of budget-conscious anglers. A local store sells groceries, drugs, suntan lotion, insect repellent, and other essentials.

The Coakley House is another lodging option for couples, groups, and families. The fully furnished three-bedroom, three-bath house overlooks the ocean flats. You can rent it as is or with maids, cooks, and other services. Independent bonefish guides can be arranged. The guides will pick you up on fishing days. The full diving program at Small Hope Bay is also available to guests renting the house.

A mile and a half south of Andros Town is the main base for the Atlantic Undersea Test and Evaluation Center (AUTEC). This area is off-limits and should be avoided.

Dock at Lighthouse Yacht Club and Marina in Fresh Creek.

The U.S. Navy uses this base for submarine warfare testing. Helicopters, destroyers, and support ships are all a common site along the eastern shoreline of Andros.

Some of the best oceanside flats in Andros begin about two miles south of AUTEC. The shorelines inside Plum Cays and Mastic Cays are a maze of mangroves that provide food and shelter to thousands of bonefish. Ambushing these fish on the open flats and around the cays as they tail their way in and out is incredible sport.

More outstanding oceanside flats begin again around Kits Cay and continue to White Bight. Man-O-War Cay, Kiss-it Cay, and Simms Cay are the heart of this wade fishing paradise. The best times to fish low incoming tides are in the early morning and late afternoon, but the fish will come anytime the tide is right.

We have often waded for tailing bones for five hours at a time in the Simms Cay area. The golden sand bottom is like walking on carpet, and the dark ocean bonefish can be spotted a hundred yards away. On calm days you can see tails, dorsals, and wakes in every direction. A five-pound fish is on the small side here, with seven pounds average, and we've caught fish up to fourteen pounds here, having first seen their bodies half exposed in ankle-deep water.

Some of these ocean flats can be accessed from shore around White Bight, but most of the shoreline and land area is too dense with vegetation to pass through from the highway. The best flats are outside across channels that are too deep to wade, and caution is always necessary due to the number of aggressive blacktip sharks.

Bruce Farrington recently finished building White Bight Lodge, which is a good base for anglers who want to wade on their own. The small lodge features nice two-room cottages steps away from the beach. Anglers can also book independent guides.

One drawback to fishing White Bight and Kiss-it Cay is the number of guides now working the area. Guides from Small Hope, Andros Island Bonefish Club, and Tranquility Hill all use the same area for their wade fishing clients. Consequently, the bonefish here are super-spooky, and extremely particular about the flies they will eat.

Another AUTEC base is positioned just north of Salvador Point. Around the point is Cargill Creek, whose entrance cuts through two light-bottomed bonefish flats. The Andros Island Bonefish Club is on the northern shore where the creek widens. Cargill Creek Lodge is adjacent, on the creek to the west. Cargill Creek Lodge closed in July 1998, and it is up for sale.

Captain Rupert Leadon runs a top-notch fishing operation at the Bonefish Club. Air-conditioned rooms are spacious and comfortable, with two double beds, mini-refrigerator, and private bath. Full bar service, good food, and satellite television round out the amenities. Rupert's top guides are excellent, and his staff is friendly and helpful. With Cargill Creek Lodge closed, Rupert has gained chef Iyke Moore, whose Key lime pie is unquestionably the best in the business.

The Bonefish Club and Tranquility Hill Lodge have larger boats for reef and off-shore fishing. Crews from both lodges are expert in the use of conventional tackle, and adequate with fly-fishing gear. Dolphin is the most abundant offshore species, with wahoo, tuna, and billfish available in season. The reef fishing for grouper, amberjack, sharks, and barracuda is also excellent.

South of Cargill Creek is Behring Point and the entrance to the North Bight. Tranquility Hill Fishing Lodge rests on a hillside clearing overlooking the ocean and the Bight. Owned and operated by the Neymour and Mackey families, this is one of our favorite lodges. Service and food are excellent, and all guests are made to feel at home. Legendary guide Ivan Neymour runs a first-class fishing operation suited to the most demanding anglers. Spending a day in a boat with Ivan is always a memorable experience.

Down the road from Tranquility is Charlie's Haven, the home and lodge of another bonefishing legend, "Crazy" Charlie Smith. Charlie has explored and guided in

Tranquility Hill Lodge.

the Bights for more than thirty years. His enthusiasm for fishing is infectious, and he guides a very loyal clientele.

Charlie is an amazing personality who can keep you entertained for days by passing on the fishing lore of Andros. He started his career on Andros as a chef, and he still cooks for his guests. Accommodations are in comfortable rooms with private baths, some with air-conditioning.

Another interesting place to stay in terms of local flair is Nottages Cottages, located at the end of the Behring Point settlement road, a short walk past Charlie's Haven, on the north shore of the North Bight. An expansive bonefish flat is right out front. Easy wading and good fishing are possible during low incoming tides.

Nottages has five basic motel-style rooms with air-conditioning, private baths, and a dining room/bar. The beautiful landscaping, including aloe trees, coconut palms, and a variety of orchid plants, is maintained by the owner, the famous Daisy Nottages.

Daisy can go out and catch grouper off the reef, or mix a potion to cure whatever ails you with equal ease. Her health potions are for sale, including her famous potency formula.

The North Bight fishery is consistently one of the best in the Bahamas, and it's the home of the original Bang Bang Club on Pot Cay. Charlie Smith has rebuilt much of the club, and is now booking anglers. This Pot

The owners and crew at Tranquility Hill Lodge— Ivan Neymour, Raymond Mackey, and crew.

Ric Fogel

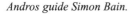

Andros guide Simon Bain.

Cay location would allow anglers to stay right on some of the best North Bight flats.

Other famous old-time guides include Rudi Bell and Errold Braynen. Errold is one of our all-time favorites. We have enjoyed some of our best-ever bonefishing days with Errold on the West Side. This tradition of guiding as a profession has led to a new generation of guides on Andros that is among the best in the Bahamas.

Guides like Charlie Neymour, Andy Smith, Simon Bain, Barry Neymour, Prescott Smith, Dennis Leadon, Dwain Neymour, and others have developed loyal followings of their own. Look at the last names of these guys and you can make a good guess who helped develop their skills.

These independent guides can be booked through Westbank Anglers at 800/922-3474. Due to their repeat clientele, we recommend booking them at least six months in advance.

Just across a channel from Pot Cay is Pine Cay, the north shore of which is a series of connected light-bottomed flats, small bays, and coral points that draw incredible numbers of big bonefish into skinny water. Over the years we have had some of our best fishing for tailing bones in the ten-pound class on these flats.

The entire north shore of the North Bight provides a lee for fishing during cold fronts, or when high winds pick up out of the northeast. Areas like the Dressing Room, Soft Mud Bight, and Yellow Cay can be fished all day on the proper tide. The numbers of fish in these areas defies imagination, but even better, these fish are aggressive to a fly.

Across the entrance to the North Bight is Big Wood Cay, which is another story. The hard white sand flats are easy to wade, and you can spot bonefish a long way out. Australian pines, casuarinas, coconut palms, and mangroves line the gold sand beaches where big bones cruise in six inches of water to feast on sea crabs. If you're looking for big bones that are a challenge to catch, this is a great place. If spooky, finicky fish easily frustrate you, you should avoid this area.

A fun option for catching a variety of fish is the Shark Hole, located in the middle of the North Bight between Nottages Cottages and Big Wood Cay. Blind casting a variety of saltwater streamers or poppers can produce jacks, mackerel, snapper, barracuda, and sharks.

The oceanside flats of Big Wood Cay between the North Bight and the Middle Bight are fished by only a few guides. Long stretches of white sand are fun to wade on incoming tides in the morning or late afternoon. This is also an excellent area to fish for permit on a high tide when the wind is blowing out of the west.

Cruising outside Big Wood Cay is the easiest and fastest way to reach the Middle Bight from Behring Point if the wind is down. Isolated coral heads and sand bars make it necessary to stay well off the shoreline, however. If the wind is up this is dangerous choppy water for a flats boat, though larger vessels can make the passage outside the reef without problem.

During rough weather flats boats take the inner passage through the North Bight, past Pot Cay, around the western end of Big Wood, past Kim's Cay, then either through Blue Creek or straight past the grounded naval buoy to reach the Middle Bight. Navigating this passage requires extensive local knowledge, as does fishing anywhere in the Bights. We believe the only way to safely fish the Bights is with a local guide.

Assuming you can take the outside route, another AUTEC base is located on the southeastern corner of Big Wood Cay at the mouth of the Middle Bight. Deep blue water signals the channel entrance to the Bight with Gibson Cay to the south. The inside flats off Gibson Cay are easy to wade on a low incoming tide, and you can count on seeing waves of bonefish tailing over the light sand bottom.

Ric Fogel

Andros guide Charlie Neymour.

Many people believe the Middle Bight is home to the largest bonefish in the world. We tend to agree. The names of the flats—"the promised land," "land of the giants," "land of a thousand tailing bones"—conjure images that make anglers weak in the knees.

For this reason, guides from Cargill Creek and Behring Point make the thirty- to fifty-minute run down here whenever the weather is good. Moxey Creek, Fever Creek, Fever Cay, and Blue Creek are fished on a regular basis. While these flats are still among our favorites, the bonefish here are educated. Longer casts and excellent line control are required to catch fish, especially the big boys.

Beginners fishing this area will do best by wading. Wading Fever Creek on the last half of the falling tide will produce multiple shots at fish in the five- to seven-pound range, and that magical ten-pounder could turn up anytime.

The last half of the falling tide is generally our favorite time throughout this area. Mangrove shorelines and back bays draw huge numbers of bonefish to feed on sea crabs. If your timing is just a touch off you won't catch these fish going in. Waiting for them to come out is more effective. There are a number of good ambush points to intercept fish returning to the deeper channels. On bad weather days, days that are dark and windy, we often fish ambush points because the fish are easy to spot as they work their way out of the mangroves.

Many anglers fish Andros specifically for big bonefish. Of course, everyone would like to catch a big fish, a fish ten pounds or better. But pursuing big bonefish is different from just going bonefishing, requiring incredible patience and selectivity. Usually, you fish different types of flats and deeper water when you pursue big bones. It's harder to spot fish in deeper water, and you need to fish a fly that will sink fast,

Brian O'Keefe

Many anglers in Andros fish specifically for big bonefish.

like a Clouser Minnow. You probably won't see as many fish as you would on a "regular" bonefish flat: You are sacrificing numbers for size.

We often hear anglers at the lodges lamenting the fact that they aren't catching any "big" fish. While it is possible to catch big bones fishing the regular flats, you usually have to make a special effort. When you see a group of fish, don't make an indiscriminate cast. Take a few seconds to scan the fish and pick out the biggest one. Make your cast specifically to the biggest fish, and away from the smaller fish. Smaller fish are faster, and often more aggressive, so if you cast near them, they will get your fly first.

Sometimes this strategy means not casting at all. If you see some smaller fish on a big bonefish flat, don't cast! If you hook one, you can be sure of seeing a ten-pounder a minute or two later while you're playing that smaller fish. We often pass up shots at bonefish in the eight- and nine-pound class while stalking the really big boys.

Keep in mind that big bones are a challenge to catch. We define big bones as ten to eleven pounds. Giant bones are twelve pounds and up. These fish are their own separate breed. Think of giant bones as being tougher to catch than permit, and you'll have a true idea of the challenge.

Mangrove Cay forms the southern shoreline of the Middle Bight. The cay features tall green hills that are set back from white sand beaches and massive black coral outcroppings. Moxey Town is on the northeastern corner of the cay. Known locally as Little Harbour, the town is marked by groves of coconut palms and sandy beaches. Anchorages are available in the cove off Moxey Town and around the government dock, though this area is rough during high northeastern winds.

Fuel, water, groceries, liquor, and hardware are available in Moxey Town. The Mangrove Cay airport is a two-minute car ride from town. Bahamasair operates here through a relationship with Congo Air. Charter air service is available through a number of carriers.

Operated for twenty-five years by Leonard and Pearl Moxey, Moxey's Guest House & Bonefishing Lodge is in the center of town, directly across from the harbor. Recently renovated by brothers Joel and "Big" Lundy Moxey, this is one of the best places to stay for anglers who want to fish the Middle and South Bights.

Accommodations are comfortable, plus the food and service are outstanding. Pearl, who still does some of the cooking, is justifiably famous for her Johnny Cake and conch chowder. True Bahamian charm and hospitality are never in short supply.

Pearl is also a kindred spirit to Daisy. She brews a delicious bush tea. If you have any ailments, including a head cold or sinus problem, Pearl will conjure up a mixture of local shrubs and herbs that would make any pharmacist jealous.

Moxey's Bonefish Lodge.

Joel runs a training program for young local guides looking to fill the flats booties of famous "old-time" guides like James and Ralph Moxey, and Carl "John Wayne" Moxey. We have assisted with the training and have been impressed with the work ethic and enthusiasm of the younger guides.

The advantage Moxey's holds over other Andros lodges is strategic location. The best Middle Bight flats are as close as five minutes away, and no more than fifteen minutes away. If you want to fish an early morning or late afternoon incoming tide on Gibson Cay, you can't do it if you're staying up north. Gibson Cay is one of our favorite spots for reasons other than the fishing. A pristine beach covers an oceanside section of the cay, and at low tide you can gaze across the exposed inside flats at thousands of purple-tinted Queen conch shells. In the late afternoon this flat turns silver, and literally glitters in the fading sunlight.

The Moxey Town location is unequaled for timing any of the Middle Bight tides, or fishing deeper into the Middle Bight, and all the way to the West Side. In addition, the South Bight and Lisbon Creek are only twenty minutes away.

Reef fishing off Moxey Town and Middle Bight Cay is excellent. Local commercial fishermen often supply their northern neighbors with grouper, snapper, barracuda, conch, and lobster. Several AUTEC buoys straight out from Gibson Cay are the best dolphin magnets we've ever seen. When the seas are relatively calm, it is common to hook lots of dolphin using WBA mullets, offshore deceivers, or saltwater poppers and a 10-weight fly rod.

Continuing south of Moxey Town inside the reef is easy for boaters. There are a few coral heads and sand bars but nothing like up north. Numerous settlements run the length of Mangrove Cay. There are several lodging options along this pleasant stretch of coconut palm shaded beaches, though these cottages and motels open and close on erratic schedules.

We consider South Andros to run from the South Bight, which includes Lisbon Creek, past the end of the island proper, to the Grassy Cays and Water Cays.

Victoria Point, White Bay Rock, and Flat Rock signal the entrance to the South Bight from the north. The entrance to Lisbon Creek is just inside the South Bight on the northern shore. Dredging has created a deeper channel into Lisbon Creek, where the mail boat and commercial fishermen use the concrete government dock.

The settlement is quiet and charming, shaded by pine and palm trees. The Bannister House furnishes comfortable accommodations. The Bannisters also own the

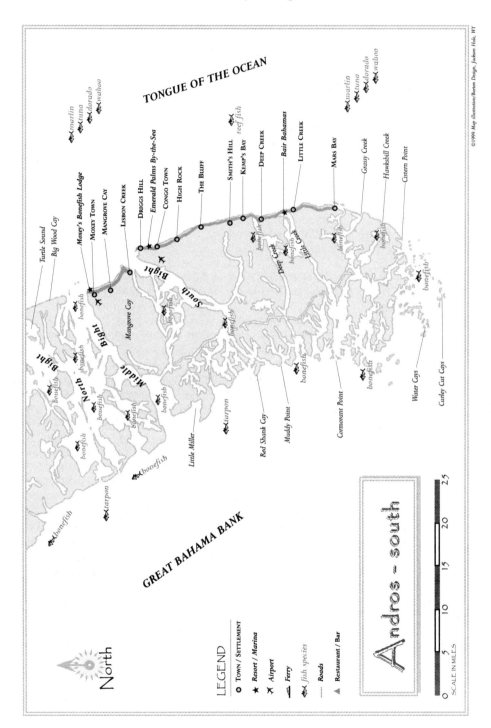

©1999 Map illustration/Burton Design, Jackson Hole, WY

Aqua-Marine Club, which is open sporadically, so call ahead if you need a meal or a Kalik.

The bonefishing in Lisbon Creek is temperamental. When it's on, it's awesome, with lots of fish, and big fish. When it's off, you'll catch some smaller fish while trying to figure out what's happening. Regardless, spending part of a day in the creek is always enjoyable. Miles of mangrove-lined flats and protected bays produce abundant food and shelter for game fish. Parts of Lisbon Creek are much like Stafford Creek, with high pine-covered hills that provide protection even on gale force days.

You could spend weeks exploring the back marls that penetrate deep into Mangrove Cay in a maze of small creeks, channels, flats, and lakes. Several channels connect to a main channel leading back to the Middle Bight. These areas hold good numbers of permit at times, though we haven't figured out any pattern for predicting their movements. We have spent some time hiking through mucky mangroves to reach tailing fish in shallow lakes that fill only on the highest tides. These areas are so dense with crabs that you can't help stepping on them as they try to scamper out of your way.

Fishing with a guide is essential in this area, as it is easy to become stranded when the tide is falling. A low incoming tide and the last half of a falling tide will produce the best bonefishing. During higher tidal periods the fish push as far back into the mangroves as they can, which often makes them unreachable.

We haven't spent much time fishing for tarpon in Lisbon Creek, but our moderate success leads us to believe that tarpon migrate through this area on an annual basis, and that smaller resident tarpon are in the creek year round.

This is definitely true of the South Bight, especially toward the West Side. South Bight tarpon fishing can be spectacular, though few local guides understand the tarpon fishery from a fly-fishing perspective. We've done most of our South Bight tarpon fishing with independent guides from Behring Point and Cargill Creek. This makes for long days and long runs, but the results are usually worth it.

The South Bight doesn't have the reputation of the North and Middle Bights, but don't tell that to the bonefish. Good numbers of fish, plus giant fish, roam these coral and sand flats. Many areas offer excellent wading for tailing fish, especially on the incoming tide. And if you're looking for permit, this is the only Bight where you can realistically expect to see them on a regular basis.

The South Bight cuts all the way through to the West Side like its northern cousins, exiting at Miller Creek and Red Shank Point. The boat ride through always feels like an adventure into primordial times. The water blends intense shades of blue and green over lush bottom structure. Green, yellow, and gold shorelines narrow as you head west past thirty or so blue holes that can boil with jacks, snappers, and barracuda. If you're looking to catch a variety of fish, you can work the blue holes with Deceivers, Glass Minnows, and Clousers until the quaking muscles in your arms tell you you've had enough.

Back on the eastern side of the island, Driggs Hill is situated on the southern point entrance to the South Bight directly below the AUTEC base on Golding Cay. A dredged harbor has been carved into the land here and, unfortunately, there are plans to bring in cruise ships. While we don't see that happening any time soon, the idea is horrendous.

Recreational boaters would be better served by anchoring around the corner in the South Bight. Boaters can continue south of Driggs Hill inside the reef with normal precautions. Coconut palms and white sand beaches make up the shoreline. A couple of miles south is Emerald Palms By-the-Sea, a nice oceanside hotel with air-conditioned

Guide Andy Smith with a barracuda caught in one of the creeks on the West Side.

rooms and a surprisingly good restaurant. The Bahamian government owns the hotel, but there are always rumors of an eminent sale to a private investor.

Anglers regularly use the hotel as a base for bonefishing, though this is also a remote spot for a relaxing beach vacation. Local guides like Stanley Forbes live in Congo Town and can be booked by the hotel. Congo Town is just another mile down the road. The Long Bay/Congo Town airport is a couple of minutes away by taxi. Congo Air and numerous charter services can be used to fly in here.

South of Congo Town are the Long Bay Cays, which provide a nice lee anchorage for boaters. Directly inland is the settlement of The Bluff, a fishing community that sits on a sand bluff overlooking a broad beach. Silvia's is one of the better local restaurants, though hours of operation are inconsistent. If you need a post office, clinic, telephone/fax office, or library, this is also the location of the South Andros government complex.

Another short run south brings you to Kemp's Bay. An abandoned AUTEC base was the reason for a dredged channel leading into the concrete dock used by the mail boat and a variety of local fishing vessels. Diesel fuel, gas, water and ice are available, though you should arrange for supplies ahead of time, or be prepared to hang out and be patient.

Supplies are best arranged for with Rahming Marine. The Rahming family runs a hardware store, grocery, laundry service, and you might even be able to rent a car from them. Make sure to confirm this in advance.

The Rahmings are also in the flats skiff business, building durable fiberglass boats capable of poling into very skinny water. Their original boats are ideal in South Andros, where guides rarely have to cross rough water, and often pole into the shallow mangrove backcountry. Due to the flat bottom of their original design, these boats will give you a pounding in deeper water when the wind is up. Recently, the Rahmings added a deluxe V-hull design to their inventory. This boat is a fly-fishing machine and includes a poling platform, a double-cushioned seat with a sturdy back mounted on a forward cooler, and a clean forward casting area. These boats are showing up all over the Bahamas. We just fished in one out of Long Island, and it was the most comfortable flats boats we've fished in.

The Royal Palm Beach Lodge, a short walk from the concrete dock, is a good spot for experienced anglers looking to fish the remote areas of South Andros. The lodge has a restaurant open to the public, but we suggest you call to make sure they'll be open, otherwise you could go hungry.

South of Kemp's Bay is the settlement of Deep Creek, and the entrance to the creek itself. Many of our friends and clients enjoy this area as a change of pace, a remote place to catch lots of fish in the three to four pound range. Both Deep Creek and Little Creek, about a twenty-minute run to the south, offer protected fishing in bad weather.

Bair Bahamas Guest House, inside Little Creek, is the best bonefishing operation in South Andros. The three-bedroom air-conditioned guesthouse was remodeled in 1996 and can take six anglers. Operated by an American couple, Stanley and Andy Bair, the food and service here are excellent. Anglers depart each morning from the dock right out front, fishing with well-trained guides. The wade fishing throughout South Andros is outstanding, though guides here will also pole clients through the backcountry.

South of Little Creek the barrier reef turns out away from land around High Point Cay. Numerous sandbars appear like white islands in the green water. On land, the road ends in the serene settlement of Mars Bay. The bay is really a blue hole encircled by shallow light-colored flats and bars. Permit feed around the bars consistently at high tide. It is possible to stay in Kemp's Bay, then hire a taxi to drive you to Mars Bay to meet your guide. This option lets anglers avoid a long bumpy boat ride and still fish the remote southern tip of Andros.

Grassy Creek is a short run south of Mars Bay, and the site of past oil exploration. A concrete dock inside the creek marks on old drilling location. Aside from this ugly landmark, the creek is a beautiful wilderness bonefish area. Schools of fish numbering in the thousands move in and out of this area throughout the year.

Grassy Creek Cays is just offshore. Good anchorages are available for boaters and the snorkeling is sensational, though you have to pay attention for sharks. The cays are surrounded by flats that are easy to wade and covered with aggressive bonefish that have rarely, if ever, seen a fly. The reef fishing is world class. Once you have a chum line going you will be amazed at the numbers and variety of fish you can catch with flies or conventional gear.

Hawksbill Creek lies farther south along the coast and is another bonefish haven. Flats boats can maneuver in over the shallow sand bar at the entrance on the right tides, but careful planning is necessary to avoid becoming stranded.

Jack Fish Channel is at the very southern tip of the island. Miles of wadable sand flats, little creeks, channels, and islets create a home for bonefish that make the numbers of fish at Christmas Island look only fair. We have seen schools of bones color acres of white sand flats shimmering silver. These masses of fish swim in waves that ripple the water across a hundred square yards. The fish in these schools average one to three pounds, which leads us to believe this area is a vast bonefish nursery.

For bigger fish we work the deeper channel edges and the many sand bars that drop off into turquoise cuts. On occasion we have seen permit when pursuing the bigger bones.

This habitat continues around the tip of the island, then up along the West Side to the Water Cays. This is the area where Stanley Bain located his Grassy Cays Bonefish Camp, which has now been closed for several years. We often hear talk of reopening the camp, or leasing the camp to an outside operator, but we are not aware of any serious plans for the camp to operate again.

Shallow water, sandbars, and tricky varying tides are a hazard to boaters in this area. We have found that published tide charts are not reliable for navigating here, and

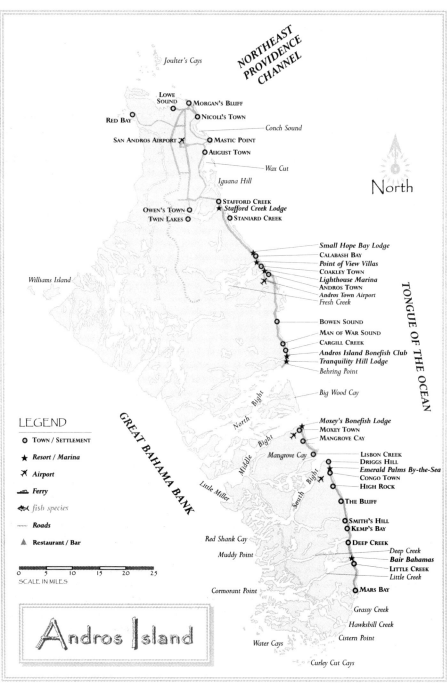

Joulter's Cays

LOWE SOUND
MORGAN'S BLUFF
NICOLL'S TOWN
RED BAY
Conch Sound
SAN ANDROS AIRPORT ✈
MASTIC POINT
AUGUST TOWN
Wax Cut
Iguana Hill

North

STAFFORD CREEK
★ *Stafford Creek Lodge*
OWEN'S TOWN
TWIN LAKES
STANIARD CREEK

Williams Island

Small Hope Bay Lodge
CALABASH BAY
Point of View Villas
COAKLEY TOWN
Lighthouse Marina
ANDROS TOWN
Andros Town Airport
Fresh Creek

TONGUE OF THE OCEAN

BOWEN SOUND
MAN OF WAR SOUND
CARGILL CREEK
Andros Island Bonefish Club
Tranquility Hill Lodge
Behring Point

Big Wood Cay

Bight
North
Bight
Middle

Moxey's Bonefish Lodge
MOXEY TOWN
MANGROVE CAY

GREAT BAHAMA BANK

Mangrove Cay
LISBON CREEK
DRIGGS HILL
Emerald Palms By-the-Sea
CONGO TOWN
HIGH ROCK

Little Miller

South Bight

THE BLUFF

SMITH'S HILL
KEMP'S BAY

LEGEND

○	TOWN / SETTLEMENT
★	*Resort / Marina*
✈	*Airport*
⛴	*Ferry*
🐟	*fish species*
～	*Roads*
▲	*Restaurant / Bar*

DEEP CREEK
Deep Creek
Bair Bahamas
LITTLE CREEK
Little Creek

Red Shank Cay
Muddy Point

MARS BAY

| 0 | 5 | 10 | 15 | 20 | 25 |

SCALE IN MILES

Cormorant Point

Grassy Creek
Hawksbill Creek
Cistern Point

Andros Island

Water Cays

Curley Cut Cays

even less reliable for predicting fish behavior. Stanley Bain and his guides spent years exploring and fishing this area before they became comfortable with the unique tides and currents on the southwest side of the island. Consider this region to be unexplored territory, and use the appropriate precautions.

The West Side of Andros is uninhabited. Special attention must be given to the tides when fishing or navigating this massive area. This attention must include the understanding that tides here can vary with weather conditions more than other areas due to the vast stretches of shallow water. An uncountable number of creeks, sandbars, and back bays compose the region along the coast from the Water Cays north to Miller Creek.

During windy conditions, especially when winds blow from the west, the water along the coast turns milky white. Sight fishing during these conditions is impossible and boating is dangerous.

With the Grassy Cay Bonefish Camp closed, the only way to fish this region is by enduring a long boat ride (about two hours from the Bights), or taking a float plane or mother boat. The Bahamian government has set specific rules for float plane and mother boat fishing throughout The Bahamas. It is strictly illegal to fish with a commercial float plane or mother boat outfitter without using Bahamian guides. Any outfitter who claims otherwise is not telling the truth, period!

Any angler who wants to book a float plane trip, or mother boat trip, is strongly advised to confirm with the outfitter that only Bahamian guides will be employed on the trip.

There are only a handful of guides who are qualified to take anglers into this area. The fishing for bonefish and tarpon in the creeks and back bays is excellent, but it is easy to become lost or stranded by an outgoing tide. For do-it-yourself experienced boaters and anglers, the use of sea kayaks deployed from a mother boat is a good method for fishing this region. Sea kayaks give you mobility in any tidal situation, and flexibility if you make a navigational mistake. Sea kayak camping is another good option, but doctor flies and no-see-ums can be fierce when the wind is down, or any time in spring. Even anchoring well offshore will not protect boaters from the ravaging bugs at this time.

The Miller Creek and Little Miller Creek areas offer good tarpon fishing on the proper tides. Miles of white sand flats that average four to six feet in depth are home to tarpon that run between sixty and one hundred twenty pounds. These are resident fish that swim between the creeks and the outer banks on a regular basis. Whenever water temperatures reach 75°F or higher, these tarpon will be on the flats. Larger migratory tarpon running up to two hundred pounds are present from May through November.

Anglers staying in Lisbon Creek or Driggs Hill can access Miller Creek by running through the South Bight. Running time will depend on your flats boat and the size of its engine, so count on anywhere from forty to ninety minutes. Only a couple of guides are qualified to fish for tarpon in the Miller Creek area, though most guides will swear they know it well. Buyer beware is a good motto, and as a safety precaution make sure your guide has plenty of gas, a radio, and a supply of flares before you leave your home dock.

Miller Creek pours out onto the West Side flats in the center of a huge bay, with Red Shank Point an obvious landmark to the south. Several other smaller creeks enter the bay and all are tarpon magnets. Sea turtles are abundant in this area. They commonly roll on the surface, which can trick you into thinking they're tarpon if you don't get a good look. Remember that tarpon like to follow land and bottom contours. They are also creatures of habit, and these habits are influenced by wind direction. We prefer to fish lee shorelines, poling into the incoming tide.

Another large bay is north of Miller Creek, and several more creeks feed this area. We have only fished here a few times, but have caught tarpon on each occasion. The long mud bank and mangrove shoreline continuing north is home to a parade of bonefish and an occasional permit.

At the end of this shoreline is a wide mangrove-covered point, which signals another massive white-bottomed bay. Little Miller Creek is at the back of the bay, and there are four other significant creeks that feed these flats. Fishing either the north or south shoreline is the best way to play the odds on an incoming tide.

North of Little Miller is the expansive opening to the Middle Bight. Deep blue channels cut into white sand flats that are some of the most beautiful in the Bahamas. Running out here in a flats boat on a calm day is an ultimate thrill. The vast serene ocean melts into the sky. You could be the only people in the world. Imagine complete peace. Daydreams blossom. Thousands of bonefish and tarpon roam on every tide.

Miles of white sand flats, hard enough to wade in most places, run along the low limestone, coral, and mangrove shorelines on the way north to Spanish Wells and Yellow Cay. These flats are rarely fished, as most guides concentrate their bonefishing efforts farther north. For shear numbers of fish, these flats are as good as any in the world.

Spanish Wells and Yellow Cay form their own complex mini-ecosystem. This area is easily reached for day fishing from Behring Point or Cargill Creek. Hundreds of cays and many creeks throughout Spanish Wells connect to sand and grass flats, many of which are protected on windy days, while on calm days tarpon roll in the deeper bays and cuts.

Yellow Cay draws high numbers of bonefish, but the real fun here is hunting big bones. Fish in the seven- to ten-pound range feed along the shorelines on a consistent basis. When the wind blows hard, the water on some of these flats turns a milky yellow color that can make seeing fish difficult.

Little and Big Loggerhead Creeks lie to the north, and both creeks connect the North Bight to the West Side. Little Loggerhead is a straight shot between high mangrove banks. When the tide is moving, this creek is like a ripping river. On bad weather days this is a fun place to anchor up and blind cast for a variety of species. Jacks, mackerel, sharks, tarpon, and barracuda are always in the creek. We like to blind cast an orange Popovic's Banger for sharks and barracuda. For jacks and mackerel, we usually go with Sardina or Glass Minnow patterns.

Outside Big Loggerhead is a massive sand flat that curves to the north away from the shoreline, with water depths averaging eight feet, and dipping to

Brian O'Keefe

Boats from Cargill Creek, headed toward Spanish Wells.

twelve in spots. We've fished this outside flat on numerous occasions when hundreds of rolling tarpon turn the water surface silver.

A quarter of a mile north is a sand and coral point that tarpon in the 150-pound and up class consistently swim past between May and October. In spite of how good the tarpon fishing has been in this area, it is not one of our favorite places because of the boat traffic. This section of the West Side is the most heavily fished, though "heavily fished" is certainly a relative term in this case.

The Andros Island Bonefish Club sends guides out this way almost every day for bonefishing, and we can't blame them as the bonefishing along the shorelines all the way to Cabbage Creek is sensational. Fish swim in waves along the sand and coral banks. Double hookups are common. When the wind is from the northeast, and you're fishing an incoming tide, you can count on high numbers of bones, with fish averaging close to five pounds.

We consider Cabbage Creek the cutoff point for day trips from Behring Point and Cargill Creek lodges. Even in a fast boat this is an hour-plus one-way run. There are guides, however, who have boats capable of fishing Wide Open and Williams Island when the weather is good.

The territory from Cabbage Creek to Williams Island is relatively unfished. This is a superb area for anglers to book an overnight camping trip. These trips are available with independent guides or through Small Hope Bay Lodge. The highlight of a camping trip is sightcasting to tailing bonefish in the early morning and late evening. Virtually every scale on every fish is visible in the clear skinny water, and the blue accents of their fins glimmer in mesmerizing contrast to the silky white bottom.

Williams Island itself holds innumerable bonefish. The numbers of fish can be overwhelming, and surprisingly, there is a high percentage of fish over eight pounds. Permit also inhabit the deeper flats around the island in good numbers.

The area between Williams Island and Red Bay is the substance of a saltwater angler's dreams. While our experience here is limited, we have plans to change that in the immediate future. High concentrations of bonefish, permit, and tarpon make this grand-slam territory. Creeks and back bays cut into the shoreline for miles. Sea kayaking and camping would be an ideal way to explore the area.

Guides from Stafford Creek Lodge are currently trailering their boats to Red Bay then fishing south toward Williams Island. In spite of its size, this is a fragile fishery than cannot sustain a lot of pressure. The Andros Island Guides Association is working with the government to protect this amazing natural resource.

FISHING HIGHLIGHTS

Traditionally, the best times to fish Andros are March through late June, then again in October and November. December, January, and February can be excellent, though these months have a greater chance of suffering through cold fronts that can bring high winds, cloud cover, and chilly temperatures. July, August, and September are the main tropical storm and hurricane months.

With due consideration given to the so-called best times for good fishing and good weather, we'd like to say that all saltwater flats fishing is at the whim of Mother Nature. The weather can be good or bad any time. We have given up any attempts at predictions. The weather is the weather, so learn to deal with it. Expect windy conditions at all times. Hope for sun but be prepared for clouds, which makes seeing fish extremely difficult. Be ready for any condition, then you will feel particularly blessed and appreciative on those gorgeous calm days.

Brian O'Keefe

*A huge barracuda; when the bonefishing is slow,
'cudas will often take up the slack.*

That said, let's get back to January and February. If these are the only two months you can go flats fishing, Andros is a great place to take your shot, especially if you are after big bonefish. More double-digit bonefish are landed in February than any other month. Also keep in mind that Andros covers a vast fishing area. There are miles of creeks, especially on the northeast coast, where anglers can fish in relative calm even on the windiest of days.

Remember too that the term "cold front" is a relative term. While a cold front can plunge air temperatures into the high 40s for a day or so, a tropical climate sets the tone. Andros temperatures average 78°F, with daytime temperatures usually in the 80s. Average water temperature ranges from 70° in January to 90° in August.

The Andros fishery is one of the most varied on earth, yet it can be analyzed with some general rules in mind, as can most other Bahamian fisheries. Flats that drop off into oceanside areas or deeper creeks and channels tend to fish better on the incoming tide. These flats are also better in poor weather conditions, especially when air temperatures drop or rise dramatically. Interior flats and creeks lined with mangroves are usually better on falling tides, and in more stable weather conditions.

We prefer to fish spring tides in Andros as they produce stronger currents and greater changes in water depths. This allows more bonefish to move onto the flats, and to penetrate deeper into remote areas in search of sea crabs. Neap tides, especially in lower tidal periods of the year, bring fewer fish onto the flats, and reduce the fishing area. May has some of the lowest tides of the year, while October has the highest.

Fish are creatures of habit. You need to be observant and patient for maximum success. Make notes in a journal, then try to make predictions about a particular area and a particular tide. This kind of game is lots of fun, and extremely satisfying when your predictions turn into fishing success.

If you spend some time on Andros, or any other Bahamian island, you will discover a variety of flats, and each must be viewed as distinct when piecing together your angling strategy. If you are a freshwater angler, think of the flats as being like big rivers, small rivers, streams, spring creeks, or lakes, each with its own characteristics and tactical demands.

Different types of flats include ocean flats; reef flats or transition flats between reefs; interior flats; mangrove flats that extend from land or cays; and island or cay flats surrounded by deep water. Each type of flat can have different types of bottoms.

Ocean flats tend to have hard sand or coral bottoms that can be waded. The White Bight area, for example, has a mixture of hard sand and pulverized coral sprinkled with brittle crunchy coral. This habitat is loaded with shrimp and crabs. On an incoming tide, this area offers some of the best wade fishing for tailing bonefish you can imagine.

Reef or transitional flats are usually hard-bottomed also, but they can be very difficult to wade due to uneven contours and sharp protruding coral. Contours, troughs, holes, and little caves are safe havens for bait fish and crustaceans. Larger game fish like jacks, snappers, and mackerel are lured to these areas on a regular basis.

Interior flats tend to have soft mud or ooze bottoms, and can be impossible to wade without sinking up to your hips in goo. These flats are best fished from a poled skiff. Interior flats in the Middle Bight area are home to countless numbers of double-digit bonefish who punch fist-size holes in the bottom while routing for shrimp and crabs.

Mangrove flats are usually fed by creeks and can be soft or hard-bottomed. The key to fishing these flats is to figure out the path bonefish will take in and out. This can be difficult on an incoming tide, especially if your timing is even slightly off. On a falling tide, however, you can set up ambush points that yield amazing results.

The importance of water temperature can't be emphasized enough. It is the key to finding fish. It is also the key to determining when to pursue larger bonefish. Larger bonefish either like, or can tolerate, colder water than smaller fish. This is a primary reason why the largest bonefish in Andros are consistently caught in February and March, and at other times of the year after a cold front.

Water depth is another important factor in fishing any flat. Bonefish like to move and feed at a constant water depth. They will congregate in pockets, channels, and creeks waiting for the incoming tide to reach the proper depth before they move onto a flat. Conversely, bonefish will wait for a falling tide to reach a specific depth before moving out of the mangroves. We have seen large bones wait until the water barely covers their shoulders before making a dash for deeper channels.

Like trout in streams, bonefish are drawn to structure. Andros possesses thousands of mangrove-lined or coral-lined white-bottomed bays, and these bays are linked by coral points. Count on finding bonefish near each point, and at the start and end of each bay. The bones will be hunting large shrimp and a variety of crabs, so consider matching your fly to these food sources.

Tides influence flats fishing more than any other type of fishing. Tides dictate where and when fish will be, and vary greatly from area to area. It is vital to be observant. You cannot rely on fish to be on the same flat at the same time each day because tides move forward approximately fifty minutes every day. Also, wind and current conditions vary, as does water depth and volume. Remember this when you want to return to a place where you experienced good fishing, and your guide decides to take you somewhere else. There is a reason for this. The guide understands the tides.

Most areas of the Bahamas, including Andros, have two high tides and two low tides, semidiurnal tides, during a day. The moon is the biggest influence on tides, and its relationship to the sun is also significant. This relationship produces higher highs and lower lows at specific times of year. As we mentioned before, the highest highs of the year in Andros are in October.

Tides dictate where and when the fish will be.

Spring tides occur with the full moon and new moon, when the sun and moon are in direct alignment with the earth. This alignment causes higher tides than neap tides, which are first and third quarter periods, with the moon positioned at right angles to the alignment of the earth and sun.

Tides rotate on a two-week cycle, meaning fishing conditions on a given flat will be approximately the same every two weeks. Opposite fishing conditions will exist on a given flat in one week. Every day one high tide is higher than the other high, and one low tide lower than the other. If you can make these distinctions, and note game fish behavioral differences, you can increase your fishing success.

Barometric pressure affects tides along with the wind. High pressure inhibits tidal flow onto the flats. Wind direction, speed, duration, and fetch (the distance over which the wind blows) all affect the tidal ranges. Charlie Smith believes that barometric pressure is more influential on bonefish behavior than water temperature. Smith is convinced that low summertime pressure drives fish off the flats, not high water temperatures. Smith has proven his theory for more than thirty years by consistently catching fish throughout the summer season, even in the middle of the day, when no other guides will venture onto the flats.

Remember, too, that tides do not rise and fall at a uniform rate. There is usually a slack period at both the top and bottom of a tidal change. It is common for a two- to three-hour period of either a rising or falling tide to produce the best fishing, while the other hours produce slower fishing. In Andros this slower fishing scenario can often be avoided by running east or west through the Bights.

Wind and weather are part of the habitat and creators of the fishing conditions. Bonefish are schizophrenic when it comes to the weather. They "smell" weather coming according to our Andros guides, and we have come to believe this over the years. It might be a gorgeous sunny day with calm winds but the bonefish won't touch a perfectly presented fly. They spook two hundred feet out. When bonefish "smell" bad weather they move from the interior flats to the outside ocean flats and then to deeper water. Conversely, when you see bonefish streaming into the Bights you can bet good weather is coming and will stay for a while. When you catch bonefish moving in expectation of good weather, you will experience fishing beyond compare.

We prefer at least a little wind, as fish are less spooky and a breeze can keep the bugs down. We have poured buckets of sweat when bonefishing on calm days, and have actually started up our motor to take a twenty-minute run, abandoning awesome fishing for the relief of rushing air.

Bonefish tend to swim into the wind. Wind calms them because they know it makes them harder to see. A good guide takes advantage of this phenomenon and sets up anglers to cast downwind. On larger wadable flats, however, bonefish will disperse in ways that make casting into the wind the best option. Understanding changing conditions and remaining flexible in your strategy is a key to success.

Bait fish and other food sources don't fight the tides, they go with the flow. All predatory fish know this. Barracuda, for example, are great ambush artists. They can be so still that they become invisible. The next time you're out on the flats, count how many barracuda you spook before you see them.

The strength of a tidal current is important in analyzing how game fish will pursue their food. Stronger currents carry food scents farther and faster and bring in more and larger bonefish and permit. Strong tidal currents correspond to spring tides, while lesser currents are present with neap tides.

The most common flats foods include mantis shrimp, snapping shrimp, swimming shrimp, grass shrimp, swimming crabs, sea crabs, mud and stone crabs, clams, mussels, and gobies. Snapping shrimp are more common in Florida and the northern Bahamas, but these burrowing miniature lobster look-alikes are also found throughout Andros. Clouser Minnows and Borski's Swimming Shrimp are extremely effective in imitating these food sources in deeper water. For skinny water we prefer a Blind Gotcha, Horror, Bonefish Special, or Mihive's Flats Fly. Swimming shrimp are great people food, too.

Grass shrimp are inclined toward areas of turtle grass and higher than normal salinity common to Grand Bahama and Abaco. There are few areas like this in Andros, though these shrimp do like to hang around mangrove roots where larger bonefish actively seek them out. Remember this when fishing for the monster bones in the Middle Bight.

There are more than sixty species of mantis shrimp in the Caribbean. They prefer to burrow in mud and sand bottoms. In Andros, mantis shrimp grow to three inches in length and look like small lobsters with their sharp claws and fan tails. Large bonefish often cruise in deeper water, three to six feet, over these types of flats. We like to fish heavy lead-eyed Gotcha Clouser Minnows or Bunny Gotchas because they sink quickly and kick up mud when we bounce them off the bottom. When you can clearly see a bonefish pick up your fly off the bottom in five feet of water, you know it's a big fish.

Crabs live primarily in shallow-water habitat and are a key reason bonefish risk moving into skinny water. Fly imitations need to be the right size and color. We prefer small Tan Yarn Crabs for fishing tailing fish on the ocean flats. It's an amazing sight to see a huge bonefish attack a Yarn Crab with reckless abandon in ankle-deep water.

Swimming crabs and sea crabs are the most common varieties on Andros, with the blue crab the most common of these. Blues are very aggressive and will defend themselves against attack. Bonefish are used to being pricked by crab claws as they subdue this food source. This explains why a missed hook set that sticks the bonefish will not scare the bonefish away. The fish will actually become more eager to eat the fly a second or third time.

Mud and stone crabs are also prolific in Andros and throughout the Bahamas. They live in the intertidal coral areas that are mixed with mud and sand. Bonefish crave these crabs, and will eat all they can in a given area. You should never underestimate a bonefish's ability to reach a crab on dry land, either. Kim once hooked and landed a ten-pound bone just after we watched it wriggle up onto a small cay and munch a sea crab off the white mud bank.

Gobies are the most common flats bait fish in the Bahamas. They prefer intertidal waters with sand, mud, or coral bottoms. Their ventral fins form a suctionlike disc that allows them to hold to any stationary bottom, which comes in handy during strong tidal fluctuations. Gobies can also live out of the water for several hours. It is common to see them laying on wet sand flats at low tide.

Needlefish are ubiquitous on Andros, and a favorite food for big bonefish. Pipefish and sea horses are found in the few areas of grassy bottoms. A sea horse is really a curled pipefish with a slanted head. Pipefish and sea horses move slowly and are easy prey when their chameleonlike attempts at camouflage fail.

Mollusks include snails, clams, mussels, squid, and octopus, and Andros has plenty of each. When bonefish or permit feed on mussels and clams they can become very finicky. Squid and octopus are also favorite foods for offshore gamefish including dorado, wahoo, and billfish.

White worms are another key part of Andros bonefish diets. Bonefish really focus on this food source in May, October, and November. Why? We have no idea. This is just a behavior we have observed over the years, and our fishing success improved dramatically because of the observation. Successful flats guides and anglers are good students of gamefish behavior, and are always ready to adapt to a given situation.

A unique feature about Andros is the character of the Bights. There is always a high *and* low tide somewhere, and every tidal stage in between. For example, when the tide is at its highest on the east coast, it is at its lowest on the West Side. As a boat progresses from east to west, the tide is at varying stages of rising and falling.

For anglers looking for specific tidal conditions, this is an exciting situation. With the aid of a fast boat, anglers can fish an incoming tide most of the day, or a falling tide, or any stage of the tide that seems desirable.

One of our favorite fishing day options is to stalk tarpon on the last half of the incoming tide on the West Side in the morning, then dash to the east coast to fish the incoming tide on the ocean flats for big bonefish. In this scenario, we have experienced days in which we battled tarpon over one hundred pounds, then bonefish over ten pounds. This strategy has also put us in position to finish the day going for permit on a high oceanside tide. Unfortunately for us, the huge Andros permit have never been hungry for our flies on a day we had success with tarpon *and* bonefish. So . . . we're still pursuing that elusive Andros grand slam.

The scenario above is just one of a countless number of daily strategies that can be pursued in Andros for a variety of species. In choosing a strategy remember that the time of day a tide occurs is more important than the strength of the tidal flow. In Andros it is easy to make the time of day factor work, but at most saltwater flats destinations this is not the case. Don't just plan a trip based on a spring tide or neap tide. Consider the time of day the tides occur, too.

Another feature unique to Andros is the amount of fresh water that influences food sources, water salinity, and the migratory patterns of the game fish. Countless miles of creeks penetrate the landmass of Andros from every point of the compass.

These creeks sometimes turn yellow with fresh water after a heavy rain, creating additional habitat for crabs and shrimp. After several days of tidal changes, the scent of these crabs lures bonefish and other game fish deep into the backcountry. These areas also become the breeding grounds for bait fish and bonefish.

The relationship of the nursery areas in Andros to other islands, and the overall Andros fishery, is not well understood. Through continued observation, however, we have been able to predict some migratory patterns and spawning behaviors for tarpon and bonefish. These predictions are based on specific areas at specific times of year. The West Side of the island has been the focus of much of our attention, especially in the vast areas south of the Middle Bight. We plan to shift this focus in the coming years to the northwest side, in the Red Bay and Williams Island region.

We have seen concentrations of permit in Red Bay that rival the best areas of Ascension Bay, Mexico. Smaller bonefish literally carpet the flats, and on calm days

Stephen and guide Charlie Neymour with a nice tarpon.

tarpon can be seen rolling everywhere. Sound like a dream? It can be, though access is a significant challenge, and predicting the behavior of the fish on a consistent basis will require a lot more time and effort.

A final note on the unique features of Andros deals with the landlocked lakes. Many of these lakes have never been fished or explored. Others were fished thirty or forty years ago but not since. Duck hunters have enjoyed great sport on these lakes over the years without ever wetting line.

Some of the lakes have a high salinity level while others are brackish or completely fresh. Rain changes the salinity in all the lakes on a regular basis. Access to most of these waters is difficult, though old logging roads come to within several hundred yards of a couple of the northern lakes.

Our recent explorations have been on foot, hiking thirty minutes to two hours through mangroves, broken coral, and muck to reach a given lake. At times the rewards have been spectacular. Can you imagine wade fishing for hundred-pound tarpon, for cubera snappers that go from thirty to one hundred pounds, for voracious jacks, and for permit?

File this away in the back of your mind as one of the last frontiers of saltwater fly-fishing. And keep in touch with us for continued updates.

It is no surprise that bonefish are the number-one flats game fish in Andros, and throughout the Bahamas. The overall coral, mud, and sand composition of the flats

A cubera snapper, caught from one of the island's many inland lakes.

in Andros inspire bonefish to forage for food. As bonefish move over these flats they exhibit a rooting behavior, and are often seeking out specific foods such as crabs, clams, and mussels. Bonefish prefer these bottom-dwelling mollusks and crustaceans, but will pounce on flies that look nothing like their preferred foods. Still, matching flies to food sources is important in terms of size, silhouette, and color, just as in trout fishing.

The Middle Bight is a classic area where dense crab populations live in shallow water along the banks and mangroves. When you roam the wadable flats around Fever Cay on a low tide you'll see thousands of crabs trapped between glistening humps of coral and sand scampering through puddles of water.

While we've seen bonefish on the flats in 66°F water, 70° is the minimum we prefer. We fish the outside ocean flats when the water is in the cooler ranges. As water warms, between 75° and 85°, the interior flats really turn on. Fish pour into the Bights from the east and west, and appear out of the deeper creeks and channels. Above 86° fish usually move back to deeper water or to the oceanside flats. In May and June it is common to see huge areas of mud in the deeper channels inside the bights. These muds are made by huge schools of bonefish tearing up the bottom in search of food.

Oxygen levels are also an integral part of this temperature factor. The more tidal flow that exists, the more oxygen the water carries. This is another reason we prefer spring tides in Andros, and ocean flats in hot weather.

The color of a bonefish varies depending on location. Outside ocean fish have dark green backs that sometimes appear black in the water. These fish usually swim over darker coral bottoms, and they are super-strong. These dark green fish will often rip off two-hundred-plus yards of backing on their first run. Concentrations of these fish live all along the eastern coast, especially around Long Bay Cay, White Bight, Big Wood Cay, and the mouth of the Middle Bight.

Inside fish, fish that spend most of their time in the Bights and creeks, are light in color, ranging from tan to a silvery white. These fish are much more difficult to see than their ocean cousins. Fish on the West Side have this color scheme also. The West Side is similar to an endless inside flat because of its shallow depth and bottom character, which is a mixture of white gooey mud and hard coral sand that stretches almost to Cuba.

Spotting bonefish is a developed skill, just like casting and line control. Total concentration is much more important than an angler's vision quality. Being observant is critical and learning to spot slight changes in color or hints of movement are the keys to developing your vision.

Spotting bonefish over light-colored bottoms is much easier than seeing them over dark turtle grass. Since most bottoms in Andros are light in color, it is an ideal place for beginning saltwater flats anglers. In focusing on the bottom, look for signs of feeding. A puff of mud will indicate that a bonefish is very close. Look for a flash, a change of color, a sign of movement. In shallow water, especially on calm days, you can see surface signs like nervous water, wakes, or actual bonefish tails and fins.

Tune yourself in to the world of flats game fish, allow yourself to be absorbed by it, and your fishing success will improve dramatically.

Resident tarpon are plentiful year round in Andros. The best fishing is weather dependent, with calmer weather providing ideal conditions. Tarpon will first appear on the flats when the water temperature reaches 75°F. A degree or two colder and the fish will stay in the creeks or on the outside banks. This minimum temperature is reached in Andros at some point every month of the year. A couple of warm, calm days in a row is all it takes.

A common misconception about the Andros tarpon fishery is that the fish are just in the creeks. And it's true, there are lots of tarpon in the creeks, and you can blind fish for them anytime. You

Stephen with bonefish, while Charlie Neymour looks on.

can also sight fish to rolling fish, but Andros tarpon move across vast stretches of white sand flats on the tides. You can see them swimming hundreds of yards away. There are only a few guides on Andros who understand the tarpon fishery. If you want to experience some of the best tarpon fishing in the world, you'll have to book one of these guides. They can be booked by calling Westbank Anglers at 800/922-3474.

Remember that good fishing is based on the number of opportunities that are available. Good catching depends on an angler's ability and some good luck. Many anglers are not yet prepared to hook and then land a tarpon on a fly. Beginning tarpon anglers need to work their way up the skill ladder. Be happy when a fish explodes on your fly. Be ecstatic when you first feel your hook tight against the tarpon's mouth. Go nuts when the fish jumps. Don't despair when the hook flies free and your line goes slack. If anything, jumping and losing a tarpon should make you more determined at the next opportunity.

Permit fishing has changed dramatically in the past several years on Andros, or we should say, our perception and awareness of it has. While fishing central Andros, the outside flats along the east coast, or the Bights, you might see an occasional permit. However, these areas would not be high on anyone's list of hot permit spots.

Sure, there are places like Black Rock and Sunken Rock where you can count on seeing a few permit on the high tide in calm conditions. There are some spots on the West Side and in the South Bight where you should have your permit rod rigged. But if permit are your main quarry, you'll be better off fishing somewhere else.

For permit, consider the Joulter's Cays or Red Bay. These areas have good concentrations of fish. An average permit here is twenty pounds, with many fish thirty-five to forty pounds. The prime months are May through August, with April, October, and November very good.

It is not practical to stay in the Cargill Creek/Behring Point area and fish the Joulter's. If you want to fish north Andros, you should to stay up north, either at Stafford Creek Lodge, in Nicholl's Town or Lowe Sound. If you really want to fish for permit, we recommend breaking up your trip by fishing a few days in the Joulter's and a few days in the Bights. This is an ideal weeklong itinerary that can give you shots at bonefish, permit, tarpon, and other species.

Snapper fishing is a lot of fun, something we enjoy on every trip. Mutton snapper is the real prize here, though March and April are the only months you can count on for concentrations of fish in shallow water. Bonefish tackle and flies work well, with our favorite fly being a Pink Clouser Minnow. Mangrove snappers are ubiquitous year round, and as their name implies, they concentrate around mangroves, especially in the deeper pockets around the root systems. They also like to hang out in the coral pockets off the points of connecting bays, and in the many creeks, with their yellow-tail cousins. If the weather is tough, and bonefish are scarce, you can still have a blast catching mangrove snappers that can run up to five pounds.

For adventurous anglers, the cubera snapper fishing in the landlocked lakes is the ultimate thrill. Reaching most of the lakes involves some tough hiking, and sometimes the cuberas do a good job of hiding. When you find them, however, they'll put as much pressure on your 10-weight rod as any tarpon.

Barracuda can also turn a slow day into a fast-paced one. These sleek lightning-fast fish deal with cold weather better than most other game fish. The winter months are especially good, and many otherwise fishless days have been saved by barracuda. We often carry a rod rigged just for cuda. Four to six inches of wire tip-pet is all you need to add to a seven-foot leader. Our favorite fly is an Orange Popovic's Banger. While sight fishing is what we enjoy most, blind fishing the many creeks throughout the island will produce large barracuda, as well as blacktip and lemon sharks.

Sharks produce exciting sport, and are often overlooked by fly anglers. These predatory fish prefer warm weather, and warm water. When water temperatures are below 70°F sharks will stay in deeper areas, including the creeks. When temperatures warm to over 75° on the flats you'll see lots of lemon and blacktip sharks cruising the shallows. When it comes to a wild, jumping fighting fish, a blacktip shark rates with the best of them.

The Tongue of the Ocean pushes in along the eastern shore, dropping to depths of six thousand feet along the world's third largest barrier reef. The reef extends for over 140 miles and has few openings for boats that are not blocked by the inner reef. Just off the outer reef are fertile fishing grounds for marlin, sailfish, dolphin, tuna, and wahoo, while minutes away over the inner reef, sharks, barracuda, amberjack, mackerel, grouper, snapper, and rockfish can be found in abundance.

January is when the grouper fishing reaches it peak. Conventional angling gear works best in deeper water around the reefs and drop-offs. Wahoo are also around in good numbers January through March, and are best pursued with conventional gear along the outside edges of the Tongue of the Ocean reefs. By using chum, it is possible to take a wahoo on a fly during this period. Wahoo run between thirty and forty pounds, so go with a 10-weight fly rod and wire shock tippet.

Billfishing for sails and marlin begins in March, with May through July being the prime months. There are few fly-fishing savvy crews, so most billfishing is with conventional gear. If you have experience fly-fishing for billfish, you will be able to get in some shots during June and July with traditional teasing methods.

April through July is the prime period for dorado, especially around the naval buoys off the eastern coast. It is not uncommon to catch between twenty and forty dorado in a day on a variety of surface poppers and mullet patterns fished on a 10-weight fly rod. When fish are around the buoys you can either blind cast, or pick out specific fish and sight cast. Traditional trolling methods are also effective along the reef.

Mackerel fishing with an 8-weight fly rod is good throughout spring over the reefs. Using chum to get these voracious feeders into a frenzy is the best method. Remember to use wire tippet against those razor-sharp teeth. Best flies include Glass Minnow patterns, Abel Anchovies, and Popovic's Candy Eels.

Amberjack are one of our favorite reef fish. These ferocious fighters are best pursued with a 10-weight rod and at least forty pound shock tippet. Using chum is the best method for luring amberjack into casting range. A few fish show up in February, but March is when the fishing turns on; prime conditions usually last through summer.

Allison tuna also show up in February, with good numbers beginning in March and running through June. Blackfin numbers increase in May, and reach their peak in June and July. Bluefin numbers are fair in April and good in May. Bonito start running in May, with peak numbers in June and July.

OPTIONAL ADVENTURE ACTIVITIES

Small Hope Bay Lodge, Point of View Villas, and Kamalame Cove are the best lodging options for visitors looking for nonfishing adventure activities. Small Hope is Andros' diving and snorkeling headquarters. Experienced divers from all over the world travel here for the "Over the Wall" and blue hole dives featured at this resort. Small Hope is also an excellent choice for beginning divers, and for people looking for certification.

Activities programs at Small Hope, Point of View, and Kamalame include sailing, windsurfing, sea kayaking, ecotours, biking, hiking, and wilderness camping. Andros should be considered a remote location, with many areas pristine and unexplored. If you're looking for any kind of shopping, nightlife, golf, or other related activities, this is not the place for you.

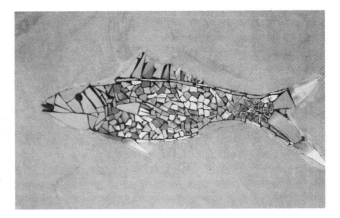

Bonefish art at Point of View Villas.

LODGING AND SERVICES

FEATURED LODGES AND ACCOMODATIONS

Tranquility Hill Fishing Lodge

Behring Point   Owned and operated by the Neymours and Mackeys, this comfortable lodge features air-conditioned rooms with private baths, a pleasant dining room/bar area with satellite TV, and an outdoor deck overlooking the North Bight. Wadable flats are right out front. Ivan Neymour runs the fishing program, which is one of the best in the Bahamas. Guides are flexible in their fishing hours, meaning you will fish the best tides at the appropriate times. Fishing areas include the North, Middle, and South Bights, outside ocean flats from Bowen Sound to Moxey Town, and the vast West Side region. Bahamian charm and hospitality are in abundant supply here. Guests are made to feel like part of the family and the food is especially good.
Season: October through June.
Suitable For: Anglers only.
What's Included: Bonefish packages feature air-conditioned rooms with private baths, 3 meals daily, Bahamian taxes, and guided fishing. Trips of any length are available.
Not Included: Airfare to Andros Town, taxi transfers, alcoholic beverages, gratuities, fishing tackle.
Pricing: $$
Contact: Reservations and information, telephone/fax 242/368-4132 or 800/922-3474.
E-mail: tranquil@grouper.batelnet.bs

Stafford Creek Lodge

Stafford Creek   Prescott and Samantha Smith's lodge is situated on a gorgeous bend in Stafford Creek, overlooking the water and the surrounding pine forests. The deluxe lodge accommodates only 6 anglers in private guest rooms with ceiling fans and air-conditioning. Great personal service and premiere fishing are the focus here. Fish outside ocean flats, various creeks that offer good fishing even in bad weather, virgin landlocked lakes, Red Bay, and the Joulter's Cays. The newly developed permit fishing in the Joulter's is very good, and the wade fishing for bonefish is amazing for numbers of fish and large fish. This lodge books up months in advance so plan ahead. Minimum stay is 3 nights/2 days fishing.
Season: October through July.
Suitable For: Anglers only.
What's Included: All packages feature accommodations in air-conditioned rooms with private baths, 3 meals daily, Bahamian taxes, and guided fishing. Single rates are available.
Not Included: Airfare to/from Andros Town, taxi transfers, alcoholic beverages, gratuities, fishing tackle.
Pricing: $$–$$$
Contact: Reservations and information, telephone/fax 242/368-6259 or 800/922-3474.

Andros Island Bonefish Club

Cargill Creek   Owned and operated by Captain Rupert Leadon, the Bonefish Club has a long tradition of serving anglers. The lodge features air-conditioned rooms with private bath, a dining/bar area with satellite TV, and a large deck overlooking Cargill Creek. There are wadable flats just across the creek. Fishing areas include the North and Middle Bights, outside ocean flats from Bowen Sound to Moxey Town, and the vast West Side region. The atmosphere at this lodge is fun and lively.
Season: October through June.
Suitable For: Anglers only.
What's Included: Bonefish packages feature air-conditioned rooms, private bath, 3 meals daily, Bahamian taxes, and guided fishing. Trips of any length are available.
Not Included: Airfare to Andros Town, taxi transfers, alcoholic beverages, gratuities, fishing tackle.
Pricing: $$–$$$
Contact: Reservations and information, 242/368-5167 or 800/922-3474, fax 242/368-5235.

Moxey's Bonefishing Lodge

Mangrove Cay   The renovated lodge is located in the fishing settlement of Moxey Town on the south side of the eastern entrance to the Middle Bight. The comfortable lodge features air-conditioned rooms, satellite TV, and some of the best Bahamian food in the islands. Renowned guide Carl "John Wayne" Moxey leads the guiding team along with Joel Moxey, using Carolina and Backcountry flats boats. Independent guides can also be booked. Good access to the West Side, South Bight, and Lisbon Creek provides outstanding variety. This is the best location for fishing the Middle Bight.
Season: October through June.
Suitable For: Anglers only.
What's Included: Airport transfers Mangrove Cay airport, air-conditioned room, all meals, guided fishing, and Bahamian taxes. Trips of any length are available.
Not Included: Airfare to Mangrove Cay, alcoholic beverages, gratuities, fishing tackle.
Pricing: $$
Contact: Reservations and information, telephone/fax 242/369-0023 or 800/922-3474.
E-mail pax@bahamas.net.bs

Small Hope Bay Lodge

Fresh Creek   Small Hope specializes in diving and snorkeling. Twenty cottages are situated right on the beach, each with private bath, double beds, and ceiling fans. The magnificent Andros Barrier Reef is one mile offshore, about a 10 minute boat ride. For the ultimate in diving, try the "Over the Wall" dive. Descend up to 185 feet along the 6,000 foot vertical drop of the Tongue of the Ocean. Excellent bonefishing options with independent guides are available in the Fresh Creek, White Bight, Staniard, and Stafford Creek areas. Full- and half-day reef or offshore fishing trips are available. Small Hope provides air charter service from Ft. Lauderdale to Andros Town. This is a reliable economical way to travel to and from Andros.
Season: October through June.
Suitable For: Anglers and nonanglers.
What's Included: Round-trip airport transfers, beachfront accommodations, 3 meals daily, afternoon snacks, all bar drinks and beverages, service charges, Bahamian taxes, introductory scuba lessons, and free use of snorkeling equipment, bicycles, sailboats, and wind-surfers. Trips of any length are available.
Not Included: Airfare to Andros Town airport, gratuities, guided fishing.
Pricing: $$–$$$
Contact: Reservations and information, 800/223-6961 or 242/368-2014, fax 242/368-2015.
E-mail: SHBinfo@SmallHope.com
Internet: www.SmallHope.com

Point of View Villas

Fresh Creek   This luxury resort features 14 2-bedroom villas with central air-conditioning, swimming pool, lighted tennis courts, fine restaurant and bar, all situated right on the oceanside beach. From this location you can fish the Joulter's Cays or the famous North and Middle Bights. Our best independent guides fish both locations. There is a 1-hour drive each way in a comfortable limousine to fish the Joulter's, and a 30-minute drive each way to fish the Bights. Or you can choose to fish the outside ocean flats right around the lodge, or take a day to fish nearby Fresh Creek. The variety of fishing options, combined with great diving, snorkeling, picnicking, touring, or just relaxing, makes this an ideal trip for anglers and nonanglers. Any length of stay is available.
Season: October through July.
Suitable For: Anglers and nonanglers.
What's Included: All fishing packages feature accommodations in air-conditioned villas with private bath, fishing lunches, guided fishing, tennis, and Bahamian taxes. Single rates are available.
Not Included: Airfare to Andros Town, taxi transfers, breakfast and dinner, alcoholic beverages, gratuities, fishing tackle, optional activities.
Pricing: $$–$$$
Contact: Reservations and information, 242/368-2750 or 800/922-3474, fax 242/368-2761.
E-mail: ptofview@batelnet.bs

Bair Bahamas Guest House

Little Creek   This comfortable guest house was remodeled in 1996 and features 3 air-conditioned bedrooms with ceiling fans and private baths. The lodge can accommodate up to 6 anglers at a time. Excellent meals are served in the dining room, with owner/chef Stanley Bair preparing fresh seafood, fried chicken, steaks and other delicious treats, including scrumptious Key lime pie. Stanley and her husband, Andy, run the type of lodge that brings clients back again and again. The fishing program covers miles flats and creeks around South Andros. Deep Creek, Little Creek and Grassy Creek offer protected fishing in rough weather. If you like to wade fish, this is an ideal location for large schools of smaller bones or larger fish cruising alone or in pairs. The well-trained guides are friendly and knowledgeable. Excellent reef and offshore fishing is also available nearby.
Season: October through June.
Suitable For: Anglers only.
What's Included: Accommodations, all meals, open bar, guided fishing, airport transfers to/from Congo Town, and Bahamian taxes. Single rates are available.
Not Included: Airfare to Congo Town, alcoholic beverages, gratuities, fishing tackle. Congo Air services Congo Town from Nassau. Charter flights are available from Nassau and Ft. Lauderdale.
Pricing: $$$
Contact: Reservations and information, 242/369-5060 or 800/922-3474, fax 242/369-5080.

ADDITIONAL ACCOMMODATIONS

Charlie's Haven and the Bang Bang Club

Behring Point, Pot Cay   Comfortable rooms, some with air-conditioning, and good food, but the reason anglers book here is to fish and visit with the legendary Charlie Smith. Charlie's Haven is near the water with access to wadable flats when the tide is right. The Bang Bang Club on Pot Cay is ideally situated in the North Bight, with great wadable flats nearby.
Pricing: $$
Contact: Reservations and information, 242/368-4261 or 800/922-3474.

Nottages Cottages

Behring Point   Motel-style air-conditioned rooms, good meals, full bar, nice landscaping, on the water with access to wadable flats when the tide is right. You can stay here and book independent guides.
Pricing: $$
Contact: Reservations and information, 242/368-4293.

Conch Sound Inn

Conch Sound   Fourteen comfortable air-conditioned rooms, restaurant, bar, and swimming pool, located 5 minutes from the water, and a 10-minute drive to the boat launch at Lowe Sound. Fishing guides can be arranged.
Pricing: $$–$$$
Contact: Reservations and information, 242/329-2060.

Kamalame Cove

Staniard Creek   Can accommodate 14 anglers and/or nonanglers in beautiful air-conditioned cottages with access to the water and a nice beach. A full fishing program, including a meal plan, is available. This is a good location for nonanglers to enjoy themselves while friends or family members are fishing. The guides here need work, but are competent.
Pricing: $$$$
Contact: Reservations and information, 242/368-6281.

Lighthouse Yacht Club & Marina

Fresh Creek Twenty nice air-conditioned rooms, restaurant, bar, and swimming pool. A meal plan is available and fishing guides can be arranged. The 18-slip marina offers full service to boaters. This is a popular marina, so slip reservations are necessary.
Pricing: $$–$$$
Contact: Reservations and information, 242/368-2305 or 800/688-4752, fax 242/368-2300.

Chickcharnie Hotel

Fresh Creek Ten of the small rooms are air-conditioned and have private baths. This is a good location right on Fresh Creek for anglers on a budget. The restaurant serves excellent spicy seafood. Fishing guides can be arranged.
Pricing: $–$$
Contact: Reservations and information, 242/368-2025.

Emerald Palms By-the-Sea

Driggs Hill A nice beachfront hotel with air-conditioned rooms and a surprisingly good restaurant and bar. Fishing guides can be arranged. A meal plan is available.
Pricing: $$–$$$
Contact: Reservations and information, 242/369-2661, or 800/688-4752, fax 242/369-2667.

SERVICES

Independent guides: Charlie Neymour, Simon Bain, Andy Smith, Barry Neymour, Frankie Neymour, Dennis Leadon, Dwain Neymour, Deon Neymour, Ricardo Mackey and the other independents can be booked by calling 800/922-3474. Being independent means these guides do not work directly for any lodge or agent; own their own boat and other equipment; set their own prices; set their own business and cancellation policies.

These and other independent guides can sometimes be booked through the hotels and lodges mentioned above, and anglers can call them directly. We cannot be more specific than this because telephone numbers and lodge relationships change often. For up-to-date information see our Web site at www.bahamasflyfishingguide.com, or cruise the Net.

Restaurants: Most lodges offer meal plans. When we are not on a meal plan, our favorite place to eat out is the dining room at Point of View Villas. In Andros Town/Fresh Creek the two favorite local restaurants are Hank's Place and the Chickcharnie Hotel. Both serve excellent Bahamian food.

Diving and snorkeling: Small Hope Bay offers one of the best dive programs in the Bahamas. Contact them directly at 242/368-2014. Most lodges can make these reservations for you, but it will usually be through Small Hope.

Car rentals: This is not easy on Andros. Your best bet is to arrange a rental through your hotel or lodge.

Taxi service is very good on Andros. Your lodge can arrange for a taxi to take you most places on the island. Be sure to ask about the cost up front. The taxi driver we use most often is "Doy" Leadon. He can be contacted directly at his airport telephone 242/368-2339 or at his home number 242/368-5042.

Grocery and liquor stores are available in most of the major settlements on the island.

There is a bank in San Andros and one in Fresh Creek. These banks are usually open only one day a week, Wednesday, though this is not guaranteed. There are no ATMs.

Government clinics are located in Lowe Sound, Nicholl's Town, Mastic Point, Fresh Creek, and on Mangrove Cay. All are nurse-staffed, except a doctor is usually available in Fresh Creek.

NEW DEVELOPMENTS

It seems as if everyone is building a new bonefish lodge on Andros, or calling their current motel a "Bonefish Club." We use the term "lodge" loosely here, and urge caution in dealing with new "Bonefish Clubs." If you have any questions about new lodges or clubs, consult with your travel professional, give us a call, or visit our Web site at www.bahamasflyfishingguide.com.

A fine new lodge is under construction west of Moxey Town on Mangrove Cay. Steve McGrath is the owner along with his Bahamian partner, Liz Bain. Liz was formerly the manager of Cargill Creek Lodge, and she is very capable in dealing with lodge operations and fishing guides. The proposed name of this lodge is the Mangrove Cay Club. McGrath and Bain plan to open the lodge in spring 2000. We believe this will be a first-class operation that will quickly develop a loyal clientele. For additional information call McGrath at 800/626-3526 or Bain at 242/368-5097.

Legendary guide Charlie Smith is planning to open his newly renovated Bang Bang Club on Pot Cay late in 1999. This is a splendid location with lots of history behind it, and close access to some of the best big fish flats on Andros. All rooms have a beautiful view of the water, and we can't imagine a more idyllic place to sip a cold Kalik after a day of fishing. For additional information call Charlie Smith at 242/368-4261.

Mars Bay Bonefish Villa is a new operation at the end of the road in south Andros. This deluxe villa can accommodate four anglers at a time, and is the closest operation to the fabulous fishing at the southern tip of the island. We have been told that the Mars Bay operation will be in full swing by late 1999. You can check out developments at www.androsbonefish.com.

For ongoing updates on the happenings on Andros Island please log on to our Web site at www.bahamasflyfishingguide.com.

Andros guide and lodge owner Charlie Smith working on a dock at the new Bang Bang Club.

5

Grand Bahama Island

Grand Bahama Island is a ninety-mile-long strip of low-lying land fifty-two miles east of Palm Beach, Florida, and eighty miles northeast of Miami. When we first mention Grand Bahama to people, they often look puzzled; then we say Freeport, and instant recognition sets in.

Freeport/Lucaya is the Bahamas' second-largest city, with a more casual cosmopolitan atmosphere than the frenetic sophistication of Nassau. The feel of the city is breezy and welcoming. The streets are wide, with numerous roundabouts, and are often bordered with well-manicured Bermuda grass, casuarina trees, or Australian pines. In the center, traffic builds up for ten to fifteen minutes in the morning and late afternoon. Nothing to sweat, mon. You can drive the length of the island in an hour and a half.

None of this is an accident, as Freeport/Lucaya was created from scratch thanks to Wallace Groves's idea for a free-trade center, and the subsequent passage of the Hawksbill Creek Agreement in 1955. Since the city was also built to attract tourism, it's no wonder it has done just that, becoming an outdoor enthusiast's playground, with championship golf courses, tennis, scuba diving, and some of the best fishing in the islands. Toss in casino gambling, duty-free shopping, good restaurants, and lively nightlife, and you have a winning combination for a wide range of vacationers.

The city's goal of becoming a major international seaport and free-trade center was accomplished in 1997 when Hutchison Port Holdings officially opened the $78 million Freeport Container Port. This facility is one of the world's key trans-shipment centers, and Hutchison has plans for further expansion that will make the port the largest in the Western Hemisphere.

Hutchison Ports Properties also bought the Lucayan Resort Hotel and Marina, adjacent to the Bell Harbour Channel, plus other properties on this long stretch of white sand beach. The hotel has been demolished, and a new mega-resort and casino, with international convention facilities and the Bahama Reef golf course, is under construction. The first phase of the new Lucayan Resort opened in April 1999, with the entire resort scheduled for completion by April 2000. While this area had become run-down, and was in need of renovation, we are concerned that the resort may have a negative impact on the West End fishery.

Aerial view of Freeport and the flats fished at Pelican Bay.

From the standpoint of the local economy, however, this development will be a tremendous boost. Of the more than 40,000 residents of Grand Bahama, most live in Freeport. This population figure is an increase of 40 percent over the past ten years, with similar projections for the future.

On the West End of the island, the old Jack Tar Marina is also undergoing renovation and development under new ownership. The new name of this location is Old Bahama Bay, with the marina now carrying the same name. We have watched this happening with great interest, as we often fish this area. Once the marina and new luxury resort are complete, Old Bahama Bay will be its own destination, with many upscale private homes as part of the project. No doubt this will affect the West End fishery even more than the projects at Bell Harbour and Port Lucaya.

All this development has kicked up the energy level of Freeport and its residents. Taxi drivers are quick to engage you with their opinions, yeah or nah, about what's going on. If you need information, definitely ask a cabby, or a waiter in one of the better restaurants.

Other service personnel working in a variety of tourist-related businesses exude a similar enthusiasm. Entrepreneurs are everywhere, and notably so in the fishing business. We've heard lots of talk about people wanting to buy a boat and become a fishing guide, or maybe build a new fishing lodge. Diving and snorkeling companies are doing killer business. The same is true for the party boats that put on sunset and other day cruises.

Freeport isn't all there is on Grand Bahama. Though the West End is being developed, it still has a renegade feel left over from the rumrunning days. Old Bahama Bay Marina is a port of entry for boaters, offering convenient water access from Florida, and a stopover point for cruisers getting ready to cross the Little Bahama Bank.

The largest part of the island, to the east of Freeport, can serve up an Out Island experience if you want it. Once you drive east past the roundabout leading to Port Lucaya, you're out in the country. You'll cross several causeways spanning miles of manmade channels where homesites are being offered, before reaching Lucayan National Park.

The park features a pine forest with nature trails and deserted beaches, plus observation decks to view the world's longest charted cavern system. North Riding Point Bonefishing Lodge is here also, at Burnside Cove. Then you have a straight shot past miles of incredible beaches until you reach McLean's Town, and the dock used by Deepwater Cay Club to pick up guests for the short boat ride to their private island.

Throughout this region of Grand Bahama you can find remnants of the earliest Arawak civilizations, and evidence of the infamous pirate days. The ocean out here is remarkable, with some of the most vivid colors we've seen anywhere over reefs, turtle grass, and white sand bottoms.

Talk to the people in McLean's Town and you could be talking to the people of Long Island or Exuma. Friendliness runs in their blood, as does maintaining a relaxed attitude. These are the qualities of Grand Bahama that combine with the growth of Freeport to make this island a great compromise for anglers and their nonfishing companions.

The Freeport International Airport provides the convenient air access that makes all the island's growth possible. Direct flights from Miami, Ft. Lauderdale, and West Palm Beach are available on American Eagle, Bahamasair, Comair, and Continental/Gulfstream. Laker Airways provides jet charter service from many cities. This service was improved dramatically in the summer of 1999 when TWA, Delta, and British Airways began regular flights. We also use several air charter companies out of West Palm and Ft. Lauderdale. This becomes more economical if you have a group of four or more.

Bahamasair, out of Nassau, and American Eagle, out of Miami, offer the most flights. If you want to fish on your arrival or departure days, you will probably have to book on one of these airlines.

AROUND THE ISLAND

The West End of Grand Bahama sits just off the edge of the Little Bahama Bank, making it prime habitat for bonefish, permit, tarpon, and other game fish.

Old Bahama Bay Marina, and the new resort, are works in progress. Full services are available for boaters, but be prepared for a construction mess that could continue through 2000. Boaters should use VHS channel 16 to communicate with the marina, and ask about recent changes.

The strong tidal currents that run between West End and Indian Cay sweep bait fish in and out of this channel. Tarpon, barracuda, and blacktip and lemon sharks use the channel for breakfast, lunch, and dinner. The tarpon cruise the bank north up to Wood Cay and Sandy Cay, and often enter the flats in this area through the cuts and creeks.

Permit follow similar patterns, penetrating farther into the flats and working along the banks where deeper water pushes up against mangrove-lined cays.

There are countless cays, rocks, creeks, flats, and shallow bays in this area that contain habitat loaded with bonefish averaging five to six pounds. Bottom structure varies from hard white sand to irregular corral and lots of turtle grass. Grass, mantis, and snapping shrimp provide a tremendous food source for bonefish all along the northwestern shoreline.

Rich flats spread out from the mainland all along the indented shore.

Moving from West End to Settlement Point and the government wharf, this habitat continues, though more creeks and mangrove-covered cays begin to create more of a blue-and-green-colored maze. Cruising boaters traveling past the government customs station need to take a wide loop north before attempting to turn back in to Hawksbill Creek.

There is a huge area of rich bonefish flats that spread out from the mainland all along the indented shoreline. Guides from Pelican Bay in particular fish here often. So far, the fish here have remained incredibly aggressive, and even fish over ten pounds will charge after a fly that misses its target area by as much as ten feet. How long this will last is anyone's guess, but for now it's awesome.

The highway from Freeport to West End is in good shape, but provides little access to the water as the shoreline is dense with mangroves and other vegetation. There are two hidden bays we fish from this area that reach within fifty feet of the road, but unless you stopped and looked hard, you couldn't see the water from the highway.

Most of the bottom structure is grass and coral until you near boating markers that indicate the entrance to Hawksbill Creek. Here, a number of gold and white sand flats blossom from the mainland. The northern end of the creek, which provides access to the Little Bahama Bank, is only accessible to smaller boats on the proper tide. Pelican Bay guides launch and retrieve their Maverick flats boats inside the creek at Queen's Cove.

Backing up to West End, boaters proceeding on the southern side of the island will reach an elbow joint of land that is the entrance to Freeport Harbour. The harbor was originally formed by the southern section of Hawksbill Creek. This is a massive commercial harbor, jointly owned by the Grand Bahama Port Authority and Hutchison, and is used primarily by ocean-going container ships and commercial cruise ships.

While eating at a popular restaurant on the harbor, Pier 1, it is a stunning sight to look out into the night and see one of the world's largest cargo ships rumbling by, being escorted by half a dozen tugboats lit like Christmas trees. The ships pass so close you could almost touch them.

The main highlight of eating at Pier 1, however, is the shark feeding frenzy. Every hour on the hour a ship's bell clangs and pounds of chum and bread are tossed out into the clear floodlit water. The resulting feeding frenzy is an awe-inspiring site, though not because of any sharks. Huge jacks, horse eye, and crevalle slam the surface with ferocious intensity. And then there are the permit, so many permit. Every time we see this we talk about renting a boat and laying off the restaurant with our 10-weight rods and surface poppers. One night we are going to do this, though we'll keep a sharp eye out for those monster container ships.

The towering orange cranes used to move tons of cargo can be seen for miles from both sides of the island. Boaters can stop in Freeport Harbour to clear customs, but it is recommended that recreational boaters use Xanadu Marina, Port Lucaya Marina, or Lucayan Marina Village to clear customs and to engage services.

Private homes, condominiums, and new resort developments flank the white sand beach-

The marina at Port Lucaya.

fronts between the channels leading to these marinas. Bell Channel is the entrance to the Port Lucaya Marina and the Lucayan Marina Village. Boaters turning left once inside the bay will cruise past Pelican Bay Hotel and the UNEXSO Dive Center before reaching Port Lucaya Marina. The marina offers more than one hundred slips with full services for boats up to 175 feet. We've seen several this size cruise in while enjoying happy hour around the pool at Pelican Bay. Our conversation quickly turns to what a great mother boat that would make for fishing remote areas of the Little Bahama Bank.

The marina adjoins the Port Lucaya Resort Hotel, the Port Lucaya Marketplace, and Count Basie Square. The casual hotel offers comfortable air-conditioned rooms, swimming pool, restaurant, and bar, with boat slips around three sides. The marketplace is a pleasing maze of eighty stores, shops, and boutiques, plus a colorful straw market, and at least twenty cafes and restaurants. For our money, this is the best shopping area in Freeport/Lucaya, surpassing the famous International Bazaar.

Count Basie Square, ringed with bars and restaurants, is our favorite spot for nightlife. You can walk here in less than five minutes from Pelican Bay. The Square features live music every night, and some of the most incredible limbo dancers you can imagine. Would you believe limboing under a cane bar set on top of two Kalik bottles? You can join in the dancing or just hang out in the festive atmosphere while sipping a cool drink and smoking a Cuban cigar.

Our favorite restaurant on Grand Bahama, Luciano's, is on the corner of the square overlooking the marina. La Dolce Vita, the Pub at Lucaya, Zorba's, and Pisces are other marketplace restaurants we have enjoyed on a regular basis.

All this activity is just down the way from the Pelican Bay Hotel, which runs a top-notch bonefishing program. The hotel features forty-eight oversize air-conditioned rooms with private baths, refrigerators, coffeemakers, satellite TV, and private balconies overlooking the pool, Jacuzzi, and marina. A poolside bar serves great rum drinks and snack foods, and is an ideal place to relax after fishing. The Ferry House restaurant serves tasty fresh pastries at breakfast, and features an appetizing dinner menu.

A free ferry service runs from the hotel to the Lucayan Village Marina, which is flanked by some of the most luxurious condominiums anywhere. Full service for boaters is available here, and amenities include golf at the Lucayan Country Club.

Entrance to the Pelican Bay Hotel.

Up the street and across the road from Pelican Bay and the Port Lucaya Market-place is the location of the new Grand Bahama Lucayan Resort. When the resort is completed we believe this area will offer the best tourism-related facilities on the island, and will rival anything in Nassau.

Currently, the center of tourist activities is a ten-minute taxi ride away, at the International Bazaar and the Princess Hotel and Country Club complexes. The Princess casino is the hub of gambling activity, but we expect this to shift to the new Lucayan Resort until major upgrades are made. In fact, our general feeling for this entire area is that it will have to undergo significant renovations to compete with the Lucayan Resort and the multimillion-dollar improvements that have been made throughout Nassau. Even with major upgrades this area is inland, so it will have to compete on price point rather than with glorious sea views.

Now back to the ocean. While the run for boaters on the southern side of the island from Bell Channel to McLean's Town offers splendid views of beautiful beaches lined with palms and Australian pines, there are no good harbors. The only fishing options are trolling lures or bait, which can produce an evening meal of mackerel or snapper. When the weather is calm there are several reefs that can be fished with poppers and Clouser's Minnows, but this is not an area we would spend any real time fishing.

This assessment changes dramatically once you reach McLean's Town. Deepwater Cay Club, one of the most venerable bonefishing destinations in the Bahamas,

is located on a private island across from the settlement. Anglers can drive from Freeport to the McLean's Town dock, then take a boat ride across, or take a charter aircraft directly to the resort's private airstrip.

Excellent white sand and turtle grass flats are

Ferry House Restaurant at Pelican Bay.

sprinkled throughout this area. While bonefish are plentiful, so are many other game fish species. The deeper creeks, cuts, and bights between the sizable cays stretching to the south are loaded with jacks, cubera snapper, barracuda, sharks, tarpon, and some permit.

Deep Water Cay Club.

To the north of Deepwater Cay the island forms a point ending with Grassy Cay, which leads into another string of cays running across to Little Abaco. This is the boaters' northern entrance to the Bight of Abaco, and one of the best and most underfished flats areas on the Little Bahama Bank. Guides from Deepwater fish this area in good weather, and also run south to Sweetings Cay, East End Bush, and Red Shank Cay in search of permit and big bonefish.

Heading back west, the northern coast of Grand Bahama is a flats fisherman's dream. This untouched area is one of the main reasons the North Riding Point bonefishing operation began. North Riding Point guides trailer their boats to four different launch sites to access the north coast, including areas of the Water Cays, and all the way out to Mangrove Cay during calm weather.

Turtle grass and dark coral make up most of the bottom structure, though there are areas of white sand, including an amazing white sandbank at Mangrove Cay that is home to huge bonefish and permit.

While fishing throughout the Water Cays we have had a number of experiences with tailing bonefish going over ten pounds. We won some and lost some, but in every case it was a heart-pounding thrill to see such impressive fish with blue tails and silver dorsals waving at the deep azure sky.

Bonefish flats continue west toward Cormorant Point, where the fishing grounds for Pelican Bay and North Riding Point intersect, though Pelican Bay guides also fish the Water Cays. There are more sandy-bottomed flats in this area all the way to Dover Sound, which is the entrance to the Grand Lucayan waterway. The waterway is a seven-and-a-half-mile-long canal that bisects Grand Bahama. It offers good anchorages and wind protection for boaters, plus forms a miles-long maze of back channels with hundreds of waterfront lots for sale.

Around the point from Dover Sound are several miles of mangrove-lined shorelines, Crab Cay and Little Crab Cay. It's hard to keep track of all the Crab Cays in the Bahamas, isn't it? Though this area produces excellent bonefishing, including some big fish, it is not visually appealing. There are some huge sandpiles with accompanying gravel pits, cranes, and other heavy machinery at work here. Planes are constantly taking off and landing at nearby Freeport International Airport. In bad weather, however, this is a fairly protected area, only a short run from Queen's Cove and Hawksbill Creek. And if you catch a nice fish here, you can take the photograph looking out to sea. Yep, we're guilty on that count.

A nice Grand Bahama bonefish.

FISHING HIGHLIGHTS

Grand Bahama's relatively northern location puts it in the path of strong winter winds and cold fronts moving across from Florida. These cold fronts are common from mid-November to the end of March, though they can occur from October into May.

A major cold front can last four to five days, while weaker fronts can be through in a couple of days. Anglers fishing from the West End out to Cormorant Point will have little protection from these winds. Since this is the primary fishing grounds for Pelican Bay and Grand Bahama Bonefishing, people fishing here are affected most by bad weather. Guides usually fish west of Hawksbill Creek during bad weather to gain some lees in the series of mangrove cays running parallel to the shoreline. It is possible to run east, though the pounding you would take from the prevailing northern winds is not worth it. On the plus side, this area has more than its share of bonefish in the eight- to twelve-pound range, and these fish have a high tolerance for cold weather and water. If you've worked on your casting in the wind, you can turn a rough day into a big success by catching a couple of hefty bonefish.

North Riding Point guides and anglers are also hampered by cold fronts, though one of their launching sites is in a more protected area on the north coast. This launch site is somewhat dependent on the tides, but it can be made to work for at least part of the day.

Deepwater Cay Club has the most options for protected areas in bad weather. Rummer Creek, Big Harbour Creek, and other similar areas are easily accessible from the club dock, plus there are wadable flats nearby.

The shoreline flats around Grand Bahama are mostly lined with mangroves. Bottom structure is predominantly irregular coral of varying dark colors and turtle grass. Due to this structure, anglers fish much more from flats boats than by wading.

The grassy bottoms interspersed with massive mangrove root systems create a rich diversity of food, including a variety of shrimp. Because of this, bonefish can be very selective in what they eat when feeding on these flats. Look more for grass shrimp around the mangroves, and snapping shrimp in the turtle grass. A Borski's Fur Shrimp or Bonefish Critter is a good fly pattern in both areas.

Crabs tend to be more prevalent on the coral flats, with clams and mussels abundant on the many gold-colored sandy flats. Bonefish are opportunistic feeders in these areas. Fly choice is a matter of picking a pattern that will get down fast into the feeding zone, which makes lead-eyed flies the way to go.

If you're planning a visit to Grand Bahama, remember that the best months for bonefish are April through July, and October and November. While some islands farther south tend to close up in July, this is a great time to fish Grand Bahama, especially the West End area.

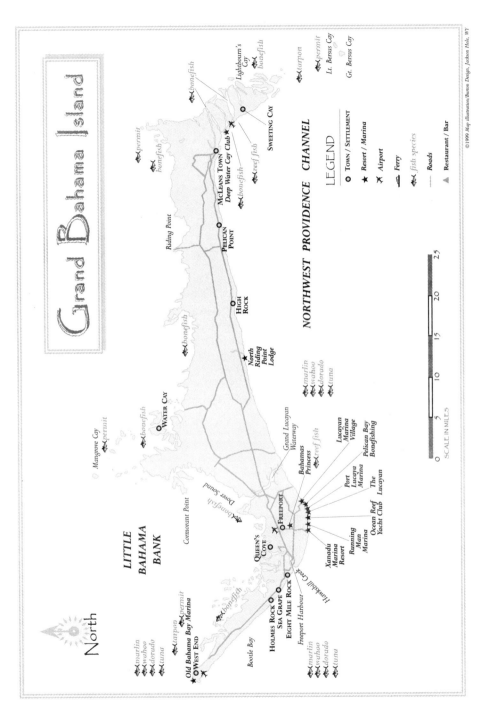

Grand Bahama Island

NORTHWEST PROVIDENCE CHANNEL

LITTLE BAHAMA BANK

North

Lighthbourn's Cay
Lt. Bersus Cay
Gt. Bersus Cay
Sweeting Cay
McLeans Town
Deep Water Cay Club
Pelican Point
Riding Point
High Rock
North Riding Point Lodge
Water Cay
Grand Lucayan Waterway
Mangrove Cay
Cormorant Point
Dover Sound
Freeport
Queen's Cove
Holmes Rock
Sea Grape
Eight Mile Rock
Hawksbill Creek
Freeport Harbour
Bootle Bay
West End
Old Bahama Bay Marina

Xanadu Marina Resort
Running Man Marina
Ocean Reef Yacht Club
The Lucayan
Port Lucaya Marina
Bahamas Princess
Lucayan Marina Village
Pelican Bay Bonefishing

LEGEND

○ TOWN / SETTLEMENT
★ Resort / Marina
✈ Airport
⛴ Ferry
🐟 fish species
----- Roads
▲ Restaurant / Bar

SCALE IN MILES
0 5 10 15 20 25

permit
bonefish
tarpon
bonefish
reef fish
bonefish
bonefish
permit
marlin
wahoo
dorado
tuna
bonefish
reef fish
permit
bonefish
Bonefish
bonefish
marlin
wahoo
dorado
tuna
permit
tarpon
marlin
wahoo
dorado
tuna

©1999 Map Illustration/Barton Design, Jackson Hole, WY

North Riding Point Lodge.

March is also a prime month, but those cold fronts can get you. If this is the only time you can go, pack your bags and give it a shot. August and September can be good, though this is hurricane season. The period from December through February is a crapshoot with the weather for fishing, though non-anglers can enjoy themselves with a variety of activities. During these months it makes sense to plan a general vacation, with fishing just one of your activities. When you hit nice weather, get out on the flats in a hurry because the bones will be feeding with a vengeance.

Our favorite flies for bonefish change as we move across the island. Fish are more aggressive from West End to the Water Cays as they have not suffered much fishing pressure over the years. We prefer larger flies, #2-4, that get down in a hurry. We also like sparsely tied flies, preferably orange in color. An Orange Christmas Island Special can be dynamite. So can an Orange Gotcha with lead eyes. We like nine-foot leaders with 12-pound tippet.

Fly fishers out of Deepwater Cay will face bonefish that have been educated. They tend to be on the spookier side closer to the lodge, less sophisticated the farther you run. Numbers of fish are far greater here than back toward West End, though the average size of fish is a touch smaller. We fish more with #4-6 Gotchas or a Miheve's Flats Fly here, and with a variety of eyeless flies like Bonefish Puffs, Snapping Shrimp, and Horrors. Sometimes we use long leaders, up to twelve feet, especially for tailing fish.

We prefer to fish incoming tides throughout Grand Bahama, though many areas never have a full incoming or outgoing tide. This often happens in April and May, when you have the lowest tidal movements of the year.

We also prefer a neap tide to a spring tide due to the generally lower water levels. Because both ends of the island are near edges of the Little Bahama Bank, lower water doesn't hurt game fish or bait fish movement.

Spring tides are still good, but they force more bonefish into the mangroves along the shorelines. You can go in and get them, but you'll break off more than you will land. A spring tide presents a prime opportunity to fish some of the cays farther off the mainland, especially the Water Cays and the cays north of West End.

Spring tides are also the best times to fish for permit, with April through July being the best months. While we have seen permit on many flats across the north shore of the island, fishing the far ends will give you the best chance to hook up. Several of our friends and clients have landed permit up to thirty-five pounds near West End using crab patterns. When in doubt, go with a #2 Del's Merkin.

Anglers staying at Deepwater Cay will also have shots at permit during these months, especially during calm weather, when the guides can run down to the Red Shank banks. Permit laze along here on the high tide, feasting on blue crabs. This

Educated bonefish are spooky, and often require longer leaders.

area, which runs along the edge of the Little Bahama Bank all the way to Moore's Island, has permit that average thirty to forty pounds.

Tarpon can be caught on both ends of the island, but we'll vote for West End as the best area for the silver king. May through July are the best months, with October and November decent. On occasion the guides here will make an effort to look for tarpon, but tarpon are usually incidental around Grand Bahama. Carry a 10-weight in the boat rigged with a Fernandez Shallow Water Cockroach or a Red/Black Sea Bunny, just in case. You definitely want to fish tarpon on the incoming tide, so time your bonefishing accordingly, then head out to the deeper tarpon flats, channels, and edges.

The 10-weight tarpon rig will also be a good all-around utility rod for sharks, barracuda, jacks, and cubera snapper. You can use the 80- to 100-pound shock tippet you use for tarpon on these fish, though we recommend wire shock tippet for sharks and barracuda if these species are your primary targets. If you don't have a 10-weight rod, a 9-weight will get you by.

Sharks are often overlooked as a fly rod game fish, but they provide exciting sport. Sharks prefer warm weather, and warm water on the flats. Though they are available year round, April through June are the best months for them. Lemon and blacktip sharks inhabit most bonefish flats and ambush points around those flats. When you see these sharks on a flat, you can take this as a sure sign bonefish are in the vicinity.

When it comes to a wild, jumping, fighting fish, a blacktip shark rates with the best of them, and if you want to settle in for a long bulldog battle, hook up a lemon. Our favorite way to catch sharks is with a Popovic's Banger. Watching a shark slash at a surface popper is a thrill, even though they often miss the target. Large streamers like Deceivers, especially in orange or red, will get you more hookups.

An Orange Popovic's Banger, or a Foam Boilermaker, are our favorite flies for catching barracuda, too. Barracuda hit their prey with ferocious intensity and are equally fun to catch on fly or spinning tackle. If fishing is slow and you need to connect with something, tossing a green tube lure on spinning tackle to a barracuda is like money in the bank. Barracuda don't mind cold water, so you can find them on the flats throughout the winter. They cruise the flats in warmer months also, though that is a time they like to congregate around reef structure.

The best fishing for gray, mutton, and cubera snappers is out of Deepwater Cay, and is equally fun with fly or spinning gear. Cubera snapper are the trophies here. These fish run thirty to eighty pounds, so you'll need your 10-weight if you want to land one.

Cuberas have huge canine teeth, and they strike with the killer instinct of a barracuda. We recommend at least 40-pound wire tippet, though 100-pound mono shock

Brian O'Keefe

Barracuda are fun to catch on fly or spin tackle.

sometimes works. You'll find cuberas in many of the creeks and deeper cuts around Deepwater Cay year round, with April through June being the best months. #2/0 Clouser's Minnows in a variety of colors are our favorite flies for these voracious fish, but any well-presented fly will usually provoke them.

You'll find a variety of jacks living in the same areas as the cuberas. Deepwater Cay is famous for large bar jacks and horse-eyed jacks, both of which are aggressive to flies. While we recommend 30- to 40-pound shock tippet when going after these bullies, you can catch the smaller ones on the flats with your bonefish outfit.

The West End of Grand Bahama enjoys very good offshore fishing due to its proximity to the Northwest Providence Channel and the Straits of Florida. April through June is the best period for most species, including blue and white marlin, sailfish, dorado, blackfin, bluefin, and Allison tuna.

We do not know of any fly-fishing–savvy offshore crews on Grand Bahama, so fishing is done with conventional gear. Old Bahama Bay Marina has boats for hire with all tackle and bait provided. You can ask at the marina if anyone has fly-fishing experience. Xanadu, Running Mon, and Port Lucaya marinas also have boats available for fishing charter. From these marinas you might also want to try reef fishing for grouper, amberjack, and kingfish. Use chum over the reefs if you want to fly-fish.

Dorado and wahoo are our favorite blue-water fish to pursue from Grand Bahama. January is an incredible month for wahoo off West End, though the weather can be tough. With conventional gear you can hook up more than twenty wahoo some days, and you can have multiple shots with flies if you have a good fishing partner for teasing. Dorado are also plentiful in January, though April is the best month we've seen.

When we think of Grand Bahama, we see three quality bonefishing operations evenly spaced across the island. Pelican Bay, North Riding Point, and Deepwater Cay each has unique qualities, offering anglers of all ability levels the opportunity to fish with high-caliber guides.

Now add in ease of access from the States, a blend of city life and Out Island charm, first-class accommodations, and a variety of activities for nonanglers, and Grand Bahama makes its case for being one of the top fishing destinations in the world.

OPTIONAL ACTIVITIES

Diving and snorkeling are at the top of the list of nonangling activities, as they are on most other islands. Grand Bahama is the only location we know of where you can dive

The Dolphin Experience at UNEXSO in Freeport.

with dolphins in the wild. This is done through UNEXSO's "Dolphin Dive" program. Resident dolphin from The Dolphin Experience Center rendezvous with divers at a reef about a mile offshore. If you want a less adventuresome dolphin experience you can visit the UNEXSO dolphin center for two hours, or make a day of it. The center is a well-organized series of pens with interspersed floating docks inside Fortune Bay.

If you want to dive with sharks (we don't), there are two feeding programs, one with UNEXSO and the other with Xanadu Undersea Adventures. In both programs, you can watch an experienced diver hand-feeding bait fish to a swarming school of reef sharks. We've only seen the pictures, which are amazing and scary.

Grand Bahama features a number of blue holes inside reefs where experienced divers can descend along the rich coral walls. Cave diving is also spectacular here as the reef structure sits atop a massive limestone base that is carved into the second largest underwater cave system in the world. Located in Lucayan National Park, the caves are still being explored, and there are special dive programs hosted by UNEXSO that can take certified divers inside.

Additional watersports include sailing, boating, jet skiing, windsurfing, and swimming. Rental equipment is available at the various marinas, and at some resorts.

Golf is a highlight for many visitors to Grand Bahama. The five courses are the Bahamas Princess Emerald and Ruby courses, the Lucayan Country Club course, the semiprivate Fortuna Hills course, and the new Bahama Reef course at the Grand Bahama Lucayan Resort.

Tennis courts are available at the Lucayan Country Club and at the Princess Club and Towers.

Any exploration of Grand Bahama usually begins at Lucayan National Park. Pine forests laced with nature trails and limestone caves are two of the highlights. The small park also provides a sampling of 250 species of plants, making it an ideal outdoor classroom for visitors interested in learning more about the flora of the Bahamas.

Loading up for a morning of fishing out of Pelican Bay Hotel.

Legend says the Park contains an ancient cemetery of the Lukka-Cairi, the Arawak Indian tribespeople who lived on the island long ago. Remnants of their civilization have been found in Ben's Cavern, the most famous of the Park's caves.

The Rand Nature Center is another favorite site for visitors. Nature trails wind through one hundred acres of Bahamian forest that are home to pink flamingos and over twenty different species of native orchids.

Shopping is a favorite pastime for many visitors. The International Bazaar was designed and decorated by a Hollywood set director to be a world village depicting the cultures and architecture of different countries. Narrow streets wander in every direction, lined with shops, restaurants, and cafes. While there are some nice stores in the bazaar, we think the place has become a little run-down, though renovation plans are in the works. Mall hours are 10:00 A.M. to 6:00 P.M.

The Port Lucaya Marketplace is Kim's favorite place to shop, maybe because it's convenient to hit after a day on the flats, and definitely because of all the jewelry stores. Some stores and all of the restaurants stay open most evenings until 10:00 P.M. The atmosphere is lively and fun, and is enhanced further by the marina location. Several stores carry a good selection of Cuban cigars. If you're looking for a gift to take home to your family, you'll be able to find something here.

LODGING AND SERVICES

FEATURED LODGES AND ACCOMMODATIONS

Pelican Bay Bonefishing

Lucayan Marina   This is an excellent choice for great bonefishing combined with a variety of vacation services. Fish average 5 to 6 pounds, with many fish 8 pounds and up. Guided fishing is done from Maverick Mirage flats boats. Anglers are picked up at the hotel each morning and driven 15 minutes to the Queen's Cove launch site. Pelican Bay Resort is a 48-room hotel on the marina with a freshwater swimming pool, Jacuzzi, restaurant, and bar. Deluxe rooms feature air-conditioning, private baths, balconies, and satellite TV. Twenty restaurants and 80 shops are located around Count Basie Square at the Port Lucaya Market-place, a 5-minute walk from the hotel. We recommend booking this location well in advance.

Season: October through July.

Suitable For: Anglers and nonanglers.

Optional Activities: 5 championship golf courses, tennis, casinos, swimming, hiking and exploring, sailing, beach sports, Dolphin Experience, snorkeling, diving, and shopping.

What's Included: Airport transfers, accommodations, guided fishing, breakfast and lunch, and Bahamian taxes.

Not Included: Dinner, alcoholic beverages, optional gratuities to guides, optional activities.

Pricing: $$$

Contact: Reservations and information, 912/634-8051 or 800/922-3474, fax 912/634-8052. In the Bahamas, 242/373-9550, fax: 242/373-9551.

Deep Water Cay Club

McClean's Town Located on a remote cay off the east end of Grand Bahama, this world-renowned bone-fishing destination was established in 1958 by Gil Drake, and it remains one of the best flats fishing destinations in the world. We like it for the overall variety of fishing. Superior habitat from flats to creeks to reefs and blue holes stretches over 250 square miles, creating a fishery for permit, sharks, barracuda, snappers, and jacks in addition to all the bonefish. Guides from McLean's Town have fishing in their blood, and they present themselves in a professional manner at all times. Eleven air-conditioned rooms can accommodate up to 22 anglers. The deluxe clubhouse is spacious, with bar, dining room, game room, and amazing views out over the turquoise water. We recommend booking well in advance as repeat clientele keeps the lodge busy.

Season: Mid-September through July.

Suitable For: Anglers and nonanglers.

Optional Activities: Snorkeling, swimming, relaxing in beautiful surroundings, or taking trips across the island to Freeport.

What's Included: Oceanfront air-conditioned rooms, all meals, guided fishing, staff gratuities, and Bahamian taxes. Friday and Monday arrivals and departures only.

Not Included: Air or ground transfers to the lodge. (We recommend the charter flight from Ft. Lauderdale or West Palm Beach directly to Deepwater Cay, though a taxi transfer from Freeport is available.) Alcoholic beverages, optional gratuities for fishing guides.

Pricing: $$$–$$$$

Contact: Reservations and information, 242/353-3073, fax 242/353-3095. In the U.S.: 954/359-0488, fax 954/359-9488.

E-mail: Bahamabone@aol.com

Internet: www.deepwatercay.com

North Riding Point

Burnside Cove The gorgeous beachfront location will put a smile on anyone's face, as will the elegant air-conditioned rooms and main lodge. The fishing program focuses on the central portion of the northern coast, with four access sites for fishing the best tides. Dover Sound, the Water Cays, and the North Riding Point areas are highlights. The guides drive the clients from the lodge each day, 15 to 30 minutes, to the launch sites. Bonefish average 5 to 6 pounds, with fish over 10 pounds possible. Dining is a highlight with special pride taken in presenting a variety of excellent food. A freshwater swimming pool overlooks the white sand beach, and all the amenities of Freeport are only a 20-minute drive away.

Season: Mid-September to mid-July.

Suitable For: Anglers and nonanglers.

Optional Activities: Diving, snorkeling, hiking through nearby Lucayan National Park, swimming, relaxing in beautiful surroundings, or taking short trips to Freeport for anything from golf and tennis to shopping and nightlife. It is hard to get space at North Riding Point, as repeat clientele book way in advance. A year ahead for prime dates is the way to go.

What's Included: Freeport International Airport transfers, deluxe accommodations, all meals including wine and liquor, guided fishing, and Bahamian taxes.

Not Included: Optional gratuities to guides and staff.

Pricing: $$$$

Contact: Reservations and information, telephone/fax: 912/756-4890.
E-mail: northrpc@aol.com

ADDITIONAL ACCOMMODATIONS

Port Lucaya Resort and Yacht Club

One hundred fifty air-conditioned motel-style rooms on the marina. Large swimming pool, Jacuzzi, restaurant, and bar. Great location on the marina, adjacent to the Port Lucaya Marketplace and Count Basie Square. Five-minute walk to the UNEXSO Dive Center. Across the street from The Lucayan, the new mega-resort, casino and golf complex.
Pricing: $$–$$$
Contact: Reservations and information, 242/373-6618 or 800/582-2921, fax 242/373-6652.

Bahamas Princess Country Club and Princess Tower

This is a major resort complex. The casino is located in the Tower, the country club is across the street. The complex contains almost one thousand air-conditioned rooms and suites. Nine restaurants are available, including the Crown Room. Amenities include 6 bars, 2 swimming pools, Jacuzzi and sauna, 2 18-hole golf courses, 9 tennis courts, and exercise room. The staff can arrange most activities. This place needs renovation, and will have a hard time competing with the new Lucayan resort without it.
Pricing: $$–$$$
Contact: Reservations and information, 242/352-6721, 242/352-9661 or 800/545-1300, fax 242/352-6842.

The Lucayan, A Harbor Plaza Resort

This new mega-resort opened in April 1999, and is scheduled for completion by April 2000. The beachfront location is spectacular. This 1600-room resort will feature a huge casino, shops, restaurants, bars, a variety of deluxe rooms and suites, swimming pools, water sports, health club, golf course, tennis courts and more.
Pricing: $$$–$$$$
Contact: Reservations and information, 800/LUCAYAN.
Internet: www.thelucayan.com

MARINAS

Grand Bahama Island currently has 7 marinas. Four are official ports of entry: Old Bahama Bay Marina, Xanadu Marina, The Lucayan Village Marina, and Port Lucaya Marina. Freeport Harbour, even though not a marina, is also an official port of entry.

All visiting boaters should call on a recognized port of entry upon arrival in the Bahamas. If you arrive at a marina that is not a port of entry, you can clear your boat by contacting Bahamas Customs and Immigration and arranging to have officers visit your vessel.

Boaters should contact harbor control or marina offices en route on VHF channel 16 to provide pre-arrival information of your vessel's name, registration number and last port of call. Similarly, providing predeparture information to the marina officials is your responsibility.

Ocean Reef Yacht Club

Fifty-two slips, with vessels up to 180 feet. Depth dockside is 6 feet. Electricity, water, ice, showers, cable and satellite TV. Charters arranged; boat rentals, tackle and bait are available. VHF channel 16. One-, 2-, and 3-bedroom air-conditioned suites and villas are also available. Amenities include a swimming pool, Jacuzzi, and tennis courts.
Contact: Reservations and information, 242/373-4662, fax 242/373-8621.

Port Lucaya Resort & Yacht Club

One hundred slips, with vessels up to 175 feet. Water, ice, showers, laundry, marina supplies, and groceries. Charters arranged and boat rentals are available. Telephone and cable TV hookups. Adjoins Port Lucaya

Marketplace with shops, restaurants, bars and entertainment. Next door to Underwater Explorer's Society (UNEXSO). VHF channels 16 and 72. Port of entry.
Contact: Reservations and information, 800/582-2921 or 242/373-9090, fax 242/373-5884.

Running Mon Marina & Resort

Sixty-six slips. Electricity, water, ice, showers, laundry, satellite TV. Tami-lift to 40 tons. Tackle shop with bait. Charter fleet on site. Thirty-two nice air-conditioned guest rooms are also available.
Contact: Reservations and information, 242/352-6834, fax 242/352-6835.

Xanadu Beach Marina & Resort

Seventy-seven slips, with vessels up to 200 feet. Depth dockside is eight feet. Fuel, water, ice, laundry, showers, telephone, satellite TV. Restaurant and bar. Marine and tackle shop, gift shop, pharmacy. Sport-fishing charter boats available. Diving and snorkeling trips arranged. VHF channel 26. The accompanying hotel tower features 108 air-conditioned rooms, restaurant, 3 bars, swimming pool, tennis courts, and beach access. This place needs renovation.
Contact: Reservations and information, 242/352-6782, fax 242/352-5799.

Lucayan Village Marina

One hundred fifty slips, with vessels up to 150 feet. Full services for boaters include fuel, water, ice, bath house, electricity, phone and satellite TV hookups, swimming pool. Open 24 hours. Port of entry and immigration services. VHF channel 16. This is one of the most deluxe service-oriented marinas anywhere.
Contact: Reservations and information, 242/373-7616, fax 242/373-7630.

Old Bahama Bay Marina

One hundred slips, with vessels up to 120 feet. Full services for boaters include fuel, water, ice, showers, laundry facilities, electricity, phone and satellite TV hookups, swimming pool, beach access. Port of entry with customs and immigration on site. The restaurant, bar, and 50-suite cottage complex is scheduled to open sometime in 2000. Flats and offshore fishing can be arranged. VHF channel 16.
Contact: Reservations and information, 242/346-6500.

SERVICES

Caribbean Divers

Located at the Bell Channel Inn. Diving facility within a resort. Certifications as well as a la carte diving.
Contact: Reservations and information, 242/351-6272, fax 242/351-6272. In the U.S., 757/427-7096, fax 757/481-9116.
E-mail: caribdiv@batelnet.bs

Underwater Explorers Society (UNEXSO)

Located next to the Port Lucaya Marina inside Bell Harbour. Adventure diving with world-class professional staff. Dolphin encounters and shark-feeding dives. Instruction for all levels. Photo lab. Snorkelers and beginner divers welcome.
Contact: Reservations and information, 242/373-1244, fax 242/373-8956.
E-mail: unexso@netrunner.net

Xanadu Undersea Adventures

A complete dive center for beginning and experienced divers, located at Xanadu Beach Hotel. World famous shark dives. Nitrox available.
Contact: Reservations and information, 242/352-3811 or 242/352-5856, fax 242/352-4731.
E-mail: divexua@batelnet.bs

Grand Bahama Bonefishing Ltd.

This is an independent guide service operated out of the Freeport area by the Pinder brothers. David Jr., William, Jeffrey and their associates offer bonefishing packages using various hotels to house their clients. **Contact:** See our Web site at www.bahamaflyfishingguide.com.

Restaurants: Our favorite restaurants are in the Port Lucaya Marketplace area: they include Luciano's, the Ferry House at Pelican Bay, La Dolce Vita, Zorba's, Pisces, and The Pub. The Crown Room at the Princess Country Club is very nice, serving fresh beef and seafood. The Arawak Dining Room at the Lucayan Country Club is excellent for lunch and dinner. The Stoned Crab on Taino Beach serves good seafood in a beachside setting. Pier 1 at Freeport Harbour is a fun experience. You should eat here just to see the shark feedings. Things are always changing, so we recommend talking with the staff at your hotel to get their suggestions.

Car Rentals: The big agencies like Avis, Dollar, and Thrifty have offices at the airport. A local agency is Bahama Buggies near the International Bazaar, 242/352-8750. We recommend booking your rental car in advance, or through your hotel after you arrive.

Taxi service is very good on the island, with zone fares regulated by the government. We still advise asking about fares up front.

Grocery stores, liquor stores, pharmacies, cigar shops, and just about every other kind of shop you would need are available in Freeport and Port Lucaya. Once you drive east, services and stores will be limited, as they are on the Out Islands.

The government-run Rand Memorial Hospital is a good medical facility with seventy-four beds. Ambulance, police, and fire department services are available in Freeport and Port Lucaya.

A number of banks are open 9:30 A.M. to 3:00 P.M. Monday through Thursday, and 9:30 A.M. to 5:00 P.M. on Friday. Several ATMs are available, but don't count on them.

NEW DEVELOPMENTS

The Lucayan, being developed by Hutchison, wins the biggest prize here for tourist-related accommodations and facilities. Part of the resort is open now, with the remainder scheduled for completion by April 2000. This resort will have a wide-ranging impact on the island, and more specifically on the northwestern fishery. The Old Bahama Bay Resort and Marina will effectively reopen the West End, and bring the possibility of a new fishing resort or lodge there.

The Bahamas Princess is planning a major renovation project. We have heard that the property could close for up to a year during this process. We do not know when this project is scheduled to begin.

We believe a significant independent guide movement could spring up around the Freeport/Lucaya area to accommodate day fishing tourists not interested in fishing packages. We will keep track of how this develops, and also watch to see if the government steps in with some sort of licensing or regulation program.

This area of Grand Bahama has a distinct angling tourism advantage over Nassau due to its extensive nearby flats habitat. Depending on the number of independent guides who think they can make a living here, there could be a significant impact on the fishery. Bad weather days could create crowding problems, as there are very few protected areas throughout the northwestern flats region.

We have heard a number of rumors about new lodges on the East End, but nothing concrete. Log on to our Web site, www.bahamasflyfishingguide.com, for the most up-to-date information.

6

The Abacos

Abaco is a mini-archipelago that stretches in a languid crescent for more than 120 miles, beginning with Walker's Cay in the north, and running to the end of the Little Bahama Bank in the south at Sandy Point and Hole in the Wall.

Palm Beach, Florida, lies just under two hundred miles to the west, while Abaco's sister island, Grand Bahama, is a short boat ride away from Coopers Town and Little Abaco.

The three distinct regions that comprise Abaco are Little Abaco, Great Abaco, and the offshore cays. Including these cays, Abaco encompasses roughly 650 square miles, with a population of about ten thousand full-time residents.

The dazzling offshore cays bob in the Atlantic mostly east, and some north, of Great Abaco. The larger populated cays include Walker's, Green Turtle, Great Guana, Man-O-War, and Elbow. The majority of the cays are uninhabited, and together, these cays provide a one hundred-mile-long sheltered cruising area for boating and fishing enthusiasts. This is one reason why Abaco is dubbed "The Sailing Capital of the World," though the people of Great Exuma would argue that point. There is no arguing, however, that Abaco's protected waters, safe harbors, deluxe marinas, charming settlements, secluded coves, and sparkling sand beaches make this little archipelago a dream destination.

A warm and welcoming people, Abaconians are resourceful by nature, necessity having dictated their vocations toward boat building, farming, sailmaking, and crawfishing. We may start to sound like a frozen CD, but meeting the people of Abaco is one of the highlights. Their forebears date back to 1783 when Loyalists and slaves arrived after being forced out of the Carolinas and other colonies at the conclusion of the American revolution.

Abaconians are industrious, church-going people with a strong sense of loyalty and a belief in self-reliance. Looking around the island it is easy to see that a pride in craftsmanship, in everything from home construction to crafts to shipbuilding, is central in their daily lives.

The tranquil local atmosphere is a great tonic for any business or other problems you may have left back home. This sense of well-being often seeps into visitors a day or two after arrival without any awareness. All of a sudden you just feel more relaxed,

Kim and Nettie Symonette at Nettie's Different of Abaco Lodge.

more at peace. Eating the local food helps, as it focuses on fare from the sea, and is prepared in a variety of spicy recipes.

When you look around you see people going about their daily lives with a simple sense of purpose. There is little unemployment on Abaco. This admirable work ethic has brought considerable prosperity to the island, most notably due to tourism. High-quality service is the key to success in the tourism industry, and Abaconians excel in reliable friendly service. If you have questions, it's easy to find someone with the answers. It's also nice to realize that people here have not become jaded by tourism, as have people in other countries with tourist economies. This is a place where you can feel safe in an uncrowded environment, yet still have access to whatever level of accommodations and services you desire.

The local government also plays a big role in daily life. When the central government in Nassau put more authority in the hands of the Out Island people, they made a giant stride forward in awakening social awareness. If you want to learn about local politics, just ask anyone. The people really feel involved in their communities, and they all have opinions they're happy to discuss.

While there are good qualities about Abaco from head to toe, we have to confess to a special feeling for Treasure Cay, and its offshore neighbors, Green Turtle, Great Guana, Man-O-War, and Elbow Cays. Great fishing opportunities combined with wonderful accommodations, plenty of activities and mind-melting serenity make this area unique in all the Bahamas.

Sailing, boating, diving, snorkeling, fishing, and other water-related activities are undoubtedly the focus of most visitors. An activity we highly recommend is exploring the offshore cays, finding your own deserted beach, and spreading out a great picnic on the pristine sand. Then, if you have a fly rod, wander over to a secluded cove and catch a few tailing bonefish.

Ecotourism is booming. Hiking and biking is popular through natural areas ripe with bird and plant life. Sea kayaking through a number of protected areas provides a rewarding sense of adventure. More conventional activities include golf, tennis, and beach volleyball. And if you don't feel like doing anything, that's a highly rated activity, too.

The commercial hub of Abaco, and third largest town in the Bahamas, is Marsh Harbour. The town offers a full array of services to visitors, including one of the best medical clinics in the islands.

Convenient commercial air service to Marsh Harbour and Treasure Cay airports, from Florida or from Nassau, make Abaco an easy destination to reach. American Eagle flies daily to Marsh Harbour from Miami. Bahamasair flies daily from Nassau to both airports. Air Sunshine flies to both airports from Ft. Lauderdale. Continental/Gulfstream flies to both airports from various Florida airports.

We also use several air charter services from Florida and Nassau for families or fishing parties who prefer this extra convenience. If you want to take the casual approach, scheduled mail boats from Nassau visit ports up and down the island on a weekly basis. Ferry service from Marsh Harbour and Treasure Cay to the offshore cays is very good, or you can choose to rent your own boat.

Most ferry boats are covered, so you stay dry even in rough weather crossings, but we still like to be prepared for bad weather. We always take rain jackets with hoods on the ferry boats just in case, and we wear either sandals with good support, or tennis shoes because the gunwales of the ferries and the docks are usually slippery. Good traction soles are a must.

AROUND THE ISLAND

Walker's Cay is the northernmost inhabited cay in the Abacos and the Bahamas. It lies on the northeastern edge of the Little Bahama Bank, a short distance from some of the best blue-water fishing in the Atlantic Ocean.

This resort cay has long been famous as a boaters' haven, and for its billfish tournaments. More recent notoriety has been achieved from Flip Pallot's ESPN television series, *The Walker's Cay Chronicles*.

The Walker's Cay Hotel and Marina dominates the island, with the hotel itself perched on the highest ground overlooking the aqua-colored water covering the shallow banks to the west. The hotel and marina serves a variety of boaters interested in cruising, diving, and fishing. The marina has space for seventy-five boats, and offers a full array of services. Hotel amenities include a restaurant, bar, two swimming pools, and a tennis court. Accommodations are in deluxe rooms and larger villas.

The airstrip is used by the resort's aircraft, bringing in vacationers from Florida, though it is available to commercial charters and private pilots. The customs office is located nearby.

Complete diving and fishing packages are available through the Walker's Cay Hotel. It is possible to combine blue-water fishing for billfish, tuna, and dorado, with flats fishing for bonefish, permit, barracuda, and sharks. Reef fishing throughout the area is also sensational.

Flats fly fishers should be aware that bonefishing right around Walker's is not very good. Runs of twenty minutes to an hour to Tom Brown's Cay, Grand Cays, and even Double Breasted Cays produce the best bonefishing. If the weather is rough, these runs can be uncomfortable, or even impossible.

Grand Cays are southeast of Walker's, and the grouping of small islands covers a considerable area. The shallow water within the islands is ideal habitat for bonefish and a variety of snappers. Pretty beaches face the ocean side of the cays, while mangrove-lined creeks snake in every direction. The wider lagoons and broader sounds have skinny water flats that are bonefish magnets. Navigating these areas is tricky at best, and we recommend using a local guide. If boaters wish to try it on their own, take a little Avon dinghy and your GPS, and be careful.

There is a good harbor for boaters next to the Grand Cays settlement. Space for about a dozen boats is available at the dock facilities of the Island Bay Front Hotel.

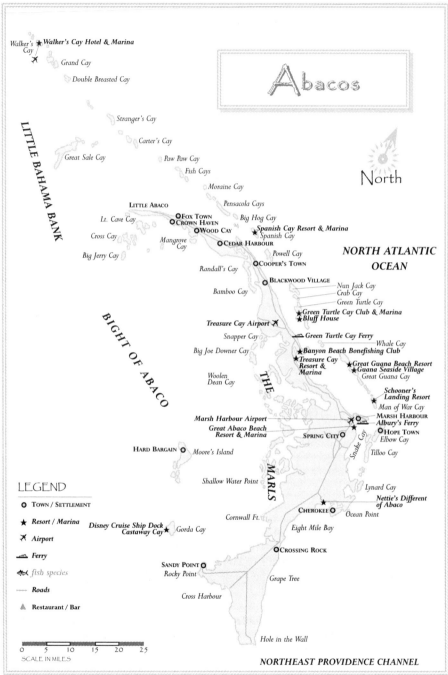

For big bonefish, it's tough to beat Abaco.

Brian O'Keefe

The hotel offers basic air-conditioned rooms, plus fuel, water, and ice for boaters. Rosie's Place serves good local dishes, including some of the best grouper and snapper we've tasted. Two smaller grocery stores have a decent selection of the necessary foods plus some over-the-counter drugs and medicines. There is also an excellent bakery. A freighter from Nassau arrives at the cay about every ten days, so the stores are stocked when the boat arrives, and then become sparse as the days pass before the next boat.

The settlement population is three to four hundred people who make their living fishing or as resort employees at Walker's Cay. These are exceptionally friendly people, who can tell you stories for hours, while never missing a beat in a domino game. Bring up the subject of fishing and you'll hear incredible tales of giant bonefish, permit, jacks, and cubera snapper.

Grand Cay is an excellent base for adventurous fly fishers cruising the cays of the Little Bahama Bank during April, May, and June. While offshore fishers would be better served at Walker's Cay, flats fly fishers will do better stationed here. There are miles of soft grassy flats and harder wadable sand and coral flats that are home to countless bonefish that rarely, if ever, see a fly. Shrimp and crab populations are amazing, as you can see in many areas at low tide. Creek, cut, and reef fishing is also outstanding. Grey snappers line the mangroves, while jacks, cuberas, and barracudas fill ambush points during the last half of falling tides.

Local guides are available in Grand Cay and can be contacted through the hotel or through Rosie's. The best means of communication throughout the Cays of Abaco is by VHS radio. Channel 68 is the general hailing and emergency channel in this area, so it should be used only when necessary. Rosie's can usually be reached on channel 16.

A little farther southeast, Double Breasted Cays are composed of countless rocks, sandbars, channels, cays, and cuts. White sand beaches dot many of the cays. Navigating larger boats is tricky in this area, so we would recommend finding a safe anchorage, then exploring the flats and creeks in a dinghy or smaller launch. Bonefishing here is excellent, especially during neap tides, when the incoming tide is in the morning or late afternoon.

A long series of cays and rocks continues in a southeasterly direction toward Great Abaco. Stranger's Cay, Joe Cays, Carter Cays, Fish Cays, and Moraine Cay are some of the more notable. While we have not fished any of these cays, several of our

Heading out for a day of sun, relaxation, and hopefully a few 10-pound bones.

boating friends have told us some great bonefish stories. One of the most impressive was about the sandbars and grass flats around the boating entrance to Little Carter Cay. Tidal currents in this area can be like a fast-moving trout stream. During the last couple of hours of the falling tide one of our friends stood on a sandbar and hooked up retreating bonefish averaging six pounds until the bar was dry. He then turned around, rested his arm, then started casting to tailing bones waiting for the tide to turn back in.

While this type of fishing is hit-or-miss without specific local knowledge, boating anglers can find these opportunities throughout this region. You just have to have your mind in tune with the habitat, paying specific attention to the bottom structure. A common denominator we look for is a combination of deeper water feeding shallower flats. Check out the tidal flow direction and this will tell you where to look for approaching bonefish.

The largest cay in the area, lying southwest of the Carter Cays, is Great Sale Cay. This low-lying cay is about five and a half miles long with huge marshy areas that are prime spawning grounds for a variety of crabs, shrimp, and bait fish. Many of the marshes are lined with thick mangroves, and off the mangroves are wide areas of grassy flats. Essentially, this is a food factory for bonefish, snappers, barracudas, sharks, and rays.

The dark grass flats make it hard to spot bonefish without good sunlight, though during calm conditions you can see tails and wakes in every direction. If you just want to catch a lot of bonefish, with fly or conventional gear, wait for high tide, especially during spring tides, and you'll see bonefish muds the size of large sandbars.

Great Sale Cay is often used as a stopover point for boaters traversing the Little Bahama Bank from West End, Grand Bahama to the northern Abaco cays and Little

*A careful release will
ensure that this bonefish
lives to fight another day.*

Abaco. The West End Bars of Little Abaco are a short boat trip southeast of Great Sale Cay.

Boaters can cruise along the eastern length of the bars to Hawksbill Cays or to Fox Town in water that averages ten feet deep. This direction is traveled more by boaters because it feeds the protected waterway between the offshore cays and Great Abaco.

Boaters can also take the route along the leeward side of the West End Bars into the Bight of Abaco. Water depths are skinnier on this side, and navigation requires constant attention over various shallow bars. Taking a path on either side of Cave Cays is the way to go. Fly fishers will want to proceed between Cave Cays and Cashe's Cay as the bonefishing in this area is fantastic. Permit are available here as well. Boaters should find a safe anchorage around Cave Cays, then use dinghies or launches to explore the series of cays running in toward Crown Haven.

There are wadable flats throughout the area with bottom structures ranging from hard white sand to uneven coral. Wading is especially good around Brush Cay. The turtle grass flats are usually too mucky to wade, but bones love to tail in the dark fertile grass during the low incoming tide. Using a sea kayak here would be a good option.

Land-based anglers can reach Crown Haven and Fox Town over the new highway. Several independent guides are beginning to operate in this area. Accommodations are available in Crown Haven at the Trade Winds Motel.

Fox Town is the main settlement at the north end of Little Abaco. Services for boaters are available at the government pier, and at the Shell station dock. As it is throughout the Abaco Cays, VHS radios are used more frequently than telephones. Channel 16 will reach the Shell Station, and the manager can help you with most anything you need.

There are a couple of good restaurants near the harbor, a general store, and telephone services at the Batelco office.

Boaters heading south from Fox Town navigate northeast around Hawksbill Cay before making the turn toward Crab Cay. The grouping of rocks and small cays on the north end of Hawksbill Cay create a number of irregular flats, some no wider than a medium-range cast. These flats, all fed by deeper water, draw decent numbers of bonefish, but more important, they draw huge bonefish. This type of flat is generally overlooked throughout the Bahamas because it requires a lot of hopping around and running, and only a little fishing, but for anglers looking to hook up some huge bones, it's worth the time.

Little Abaco fattens out before it joins Great Abaco via a narrow causeway that is part of the Great Abaco Highway leading south to Coopers Town. A small series of cays strung along the road, including Wood Cay, are connected by beautiful bonefish flats that are easy to wade.

On the windward side, Cedar Harbour, the Riding Rocks, Crab Cay, and Angel Fish Point create a small bay that is laced with creeks, cuts, and flats. When the wind is down, this area produces spectacular fishing for bonefish, jacks, snappers, sharks, and barracuda. This is an area the independent guides from Coopers Town are developing for their fly-fishing clients.

Boaters cruising south past Angel Fish Point can choose to veer eastward to Spanish Cay, which was once controlled by Clint Murchison, a past owner of the Dallas Cowboys football team. The five-thousand-foot runway was built by Murchison for his private jet, and the jets of his internationally famous friends. The island is now open to the public. The marina includes a sturdy breakwater, slips, and full services. This cay is a self-contained vacation destination that includes a couple of good restaurants, deserted beaches, rental condos and houses, tennis courts, a dive center, and boat and bike rentals.

A potential danger to boaters, but a bonanza for fly fishers, is a large shallow bank with accompanying flats stretching southwest from Spanish Cay. Several of our boating friends have caught permit here during the last part of the incoming tide, and good numbers of bonefish are readily available. If you are just cruising through this can be hit-or-miss, but if you're staying on Spanish Cay, and you put in some time here, the results should be worthwhile. These flats can also be accessed from Coopers Town, though the fishing on the leeward side is so good that anglers rarely head in this direction.

Coopers Town is a well-established community based around a fishing economy. While conch, grouper, snapper, and a variety of other fish produce food and income, lobster, or crawfish as it's called locally, is the high-dollar ticket. The commercial crawfish season runs from August 1 to March 31, and it is not uncommon for entire families to stop everything else and go harvesting during August.

Tourism is becoming a bigger part of Coopers Town life, but with no special hotels or resorts, sportfishing, and especially bonefishing, is leading the way. Arriving boaters can find all services at either Murray's dock or the Shell station pier. VHS channel 16 is the best way to contact both facilities. Grocery stores, restaurants, bakeries, a laundromat, and telephone services are all within walking distance of the docks.

For fly and conventional fishers, the action here is on the leeward side of Coopers Town. O'Donald Macintosh is the best guide in the area, and one of the most interesting guides to fish with anywhere in the Bahamas. He is also an elected member of the local government, and one of the community leaders. Two of O'Donald's sons, Kirk and Drexel, have joined him in the guiding business.

A number of dirt tracks, some of which can be called roads, lead out to the leeward side of the island. The fishing grounds in this area are spectacular. Bonefish cruise right into the shoreline to feed, and we often see tailing bones at the small dock where O'Donald keeps his boats. A five-minute run to a crescent-shaped group of cays split by a deep creek puts anglers onto large numbers of aggressive bones in the three- to six-pound range.

Mangrove-covered cays, some with blue holes, stretch for miles in every direction, the largest being Randall's Cay to the south. Flats, creeks, and deeper channels fill in the space between the cays with shades of blues and greens that are ever changing.

We fish the turtle grass flats from boats, but much of our fishing time here is spent wading. Hard white sand flats interspersed with crunchy coral and grass provide miles of ankle-deep water for tailing bonefish on the appropriate tides.

When approaching bonefish in thin water like this, silence is indeed golden.

Occasionally, we have seen float planes from the States drop off anglers for the day, so we must issue this word of caution to anglers choosing this option. Make sure the float plane operators show you their Bahamian license to operate, and make sure they know the tides. Just fishing a neap tide is not enough to ensure low water, and fishing a spring tide is tricky at best. The time of the day for the tides is the most important factor. If your timing is wrong, you will spend your day struggling through deep water, with limited access to the better fishing areas, and you probably won't catch any fish.

This is not an area we recommend for fishing on your own unless you have a boat. Even then, good local knowledge is critical, so we recommend fishing with a professional guide. For anglers staying in Treasure Cay, or on the nearby offshore cays, fishing this area with O'Donald will be a highlight of your trip.

Boaters heading south from Coopers Town will find small bonefish flats and good reef fishing around Powell Cay, which is a private island, and then at Manjack, Crab Cay (yes, another Crab Cay), and Fiddle Cay, on the way to Green Turtle Cay.

On land, the Great Abaco Highway takes you south to the Treasure Cay Airport, the Green Turtle Cay Ferry, and then to the resort of Treasure Cay, for a total driving time of about twenty-five minutes to the resort proper.

Treasure Cay is one of our favorite places in the Bahamas, both as a base for fishing, and for just chillin', mon. The large marina offers full services to boats of all sizes, and you can be sure to see some eye-popping yachts here any time of the year. Boaters have access to all the marina facilities including the swimming pool, bar, Spinnaker's restaurant, and a complete dive shop.

Condos and villas ring the marina and spread into the gardens that include clay and hard-surface tennis courts. A huge grass park in the center of the resort is ringed by a Little Switzerland gift shop, Florence's Café, a laundromat, golf cart and bike rental shops, a small market, plus a larger grocery and liquor store.

Just across the main road is Three-Mile Beach, often rated among the top ten beaches in the world. Erosion has washed away a lot of the sand, but this beach is still dazzling. The Banyon Beach Club, a nice condo complex, is located here, along with a number of houses available for rental. The Banyon Beach Bonefishing Club is one of the newer bonefishing operations in the Bahamas, and is ideally suited to accommodate anglers traveling with nonangling companions. More rental houses are available farther along the road, including the Treasure Houses, and all the way out to Windward Road, which faces Green Turtle, Whale, and Great Guana Cays.

An eighteen-hole Dick Wilson golf course rounds out the resort's amenities. At the far southeastern end of the golf course are bonefish flats that produce good fishing for the first few hours of the incoming tide.

Treasure Cay Resort & Marina has bonefish guides and offshore boats available. One of the Resort's bonefish guides is Orthenell Russel, the "Bonefish King." Orthenell is a character, one of the old-time guides with plenty of stories to keep you entertained. The offshore boats fish the reefs for jacks, barracuda, cubera snapper, and mackerel, and fish the blue water for marlin, sailfish, tuna, and dorado. Most of this fishing is with conventional gear, slinging plugs, and spoons over the reefs and using trolling lures in blue water.

The people we know who cruise in this area drag some kind of lure or bait behind their boats most of the time. They catch a variety of fish throughout the day, and usually keep enough for dinner.

While Treasure Cay is a great base, Green Turtle and Great Guana Cays are just as good if you want a more remote location. Green Turtle Cay is three miles long and about a mile and a half wide. The irregular coastline consists of spectacular beaches, a number of deep bays that provide protected anchorages, plus shallower bays and sounds. Growing pineapples, salvaging wrecked ships, and fishing have supported the locals over the years, but tourism leads the economy today.

New Plymouth, located near the southern end of the cay, is a picturebook New England–style settlement, with a main cement dock that is used by the weekly mail boat and the commercial water taxis. Lowe's water taxi service makes the two-mile run from Abaco on a continuous basis throughout the day. People coming from Treasure Cay can be dropped off for a couple of hours to look around New Plymouth, take the next ferry over to the Green Turtle Cay Club for lunch or a walk, then take another ferry back to Abaco later in the day.

New Plymouth is a port of entry with full services for boaters, vacationers, and day visitors and includes a marine hardware store, grocery and liquor stores, a post office, a bank open two days a week, and Batelco telephone and fax services. A two-hour stroll through the narrow maze of clean streets will take you to many interesting shops and a stop at the Albert Lowe Museum, located in a one-hundred-fifty-year-old house. The restored museum displays Alton Lowe's paintings, plus model ships and an amazing collection of photographs depicting the history of Abaco. At the end of your walk there are several restaurants and bars you can choose from for a snack, rum drink, or a Kalik.

We prefer to get back on the ferry and head over to the Green Turtle Cay Club. Black Sound is on your right as you cruise north toward the Club. Two marinas and additional services for boaters are located here, including boat storage facilities.

Green Turtle Cay Club is at the northern end of White Sound, which is cut in two by a strip of land that separates the deeper water from a large shallow back bay lined with mangroves. The club has an atmosphere of casual old-style elegance, with dock space for thirty-five boats, villa and suite accommodations, a swimming pool, beach, two bars, and an excellent restaurant.

While any beach-loving vacationers would be happy here, so would anglers. A short walk up over a moderate hill will bring you to Coco Bay. You can have at least two good hours of bonefishing here most days. The bottom structure is a combination of sand and grass, and wading is easy in most parts of the bay. It is a little more difficult, but anglers can also walk to Bluff Harbour Bay and catch bonefish cruising the shorelines on the incoming tide. Bonefish will also lay up in certain areas here during the high tide.

Across the sound, perched on top of an eighty-foot-high hill is the Bluff House, a very nice hotel with villa and deluxe room accommodations. The views are spectacular from the restaurant, which is one of our favorite places for dinner. You will need reservations during the season.

South of Green Turtle are several private cays, Whale Cay and then Great Guana Cay. In good weather this is a fun area for recreational boating and reef fishing, though the Whale Cay Passage can be dangerous due to strong cross-currents that can create unpredictable waves. All boaters should familiarize themselves with the potential problems before cruising here.

Great Guana Cay is one of the most beautiful little islands anywhere. The small settlement is like something you would imagine in a South Seas dream; coconut palms, Casuarinas, turquoise water, a crescent beach, and welcoming locals. The Great Guana Beach Resort & Marina has its own dock adjacent to the government dock, with about twenty boat slips and a dinghy tie-up area for visitors. This is another of our favorite lunch spots on days we go cay hopping. Daily ferry service is available from Marsh Harbour, and the mail boat calls weekly.

Guana Seaside Village is a newer resort, small and intimate, built in 1996. If you're looking for a romantic getaway, you can't beat this location. The windward side beaches run for seven miles, the length of the cay, so you can find a spot all to yourself anytime of the year. In places rocky sections of the reef run in to the beach, forming pools and drop-offs. On calm days you can fly fish these areas for small jacks, snappers, and grouper.

There are also a couple of leeward bays that offer excellent fishing for tailing bonefish. Bonefish and reef guides are available through both Great Guana resorts, or you can take the ferry across to Abaco and meet O'Donald Macintosh for a day of guided fishing in The Marls.

Man-O-War Cay is the next significant island on the way to Marsh Harbour and Elbow Cay.

Solitude on the sand.

Two and a half miles long, the enchanting cay is famous for its shipbuilding tradition. The hardy locals can trace every one of the their ancestors back to their initial arrival. They credit their strong religious beliefs for their survival through long periods of hard times, which is the main reason the sale of liquor and tobacco is not permitted on the cay.

Man-O-War Cay has two of the best safe harbors in the Bahamas. If you turn left after passing the main harbor entrance, you head into North Harbour. The sixty-slip Man-O-War Marina is the first major facility you encounter. The marina offers full services to boaters, including fuel and dingy docks, a pavilion restaurant, dive shop, and bank. The restaurant is a fun place for lunch, serving great cracked conch plus barbecued meats on weekends.

Albury's Ferry Service has a fleet of water taxis at the marina for trips to Hope Town, Marsh Harbour, and the surrounding cays. VHS channel 16 is the best means of communication here, as it is in all the other offshore cays.

A little farther into the harbor is the government wharf, which is flanked by two shipbuilding yards. The friendly settlement contains a good grocery store, a couple of restaurants and delis, bakery, post office, and telephone station. The atmosphere here is peaceful and content. Just wandering around the narrow streets, all lined with brightly painted houses, is a nice way to pass some time. You can also walk across the island on coconut palm–lined paths to some gorgeous windward beaches.

Small boats, motorbikes, and golf carts are the main mode of transportation around the cay. Along the northern shore, on the leeward side, are several bonefish flats that are best accessed by boat. You have to take note of the tides, however, or you can become grounded as the tide falls. This is true for all boating anglers throughout this region. We have talked to plenty of people who have spent up to six hours stranded on a bar or flat because they didn't anticipate tidal movement.

Back on the mainland of Abaco, the highway south from Treasure Cay to Marsh Harbour is in great shape. The drive takes less than an hour. Taxi service is available for this trip, though we recommend renting a car if you prefer traveling by land. You can also reach Marsh Harbour by boat or ferry, either directly, or with stop-offs on the offshore cays.

Many people staying in Treasure Cay or on the offshore cays rent boats, and a number of good rental agencies are available. A twenty-three-foot runabout is ideal for transportation, cay hopping, and reef fishing. In good weather the run from Treasure Cay to Marsh Harbour takes about forty-five minutes.

Marsh Harbour is the third largest town in the Bahamas, and the center of commercial activity for Abaco. The settlement was established in the late 1700s. By the late 1800s and early 1900s the settlement had grown prosperous from shipbuilding and sponging. Sponging declined after World War I, and was eventually obliterated in 1938 by a blight that wiped out sponges throughout the Bahamas. Shipbuilding also declined and sent many residents off to Nassau in search of work.

By the late 1950s, several farming projects began to take hold, and tourism started to pick up. After Castro took over in Cuba in 1959, even more sailors and vacationers began heading to the Abacos, and tourism led the way to new prosperity.

Today, the airport features convenient daily air service to Nassau and Florida. The main harbor offers easy access to a number of docks and marinas and the town itself.

Boaters entering the harbor along Pelican Shores can steer to the right through the dredged passage to the Government Customs Wharf or head straight in through the channel to the Conch Inn Marina and Hotel in the southeast corner. The marina has seventy-five slips and full boater services, though a number of the slips are taken by charter boats.

A hard-fighting jack, taken on a yellow popper.

Brian O'Keefe

Part of this charter fleet features offshore boats for both reef and blue-water fishing. None of the crews are fly-fishing specialists, though they are enthusiastic and will be happy to put experienced anglers on fish. If you just want to catch fish with conventional gear, no problem, mon.

The Conch Inn Marina is operated by the Moorings, the charter yacht company. If you're looking to rent a boat and cruise the offshore cays, this is the place. The facility also features harbor view rooms, a swimming pool, and complete dive shop.

Mangoes, a restaurant, bar, and gift shop located next to the water has a dock with space for customers to tie up while eating lunch, dinner, or just shopping. If you're boating over from Treasure Cay, this would be a good spot to come ashore, enjoy some lunch, and walk around.

To the west is the Harbour View Marina, then Triple J Marine, the Tiki Hut restaurant, Long's Landing (where you can buy fresh seafood), and the government's Union Jack dock. There are three or four additional dinghy docks through this area for visitors to tie up and walk around town.

Straight across the harbor from Conch Inn is the Marsh Harbour Marina, home of the Royal Marsh Harbour Yacht Club, and Jib Room bar and restaurant. The yellow-and-white–striped roof makes this an easy landmark to spot. The two-story restaurant offers views of the harbor, a fun atmosphere, a good variety of seafood, and excellent barbecue.

If you're driving down from Treasure Cay, make sure you get a map from your rental car agency. You will have to negotiate several roundabouts on your way to the harbor, so remember that driving is on the left. The Conch Inn Marina and the Marsh Harbour Marina are well marked on all the maps we've seen.

The town of Marsh Harbour has just about anything you would ever need, right down to a one-hour photo store. Still, using VHS channel 16 to communicate, especially if you want a taxi, will serve you better than a telephone.

The east side of Marsh Harbour can be easily reached by boat or car. If you're driving, keep going along the harbor past the Conch Inn and make a right turn following the signs for Boat Harbour Marina and the Great Abaco Beach Resort. If you're headed to the main ferry dock, keep going straight out past the Great Abaco Club.

Sugarloaf Cay sits just off Marsh Harbour's eastern shore. Development here is rampant with new vacation homes and docks. Albury's Ferry Service is located between the west end of Sugarloaf and Boat Harbour Marina. Albury's offers the most convenient ferry service to Hope Town and White Sound on Elbow Cay, plus other offshore cays like Man-O-War and Great Guana.

Boat Harbour Marina has 175 slips for boats up to 150 feet. Full services are available, including use of the Great Abaco Beach Resort's swimming pool and tennis courts. The hotel features air-conditioned accommodations, its own beach, restaurant, bar, boat and bike rentals, and a number of shops. Grocery and liquor stores are nearby.

While Marsh Harbour has changed for the better over the past few years, with many upgrades and renovations, this wouldn't be one of our choices for a fishing vacation. The town is a great hub for reaching the other more desirable regions of Abaco, and for obtaining services not available elsewhere. It's fun to visit for lunch, a look around, a little shopping, stocking up on groceries, and maybe dinner at one of the harbor restaurants.

Elbow Cay, on the other hand, is idyllic for sea and sun worshippers as well as fly fishers. Hope Town is home to the most historic lighthouse in the Bahamas, the famous candy-striped tower built in 1863. When the lighthouse was built, the locals considered it a disastrous event, as this aid to navigation put a serious crimp in the salvage business.

Today the locals look more kindly on the landmark. They recently defeated an effort to automate the lighthouse, voting instead to keep the kerosene-powered system that requires winding every hour and a half throughout the night.

Hope Town is snuggled around a picturebook harbor dotted with pleasure boats. The streets are like wide sidewalks, with no automobile or golf cart traffic allowed. The houses are well tended, with fresh bright paint, and beautiful flower gardens.

The Lighthouse Marina is just inside the harbor. Full services are available for boaters, including the only fuel service in Hope Town. Several hundred yards to the south is the long dock of the Hope Town Marina. The adjacent Club Soleil Resort features a restaurant and bar, and comfortable air-conditioned rooms with balconies overlooking the harbor. If you want to talk about reef or offshore fishing, the Hope Town Marina is the place. You can charter a boat here, or rent a boat and explore on your own.

A little farther south is the relatively new twelve-slip dock and marina for Hope Town Hideaways, owned by Peggy and Chris Thompson. This resort features two-bedroom waterfront villas with central air-conditioning, full kitchens, private docks, swimming pool, and beach, all contained on a beautifully-landscaped eleven-acre property. The Thompsons also manage and rent the most luxurious houses on the island, including houses at Tahiti Beach.

Across the harbor, on the strip of land between the harbor and the oceanfront beach, is the main settlement of Hope Town. Two grocery stores, several bakeries, a liquor store, a variety of shops and restaurants, library, and post office are all easily accessed from various waterfront docks, including the Hope Town Harbour Lodge dock.

The lodge itself offers nice air-conditioned rooms with a choice of harbor or ocean view. The swimming pool overlooks the Atlantic beach, where a live reef is thirty feet off the sand, and is a favorite with snorkelers.

Hope Town has become a favorite April and May destination for many of our friends from Jackson Hole, Wyoming. We've heard some boaters complain that the harbor has become overcrowded with boats, but we think there is just the right mix of "enough to do," with relaxing solitude, and access to great fishing that you can do on your own or with a guide. Several guides specialize in bonefishing the surrounding cays; they will also take anglers to the Marls.

South of Hope Town is White Sound, a quiet harbor with a bonefish flat stretching out from the southern tip of the boaters leeward entrance. Golf carts are the main mode of land transportation from Hope Town to the White Sound and Tahiti Beach areas, though the two resorts, Abaco Inn and Sea Spray, provide van service to their guests from Nigh Creek. From Marsh Harbour guests can use the Albury Ferry Service to reach the Abaco Inn or Sea Spray docks directly.

It is easy boating from Hope Town to White Sound and Tahiti Beach. We highly recommend that Elbow Cay vacationers rent their own boat. Island Marine, located on Parrot Cay, is one of the best boat rental companies in the Bahamas. They also work through the Hope Town Harbour Lodge, and will deliver rental boats directly to your dock anywhere on Elbow, Man-O-War, or Great Guana Cays.

The Abaco Inn offers recently refurbished rooms, two new suites, a superb restaurant, and saltwater swimming pool, all overlooking the sound and the ocean. There are many beautiful spots throughout the offshore cays, but this is one of the most spectacular.

At the southern end of the sound is Sea Spray Resort Villas and Marina. The pleasant one- and two-bedroom air-conditioned villas offer inspiring views in a quiet tropical setting. Boaters and vacationers will find full services here including fuel, boat, and bike rentals, restaurant, bar, laundry, and villa catering.

Elbow Cay's southern tip includes two points facing Tilloo Cay, while the exclusive Tahiti Beach faces Lubber's Quarters and the Sea of Abaco. Acres of coconut palms shade a number of deluxe homes available for rent here. This is a great couples or family retreat for people who want to mix fishing with laid-back vacationing.

Fly-fishing boaters, including cay hoppers from Elbow Cay and Marsh Harbour, will want to explore the cays, flats, cuts, and mangrove-lined creeks south of Elbow all the way to Little Harbour. The cuts between the cays, including deeper areas between bars and reefs, hold a variety of snappers, jacks, mackerel, barracuda, and sharks. On the falling tide, especially when the current really moves, you'll find all these predators waiting on meals.

Snake Cay, just off the mainland, begins a series of cays that follow the shoreline southward. Many wadable flats extend eastward from the cays, and a number of creeks lead into thick mangroves. Good numbers of bonefish roam through the mangroves looking for crabs. They often wait as long as possible before heading back out to deeper water. That makes it possible to set up ambush points on the last part of the falling tide. Then you can wait for the new incoming tide to cast to tailing fish.

Brian O'Keefe

Mutton snapper, taken from one of the many cuts.

Knowing the tides in this region is vital. It's better to get skunked than to end up with your boat aground for hours—or maybe not, if you're a fishing fanatic. But remember, there is a big difference in water levels between a spring and a neap tide. If you fish this area on a neap tide, water levels won't change so dramatically. If you come back a week later on a spring tide, you'll see lots of dry flats at low tide that were previously covered with water. Professional guides Jay Sawyer and Justin Sands run trips to the Snake Cay area when the tides are right.

Long and lean Tilloo Cay has some pretty beaches for picnicking and several wadable flats, the best we've fished being at the southern point. The Pelican Cays are part of the Pelican Cay Land and Sea Park, which was founded by the Bahamas National Trust. The Trust's ongoing mission is to preserve the natural beauty of numerous Bahamian cays, reefs, and seabeds. Boaters need to read the regulations for this area, as dropping anchor in many parts of the park is forbidden.

There are several good wadable flats interspersed through the Pelican Cays, plus some reef-type banks where we have seen large permit. These banks are on the windward side of the cays and are best fished in calm weather. We recommend that day boaters pay close attention to the weather, and pick the nicer days for exploring and fishing.

Cruising boaters will be better served to explore the flats and creek fishing areas in smaller dinghies. One area ripe for this type of adventure is the Bight of Old Robinson, which is north of Little Harbour. The Little Harbour area itself has a number of creeks and cuts worth fishing a day or two. This is another area protected by the Bahamas National Trust, so read the regulations. Variety is what you're looking for here. Bonefish, permit, different species of grouper, snapper, and jacks can provide lively action on flies, lures, and bait.

Little Harbour is known as the home of Randolph Johnston, the noted writer and sculptor. Some of Randolph's most famous sculptures, including Monuments to Bahamian Women, are on display in several galleries in Nassau. Johnston died in 1992 at the age of eighty-eight, but his family members, many of whom are artists also, still own much of the land surrounding Little Harbour.

All boaters in this area should note that many cays and Harbour are privately owned and require permission to come ashore. It is your responsibility to recognize private property and not trespass. Remember that VHF channel 16 is the best means of communication. It is easy to find people willing to help with directions and other information.

We have no experience with the run from Little Harbour to Cherokee Sound, but we do know that it requires staying offshore, away from the rocks and reefs. We do not have any reports of good shallow water fishing through this area.

Nettie's Different of Abaco Lodge.

Cherokee Sound is another story. This is the home of Nettie Symonette's Different of Abaco, which is a bonefishing lodge and ecotourism resort. Fly fishers and vacationers fly into Marsh Harbour, then are driven twenty-five minutes south on the Great Abaco Highway to Casaurina Point.

Bonefishers usually stay at the Heritage Lodge, which features eight air-conditioned rooms, restaurant, bar, and game room situated on a natural lagoon a short walk from the beaches of Cherokee Sound. A second lodging option is the Sea Shell Beach Club, located on the pristine white sand beach that stretches for miles north and south. The Beach Club includes a swimming pool, Jacuzzi, and the use of bikes and golf carts for transportation to and from the Heritage Lodge, where all meals are served.

Packages are available for anglers and nonanglers. The bonefishing in Cherokee Sound is excellent, especially if you're looking for big fish. Anglers can fish with a guide, or wade for miles down the shoreline on an incoming tide. The highlight of staying at Different of Abaco, however, is being able to fish the vast central section of the Marls. Located on the leeward side of the island, in the Bight of Abaco, this huge area of the Marls was only accessible by boat until Nettie opened it up to her guests with a private road and channel access.

Most of Nettie's guides are from Cherokee Sound, which has a long tradition of fishermen and shipbuilders. Many of the guides were commercial fishermen who have adapted well to guiding. They have excellent vision and an innate sense of where to find bonefish.

The Marls habitat is one of the most fertile in the Bahamas. Miles and miles of mangroves, creeks, cays, cuts, and flats expand out in every direction. Thousands of bonefish live in this protected area. Anglers can catch high numbers of fish in the one- to three-pound range, plus larger fish ranging up to eight or nine pounds.

While there are wading flats, most fishing here is done from a poled skiff. Farther out, larger cays and deeper water lures bigger bonefish, permit, and tarpon in to feed on an array of crabs, shrimp, and bait fish over dark grass bottoms.

In spite of the guides from Nettie's lodge, and some fly fishers off cruising boats, this area remains relatively untouched. If you want proof, book a trip to Different of Abaco, and spend a few days fishing the Marls. We think you'll enjoy watching bonefish knock each other out of the way to get to your fly.

From Cherokee Sound to Hole in the Wall, the southernmost tip of Abaco, the shoreline is steep and rugged. From what we know, there is no shallow water fishing in this area. From Hole in the Wall boaters can cross the Northeast Providence Channel to Spanish Wells, or make the forty-seven-mile run to Nassau. Fly fishers would want to head northeast along the edge of the Little Bahama Bank to Sandy Point.

The easiest way to reach Sandy Point, however, is by land

Loading up to go fish the Marls, out of Nettie's Different of Abaco.

and/or air. The highway down from Casaurina Point is only a couple of years old and is in excellent condition. Travelers can fly into Marsh Harbour and rent a car for the drive, or take a charter flight to the Sandy Point airstrip. If you are on a bonefishing package at Pete and Gay's Guesthouse or Oiesha's Resort, these transfers from Marsh Harbour can be included.

The settlement of Sandy Point sits on a finger of land between two creeks shaded by coconut palms. This is a quiet commercial fishing town with nicely painted houses and well-kept gardens. Pete and Gay's Guesthouse is located at the main dock and offers splendid views of the harbor from the rooftop lounge. This is also one of the best places in the world to have a cold Kalik and watch the sunset. Fuel is available up the street at the local Esso station and hardware store. A grocery store is within walking distance of the dock.

Bonefishing has been a significant contributor to the local economy in recent years, along with completion of the Great Abaco Highway. Pete and Gay's has ten comfortable air-conditioned rooms and some of the best Bahamian food found in the islands. Anglers can book rooms here on their own and have the management arrange guides, or prearranged bonefishing packages are available.

The same is true for Oiesha's Resort, at the other end of the settlement toward the airport. Oiesha's is a newer motel with nice air-conditioned rooms, a restaurant, and bar.

Fly fishers staying at Sandy Point enjoy an excellent fishery that produces good numbers of bonefish averaging three to six pounds, plus daily shots at larger fish, including double-digit monsters. Permit cruise the deeper edges of the Sarah Wood Bars, near the outer cays like Gorda and Crab, and along the edges of the bank. On calmer days a run to Moore's Island, or maybe north to the Marls, is a fun option.

Local guides are longtime commercial fishermen who have worked hard to develop their bonefishing guide skills. Like the guides from Cherokee Sound, they have good eyes for spotting fish, a pleasant enthusiasm, and they are working to improve their fly-fishing skills. Guides use a variety of boats, some with larger V-hulls for crossing deeper and rougher water, but less well-suited for skinny water. Independent guide, Patrick Roberts, owns a twenty-eight-foot Mako with twin 200-hp outboards. This boat is ideal for blue water fishing or for cruising up to Mores Island or the Marls. For adventurous anglers, Roberts is willing to do overnights on this boat.

It will be interesting to see what happens to this area now that the Walt Disney Company has purchased nearby Gorda Cay and installed a cruise ship harbor and glitzy resort.

FISHING HIGHLIGHTS

The Bight of Abaco runs from Sandy Point in the south to Little Abaco in the north, and is flanked on the east by the Marls, and on the west by a series of cays and the east end of Grand Bahama. This area of the Little Bahama Bank is arguably the best overall shallow water fishery in the Bahamas.

There are no settlements on the west coast of Great Abaco from Sandy Point to Coopers Town, a distance of more than fifty miles. This means cruising boaters are on their own in this vast area. Navigating the Bight is a straightforward matter, though it requires diligent observation, especially in poor weather conditions. We recommend that exploring fly fishers move through this area only in daylight.

The center of the Bight holds deeper water, roughly ten to eighteen feet, with varying sand and grass bottoms. As you move closer to any of the shorelines or cays, water depths can drop quickly. This long and relatively wide patch of deeper water is the bad-weather home for bonefish, permit, tarpon, and other shallow water game fish and bait fish.

Abaco's northern location in the Bahamas means more northeast winter winds and greater chances for winter cold fronts. These cold fronts are most common from mid-November to the end of March, though they can occur from October into May. A strong cold front can last four to five days, while a weaker front can be through in a couple of days. Often, the day before a front will be beautiful, and bonefishing will be fabulous, as fish feed aggressively before moving to deeper water in anticipation of bad weather.

After the cold front has passed, fish return to shallower water and flats. Water temperatures have generally cooled, and fish begin feeding with vigor.

Moving north from Sandy Point, you reach Cedar Cays and then Big Mangrove Cay, which is the southern edge of the Marls. Ocean-type flats surround many of the outer Marls cays. Some of these irregular hard coral flats can be waded, but it's easier to fish from a boat. We like to fish crab flies, especially yarn crabs, over the coral and adjacent flats covered with turtle grass. Golden and snapping shrimp patterns are productive over the turtle grass in skinnier water.

Entering the Marls proper is awe-inspiring. Without good local knowledge it would be easy to get lost or to stick yourself on a bar. Much of the bottom is turtle grass interspersed with sand and coral. Mangroves are everywhere. Many of the green and brown clumps look like mating spiders with long legs arching toward the sky.

The closer you move toward the mainland, the softer the bottom becomes. The mangroves become more dense. Creeks and cuts slash through the vegetation in every direction. Perfectly round bays and surprisingly large flats appear out of nowhere. Countless numbers of blue crabs, some the size of footballs, skitter across the dark grass and golden coral.

This mangrove root and grass bottom structure produces millions of swimming, mantis, snapping, and grass shrimp. Grass shrimp especially love hanging around the latticework of mangrove roots, and they prefer water with a higher salinity. The salinity of the Marls changes with the amount of rain throughout the year. Factoring this into your fishing strategy and fly selection can be critical. The larger snapping shrimp prefer the turtle grass, and are a favorite food for tailing bonefish. The classic version of a Fernandez Snapping Shrimp works well as it lands softly and resists hooking up in the grass.

This unique habitat, combining abundant food and ample protection from predators, creates one of the best bonefish nurseries in the Bahamas. We have seen schools of bonefish here numbering in the thousands, where the largest fish was ten inches long!

Bonefish are the number one game fish species in the Marls, and the number-one target for shallow water fly fishers throughout Abaco. Bonefish size runs the spectrum from bait fish length to gigantic fifteen pounders. The majority of Marls' fish run one to four pounds, with a decent number of fish up to eight or nine pounds. Larger average fish, including fish over ten pounds, are found in deeper water around the outlying and offshore cays, and north of the Marls where access to deeper water is closer to the Abaco mainland.

The best months to fly fish for bones are April through July, and October and November. March is also an excellent month, but look out for cold fronts. August and September can be very good if no hurricanes are around. December through February is weather dependent, and the most common period for cold fronts. This tough cloudy windy weather makes fly-fishing difficult at best. But when you hit nice weather during this period, you'll find hungry bonefish eager to jump on your fly.

The highest concentration of bonefish is in the southern area of the Marls, though numbers are good all along the west coast. Marls fish have a well-earned repu-

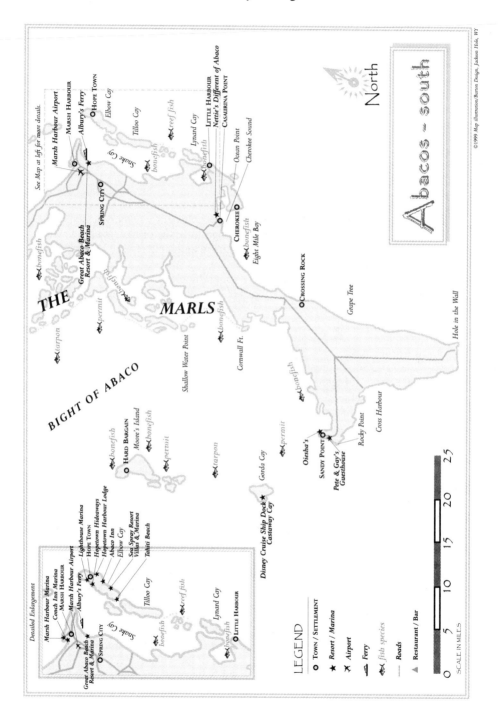

©1999 Map illustration/Burton Design, Jackson Hole, WY

tation for being super-aggressive. It is common to make a bad cast well away from your target, then watch one or more bonefish race over and gobble your fly. This may sound like fly selection is not that important, but we favor lighter flies without eyes, or with beadchain eyes. We rarely use lead-eyed flies such as Clouser's, which are our favorites in many other areas. Go with #4–6 Gotchas, Brown Epoxy Charlies, Snapping Shrimp, and Miheve's Flats Fly as a basic selection.

We prefer to fish the Marls during a neap tide. Generally lower water levels don't allow fish to get as far back into the mangrove systems, thus making them more accessible throughout the day. During spring tides you have to be especially smart and quick to put yourself into position for success on an incoming tide. If you're fishing a spring tide, you'll usually have your best fishing during the last part of the falling tide. You can set up ambush points, then cast to those beautiful silver backs and blue tails as they come swaggering out of the creeks and mangroves.

The time of day of the tide here is more important than whether it's a spring or neap tide. There are times when the tide will be high for most of the daylight hours. If this is the case, you'll have to go into the mangroves after the fish. Guides familiar with this area know how to find fish in these conditions. You can get shots in clear areas, but these bones know a good mangrove root when they see one, and most will break you off. Fish shorter leaders, heavy tippet, up to 15-pound Mason would be our choice, and use flies you don't mind losing.

Remember that all fish are creatures of habit, bonefish even more so. The guides from Nettie's and others who fish this area know bonefish behavior. Ask them questions so you can learn as much as you can about this behavior. If you're fishing on your own, make sure you know the tides, then consider access and ambush points, and you should have some success.

In working out the tides, you must factor in the barometric pressure as well as the wind. Both can hold a tide out longer, or bring it rushing in sooner. During windy conditions many areas of the Marls are well protected, which means good fly-fishing here when other areas might be unfishable. The bad news is that low pressure can drive fish out of the Marls' shallower areas and into deeper water covered with white caps. Hey, no one said bonefishing was a sure thing, which is one of the reasons it is our greatest fishing passion.

Continuing north of the Marls, bonefishing remains excellent. From Norman Castle up to Basin Harbour and on past the backside of Coopers Town is a massive area that receives little pressure and produces much larger fish. Bones up here average four to five pounds, and double-digit fish are a real possibility. This is our favorite area of Abaco, which is easily reached by anglers staying in Treasure Cay or on Green Turtle Cay. As we discussed in the Around the Island section (page 102), this is the home guiding water for O'Donald Macintosh and his sons. We always look forward to fishing with these guides, and we are especially excited about exploring more of the backside cays on Little Abaco in the next few years.

So how about permit? Anglers who fish the Marls can expect to see the occasional permit while fishing for bonefish. If permit are your goal you should move out to the deeper water along the outer cays, or fish other areas of the island. Sandy Point has good numbers of large permit, especially along the sand-bottomed edges of the Little Bahama Bank, and north up near Cedar Cays. The cays between Gorda Cay and Moore's Island are also home to big permit. To the north, the leeward cays off Coopers Town have a number of deeper creeks and cuts that give permit access to many of the flats.

The windward offshore cays, from Spanish Cay to Little Harbour, are loaded with permit. Fish concentrate around the oceanside reefs and along bars and cays with access to deeper water. Fly fishers in this area will have their best chance at hooking up during calm weather, though spinning rigs fished with live crabs are deadly

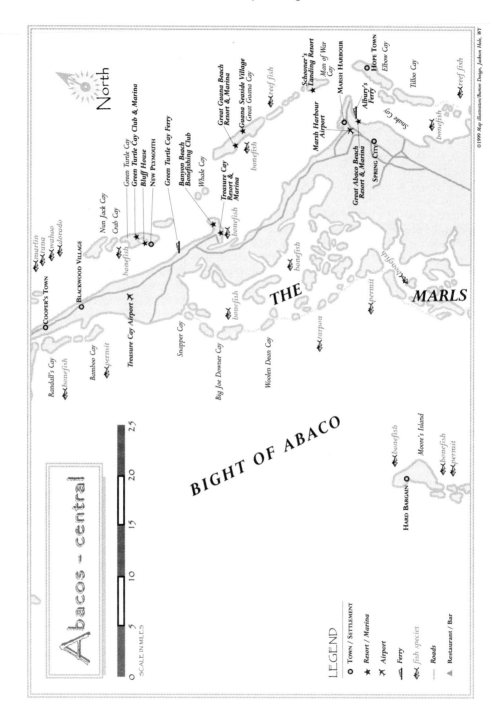

anytime. The best months for permit are April through July, though they are available year round. We especially like to fish for permit after a heavy rain. The rainwater reduces salinity, and brings out all the crabs. This scent, unleashed upon the tide, brings the permit running. It doesn't make them any easier to catch on a fly, but just getting a shot or two will guarantee an adrenaline rush.

Our favorite permit flies include #4 Yarn Crabs, a #2 Del's Merkin, and a #2 Gotcha Clouser.

There are resident tarpon in the Bight of Abaco, plus migratory tarpon that move along both coasts from April through August, but the numbers are not high as far as we know. We have talked with many boaters who report seeing tarpon roll all through the offshore cays region, but few have fished for them, and even fewer have jumped or landed any. Local guides have reported similar observations.

We have caught a few tarpon here and there in the northern Marls, and we've jumped some fish between Green Turtle and Elbow Cays, but in all these cases we were not specifically fishing for tarpon. We had a tarpon rod rigged, and took the opportunity when we got lucky and saw fish.

When we look at the habitat, and the relatively northern position of Abaco, the lack of tarpon in any numbers is not surprising. Still, we plan to spend some time in the future looking harder, especially in June.

If you just want to catch fish, fishing for snappers with fly or spinning gear is a blast. Mutton snapper are the real prize, as they are great fighters and make a delicious meal. Gray snappers, or mangrove snappers as they are more commonly known, are everywhere, from the mangrove-infested Marls, to the reefs of the offshore cays. Snapper fishing is good year round, with April through August being prime. April is the best month for mutton snapper. Clouser's Minnows in a variety of colors are our favorite flies for these feisty fish.

Barracuda are ferocious fish that are equally fun to catch on fly or spinning tackle, and they can deal with cold weather better than most other game fish. The winter months are especially good, and many winter fishing days have been saved by pursuing barracuda. Wire shock tippet is essential against their razor-sharp teeth. If you choose to land a fish for photos, be extremely careful, as even the little guys can do serious damage to hands and fingers.

Sharks are great sport for anglers who feel like hooking up something big. We've talked with lots of people who just get that urge to feel the weight of a wide body. Go with a 10-weight for lemons and blacktips, and use six-inch-long 40- to 80-pound wire shock tippet to protect your leader. The best flies are Offshore Deceivers in red/black and chum colors.

Sharks prefer warm weather, and warm water, so April through October will offer the best flats fishing. In deeper water and around the reefs you can catch sharks year round. Most people understand extreme caution is necessary when landing sharks, and many people just break them off at the boat. Occasionally, anglers think it's cool to land a small shark for a photo. Be aware that sharks are like snakes! Their cartilage structure is relatively soft, and it allows them to completely bend back on themselves. This means if you are holding their tail they can easily whip around and bite your hand. One of our guides almost lost a hand this way, so be careful out there.

Billfishing for sails and blue marlin begins in March, picks up in April and is prime May through July. There are very few fly-fishing–savvy crews in the Bahamas, and most fishing is with conventional gear. If you have experience with fly-fishing for billfish, you should be able to get in some shots in June and July with traditional teasing methods.

June is the month for a number of billfish and tuna tournaments, including the Green Turtle Cay Club Invitational and a leg of the Bahamas Billfish Championship

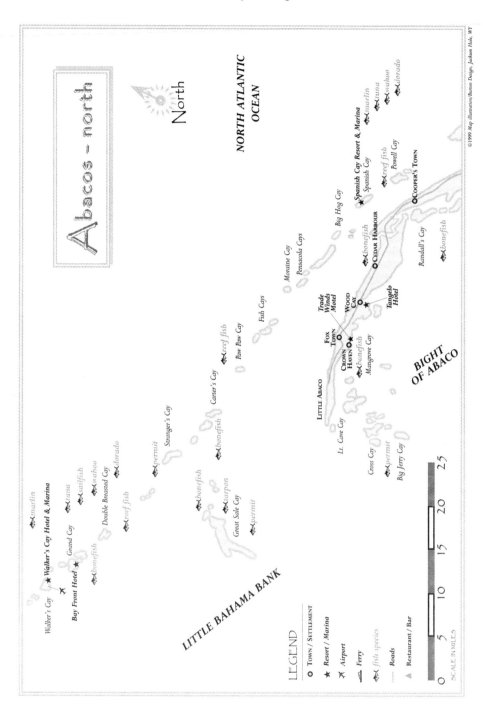

out of Boat Harbour Marina. Good offshore boats are available for charter out of Treasure Cay, Green Turtle Cay, Marsh Harbour, and Elbow Cay.

The Bahamas Wahoo Championships hold one of the five legs out of Boat Harbour Marina and the Great Abaco Beach Resort in January. January and February are the best months for wahoo, which is our favorite offshore species in the islands. When these fish are concentrated they will readily hit billfish flies and large surface poppers. Wire tippet is a must against their super-sharp teeth. And if you like to eat fish, fresh wahoo, or ono as it is called in Hawaii, is as good as it gets.

July is regatta time, with continued excellent offshore fishing, and many related activities and parties on the offshore cays. Many anglers start thinking of trout in June and July, but this is a premiere time to fish Abaco's flats and offshore waters.

April and May are prime months for dorado. You can often find scum and grass lines beyond the offshore cays where dorado hang out in good numbers. On these occasions you can cast surface poppers and large deceivers for fantastic action. Trolling will consistently bring up dorado during these months, and live bait will take the school fish on every cast.

Allison tuna show up in March, with good numbers beginning in April and prime fishing occurring May through July. This is definitely our favorite tuna to do battle with in the Bahamas, as they readily take flies and are commonly found hanging out with dorado. Our favorite flies include WBA Mullets and Abel Anchovies.

The Bahamas National Bonefish Tournament is held on each major island every year, usually in June. The winner from each island then competes for the national crown, with the Bahamian winner going on to compete in the World Invitational Bonefish Tournament.

People often ask us to name our favorite Bahamian Out Island. We usually hedge a little, and qualify our answers based on what each island has to offer. We've already mentioned that Andros is our favorite island for pure fishing and hanging out. That said, we'll go out on a reef and say Abaco is our favorite overall when you put the big picture together.

The day begins.

Ease of access by air and boat, combined with a variety of high-quality accommodations, starts it off. Then you have the flats of the Marls, the offshore cays reef fishing, and world-class blue-water fishing, combined with a number of good guides, and a dizzying array of nonangling activities. Not a bad combination if you're looking for a vacation to satisfy a wide range of people.

OPTIONAL ADVENTURE ACTIVITIES

We don't know of any other Bahamian island where you can rent your own boat, take a short orientation session, then head off over calm protected waters for secluded beaches, neon-colored reefs, quiet settlements on remote cays, or to superior fishing grounds, all on your own. You can have fresh cracked conch for lunch in a bayside restaurant, snorkel in a marine park, stroll through shops and galleries in a picturebook settlement, catch rays on beaches few people visit in a year, and do it all in one day.

Sailing is the number-one activity in Abaco, and it is a favorite destination for numerous regattas and sailing events. Regatta Time, an annual July event, attracts sailors from around the world who participate in a nine-day series of races. Contestants compete for trophies and bragging rights, but eating, drinking, and general partying seem to be of equal importance.

Diving and snorkeling are a close second to sailing in popularity. There are countless diving and snorkeling sites over coral reefs and around various wrecks, including the wreck of the USS *Adirondack,* a 125-year-old American warship lying off Man-O-War Cay.

If you want to combine boating and snorkeling you can visit Pelican Cay National Park, an underwater preserve; or Abaco National Park, a twenty-thousand-acre site in southern Abaco that includes nesting habitat for the Abaco Parrot.

Treasure Cay is the ideal spot for people who want the largest variety of activities including an eighteen-hole championship golf course, tennis courts, marina, boat rentals, offshore fishing, dive packages, good restaurants, and powder-white beaches.

LODGING AND SERVICES

FEATURED LODGES AND ACCOMMODATIONS

Treasure Cay Resort and Marina

Treasure Cay   This is a top choice for an all-around family or couples vacation. Accommodations range from marina-view rooms and suites, to villas and townhouses on one of the most beautiful white sand beaches in the Bahamas. Amenities include a swimming pool, restaurant, 2 bars, golf cart and boat rentals, golf, tennis, diving and snorkeling excursions. Bonefishing guides and offshore charters can be arranged.
Season: October through July.
Suitable For: Anglers and nonanglers.
Optional Activities: Diving through the certified marina dive shop, snorkeling, an array of beach/water sports, golf, tennis, and excursions to the offshore cays.
What's Included: Deluxe accommodations, guided fishing, meals and Bahamian taxes can be included in one package. Trips of any length are available.
Not Included: Airfare to/from Treasure Cay, optional gratuities, alcoholic beverages, and any optional activities not in your package.
Pricing: $$–$$$
Contact: Reservations and information, 800/327-1584 or 800/922-3474, fax 954/525-1699.
E-mail: info@treasurecay.com
Internet: www.treasurecay.com

Nettie's Different of Abaco

Casuarina Point   Nettie Symonette's lodge offers the only easy access to the famed central and southern Marls regions, plus great wading flats in Cherokee Sound. The variety of bonefishing options are suitable for anglers of all ability levels, especially beginners. Air-conditioned accommodations are available at the original Heritage Lodge, while oceanside accommodations are found at the Seashell Beach Club, located on a gorgeous 8-mile-long white sand beach. Excellent meals and experienced guides round out this fine fishing package. It is possible to fish on arrival and departure days.

Season: October through June.

Suitable For: Anglers and nonanglers.

What's Included: Airport transfers to/from Marsh Harbour, accommodations, all meals, guided fishing and Bahamian taxes. A golf cart is included for each room at the Seashell Beach Club for easy access to the main lodge for meals.

Not Included: Airfare to Marsh Harbour, alcoholic beverages, gratuities.

Pricing: $$–$$$

Contact: Reservations and information, 242/366-2150 or 800/922-3474, fax 242/327-8152.

E-mail: different@oii.net

Banyon Beach Bonefishing Club

Treasure Cay   Deluxe air-conditioned 1- and 2-bedroom condos on the beach, with swimming pool, restaurant, bar, and all the amenities available at the Treasure Cay Resort. You can book accommodations only, or a complete bonefishing and meal package. The guide staff works out of well-maintained "FlatsMaster" boats. The fishing program here covers the Marls and the Coopers Town area. We recommend renting a golf cart if you stay here.

Season: October through July.

Suitable For: Anglers and nonanglers.

Optional Activities: Diving through the certified marina dive shop, snorkeling, an array of beach/water sports, golf, tennis, and excursions to the offshore cays.

What's Included: Deluxe accommodations, guided fishing, meals, and Bahamian taxes can be included in one package. Trips of any length are available.

Not Included: Airfare to/from Treasure Cay, optional gratuities, alcoholic beverages, and any optional activities not in your package.

Pricing: $$$

Contact: Reservations and information, 888/883-9927 or 800/922-3474, fax 561/625-5301.

Internet: www.bigbonefish.com

Walker's Cay Hotel & Marina

Walker's Cay   Walker's Cay is approximately 110 miles east of Palm Beach and 45 miles northeast of Freeport, Grand Bahama. Accommodations are in 62 hotel rooms and 4 villas. All accommodations are air-conditioned and have private balconies. On-island facilities include a 2,500-foot paved airstrip with customs and immigration clearance 7 days a week. Amenities include 2 swimming pools, full-service 75-slip marina with commissary, and 2 restaurants with bars and a lounge.

Walker's specializes in offshore fishing, though they also have very good reef and flats fly fishing options. They also specialize in diving and snorkeling. Just a few minutes from the dock you can troll for marlin, sailfish, tuna, wahoo, and dorado, or fish the reef for grouper, snapper and yellowtail. Walker's Cay is a forty-five-minute flight from Fort Lauderdale via Pan Am Airbridge. Pan Am operates scheduled service 6 days a week utilizing its twin-pilot Grumman Mallard seaplanes. Flights depart from the Pan Am Airbridge terminal located on the North Perimeter Road at Fort Lauderdale International Airport. There is free parking at the terminal and Pan Am operates a shuttle bus service between U.S. Customs and the terminal. Of course, many people travel to the Walker's Cay Marina by boat.

Season: October through July.

Suitable For: Anglers and nonanglers.

Optional Activities: Diving through the marina dive shop, snorkeling, an array of beach/water sports, and excursions to the offshore cays.

What's Included: Deluxe accommodations, guided fishing, meals and Bahamian taxes can be included in one package. Trips of any length are available.

Not Included: Airfare to/from Ft. Lauderdale, optional gratuities, alcoholic beverages, and any optional activities not in your package.

Pricing: $$$

Contact: Reservations and information in the U.S., 800/WALKERS or 954/359-1400, fax 954/359-1414. In Walker's Cay, 242/353-1252, fax 242/353-1339.

Internet: www.walkerscay.com

ADDITIONAL ACCOMMODATIONS

Pete and Gay's Guesthouse

Sandy Point   Located at the main settlement dock, this motel offers splendid views of the harbor from the rooftop lounge, comfortable rooms, and excellent Bahamian food. Full bonefishing packages are available including accommodations, meals, airport transfers to/from Marsh Harbour, and Bahamian taxes. This is a very good fishing program at a good price.

Pricing: $$

Contact: Reservations and information, 242/366-4119, fax 242/366-4007.

Oiesha's

Sandy Point   Located at the opposite end of town from Pete and Gay's. This motel offers 11 modern air-conditioned rooms, a fun bar, good restaurant, and complete bonefishing packages. You can also book guides on a daily basis.

Pricing: $$

Contact: Reservations and information, 242/366-4139, fax 242/366-4283.

Tangelo Hotel

Wood Cay, Little Abaco   Nice oceanfront location with 12 air-conditioned motel-style rooms. Nice people and good food make this a fine place to stay while pursuing bonefish on your own or with a guide. Bonefishing packages are available and can include airport transfer to/from Treasure Cay.

Pricing: $$

Contact: Reservations and information telephone/fax, 242/365-2222.

Spanish Cay Resort & Marina

Spanish Cay   The new owners of this cay are upgrading everything to make it spectacular. Five villa-suites, several 1- or 2-bedroom condos, and several private homes are available to rent. A 70-slip marina is being remodeled to be one of the best in the Bahamas. The marina restaurant is being remodeled also, and the inside dining room will be air-conditioned. A complete dive shop is being built, and boat rentals will be available. A new swimming pool and Jacuzzi for boaters and island guests will be built adjacent to the marina. A 5,000-foot paved runway is suitable for most private jets, and is being repaved. Customs services are available. New golf carts and bicycles can be rented to explore this beautiful island. Bonefishing can be arranged with guides from Coopers Town. To reach this island you can fly in by private aircraft, or fly to Treasure Cay Airport, take a taxi to Coopers Town dock, then take the free Spanish Cay ferry to the island, about a 15-minute ride.

Pricing: $$–$$$

Contact: Reservations and information, telephone/fax 242/365-0083 or 888/722-6474.

Green Turtle Cay Club & Marina

Green Turtle Cay   Beautiful landscaping, superior service, and a casually elegant feel are the trademark of this world-class resort. Thirty-four air-conditioned rooms and cottages are spread around the waterfront property. The excellent restaurant is well known throughout the islands. Swim, dive, snorkel, relax, fish on your own or with a guide. There are 2 bays you can walk to for bonefishing on your own, or take the ferry across to Treasure Cay and fish Coopers Town or the Marls with the best independent guides. Complete packages are available, including taxi/ferry transfers to/from the Treasure Cay airport.

Pricing: $$$$
Contact: Reservations and information, 242/365-4271 or 800/922-3474, fax 242/365-4272.

Bluff House

Green Turtle Cay   Elegant yet laid-back, this resort features a great dining room with views over the Sea of Abaco. Twenty-eight air-conditioned rooms, suites, and villas offer upscale travelers all the amenities they expect. Guests enjoy easy beach access, bonefishing on their own, or with guide. All other activities can be arranged by the hotel. Complete packages are available, including taxi/ferry transfers to/from the Treasure Cay airport.
Pricing: $$$$
Contact: Reservations and information, 242/365-4247 or 800/922-3474, fax 242/365-4248.
E-mail: BluffHouse@oii.net

Guana Seaside Village

Great Guana Cay   This 7-mile-long cay is located 7 miles across the Sea of Abaco from Marsh Harbour and Treasure Cay, between Green Turtle Cay and Man-O-War Cay. This new 8-room beachfront inn features an excellent restaurant and bar, swimming pool, boat dock, and access to miles of awesome beaches, swimming, and snorkeling. You can also catch bonefish on your own in a couple of the nearby bays. Packages can include taxi/boat transfers from Marsh Harbour via Albury's Ferry service.
Pricing: $$$
Contact: Reservations and information, 800/242-0942, fax 242/365-5146.
E-mail: guanaseaside@oii.net

Great Guana Beach Resort & Boat Harbour Marina

Great Guana Cay   Eight deluxe rooms and 7 suites with kitchens are set in a beachside palm grove. The restaurant serves good seafood and Bahamian fare. The poolside bar serves snacks throughout the day. Packages can include taxi/boat transfers from Marsh Harbour via Albury's Ferry service. Miles of beach are steps away. The marina offers some services to boaters, and you can call ahead on VHF channel 16.
Pricing: $$$
Contact: Reservations and information, 242/365-5133, fax 242/365-5134.
E-mail: guanabeach@guanabeach.com

Great Abaco Beach Resort & Boat Harbour Marina

Marsh Harbour   Completely renovated in 1997, all 52 rooms and 6 villas feature ocean views. Amenities include 2 swimming pools, 2 tennis courts, a nice restaurant, 2 bars, and complimentary use of windsurfers, sea kayaks, and mountain bikes. Boat rentals and a complete dive shop are located in the adjacent full-service marina. Fishing guides can be arranged. Complete packages are available, including taxi transfers from the Marsh Harbour airport.
Pricing: $$–$$$
Contact: Reservations and information, 242/367-2158 or 800/468-4799, fax 242/367-2819.

Schooner's Landing Resort

Man-O-War Cay   Nice 2-bedroom condos overlooking the water with kitchens, TVs, and VCRs. Renting a golf cart is the way to go to get around to the gorgeous beaches, snorkeling sites, tennis, shops, and settlement activities. Guests fly to Marsh Harbour, then take Albury's Ferry to the island dock. The resort will meet you at the dock, then transfer you to the property.
Pricing: $$–$$$
Contact: Reservations and information, 242/365-6072, fax 242/365-6285.

Hope Town Hideaway

Hope Town, Elbow Cay   If you want to rent the best townhouses, villas, and homes on Elbow Cay, you should do it with Hope Town Hideaway. They will take care of everything you need, from boat and golf cart

rentals, to guided fishing trips, island-hopping excursions, scuba, and snorkel trips or whatever else you might want. Their new 12-slip marina can take boats up to 70 feet. You can also book a nice 2-bedroom villa with air-conditioning, full kitchens, and decks overlooking Hope Town harbor. Taxi/ferry transfers are available from the Marsh Harbour airport to Hope Town. The ferry ride is about 20 minutes.
Pricing: $$–$$$$
Contact: Reservations and information, 242/366-0224, fax 242/366-0434.

Hope Town Harbour Lodge

Hope Town, Elbow Cay   Eighteen newly renovated rooms feature harbor or ocean views, air conditioning and ceiling fans. The Butterfly House, a recently renovated 100-year-old Hope Town house with full kitchen, 2 bedrooms, 2 baths, and large decks, will accommodate up to 6 people. All accommodations include daily maid service. Swimming pool, restaurant, bar, and snorkeling are right out your door. Taxi/ferry transfers are available from the Marsh Harbour airport to Hope Town. The ferry ride is about 20 minutes.
Pricing: $$–$$$
Contact: Reservations and information, 800/316-7844 or 242/366-0095, fax 242/366-0286.
E-mail: harbourlodge@batelnet.bs
Internet: www.hopetownlodge.com

Abaco Inn

Elbow Cay   Set among coconut palms and seagrapes on a beautiful ridge of sand dunes. Fourteen private cottage-type rooms and 2 new one-bedroom villas with kitchenettes overlook the Atlantic Ocean to the east and the sheltered harbor of White Sound and the Sea of Abaco to the west. Great food is a trademark here, from elegant dinners to tropical lunches and leisurely breakfasts. The beach and surf are at your feet. You can swim in the pool or in the ocean, and all island activities, including fishing, can be arranged by the hotel. Taxi/ferry transfers are available from the Marsh Harbour airport to Hope Town or directly to White Sound. The ferry ride takes about 20 minutes from Marsh Harbour to Elbow Cay.
Pricing: $$–$$$
Contact: Reservations and information, 800/468-8799 or 242/366-0133, fax 242/366-0113.
E-mail: abacoinn@batelnet.bs
Internet: www.oii.net/AbacoInn

Sea Spray Resort Villas & Marina

White Sound, Elbow Cay   Located at the southern tip of White Sound Harbour, the resort encompasses 6 acres of well-groomed grounds tucked between the Atlantic Ocean and the Sea of Abaco, and is just 3 miles from Hope Town. One- and 2-bedroom villas include island-style furnishings, full kitchens, air-conditioning, surrounding patio decks, and daily maid service. The Boat House restaurant serves delicious Bahamian-style meals. Swim in the freshwater pool or in the ocean. Surfing in the Atlantic is great off Garbonzo Reef. A full watersports and diving program is available, and any other activities can be arranged through the resort office. The marina offers full services to boaters. Complete packages are available. Taxi/ferry transfers are available from the Marsh Harbour airport to Hope Town or directly to White Sound. The ferry ride takes about 20 minutes from Marsh Harbour to Elbow Cay.
Pricing: $$–$$$
Contact: Reservations and information, 242/366-0065, fax 242/366-0383.
Internet: www.seasprayresort.com

SERVICES

The Port Authority: We recommend that boaters with any questions give the Port Authority a call at 242/393-1064. They can provide all necessary information including a complete list of ports of entry.

Independent Fly-Fishing Guides: O'Donald Macintosh, Justin Sands, Jay Sawyer and others, can be booked by calling 800/922-3474. We recommend booking these guides as far in advance as possible for the months of March through May, and October and November. Some resorts and hotels can also book or recommend independent guides. Offshore guides can be booked through your resort, hotel, at the nearest marina, or by calling 800/922-3474.

Restaurants: Our favorite Treasure Cay restaurants are Spinnaker's at the marina, and A Touch of Class on the main highway. You need reservations at Spinnaker's. For breakfast you need to try Florence's. Great homemade cinnamon rolls here, plus box lunches for fly fishers.

In Marsh Harbour, Wally's is one of our favorites for spicy Bahamian food and Key lime pie.

On Elbow Cay, there are a lot of good choices, but the Abaco Inn is our favorite. For just hanging out, drinking, and simple food, the Harbor's Edge is the place.

The food at Nettie's Different of Abaco is always good, and you can eat here without staying here if you make a reservation.

Green Turtle Cay is worth a visit for lunch or dinner—even if you're not staying there—just to eat at the Green Turtle Cay Club or the Bluff House. These are the two best restaurants in the Abacos for delicious food and a wonderful atmosphere.

Pete and Gay's Guesthouse is the place to eat if you make it down to Sandy Point.

Car rentals: There are a number of small agencies you can contact through your resort or hotel. At the Treasure Cay airport—Corniche Car Rentals, 242/365-8623. In Marsh Harbour—H&L Car Rentals, 242/367-2854 or Reliable Car Rentals, 242/367-3015.

Taxi service is good on the island, with some fares regulated by the government. We still advise asking about all fares ahead of time.

Ferry service is just as important, and maybe more important than taxi service on Abaco. Albury's Ferry Service, 242/367-3114. Green Turtle Cay Ferry, 242/365-4032.

Boat rentals: Check with your resort or hotel when you book. In Treasure Cay—J.I.C. Rentals is our choice, 242/365-8465. The owner, John Cash, is very helpful. In Marsh Harbour—Sea Horse Boat Rentals, 242/367-2513. In the Marsh Harbour/Elbow Cay area—Island Marine, 242/366-0282.

Diving and snorkeling: Trips can be arranged by your resort or hotel, or at the nearest marina. In Marsh Harbour—Dive Abaco, 242/367-2787 or Great Abaco Beach Resort, 242/367-2158. In Treasure Cay—Diver's Down, 242/365-8465. On Elbow Cay—Dave's Dive Shop, 242/366-0029.

Grocery stores, liquor stores, pharmacies, and just about every other kind of shop you would need are available in Marsh Harbour. Treasure Cay also has most services. The rest of the island has limited services, though resort cays such as Green Turtle and Elbow can take care of most requests.

The Marsh Harbour Clinic is the best medical facility in the Abacos. Clinics are available in the larger settlements.

Your best bet for banking is in Marsh Harbour, though bank services are available in Treasure Cay and on Green Turtle Cay on a limited basis.

NEW DEVELOPMENTS

Seven miles west of Sandy Point is Disney's privately owned Castaway Cay, formerly Gorda Cay. The *Disney Magic,* a 2,400-passenger cruise ship, visits the cay twice a week. This is a sad event for fly fishers who used to fish around this pristine cay for huge bonefish and permit.

On a positive note, the main highway running the length of the island has been resurfaced and is in great shape. This means easier access to all of the island, which has opened up lots of new fishing areas, and made it possible for independent guides and lodge guides to begin trailering their boats to remote locations. As these guides explore and expand their programs, we believe many new areas will produce great fishing. Log on to our Web site at www.bahamasflyfishingguide.com for the most up-to-date information.

7

Bimini and Berry Islands

Self-proclaimed "the sportfishing capital of the world," Bimini actually consists of two distinct islands separated by a narrow channel that forms the entrance into North Bimini Harbour. North Bimini is a thin strip of land seven miles long and no more than seven hundred yards wide. This is where the action is, in the marinas and bars and hotels made famous by Ernest Hemingway, Zane Grey, Michael Lerner, and Adam Clayton Powell. South Bimini is the quiet cousin, with a five-thousand-foot airstrip and a couple of hotels. The storied Fountain of Youth is supposedly somewhere near the airstrip.

The Biminis are only forty-eight miles east of Miami, making them the closest Bahamian islands to the United States, but they are a world away in terms of lifestyle and atmosphere. Shirts and shoes are not required. The saying, "so close, yet so far" has real meaning here. The proximity to Florida made the islands an ideal location for illegal activities. From pirates, to Confederates, to rum- and drugrunners, this was a place to rendezvous and hide. Today, fishing is the main topic of most conversations, though divers get in a word or two on occasion, usually bringing up the legend of the lost continent of Atlantis.

Alice Town, on the southern end of North Bimini, is the main settlement. All the hotels, marinas, bars, and shops are located along the Queen's and King's highways, which run parallel to each other. It's easy to walk wherever you want to go, though renting a scooter or golf cart can be fun. While some visitors arrive via Pan Am Bridge seaplanes, most people cruise into the harbor on boats. The Bimini Big Game Fishing Club and Hotel is the happening place for anglers, and the headquarters for more than a dozen fishing tournaments throughout the year.

During tournaments the island really turns on, with nightlife going from so laid-back you could fall asleep to lots of serious partying and drinking. The Compleat Angler is often the epicenter for some wild times.

Over the years the locals have seen and done it all. People here take everything in stride, no problem, mon. Fishing and tourism keep the economy going for the population of sixteen hundred or so. As an official Port of Entry, the Biminis see a constant stream of boaters. During spring and summer, the Bahamas Boating Flings, which are organized flotillas, cruise over from Florida. These are regularly scheduled events, sponsored by the Bahamas Ministry of Tourism and the South Florida Marine Industries Association. A registration fee is required, no more than thirty boats are allowed, and vessels must be at least twenty-two feet long. To participate, call the Bahamas Tourist Office in Miami at 800/32-SPORT.

Pan Am Airbridge flies to Alice Town several times a day from Miami's Watson Island terminal. Flights are also available from Ft. Lauderdale, and from Pan Am's base on Paradise Island, Nassau. A weight restriction of thirty pounds per passenger is usually enforced. The seaplanes land in the harbor, then waddle up onto a land-based ramp. Passenger vans meet all flights, then drive you to your hotel. Charter flights are also available to South Bimini. If you land here, you take a water taxi to the hotels or marinas in Alice Town.

AROUND THE ISLAND

Whether by air or by sea, visitors usually arrive in Alice Town via the North Bimini Harbour. The Pan Am seaplane ramp and terminal are just inside the harbor next to a small customs office. Next is Freddy Weech's Bimini Dock, which can accommodate up to fifteen boats. Just north is the government dock and Customs House.

The Sea Crest Hotel and Marina offers eighteen slips, ice, electricity, and showers. The hotel is across the street, and features air-conditioned rooms and suites with satellite TV, and oceanview balconies.

The Bimini Blue Water Resort, owned by the pioneering Brown family, was one of Ernest Hemingway's favorite places. You can contact the marina on VHF channel 68. Full services are available for boaters, along with thirty-two slips and a dockside pool. Accommodations are across the street in guestrooms that include nice balconies and satellite TV. The Anchorage Restaurant, which was once Michael Lerner's home, offers views of the west side of the island, and serves excellent seafood. The restaurant will also make box lunches for fishermen.

On up the harbor is the Bimini Big Game Fishing Club and Hotel. The recently expanded one-hundred-slip marina offers full services to boaters and anglers, and just about anything else a visitor might need. Contact the marina on VHF channel 16. This self-contained resort includes the Gulfstream Restaurant, the New Sport Bar, deluxe accommodations, a swimming pool, gift shop, and the island's only tennis court. All rooms feature air-conditioning, private baths, and satellite TV. Suites and penthouses are available. The restaurant serves everything from seafood to steaks. If you want to stay here, especially during a fishing tournament, you need to make reservations well in advance.

If you're looking to book a fishing guide for bonefish, backcountry, or offshore, the Big Game Club is the place. The more famous guides like Bonefish Ansil, Bonefish Rudy, and Bonefish Cordell are booked well ahead during the prime fishing months of March through June. Not to worry, though, as there are plenty of other Bonefish Whoever's who can take you out, but if you're serious about your fishing, we suggest booking a guide well ahead along with your accommodations. Many of these guides can also be booked directly, but if you do this, be aware that double-booking practices can leave you without a guide. To avoid this problem, we recommend booking through the Big Game Club, as they have the ability to make sure you have a guide.

The post office, commissioner's office, and police stations are in the government building north of the Big Game Club. Additional services include a Royal Bank of

Brian O'Keefe

A good-sized bonefish from Bimini.

Canada, Bimini Undersea for diving and bike rentals, the North Bimini Medical Clinic with a resident doctor and nurse, a straw market, several grocery stores, and a number of shops. You can walk, bike, or golf cart to any place on the island, or take one of the Bimini buses that run up and down the island. Pay phones are scattered along the main roads, but don't always work. Using a VHF radio is the most reliable way to communicate.

Capt. Bob's is a favorite breakfast spot. A number of our boating friends say the French toast here is the best on the planet. The Compleat Angler offers calypso bands with dancing several nights a week. The historic bar features tables made of old rum kegs, and hundreds of old fishing photos. The bartenders are geniuses when it comes to blending rum drinks. Hemingway had more than his share of Goombay Smashes here while he was working on his novel *To Have and Have Not.* The Red Lion restaurant is another good choice for tasty seafood prepared Bahamian style.

Most of the locals live in Bailey Town, to the north of Alice Town on Porgy Bay. Both settlements have been spruced up in recent years, with fresh pastel colors being applied to houses and shops of varying shapes and sizes.

North of the settlements on the western shore are long stretches of shell-covered beaches. The prettiest beach is at Paradise Point, which is the location of the famous art deco mansion built in the 1950s by George Lyons. The mansion was then owned by Rockwell International, and is now run as the Bimini Bay restaurant and sometimes guesthouse by Antoinette and Basil Rolle. For people in the know, this is the best place on the island for dinner. Splendid ocean views and attentive service create an intimate atmosphere. Use VHF channel 68 to call ahead for reservations.

Just off Paradise Point are the Atlantis Rocks, the underwater formation many people claim to be the remains of a temple from the lost continent. Whether this is true or not, this is an excellent dive site. The road continues north from here, ending at East Wells.

Porgy Bay and the sound run up along the eastern shore of North Bimini, and separate the inhabited portion of the island from a large backcountry area of cays, mangrove creeks, and flats. This is where anglers will find some of the best fishing for big bonefish in the Bahamas.

Working back south, shallow open water with deeper flats and channels head to South Bimini. Another nine miles south is Gun Cay. Between the two islands are many smaller cays and rocks, and the massive, partially sunken concrete ship, *Sapona,* which was the unfortunate victim of a hurricane in 1929.

Another mile to the southeast is Cat Cay and the Cat Cay Yacht Club. This is a private club, so only members can stay overnight, but boaters can tie up during the day and enjoy a great lunch in the restaurant overlooking the marina.

FISHING HIGHLIGHTS

From a habitat point of view you couldn't ask for a better location. The islands sit on the eastern edge of the Florida Straits and the Gulf Stream, and on the northwest corner of the Great Bahama Bank. Great offshore fishing for marlin, sailfish, tuna, wahoo, and dorado is a tradition, with some of the world's best-known billfish tournaments run out of the Bimini Big Game Club.

Though several IGFA bonefish records have gone into the books here, the flats fishing has taken a back seat to the blue water challenges. From a conventional tackle perspective we understand this, but for fly fishers, the flats fishing is the thing.

The vast flats areas are northeast of Alice Town, in a wilderness of mangrove-lined creeks and cays that require local knowledge to navigate. While bonefish over ten pounds are always the talk here, you'll see good numbers of fish in the four- to six-pound range. If you want to go for the big boys, you'll have to be selective, as the larger fish often use the smaller fish for protection. An indiscriminate cast will almost always take the smallest fish in the group.

In talking with locals and regular boating visitors it's clear that James B. Orthwein is the king of the flats on Bimini. He holds three current IGFA fly rod records for bonefish; the two-pound class with a twelve-pounder, the four-pound class with a fifteen-pounder, and the sixteen-pound class with a thirteen-pounder. We understand his favorite guide is Bonefish Rudy, and his favorite fly is a Jim's Golden Shrimp. We recommend Dick Brown's books *Fly Fishing for Bonefish* and *Bonefish Fly Patterns* for a comprehensive reference to Mr. Orthwein's flies.

When we fish for big bones we like flies that get down quickly. A #2 Gold Shiner Clouser Minnow would be our first choice in most situations, though a #2 Gotcha Bunny, or Yarn Crab to match the bottom color, would be right there, too.

Bimini bonefish guides commonly take out spinning anglers who use a variety of small jigs tipped with shrimp. This is a guaranteed way to catch bonefish, even during periods of bad weather. If you have children who want to catch bonefish, but can't manage a fly rod, this is an ideal way to introduce them to the sport. This is also the time to introduce them to catch-and-release fishing, which is promoted by most guides on Bimini.

Other flats species include barracuda, sharks, permit, jacks, and tarpon. Tarpon fishing can be excellent from April through July, with June the prime month. Our favorite tarpon flies include a Shallow Water Cockroach and a Red/Black Sea Bunny. June is also the month with the most rainfall and lightning. Most guides know to get out of the way of these powerful thunderstorms, but sometimes the storms develop too quickly to avoid. Don't let your enthusiasm for catching fish get the best of your judgment. You need to head for cover when those ominous black clouds start spitting lightning bolts.

Offshore, the best months for billfish are March through July, though billfish cruise these waters most of the year. The Hemingway Championship is held in Febru-

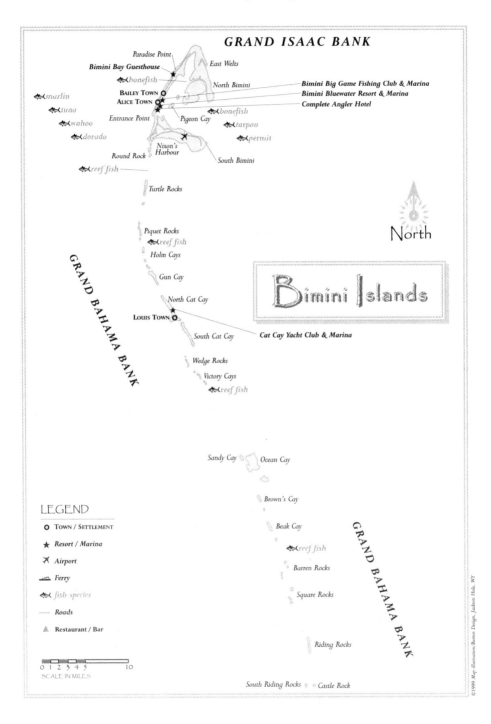

GRAND ISAAC BANK

Paradise Point

Bimini Bay Guesthouse

East Welts

bonefish

North Bimini

BAILEY TOWN

ALICE TOWN

Bimini Big Game Fishing Club & Marina
Bimini Bluewater Resort & Marina
Complete Angler Hotel

marlin

tuna

wahoo

dorado

Entrance Point

Pigeon Cay

bonefish

tarpon

permit

Round Rock

Nixon's Harbour

South Bimini

reef fish

Turtle Rocks

Piquet Rocks

reef fish

Holm Cays

Gun Cay

North Cat Cay

LOUIS TOWN

South Cat Cay

Cat Cay Yacht Club & Marina

North

Bimini Islands

GRAND BAHAMA BANK

Wedge Rocks

Victory Cays

reef fish

Sandy Cay

Ocean Cay

Brown's Cay

Beak Cay

reef fish

Barren Rocks

Square Rocks

GRAND BAHAMA BANK

LEGEND

◎ TOWN / SETTLEMENT

★ *Resort / Marina*

✈ Airport

Ferry

fish species

Roads

Restaurant / Bar

0 1 2 3 4 5   10
SCALE IN MILES

Riding Rocks

South Riding Rocks   Castle Rock

© 1999 Map illustration/Burton Design, Jackson Hole, WY

*Heading out to the fishing
grounds, early morning.*

ary, with the Bacardi Rum tournament in March and the Big Game Club Bimini Festival in May.

A variety of tuna, including giant bluefin, blackfin, and yellowfin, are best April through June, with May the prime month. Wahoo and kingfish are the prime winter species, with January and February best. The Bahamas Wahoo Championships are held throughout the islands from November through February, with the Bimini leg usually in November.

Reef and wreck fishing for sharks, barracuda, jacks, snappers, and grouper is good year round. Using chum will get the fish in the feeding mood, then you can toss out flies, lures, or bait and have a field day. Most restaurants on Bimini will be happy to cook your catch. Charter boats are available for hire through the Bimini Big Game Club and the Bimini Blue Water Marina.

OPTIONAL ACTIVITIES

Ah, the boating life for me, is the inner voice of the Biminis. The atmosphere here is a combination of the old pirating days mixed with modern nostalgia. People who leave Florida as intense American entrepreneurs transform themselves into barefoot deckhands in a mere forty-eight-mile crossing.

While fishing is the dominant activity around Bimini, just hanging out, relaxing, and socializing is a major part of daily life, especially on weekends. Long, lazy beaches offer sunning, swimming, and snorkeling. If you need some exercise you can jog or bike up the King's Highway to East Wells.

Diving enthusiasts can choose from a variety of sites rich in marine life. The Bimini Wall, Rainbow Reef, the Bimini Barge, Little Caverns, and the Atlantis Rocks are among the most popular dives. Most hotels can set up a dive package, though Bimini Undersea is the main diving operation, and you can book directly with them. Guided snorkeling and swimming with dolphins can also be arranged. Snorkeling around the concrete wreck of the *Sapona,* and all through the surrounding area is very good. All necessary equipment is available for sale or rent. Boston Whalers can be rented by the day or half day from Weech's Bimini Dock.

If you're looking for nightlife, make your visits on the weekends or during the bigger fishing tournaments.

LODGING AND SERVICES

FEATURED LODGES AND ACCOMMODATIONS

Bimini Big Game Fishing Club and Marina

This self-contained resort offers full marina services and deluxe accommodations in a casual fun atmosphere. Thirty-three air-conditioned rooms feature 2 double beds, private bath, and enough room to spread out your fishing and diving gear. Twelve larger cottages include a dining area and refrigerator. Two penthouse suites provide outstanding views of the marina and harbor beyond. All rooms have satellite TV.

Amenities include a freshwater swimming pool, fine dining in the Gulfstream Restaurant, poolside and sports bars, event barbecues, duty-free liquor store, and a logo shop for souvenirs. Meeting rooms are available for up to 30 people. Baby-sitting and laundry service can be arranged.

The newly expanded modern marina offers 100 slips, 110- and 220-amp electrical, satellite TV hookups, fresh water, ice, and Texaco diesel and gas products.

Everything in Alice Town is within walking distance, including the west shore beaches. Guided flats, reef, and offshore charters are arranged, along with diving and snorkeling packages. Calling well ahead for reservations is a must.

Season: October through July.

Suitable For: Anglers, divers, and nonanglers.

What's Included: Fishing and diving packages, including meals, are available through the resort.

Not Included: Air or boat transportation to the islands, alcohol, gratuities. Any optional activities you choose. Most people book accommodations and fishing, then do everything else on their own. We recommend booking your fishing guide or charter boat well in advance.

Pricing: $$–$$$

Contact: Reservations and information, 800/737-1007 or 242/347-3391, fax 242/347-3392.

ADDITIONAL ACCOMMODATIONS

Bimini Blue Water Resort and Marina

The hotel portion of the resort is atop a hill on the western side of the island, while the marina is on the eastern harbor. Nine regular rooms have private balconies and baths. Anchorage suites feature 2 bedrooms, a sitting room, and private balconies. You can also rent the 3-bedroom Marlin Cottage with a full kitchen, where Hemingway wrote much of his novel, *Islands in the Stream.* The west facing cottage provides a spectacular sunset view. You can swim off the beach or in the freshwater pool. The Anchorage Restaurant also presents great views of the ocean along with some of the best seafood on the island. The 32-slip marina offers full services and monitors VHF channel 68.

Pricing: $$–$$$

Contact: Reservations and information, 800/688-4752 or 242/347-3166, fax 242/347-3293.

Sea Crest Hotel and Marina

Three-story hotel with 11 motel-style rooms with satellite TV and balconies, plus 1 2-bedroom, and 1 3-bedroom suite. Short walk to the beach. Special off-season rates are offered October through February. Golf carts are available for rent. The marina monitors VHF channel 68.

Pricing: $$

Contact: Reservations and information, 242/347-3071, fax 242/347-3495.

Weech's Bay View Rooms and Marina

Five simple air-conditioned rooms and 1 apartment. Full marina services with the exception of fuel. VHF channel 68. Close to the beach.

Pricing: $$

Contact: Reservations and information, 242/347-3028, fax 242/347-3508.

Brian O'Keefe

Fly fishing for tailing bones on an incoming tide; this is what being in the Bahamas is all about.

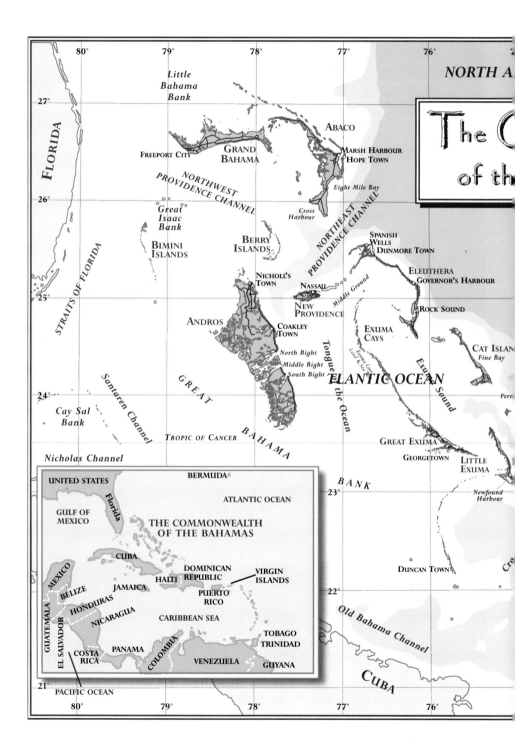

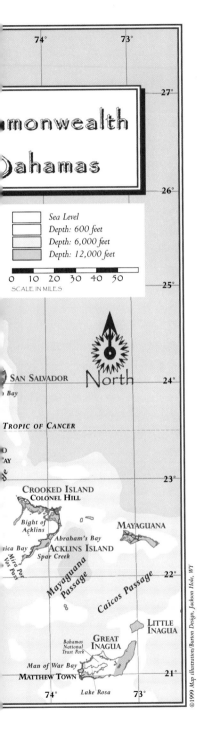

monwealth

)ahamas

	Sea Level
	Depth: 600 feet
	Depth: 6,000 feet
	Depth: 12,000 feet

0   10   20   30   40   50
SCALE IN MILES

27°

26°

25°

24°

23°

22°

21°

74°   73°

SAN SALVADOR

Bay

TROPIC OF CANCER

CROOKED ISLAND
COLONEL HILL

Bight of
Acklins

MAYAGUANA

Abraham's Bay

ica Bay   ACKLINS ISLAND
Spar Creek

Mira Por
Vos Pass

Mayaguana
Passage

Caicos Passage

LITTLE
INAGUA

Bahamas
National
Trust Park

GREAT
INAGUA

Man of War Bay

MATTHEW TOWN

Lake Rosa

North

An aerial view of Grand Bahama. Flying into the islands can be as exhilarating as actually being there.

A bonefish in eelgrass. Make any disturbance in the water, and he's gone!

Stephen Vletas with a 100-pound tarpon.

The smile on Kim Vletas' face says it all; this bonefish made her day.

Brian O'Keefe

Fishing for mutton snappers in the rocks.

A hooked dolphin goes airborne in the waters off Andros.

The waters off of Long Island offer endless flats, superb bonefishing.

Shrimp-imitating bonefish flies; the bead eyes make all the difference.

Tarpon follow each other in a daisy chain; a cast just to the side might entice one into hitting.

The Sly Fox on Andros; after a long day on the water, there's nothing like kicking back and having a cold Kalik.

A small lemon shark taken on a fly. Lemons are fun to catch, and found throughout the Bahamas.

Brian O'Keefe

Kim Vletas with Andros guide Charlie Neymour and a cubera snapper they caught from one of the island's land-locked lakes.

Wading for snappers in a creek. This is fun fishing, but just keep your eyes peeled for cruising sharks.

Brian O'Keefe

Compleat Angler Hotel

This place is a piece of history. Twelve comfortable air-conditioned outside rooms open onto a common walkway facing the bar and street. Guests can use the pool at the Blue Water Resort. If you like getting to sleep early, you might have a problem during fishing tournaments, as the downstairs partying gets pretty loud.

Pricing: $$
Contact: Reservations and information, 242/347-3122, fax 242/347-3293.

Bimini Bay Guesthouse

Interesting architecture, located on the island's best beach. Small, comfortable, and intimate. Make reservations well in advance.

Pricing: $$–$$$
Contact: Reservations and information, 242/347-2171.

SERVICES

Bimini Undersea Adventures Full diving and snorkeling services and excursions, including sales and rentals. Also rents bicycles. Call ahead for rentals during prime times.
Contact: Reservations and information, 800/348-4644 or 242/347-3089.

Pan Am Airbridge
Contact: See our Web site at www.bahamasflyfishingguide.com for up-to-date information.

Compleat Angler Golf Cart Rentals
Contact: 242/347-3122.

Bimini Tourist Office
Contact: 242/347-3529, fax 242/347-3530.

Cat Cay Yacht Club and Marina Most of Cat Cay is private, for members only, but boaters can stop in the marina to clear customs or to have lunch. The marina offers full services to boaters, a gift shop, and a small grocery store with a good array of provisions.
Contact: Reservations and information, 954/359-8272 or 242/347-3565. The marina monitors VHF channel 16.

NEW DEVELOPMENTS

A $450 million mega-resort and residential community is in the works, though the ruined remains of a similar project that ran out of money are in evidence north of Bailey Town. This complex would cover seven hundred square acres on North Bimini, and be called Bimini Bay Hotel Marina & Casino. Needless to say, the completion and opening of a resort this size would change the atmosphere on Bimini forever. Locals we have talked with say they will never allow this sort of development to happen.

We have also heard that Pan Am Airbridge is in financial trouble again, which could mean that this flight service would be interrupted or discontinued. Stay tuned at www.bahamasflyfishingguide.com, for updated information.

BERRY ISLANDS

About seventy miles east of the Biminis is a cluster of thirty islands and close to one hundred cays known as the Berry Islands. With a land mass totaling about a dozen square miles, these cays rest on the northeastern edge of the Great Bahama Bank,

Brian O'Keefe

Largely uninhabited, the Berry Islands offer
prime bonefish in an idyllic setting.

sandwiched between the deep blue waters of the Northwest Providence Channel and the Tongue of the Ocean. Starting with Great Stirrup Cay in the north, the islands extend some thirty miles to Chub Cay in the south, which is just thirty five miles north of Nassau and twelve miles from the Joulter's Cays on north Andros.

These largely uninhabited islands offer spectacular secluded anchorages, and several small resorts for diving, snorkeling, bonefishing, and offshore fishing for blue and white marlin, sailfish, wahoo, and kingfish.

At ten miles long and a mile and a half wide, Great Harbour Cay is the largest island in the chain. Most of the island's six hundred or so residents live here, in Bullock's Harbour settlement. The local economy is based on commercial lobstering, conching, and fishing, with some farming and stock raising as well. Tourism, centered around diving, fishing, and boating, is also a major factor on Great Harbour and Chub Cay.

The locals in Chub Cay will tell you that there are more millionaires per square mile in the Berry Islands than almost anywhere on the planet. When you look around at all the private islands and cays, it's not hard to believe this is true.

While most visitors arrive by boat, there are two airports, one at Great Harbour Cay and one at Chub Cay. Island Express flies charters to both from Ft. Lauderdale. Great Harbour Cay uses its own charter service, Tropical Diversions Air. A number of other charter companies fly in from Miami, Ft. Lauderdale, and West Palm Beach.

AROUND THE ISLANDS

Both Little Stirrup Cay and Great Stirrup Cay have become day stops for at least two cruise ship companies. Royal Caribbean Cruise Lines uses Slaughter Harbour for its day operations, which include jet skiing and parasailing. Bertram Cove on the north side of Great Stirrup, is also cruise ship central. Local vendors have sprouted from the sand to sell T-shirts, baskets, and other souvenirs.

Good bonefish flats, wadable at low tide, extend south of Great Stirrup to Snake Cay and Goat Cay. There is also a good anchorage for boaters on the northeast side of Goat Cay. This would be a good base from which to explore the flats between Lignum Vitae Cay and the north end of Great Harbour Cay. The water in this area is usually one to two feet deep, and some areas go dry at low tide. Using a dinghy or sea kayak would be ideal, fishing both from the watercraft and by wading.

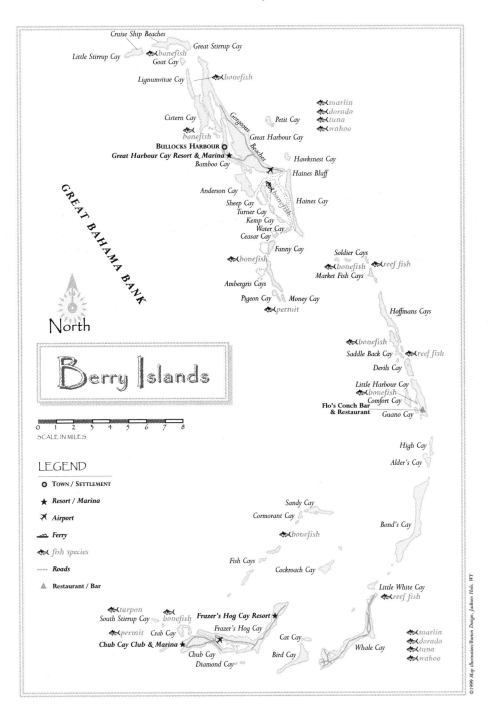

Berry Islands

SCALE IN MILES

0 1 2 3 4 5 6 7 8

LEGEND

- ○ **Town / Settlement**
- ★ **Resort / Marina**
- ✈ **Airport**
- ⛴ **Ferry**
- 🐟 *fish species*
- **Roads**
- ▲ **Restaurant / Bar**

North

GREAT BAHAMA BANK

Cruise Ship Beaches
Great Stirrup Cay
Little Stirrup Cay
bonefish
Goat Cay
Lignumvitae Cay
bonefish
Cistern Cay
bonefish
Petit Cay
marlin
dorado
tuna
wahoo
Gorgeous Beaches
Great Harbour Cay
BULLOCKS HARBOUR ○
Great Harbour Cay Resort & Marina ★
Bamboo Cay
Hawksnest Cay
Haines Bluff
Anderson Cay
bonefish
Haines Cay
Sheep Cay
Turner Cay
Kemp Cay
Water Cay
Ceasar Cay
Fanny Cay
Soldier Cays
bonefish
reef fish
Market Fish Cays
bonefish
Ambergris Cays
Pigeon Cay
Money Cay
permit
Hoffmans Cays
bonefish
Saddle Back Cay
reef fish
Devils Cay
Little Harbour Cay
bonefish
Comfort Cay
Flo's Conch Bar & Restaurant
Guano Cay
High Cay
Alder's Cay
Sandy Cay
Cormorant Cay
Bond's Cay
bonefish
Fish Cays
Cockroach Cay
Little White Cay
reef fish
tarpon
South Stirrup Cay
bonefish
Frazer's Hog Cay Resort ★
Frazer's Hog Cay
permit
Crab Cay
Chub Cay Club & Marina ★
Cat Cay
Chub Cay
Diamond Cay
Bird Cay
Whale Cay
marlin
dorado
tuna
wahoo

A maze of mangroves and creeks continues south past Cistern Cay on the way to Bullock's Harbour. This entire area offers good bonefishing on the incoming tide. Boaters must stay well off this area, as many of the sand banks go dry at low tide.

The entrance to Great Harbour Cay Marina is through an eighty-foot-wide channel on the bank side in the center of the island. The eighty-six-slip marina and resort offers full services to boaters, including a grocery and liquor store. All resort guests have the use of the freshwater swimming pool and the nine-hole golf course.

Visitors arriving by air are met at the airport and transferred to the resort. Accommodations are in privately owned villas and townhouses that feature satellite TV and sundecks; some are air-conditioned—be sure to ask for air-conditioning when making your reservations. Guests can stock up on food and cook in their units, or eat out at a variety of restaurants. If you plan on shopping for provisions, be sure to check the freight boat schedules and be at the grocery stores soon after it arrives.

One of the most popular places for lunch and dinner is the Great Harbour Yacht Club on the marina. Salads, burgers, and sandwiches are served at lunch, while seafood specialties change every night. If you are a resort guest you can eat dinner at the Tamboo Club, which offers exceptional seafood buffets a couple of nights a week. Another favorite restaurant with boaters is The Wharf, also located on the marina.

Our favorite part of Great Harbour Cay is the eastern shore, where you'll find one of the most inviting beaches in the Bahamas. The white sand runs from south of the airstrip to the northern tip of the island. The Beach Club restaurant, near the airport, is the best place on the island for lunch. You can fish the incoming tide on mangrove flats south of the airport, take a swim, do some snorkeling, and have a great lunch or afternoon drinks, all in the same day.

Great Harbour Cay is a good location for adventurous anglers looking to test their skills without a guide. Percy Darville is the man to contact to point you in the right direction. Mr. Darville can arrange for boat rentals; then, if you get frustrated, he can arrange for a guide.

The flats south of Great Harbour are best fished on the incoming tide, though the massive mangrove areas between Anderson Cay and Haine's Cay are very good during the last of the falling tide.

Miles of shallow banks, flats, and cuts continue east and south. The banana-shaped Ambergris Cays have rarely fished flats on their western side, and deeper water on the east running out to the Solider Cays and Market Fish Cays. Using chum, you can catch sharks, barracuda, jacks, and snappers in this deeper water until your arms can't take it. On the tide you can wade for several hours for bonefish that average five to six pounds. The east side of the cays, and down around Ambergris Rock, are also good permit areas, with twenty-five- to forty-five-pound fish working the last of the incoming tide.

There is a pleasant anchorage for boaters in the lee of Market Fish Cays, with good fishing for jacks, snapper, and grouper in the cuts. This type of fishing continues consistently down through the Holmes Cay, Hoffman Cay, and Devil's Cay section. The bonefish flats are inside, on the bank.

A couple of our boating friends who regularly cruise the Berrys and Andros tell us that Little Harbour Cay is one of their favorite spots, and they especially like Chester Darville and his family. The Darville family dock, and a beautiful little harbor, are located in the lee off the southern end of the cay. The cay itself is hilly and covered with dense vegetation. You can contact the Darville's on VHF channel 68. Our friends highly recommend Flo's Conch Bar and Restaurant for great lobster, grouper, fried conch, conch salad, and cold Kaliks. You'll need to call ahead for reservations.

There are a number of privately owned houses on the island, and we're told they do not welcome visitors, which is the case on many of the private islands to the south.

Just across from the southern end of Little Harbour is Cabbage Cay. A small white sand flat on the west side produces excellent bonefishing a couple of hours each day. Just north is Guana Cay, Comfort Cay, and some smaller cays that form another white sand flat in their center. This flat provides good bonefishing on both the incoming and falling tides.

Continuing south, Frozen and Alder Cays are private property. We're told the owners are busy with all kinds of construction that includes several major docks. Access to great offshore fishing, especially for billfish and tuna, is only a couple miles off these cays. To the south, Bond's Cay is also private, as are Little Whale and Whale Cays. We understand Whale Cay is also being heavily developed. Little Whale Cay was originally developed by Wallace Groves, the founder of Freeport. The bird population on this cay includes peacocks, golden pheasant, ducks, geese, and flamingos. The reef fishing off these cays is excellent. If you want to hook up a big shark, bull, or blacktip, this is one of the best places to try it.

On the bank side of these private cays are countless flats dissected by cuts and creeks running out to Cockroach Cay, Cormorant Cay, Fish Cays, and many other nameless cays. To the south and west the chain ends with Bird Cay, Frazer's Hog Cay, and Chub Cay. That's a lot of cays, and they help to create ideal habitat for big bonefish and permit.

Bird Cay is a millionaire's haven, with elegant homes, roads, and landscaping that includes groves of coconut and citrus trees. Across the channel is Frazer's Hog Cay, which is actually the eastern part of Chub Cay. Frazer's Hog Cay Resort is located to the east of the island's airstrip. This small resort specializes in taking it easy. If you really need to do something, diving, snorkeling, fishing, and watersports are available.

The Chub Cay Club and Marina is located on the southwestern tip of the island. This is a port of entry with a customs office at the airstrip. Once a privately owned resort, the Club is now open to the public. The well-designed marina can accommodate almost a hundred boats, and offers full services that include an excellent restaurant, grocery and liquor stores, and gift shop.

Visitors arriving by air are met at the airstrip and driven to the resort. Deluxe air-conditioned rooms are built around a large swimming pool. One- to three-bedroom villas are situated on a gorgeous southwest-facing beach. A good anchorage for boaters is just off this beach. Another longer beach is around a rocky point to the east, where you can enjoy snorkeling in glass-clear water. Two tennis courts, a complete diving operation, and bike rentals are available.

Bonefishing packages have been offered on and off. Right now they're off, but you can arrange for a bonefish guide or an offshore charter through the club office. We've fished the area on several occasions, running across from north Andros on calm days. While we've seen good numbers of fish, the impressive thing here is the size of the bone-

Kim with bonefish taken near Chub Cay.

fish. Fish average five to seven pounds, with plenty of fish pushing ten. A couple of our guides have landed fish around Chub in the thirteen- to fourteen-pound class. This is also a prime area for permit, though the concentrations of fish are not as high here as they are in the Joulter's.

FISHING HIGHLIGHTS

Flying over the Berry Islands is always exciting and enticing. It's the same flying over the Joulter's. The white flats go on forever, sliced up by blue cuts and creeks and green cays that create the best possible habitat for big bonefish and permit. A shallow lee bank runs the length of the chain, from Little Stirrup Cay to Chub Cay. These banks are packed with shrimp and crabs. Blue water traverses 75 percent of the chain. Miles of coral reefs are home to countless bait fish. And very few people ever fish here.

Bonefish are the primary flats game fish, with the average size being five pounds throughout most of the chain. Many of these fish are dark-green–backed ocean fish that will take two hundred yards of your backing on the first run. If you hook up an ocean fish over eight pounds, you can count on runs like this.

There are not many guides in the islands who understand the intricacies of this fishery. The area is so vast, with so much structure for fish to follow, that this type of understanding takes years of observation. Certain areas are well known, while other flats go unfished for years at a time. The mangrove areas south of Great Harbour Cay hold higher numbers of smaller fish, telling us this is a nursery area, though big fish also cruise the region. A lot of these fish tend to be lighter in color.

We prefer to fish the Berrys on a neap type. These lower tides create miles of wadable flats, and lower water levels cause bonefish to pod up in one to two foot deep troughs and depressions before dispersing onto the flats. Big bones normally prefer spring tides, but here the bigger fish have plenty of deeper water channels to use for accessing super-shallow flats. Our favorite fly for these tailing fish is a White or Tan Yarn Crab. We also take fish consistently on these light-colored bottoms with Gotchas and Gotcha Clouser's. The prime bonefishing months in the Berrys are March through June, and October and November.

Your chances for catching a permit are best in the southern Berrys, from Chub Cay west to the Rum Cay area. The fish we've seen averaged twenty-five pounds, with some monsters pushing fifty. Best months are April through July, with the fall also good. Our favorite permit fly here is a White Yarn Crab with brown rubber legs and heavy lead eyes. If you find a permit following a big stingray in this environment, you'll have an excellent chance for a hookup.

Tarpon fishing in the Berrys is fair from April on through the summer, though we suspect it could be very good if the guides tried harder to figure it out, or if some boating anglers took an interest and put in some time. The few times we've seen tarpon on the flats around South Stirrup Cay, they've attacked our flies with abandon. These fish averaged about eighty pounds, with a couple pushing a hundred. A Shallow Water Cockroach is all we've tried, so until we get a refusal we'll just stick with it.

Like the Biminis, the Berrys are best known for their reef and offshore fishing. If you're looking to catch an amberjack in the fifty-pound class, you'll have ample opportunity from November through May, with April the best overall month. April is also prime time for mutton snappers over the reefs. If you catch a few of these hard fighters, keep one for the dinner table.

Offshore fishing is the specialty out of Great Harbour Marina and Chub Cay Marina. The winter months are prime for wahoo and kingfish, with some dorado and tuna. Starting in April the dorado and tuna really pick up, with May the best time. Allison tuna are our favorites, though dealing with the ones over fifty pounds are pretty tough on a fly rod. The best fly is a WBA Mullet, though a variety of Offshore Deceivers and other similar patterns will take fish.

Blue and white marlin and sailfish are available from January on, with May and June the best marlin months. Several tournaments are held out of each marina during these prime months, but you don't have to be serious to enjoy this fishery. Cruising boaters can toss out trolling rigs almost anywhere throughout the chain and hook up something.

OPTIONAL ACTIVITIES

Sailing, boating, and just enjoying the remote beauty of the islands is the attraction here, though the diving and snorkeling doesn't get much better. In the Chub Cay area the water is so clear you can easily see small crabs moving on the bottom twenty feet below the surface. Undersea Adventures out of Chub Cay provides a full diving program. Reef, wall, and cave sites are suited to the most adventurous divers, while beginners can enjoy calm areas loaded with fish. Night dives are also available.

Secluded beaches can be found on almost every cay. If you're looking for a piece of sand all your own, you'll find it here, even on Chub and Great Harbour.

LODGING AND SERVICES

FEATURED LODGES AND ACCOMMODATIONS

Great Harbour Cay Resort and Marina

This is an ideal spot for couples and families, and a convenient location for boaters to hang out for extended periods. Anglers looking for variety, and a chance to fish on their own, will have lots of options. The resort's villas and townhouses are nicely appointed, and since they are individually owned, they are all very different. Air-conditioning is available, and all units include satellite TV and sun decks, but no telephones. The resort includes 3 restaurants, a bar, 9-hole golf course (though we've heard it's not in good shape), boat and bike rentals, and a beautiful beach. The full-service marina monitors VHF channel 68. A couple of grocery stores and a liquor store are nearby, as are other restaurants and bars.

Season: October through July.

Suitable For: Anglers and nonanglers.

What's Included: Fishing packages are available, including meals and airport transfers, though most people book accommodations first, then other activities separately.

Not Included: Airfare to/from Great Harbour, meals and optional activities. Flats, reef, bottom and offshore fishing can be arranged through the resort.

Pricing: $$–$$$

Contact: U.S. reservations and information, 800/343-7256 or 954/921-9084, fax 954/921-1004. On the island, 242/367-8838, fax 242/367-8115.

Chub Cay Club and Marina

This is our favorite place in the Berrys. The remodeled marina is one of the nicest in the Bahamas, and offers full services to boaters. The marina monitors VHF channel 68. Boaters should call ahead for slip space. The 16 deluxe air-conditioned rooms around the larger of 2 pools will make most people very comfortable. If you need something bigger, and more remote, you can rent one of the 9 villas on the beach just south of the marina. The villas include large living rooms and full kitchens. You can walk right off your deck onto the white sand beach, and take a swim in the tranquil bay. Two tennis courts and bike rentals are available. The club dining room serves fresh seafood every evening, with most dishes prepared with a distinct Bahamian flare. That means spicy and delicious. Fresh lobster is available in season. We suggest making reservations for dinner. Three bars make it convenient to get a cold Kalik or rum drink from noon until whenever. The grocery store is nicely stocked, though shopping right after the freight boat arrives is a smart thing to do.

Season: October through July.

Suitable For: Anglers and nonanglers.

What's Included: Fishing and diving packages are available, including meals and airport transfers, though most people book accommodations first, then other activities separately.

Not Included: Airfare to/from Chub Cay. Island Express flies regular charters from Ft. Lauderdale. Meals and optional activities. Flats, reef, bottom, and offshore fishing can be arranged through the club. Full- and half-day diving and snorkeling excursions are available through the dive shop.

Pricing: $$–$$$

Contact: Reservations and information, 800/662-8555 or 242/325-1490, fax 242/322-5199.

ADDITIONAL ACCOMMODATIONS

Frazer's Hog Cay Resort

If you're looking for peace and quiet you'll find it here on the east end of Chub Cay. The emphasis is on a natural Bahamian experience. Comfortable rooms feature ceiling fans and private bath. The open-air restaurant is on the beach and specializes in fresh grilled seafood. Fishing, diving, snorkeling, and watersports are the main activities.

Pricing: $$

Contact: Reservations and information, 242/328-8952, fax 242/356-6086.

E-mail: fhcresort@bahamas.net.bs

SERVICES

Tropical Diversions Air   Charter flights from Ft. Lauderdale to Great Harbour Cay.
Contact: Reservations and information, 800/343-7256 or 954/921-9084.

Elorne Rolle's Happy People on the Great Harbour Marina   They rent car, boats, motorbikes and bicycles.
Contact: Reservations and information, 242/367-8117.

Percy Darville   Mr. Darville has been involved in a number of package bonefishing operations over the years. He can assist anglers interested in fishing on their own, or he can arrange for bonefish guides. Contact him through the Great Harbour Marina. We suggest contacting Mr. Darville as far in advance of your arrival as possible.

Undersea Adventures   Operated by dive master Bill Nelson out of Chub Cay. Morning, afternoon, and night dives are available. Packages are available.
Contact: Reservations and information, 800/327-8150 or 242/323-2412.

NEW DEVELOPMENTS

We've heard all kinds of rumors about new mega-resorts, and a bonefish lodge or two, but nothing we can confirm. Major developments are definitely in full swing on a number of the private islands, but we don't know if these will remain private or be opened to the public. Stay tuned to our Web site at www.bahamasflyfishingguide.com for updated information.

8

Eleuthera, Spanish Wells, and Harbour Island

At its closest point Eleuthera lies only thirty miles northeast of Nassau, and less than thirty miles east of the northern Exuma Cays. The island spans about a hundred miles from north to south, ending in a Y-shape formed by Powell Point, Rock Sound, and Bannerman Town. While long, the island is also skinny, with an average width of less than two miles.

The terrain is a combination of tall white-faced cliffs, coral sand beaches, forests, green hills, and pristine valleys dotted with lakes. All of this is surrounded by aquamarine seas, with the deeper blue of the Atlantic Ocean pouring in over the windward reef.

The story of the Eleutherian Adventurers is well known throughout the Bahamas. Led by Captain William Sayle, a former governor of Bermuda, seventy souls seeking religious freedom set out in search of a new homeland. They originally landed in 1648 near Governor's Harbour, then discord within the group caused Sayle and some of his followers to leave and sail north. Their boat eventually ran aground on the dangerous northern reefs, but the party struggled ashore at a location that came to be

The famous pink sands beach at Pink Sands Hotel.

141

known as Preacher's Cave. Some of the group found their way to what is now Spanish Wells. Life was harsh, with starvation a constant threat.

These settlers named the island Eleuthera, from the Greek word for freedom, and continued their determined battle to survive. Sayle, realizing his new homeland needed help, sailed off to the colonies to look for support.

Though most of the original settlers returned to England by 1650, Sayle's mission was ultimately a success. Eleuthera became known as the "birthplace of the Bahamas," and was probably the first true democracy in the Western Hemisphere.

Loyalists arrived with their slaves after the Revolutionary War. They built colonial-style homes and based their economy on agriculture and shipbuilding. As with the Abaconians, salvaging wrecked ships off the reefs became an important part of their livelihood.

Growing pineapples proved to be big business for a long period of time, with many tons shipped to the United States and England. Though the pineapple business is not what it was, it is still important to Eleuthera's economy today. Tomatoes, citrus fruits, corn, and other crops are also routinely shipped to the markets in Nassau.

Spanish Wells, the settlement on St. George's Cay off northwestern Eleuthera, was made famous by the Spanish conquistadors, who stopped here to load up with fresh water for the final leg of their journey back across the Atlantic Ocean. Residents of the settlement are expert seamen, and accomplished farmers, working crops on the mainland of Eleuthera. Today, harvesting crawfish and servicing the many visiting boaters adds to the community's prosperity.

Harbour Island, or Briland, as it's called by residents, is just off the northeastern coast of Eleuthera. The island is only three miles long and half a mile wide, yet it has played an important role in Eleuthera's development. By the late 1800s, Dunmore Town, its main settlement, had grown into a renowned shipyard and sugar-processing site. The sugar business gave rise to the rum business, which made the island especially popular during Prohibition in the United States.

The Pinks Sands Hotel and the Dunmore Beach Club created a long-standing resort atmosphere for refined elegance and quiet charm, yet for years you had to be "in the know" to realize this was an option on Harbour Island. Through modern renovations and promotional efforts, both resorts are now more well-known, though the pampered feeling given to guests hasn't changed at all, nor has the vivid pink sand beach.

The current population of Eleuthera is a little more than 10,000. Without as many sailing and resort options as Abaco, Eleuthera is more quiet and unassuming. Development on the island is geared more toward private residential communities than toward resorts. Harbour Island and Club Med, which is located near Governor's Harbour, are exceptions, but they still fit in with the overall remote feeling of the island.

The entrance to Pink Sands Hotel, Harbour Island.

Like most Out Island Bahamians, the people here are extremely self-sufficient, welcoming and accommodating. Nothing seems too difficult if you ask politely. No problem, Mon. Excellent seafood can be readily found in many local restaurants. So can some of the best Johnny Cake anywhere, but the special treat on Eleuthera is pie, the best coconut and pineapple pies in the world.

Taxi service on the island is very good, or you can choose to rent a car. We highly recommend renting a car and doing some exploring on your own. To reach some of the best beaches you'll need 4-wheel drive. If you're really ambitious you can cover the island from top to bottom in about three and a half hours. Miles of pink and white sand beaches are mixed with rugged cliffs on the windward side of the island. Calm bays and bonefish flats are sprinkled in the lee. Pleasant colonial villages with brightly painted houses overlook pineapple plantations and white-capped waves crashing over the outer reef.

Think of the Old South, of the graceful illusion created in "Gone With The Wind" before the war, and you'll have a feel for Eleuthera, something that is subtly different from any other of the Bahamian islands.

Diving and snorkeling are top activities throughout Eleuthera, but surfing is also a big draw. We often encounter surfers in the North Eleuthera Airport when we're on our way to or from Harbour Island. We have received consistent reports of good surf between Glass Window and James Point, with Surfer's Beach being best overall.

Biking and hiking are especially popular on Eleuthera, with beautiful rolling terrain surrounding good roads and trails. If you want privacy, you'll find plenty of remote beaches, many with pink sand, where you can swim and picnic in idyllic conditions.

American Eagle flies daily from Miami to Governor's Harbour. Bahamasair flies daily from Miami and Nassau to North Eleuthera, Governor's Harbour, and Rock Sound. Continental Express/Gulfstream flies daily from Miami and Ft. Lauderdale to North Eleuthera. US Airways Express flies daily from Ft. Lauderdale to North Eleuthera and Governor's Harbour. Be sure to check with your resort or hotel for the nearest airport, as this will save you time and taxi fare.

Arriving and departing visitors will want to carry plenty of small bills for taxi and water ferry services. After landing at North Eleuthera or Governor's Harbour, it is common to spend $25 to $50 reaching your accommodations. These transfers are often taxi, water ferry, then another taxi, which is the way you reach Harbour Island.

We recommend soft luggage that is at least water resistant. You should also have a rain jacket handy for bad weather and ferry crossings. If the weather is calm, have insect repellent ready to apply while you're waiting for your luggage.

AROUND THE ISLAND

There are several ways for boaters to approach northern Eleuthera. One is across the Northeast Providence Channel from Abaco. Another is across the channel from the Berry Islands. The most common route is northeast from Nassau, past Rose Island, Six Shilling Cay, Current Island and other smaller cays, to the triangular-shaped landfall of North Eleuthera.

Most vacationers fly. If your destination is Harbour Island or Spanish Wells you should fly into North Eleuthera airport. Then take a short taxi ride, followed by a ferry boat ride to either island.

Flying between North Eleuthera and Nassau has always fascinated us. As we look down over the series of cays, we can see white sand flats everywhere around North Eleuthera. The southwestern point, called Current Settlement, is particularly notice-

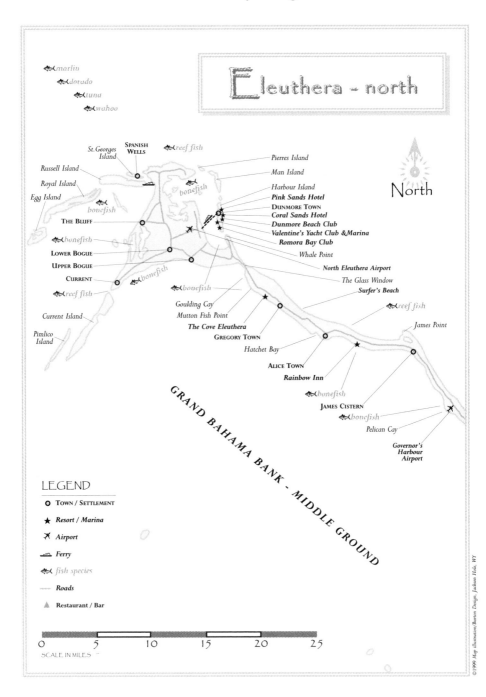

marlin
dorado
tuna
wahoo

Eleuthera - north

SPANISH WELLS
St. Georges Island
reef fish
Pierres Island
Man Island

Russell Island
Royal Island
Egg Island
bonefish

Harbour Island
Pink Sands Hotel
DUNMORE TOWN
Coral Sands Hotel
Dunmore Beach Club
Valentine's Yacht Club &Marina
Romora Bay Club
Whale Point

North

THE BLUFF
bonefish

bonefish

LOWER BOGUE
UPPER BOGUE
CURRENT
reef fish

North Eleuthera Airport
The Glass Window
Surfer's Beach

bonefish

Goulding Cay
Mutton Fish Point
The Cove Eleuthera
GREGORY TOWN
Hatchet Bay

reef fish

James Point

Current Island

Pimlico Island

ALICE TOWN
Rainbow Inn

bonefish
JAMES CISTERN
bonefish
Pelican Cay

Governor's Harbour Airport

GRAND BAHAMA BANK - MIDDLE GROUND

LEGEND

○ TOWN / SETTLEMENT
★ Resort / Marina
✈ Airport
Ferry
fish species
Roads
Restaurant / Bar

0   5   10   15   20   25
SCALE IN MILES

© 1999 Map illustration/Burton Design, Jackson Hole, WY

able from the air. The settlement is one of the oldest on Eleuthera. When you talk with the locals, they will tell you stories about the first arrivals, American Indians who were driven out of Cape Cod after a bloody slaughter.

There is not much to see in Current Settlement, but if you're looking for good fishing, diving or snorkeling, you'll find it here. The road into the settlement runs along several miles of bonefish flats that are easy to access and wade. Fishing the incoming tide will usually give you good shots at single tailing bonefish, though you'll also see schools of fish as the tide rises. The mail boat stops at the settlement dock once a week. On either side of the dock you can see the ruined remains of a small resort lodge and a marina that were destroyed by the hurricane in 1995.

For a small charge local boaters can take you across the cut to Current Island, where there are several flats adjacent to the best boat harbor. Current Cut provides one of the best drift dives in the Bahamas. The deep blue water is glass clear, and there are amazing numbers of fish. The snorkeling is also sensational.

A couple of local guides offer good bottom and reef fishing just five minutes from the dock. These guys also know where to find bonefish in the bays and around the cays up toward Spanish Wells. They'll show you the fish, then the rest is up to you. George Mullin, the owner of The Cove Eleuthera, can set up anglers with a guide at very reasonable rates.

From the Current, boaters either travel north to the Egg Islands, Royal Island, and Spanish Wells, or east to Hatchet Bay. Royal Island is gorgeous, with a protected leeside harbor, and some great beaches facing the reef. Services on the island are either unreliable or nonexistent as far as we know, but well-stocked boaters can explore some productive bonefish flats from here, including flats and reefs around the Egg Islands. The bonefish in this area rarely get fished, and are extremely aggressive to any fly they see.

Spanish Wells makes a better overall base for this area, as full services are available in the settlement. Most boaters enter the harbor between Russell Island and Charles Island, though a second entrance is available between Charlies Island and St. George's Cay. Ferry boats from the mainland use this second entrance.

Spanish Wells Marine is located in the center of the harbor at the concrete dock that is used by the mail boat. Spanish Wells Yacht Haven is farther along inside the harbor, and is recommended for recreational boaters. Fuel and petroleum products are available here along with electrical and TV hookups, water, and a laundromat. The Harbour View restaurant features a bar with pool table, and tasty seafood. When in season, the fresh lobster here is outstanding.

There are several comfortable rooms for rent at Yacht Haven, but there are no resorts or even small lodges that cater to tourists. The community is well maintained and prosperous, but it can seem like a ghost town even in the prime season of December through April. Local guides, including Woody Perry, are available to take anglers bonefishing or reef fishing. Some of the best bonefishing is across the channel along the mangrove-lined shore of Eleuthera.

Boaters can continue on from Spanish Wells to Harbour Island via Ridley Head Channel and Devil's Backbone, but it is highly recommended that you hire a local pilot for this trip due to dangerous coral heads and reefs.

We'll leave that route to adventuresome seafarers. We fly into North Eleuthera Airport, then take a five-minute taxi ride to the ferry dock, and a five-minute boat ride to Dunmore Town. No matter where you're staying on the island, a five-minute taxi ride will put you at your place of residence. The Pink Sands Hotel, Coral Sands Hotel, Dunmore Beach Club, and Romora Bay Club all provide accommodations and guest amenities that range from nice to luxurious.

Fishing for tailing bonefish off Eleuthera.

With brightly painted houses and white picket fences, Dunmore Town is not only one of the oldest settlements in the Bahamas, but one of the most charming. The concrete government wharf is the center of activity, as it is the ferry landing and the mail boat dock. This is also where we meet our bonefishing guides each morning. Legendary "Bonefish Joe," Joe Cleare, is the dean of guides. Stanley Johnson, Vincent Cleare, Stuart Cleare, Patrick Roberts, and Vincent Flucker round out the guiding team we use most often.

Some of the best fishing is just northwest across the harbor, on wide-open white sand flats where the incoming tide tempts tailing fish on a consistent basis. As the tide moves in the fish cruise the many mangrove shorelines and creeks with darker bottoms of sand, coral, and grass. One particular creek winds through the mainland for miles, with a current like a river during a spring tide. You can also fish the outside cays like Jacob Island, Man Island, and many smaller ones, all of which have bays and bars of white sand that make spotting bonefish unusually easy.

While we consider the bonefishing good here, Harbour Island is the ultimate Bahamian location for pampered beach vacationing in luxury accommodations. The three-mile pink sand beach facing the Atlantic Ocean is protected by a reef that makes swimming fun for all ages. If you like body surfing or boogie boarding, the reef break is just right. Several of the hotels, including the Pink Sands, have lighted tennis courts. The food on the island is out of this world.

Anglers and nonanglers can take equal pleasure in pursuing their own type of relaxation. You can walk anywhere on the island, though many visitors rent golf carts. If you get lost, just ask for directions. You'll find the people here will go out of their way to help you.

For boaters, Harbour Island is a port of entry. Valentine's Resort & Marina is located a couple hundred yards south of the government wharf. Full services are available including two restaurants, a bar, pool, guest accommodations, and a certified dive center. Thirty-nine slips can accommodate boats up to 160 feet. Since this is a popular spot, we suggest you call ahead for reservations. Along with the Romora Bay Club poolside bar, this is the best place on the island to watch the sunset.

The Romora Bay Club offers an excellent dive service with a PADI-trained staff that specializes in instruction and specially arranged trips to meet individual needs.

The Harbour Island Club & Marina is south of Romora Bay. Thirty-two slips offer full services, including showers and a laundromat. The restaurant here serves a good lunch, and is another nice spot from which to watch the sunset.

Unlike Abaco, Eleuthera doesn't have a long string of offshore windward cays. The deep ocean pushes in close against the protective reef that has been a hazard to sailors for centuries. For this reason, cruising boaters usually choose to navigate through the Bight of Eleuthera and along the western shoreline, where a number of bays offer good anchorages.

Visitors driving south from North Eleuthera Airport will pass the settlements of Lower and Upper Bogue before reaching a unique bridge known as the Glass Window. Sailors gave this spot its name because they could see under the span of land connecting North Eleuthera with the southern part of the island. Their view from the tranquil waters of the Bight was of the turbulent Atlantic beating across the reef.

If you get lost, just ask for directions. The people here will go out of their way to help you.

It is believed that the natural span was washed away by violent seas in the early 1900s. In 1991, a storm surge pushed a modern two-lane bridge seven feet to the south, reducing it to one lane.

The pleasant drive through this area features views of sixty-foot cliffs dropping straight down to the roiling sea on one side, and glass-clear green water rippling over white sand on the other. About a mile north of Gregory Town, is the turnoff to The Cove Eleuthera. Situated on the leeward side of the island, this intimate tranquil resort offers stunning ocean views over three rocky promontories that protect two small coves and a delightful white sand beach. Called Pineapple Cove by the locals, the resort offers air-conditioned rooms with private terraces overlooking the water, a good restaurant and bar, beautiful swimming pool, and two unlighted tennis courts. The snorkeling here is exceptional, as is the sea kayaking.

Owners George and Ann Mullin, and their staff, are among the most friendly people we've met in the islands. They can help vacationers arrange fishing, diving, and snorkeling, or point you in the right direction to explore the island on your own. The best nearby bonefishing areas run from the Current Settlement to Goulding Cay to Rainbow Bay and Pelican Cay.

Gregory Town is a pretty little settlement surrounded by pineapple fields. Amazingly, the town harbor holds a good number of bonefish at low tide. Surfer's Beach is just two miles away over a road that requires a four-wheel drive vehicle. Elvina's Restaurant and Bar is the main surfers' hangout, with good seafood, coin laundry, and satellite television. You can also rent cars here. Rebecca's General Store is Ponytail Pete's surfing headquarters, where this friendly local surfer dude posts surf conditions and tide reports. Pete's tide reports are essential for anglers fishing on their own.

For boaters and land-based visitors, the next stop down the road is Hatchet Bay. The water entrance to the bay has been enlarged, and is now ninety feet wide. Marine Services of Eleuthera offers moorings and some dock space plus fuel, electricity, and water. Rolle's Harbour View Restaurant serves spicy conch chowder, and hosts lively weekend nightlife on an irregular basis.

Alice Town is the settlement on the south side of the bay. There are a couple of grocery stores with limited supplies, a laundromat, liquor store, and a telephone office.

The fifteen-mile drive down to Governor's Harbour will take you past the Rainbow Inn, the settlement of James Cistern, the airport, and many miles of awesome pink

Decisions, decisions!

sand beaches sheltered by high limestone bluffs. Unless you rent a car and explore on your own, all of this will be lost, as many of these striking beaches are not visible from the highway. We like to take a picnic lunch and make a day of touring different beaches and flats. There are flats on both sides of the island throughout this area, so regardless of the wind direction, you can find a lee. You can also find superb snorkeling, even for beginners, while swimming and just catching rays is a great way to kick back.

But let's face it, we like to fish, too. The reef fishing here is excellent for snappers, jacks, and grouper, but the weather has to be calm to fly-fish. Clouser Minnows and bait fish imitations are the way to go. Tossing plugs and spoons on spinning gear is always deadly, even in a light wind.

For bonefishing, the last of the falling and first of the incoming tides are best. The tide on the oceanside of the island is two hours earlier than the tide on the leeward side. This gives anglers several different prime times to fish during a day. We recommend good wading booties to fish the outside ocean flats and reef areas safely.

Between Hatchet Bay and James Cistern, is the Rainbow Inn, which features one of the best restaurants on the island. Ribs on Wednesday night and steaks on Friday are local events and often include Dr. Seabreeze strumming island tunes on his guitar. Fish chowders, plus steamed and boiled fish are Bahamian delicacies you have to try. Great views and amazing sunsets can be enjoyed from the restaurant or bar. This is one of

our favorite places to watch the orange end of a perfectly relaxing day while sipping Goombay Smashes, Kim's favorite Bahamian rum drink.

Comfortable air-conditioned accommodations here are spacious, and make this a prime location to spend a few days and explore

Bungalow at The Cove Eleuthera.

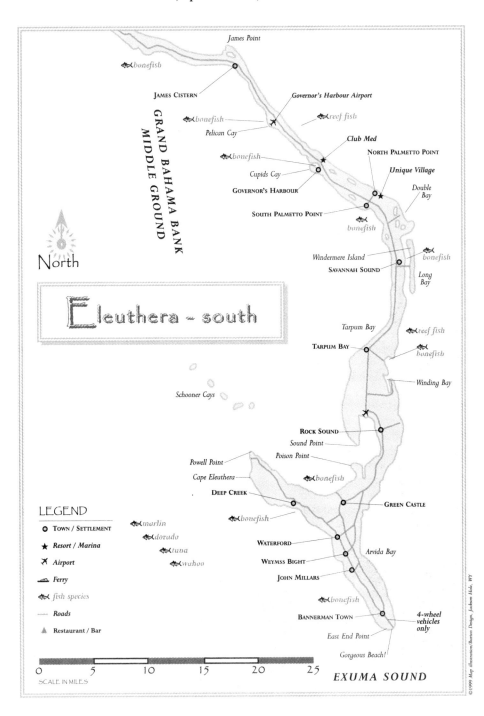

the island. Be sure to ask the staff about things to do, as they can help you plan day trips. They will also give you a free copy of "Bone Fish Graham's" personal guide-book to bonefishing on Eleuthera. We suggest you read it carefully.

Just before reaching Governor's Harbour you'll see a high pointed bluff either from the highway or from the water. Balara Bay is on the northern side of this bluff, and there are some good bonefish flats here between the tree-lined shore and Levy Is-land. These flats can be waded on lower tides. The bottom structure is a combination of coral and sand.

Governor's Harbour offers easy access for boaters, with plenty of deeper water over grassy bottoms, though this is not a good rough weather anchorage. Driving in from the north you can see across the harbor to Cupid's Cay, which many locals claim was the original settlement of the Eleutherian Adventurers. If you need to stock up on groceries or other supplies, this is a good place. Most services are available, including a post office, telephone office, government clinic, bank, and car rentals. If you don't mind a local audience while you fish, you can catch bonefish right in the harbor dur-ing the lower tidal stages.

Across town, on a stunning oceanfront beach, is Club Med Eleuthera. The beach is protected by the reef, creating ideal conditions for swimming and snorkeling. If you're looking for an all-inclusive package in a central location, and you don't mind the never-ending activities, this is a fun vacation spot. Reef and bonefishing guides can be arranged through the club. The club facilities are open to the public for lunch and dinner on a reservation space-available basis.

Driving south, Queen's Highway will take you to Palmetto Point. The place to stay on North Palmetto Point is Unique Village, set on a small green rise between a lush for-est and a pink sand beach. Hotel rooms and villas are spacious and comfortable, with villas offering full kitchens. All rooms have ocean views. The restaurant serves good local fare, and you can choose a meal plan option, or not. The Sunday brunch buffet features Dr. Seabreeze on his guitar, and the bar offers sports on satellite TV.

This is a fine base for exploring the southern region of Eleuthera and its many bonefishing options. Renting a car is a must to reach wadable flats and miles of se-cluded beaches. There is a good white sand flat marked by a high mangrove cay just north of the Palmetto settlement pier. You can walk all the way out and around this mangrove on a low neap tide. Larger bonefish like the darker deeper edges out past this mangrove. The fish are definitely not spooky here, so we like throwing Gotcha Clousers.

Tarpum Bay is the next settlement south. What a pretty little place this is, with white-walled buildings and shallow clear water covering golden sand stretching out from the shoreline. There is a good grocery store and hardware store near the main dock. Even though you will have your own car, don't forget the taxi drivers. These guys know everything about everything and are happy to talk to you. Sometimes we just park our car and have them drive us around.

This is how we were originally reminded not to forget the windward side of the island between Palmetto and Rock Sound. "You been out to the oceanside, mon? All kinds of fish out there, mon." This was in response to a question we asked about fishing the Bight side. The oceanside has at least half a dozen bays and coves where bonefish feed on the tide. And the reef fishing continues to be excellent during calm conditions.

Drive ten to fifteen minutes south and you'll be in Rock Sound. Boaters and land-based do-it-yourselfers will love the supermarket here. Fresh fruit, seafood, and other staples are in good supply. If you aren't cooking for yourself, stop in at Sammy's

If you somehow get tired of fishing, you can always go swimming—or just catch a few rays!

Place, just out of town toward the airport. The food is home-cooked, delicious, and reasonably priced.

The main road runs through the settlement along the water, where a number of commercial fishing boats and Boston Whalers are tied up. Stop by here in the afternoon and you can work out a fishing guide, or ask one of the taxi drivers to recommend a guide. Most likely the driver will steer you to one of his cousins.

South of Rock Sound is the currently closed Cotton Bay Club. The Robert Trent Jones golf course, however, is open to the public.

Most boaters travel from Rock Sound across to Powell Point, which begins the journey to the Exuma Cays or back to Nassau. We like to drive all the way south to Bannerman Town, where there are beautiful flats and creeks and lots of bonefish. On occasion we take the right fork to Greencastle, then head to Deep Creek and Cape Eleuthera. There are miles of mangrove-lined flats around Deep Creek and a maze of creeks at Cape Eleuthera that hold bonefish and tarpon.

If you drive down to Bannerman Town or Deep Creek be sure to take along a picnic lunch and a cooler with drinks, as there are no reliable food services in the area. Good wading shoes are a must, as you will often have to walk through mucky mangrove areas to reach the fishable flats, bays, and creeks. This is sometimes difficult walking with areas of soft bottom, but there sure are a lot of nice-size fish. If you have a four-wheel drive vehicle, you can drive to the end of the road past Bannerman Town. Your reward will be one of the most spectacular deserted beaches on the planet.

Another thing to remember is gasoline. Don't run out. Our motto is "never pass an open gas station without filling up, even if you only need a couple of gallons." You cannot rely on gas stations being open, even during regular business hours, and sometimes it is impossible to find gas anywhere on the weekends.

FISHING HIGHLIGHTS

The most surprising thing about Eleuthera is that it is the only major Out Island without some sort of organized fly-fishing program. The closest thing to a fishing program is on Harbour Island, where guests of the various hotels can book with the island's independent guides, or staying at Cove Eleuthera and booking these same guides. We recommend booking independent guides well in advance of your trip, either through your hotel or with one of the few agents who work with these guides.

Before we visited Harbour Island and Spanish Wells, we imagined the fishery in this area to be pretty limited. Where this idea came from is a mystery, as the North Eleuthera fishery covers a sizable area of productive flats and creeks on both sides of the mainland.

Boaters fishing on their own, exploring in skiffs or dinghies, have better access to the Spanish Wells side, due to the geography and lack of accommodations. The dangerous yet alluring reefs that guard North Eleuthera and drop off into the Northeast Providence Channel create a home for countless bait fish, and provide nearby deep water for larger flats game fish. Along with this, the dense mangrove shorelines of the mainland provide habitat for smaller fish and a variety of shrimps and crabs.

There are many areas of wide open white sand flats within the shallow water area created by the mainland, the southwest reef, Royal Island, Russell Island, and St. Georges Island. The areas from the Lobster Cays and up past Ragged Cays are some of the best. These flats are a short run from the settlements of the Bluff or the Current.

Just south of the Bluff is a massive mangrove-lined bay that is stacked with bonefish, as is the entire shoreline. Easy runs also put boats over some of the best reef fishing for jacks, snappers, grouper, and mackerel anywhere in the Bahamas. The drawback is protection from the weather, which is minimal with the wind anywhere in the north, and this is the prevailing wind direction during cold fronts. The exception is when the wind is from the east, or northeast; then anglers can gain protection for bonefishing along the mainland shorelines.

On the Harbour Island side the habitat is similar, though there are many more shallow-water back bays and mangrove systems that hold even higher numbers of bonefish. This area is more closed in, which provides some protection from the wind, but is more exposed to the northeast, which evens that score. During bad weather conditions, casting will be difficult as usual, but there are lots of light sand areas where visibility is still good enough to catch some fish.

We prefer to fish an incoming tide on both sides. The bonefish are really dialed in to move from the deeper water into the mangroves, and they are often very quick about

Brian O'Keefe

A monster bonefish: When you hook a fish like this, be ready to be into your backing in under a minute.

it. Timing is critical if you want to catch them tailing over sandy bottoms. Once the fish get into the creeks and spread out through the mangrove flats they are actually easier to hook up, but you'll break off more than you land.

No question, bonefish are the number-one flats species on Eleuthera. The highest concentration of fish live at the northern and southern tips of the island where there is more protective habitat and more food. The creeks and bays and mangrove structure from Rock Sound to Deep Creek and Bannerman Town is much like it is in the north.

The long, skinny strip of land connecting the north and south is unique in its own way. It is easy to cross between the Bight and ocean flats, and therefore easy to escape the wind. The Bight side tide is two hours behind the ocean tide, so you have at least two periods of prime fishing through the day. The Bight side holds more bonefish, but the windward side has bigger fish. The nice thing about this area is that the good flats are obvious, and many are easily accessed from land. As "Bone Fish Graham" says, you don't need a boat or a guide here, you can do it on your own.

Our favorite flies for sandy bottoms are Gotchas, Krystal and Epoxy Charlies, and Epoxy Flies, which imitate the gobies that live throughout the Bight. The most finicky fish live in the north, and on some of the most fished flats like those at Pelican Cay. The rest of the fish are opportunistic feeders. When in doubt, put on a Clouser Minnow and start casting. For tailing fish, go with a #6 Tan Yarn Crab. It's fun to watch bonefish pounce on this fly like a cat on a mouse. Over grass and broken coral we still fish Clouser's and Yarn Crabs, but if we're getting hung up we go to a Miheve's Flats Fly or a Rattle Rouser.

While we have cast to a few permit in the north, we have never hooked up. Several of our friends and clients have caught permit up to thirty-five pounds out of Harbour Island, but most were on live crabs. Bonefish Joe and the other guides say the best permit fishing is around the outer cays and over the reefs from April through July.

Other people we've talked with from Gregory Town to Rock Sound have seen permit occasionally, but the only ones reported caught were on live crabs. The commercial fishermen out of Rock Sound love to tell permit stories, seeing huge schools around the Schooner Cays and all along the Exuma Sound banks.

We've seen permit inside the windward reefs in a number of places while snorkeling and while fishing for jacks, but have never had a cast to one of these. Permit are permit, and they remain as elusive on Eleuthera as elsewhere.

Migratory tarpon move through the Bight of Eleuthera from April through October. We've talked with the guides and commercial fishermen about their patterns and habits, but we never seem to get the same story twice. Still, we have enough information from various people to suggest your best shot at tarpon would be around Current Island, setting up ambush points throughout the Current Cut channel. This is the place where tarpon move in and out of the Bight most consistently. Another good location would be in the Deep Creek and Cape Eleuthera area. Resident tarpon hang in some of the creeks, and the migratory tarpon move through in season.

We've only seen a few tarpon on Eleuthera, so we don't have any favorite flies, but when in doubt go with a Fernandez Shallow Water Cockroach or a #2/0 Chartreuse/White Clouser Minnow. Like a trout fly fisher putting on a favorite attractor pattern, these are our favorite tarpon flies throughout the Bahamas.

Sharks and barracuda are everywhere, especially around the reefs. So are jacks, grouper, snappers, mackerel, and zillions of bait fish. If you just want to catch fish, the reefs are the place. Our favorite flies are Popovic's Bangers, Crystal Poppers, Clouser's Minnows, and Deceivers.

Local fishermen from Hatchet Bay to Rock Sound love to go reef fishing. Pick a calm day, hire one of these guys, and you'll have some of the best action you can imagine. If you promise to let your guide keep the catch, he'll bring the bait and chum. Even if you don't promise, you'll have to be quick to release any of the snapper, mackerel, or grouper.

Offshore fishing is very good out of North Eleuthera. Valentine's Marina on Harbour Island is headquarters for a leg of the Bahamas Wahoo Championships in January, and the Bahamas Billfish Tournament final leg in June.

November through April is wahoo time, with January and February prime. Boats are available for charter from Valentine's and Harbour Island Marina.

Allison tuna and blue marlin are in the waters off North Eleuthera year round, but June and July are the prime months. July is also regatta time, which means lots of boaters, and even more parties. While this is off-season for general tourism, this is a great time to visit as rates at even the best hotels are at their lowest, and weather is generally at its best.

When we evaluate the overall fishing opportunities on Eleuthera, we have to give it high marks for uncrowded, unspoiled flats, good numbers of bonefish, and outstanding reef fishing. For adventurous fly fishers looking to explore on their own, this island is one of the best options.

OPTIONAL ACTIVITIES

Eleuthera is the sort of place where optional activities are often ignored in favor of lying on the beach and reading a book. Planning activities can be too taxing, so many visitors just don't bother. Those who get motivated usually decide that general exploring is the best option. You can rent a car to do this, though biking, hiking, and sea kayaking will give you access to some gorgeous remote locations.

Preacher's Cave on the northernmost coast is a standard point of interest, as are many other caves, including the ones at Hatchet Bay. Most explorers end up at one spectacular beach or another, swimming and snorkeling inside the oceanside reefs. Good diving programs are available, with the best ones out of Harbour Island.

If you are action-starved for watersports and lively activities you should book in to Club Med, where you can water ski, jet ski, and windsurf until you drop. Golf is available at the Robert Trent Jones course south of Rock Sound, and if you need to work up a serious sweat, you can play tennis during the day at a variety of locations.

There are miles of secluded beaches to explore on your own.

The Blue Bar and Restaurant on the beach at Pink Sands Hotel.

LODGING AND SERVICES

FEATURED LODGES AND ACCOMMODATIONS

Pink Sands Hotel

Harbour Island This is Kim's favorite hotel in the Bahamas, and one of her favorites in the world. This Chris Blackwell resort features 26 rooms in 18 cottage-style buildings. Large deluxe air-conditioned rooms and suites include wet bars, refrigerator, toaster, coffeemaker, CD player, Italian-tiled bathrooms, and private terraces. The open-air lobby is bright and comfortable and includes a long hardwood bar, pool table, and cocktail area. A gorgeous living room/library features satellite TV and board games. The outdoor dining area is casual and elegant, and the food is simply superb. You'll need to be on a diet either before or after this trip, and maybe both. A beachside restaurant serves great lunches, or you can order lunch down on the beach. And the pink sand beach? Yep, it's pink and magnificent. If you don't want to swim in the ocean try the freshwater pool, next to 3 lighted tennis courts. To top it off, the hotel can arrange for legendary bonefish guides or offshore fishing. Diving and snorkeling excursions are also available. The on-site staff is extremely helpful, and will do everything possible to make your trip memorable.

Season: Mid-October through July. (Low season rates are available in October, early November, and in the summer. These are great fly fishing months.)

Suitable For: Anglers and nonanglers, or anyone who wants a luxurious beach vacation.

What's Included: Complete packages include accommodations, Bahamian taxes, breakfast, and dinner.

Not Included: Airfare to/from North Eleuthera airport, taxi/boat transfers, guided fishing, and other optional activities.

Pricing: $$$$

Contact: Reservations and information, 800/688-7678 or 242/333-2030, fax 242/333-2060. To book bonefishing in advance, 800/922-3474.

E-mail: outpost800@aol.com

Internet: www.islandoutpost.com

The Cove Eleuthera

Gregory Town   Owned and operated by George and Ann Mullin, this resort sits on 30 isolated acres over-looking the Atlantic Ocean. Twenty-seven air-conditioned rooms have been recently renovated. The restaurant and bar are adjacent to the swimming pool and a huge deck for lounging or evening cocktails. Ideal snorkeling in a protected bay is right out front, off a pretty white sand beach. If you need some exercise there are 2 nonlighted tennis courts. There are miles of wadable bonefish flats nearby. You can fish on your own, or the hotel can arrange for a guide. You can fly into either North Eleuthera or Governor's Harbour, but we recommend North Eleuthera, and we definitely recommend renting a car.

Sea kayaks, bicycles, snorkeling gear, beach towels, and coolers are provided to guests at no charge. Other optional activities, including fishing guides, can be arranged.

Season: October through July.
Suitable For: Anglers and nonanglers.
What's Included: Packages are available, including special honeymoon packages.
Not Included: Airfare to/from North Eleuthera airport, taxi transfers, guided fishing, and other optional activities. Regulated taxi fares are $27 from North Eleuthera, and $42 from Governor's Harbour.
Pricing: $$
Contact: Reservations and information, 242/335-5142 or 800/552-5960, fax 242/335-5338.
E-mail: Ann@TheCoveEleuthera.com
Internet: www.thecoveeleuthera.com

Rainbow Inn

Governor's Harbour   This small oceanfront resort specializes in friendly personal service. The location makes it ideal for exploring all of Eleuthera. Comfortable air-conditioned rooms are suitable for couples, families, or hard-core anglers. The restaurant is one of the best on the island, and the bar is a great place for watching the sunset. If you're looking for a place to fish on your own, this is one of the best choices in the Bahamas.

Season: November 15 through August.
Suitable For: Anglers and nonanglers.
What's Included: 8 day/7 night packages include air-conditioned tropical studio apartment with mini-kitchen, breakfast and dinner daily, wine and drinks with dinner, unlimited tennis, use of bicycles and snorkeling equipment, car rental for the week, Bone fish Graham's guide and four bonefish flies. Nonpackage rates are available, and stays of any length are available.
Not Included: Airfare to/from Governor's Harbour airport, taxi transfers if applicable, guided fishing, and other optional activities.
Pricing: $$
Contact: Reservations and information, telephone/fax 242/335-0294 or 800/688-0047.
E-mail: vacation@rainbowinn.com
Internet: www.rainbowinn.com

ADDITIONAL ACCOMMODATIONS

Dunmore Beach Club

Harbour Island   A tradition on Harbour Island, this resort is a little stuffy for us, though they have a long list of repeat clientele. Comfortable rooms are set in beautiful gardens on the hillside overlooking the ocean. Amenities include a swimming pool and tennis court. Excellent meals are served in the clubhouse. Men must wear jackets for dinner. The club is down the beach from the Pink Sands, and next door to the Coral Sands.
Pricing: $$$$
Contact: Reservations and information, 242/333-2200, fax 242/333-2429.

Coral Sands

Harbour Island   Next door to the Pink Sands, this hotel has just been renovated and is a great economical option for staying on Harbour Island's pink sand beach. Twenty-seven air-conditioned rooms overlook the ocean. The restaurant, bar, and sundeck provide shaded comfort above the beach for breakfast, lunch, and dinner. The new swimming pool is a nice alternative to the ocean, and a tennis court is available. Fishing, diving, and snorkeling excursions are arranged.

Pricing: $$–$$$
Contact: Reservations and information, 242/333-2320 or 800/468-2799, fax 242/333-2368.
E-mail: coralsands@batelnet.bs
Internet: www.coralsands.com

Romora Bay

Harbour Island   Recently renovated, this resort faces west overlooking the harbor; the bar is the best place on the island to watch the sunset. Comfortable accommodations, a good restaurant, a new swimming pool, tennis court, and a nearby dive center are the highlights.

Pricing: $$$
Contact: Reservations and information, 242/333-2325.

Valentine's Yacht Club & Marina

Harbour Island   Twenty-one air-conditioned rooms combine with the 39-slip marina to create a center of activity on the west side of the island. Amenities include a swimming pool, tennis court, bicycles, and a complete dive center. Fishing trips, flats and offshore, can be arranged. The marina monitors VHF channel 16.

Pricing: $$–$$$
Contact: Reservations and information, 242/333-2142, fax 242/333-2135.

Unique Village

North Palmetto Point   South of Governor's Harbour, the resort's 14 air-conditioned rooms and villas are spacious and overlook a beautiful stretch of beach. The restaurant serves good steaks and seafood. The bar offers satellite TV and ocean views. Island excursions and car rentals can be arranged. We recommend staying here if you want to explore and fish southern Eleuthera.

Pricing: $$–$$$
Contact: Reservations and information, 242/332-1830, fax 242/332-1838.

Palmetto Shores Vacation Villas

South Palmetto Point   Located on the bay side of the island, the resort offers 15 1-, 2-, and 3-bedroom air-conditioned condos with kitchens and TV. Two tennis courts and a boat dock are available. Car and bike rentals can be arranged.

Pricing: $$–$$$
Contact: Reservations and information, telephone/fax 242/332-1305.

Club Med

Governor's Harbour   This all-inclusive resort is geared toward families with young children. If you're looking for activities, this place has every water sport you can think of. Daily programs keep children and adults busy. Buffet-style meals will satisfy the largest appetite. The casual atmosphere is also conducive to sitting around and doing nothing on the beautiful beach. The place is big, however, with 284 air-conditioned rooms, 3 restaurants, 8 tennis courts, and lively nightlife.

Pricing: $$$
Contact: 800/258-2633 or 242/332-2270, fax 242/332-2855.

SERVICES

Guided flats fishing: As we've mentioned, it is possible to fish Eleuthera successfully on your own, though there are a few good independent guides available. You can book them through your resort or hotel, or call 800/922-3474, to book a guide in advance. If you plan to book a guide out of Harbour Island from March through June, you will need to book well in advance.

Offshore fishing: Your resort or hotel can book offshore boats.
Out of Harbour Island, contact Valentine's Marina for reservations and information, 242/333-2309.
Out of Hatchet Bay, Captain Gregory Thompson runs a 32-foot Stamas Sportfisher. Contact him at 242/335-5357.

Diving: Out of Rock Sound, South Eleuthera Divers covers the south part of the island. We recommend booking dive trips well in advance here.
Contact: Reservations and information, 242/334-2221, ask for Tim Riley.

Out of Harbour Island, Valentine's Dive Center is the best operation for North Eleuthera and the surrounding area. Equipment is available for sale or rent. Dive packages, or daily dives, including certification, are available for all ability levels. You should book well in advance during the season. Your hotel can book diving or snorkeling for you.
Contact: Reservations and information, 242/333-2309.

Car Rentals: It's best to arrange this in advance. Most hotels and resorts are happy to make these reservations for you. Some packages include car rentals. Most car rental companies are located in Governor's Harbour, but rentals can be delivered with advance notice.
Johnson's Car Rentals—Governor's Harbour 242/322-2226 or 322-2778.
Hilton's Car Rentals—242/335-6241.
Arthur Nixon—242/332-2568. Mr. Nixon also conducts tours of the island. If you want to know everything about everything on Eleuthera, this is the man to talk to.
North Eleuthera Service Station—North Eleuthera, 242/335-1128.

Boat, golf cart, and other rentals: You're best off making these arrangements through your resort or hotel in advance.
    On Harbour Island, Big Red Rentals rents snorkeling gear, golf carts, and small boats. Contact them at 242/333-2045.

Restaurants: On Harbour Island we like to stay and eat at the Pink Sands Hotel. Our feeling here is, why leave perfection? However, we do like to try new places, so some of our favorites include Ma Ruby's for tasty seafood, and her famous Jimmy Buffet–inspired "Cheeseburger in Paradise," plus killer Key lime pie; Angela's Starfish for fresh conch ceviche; the Dunmore Deli for good boxed fishing lunches. Definitely have sunset drinks at Romora Bay.
    If you're cruising around Eleuthera, stop for a meal at The Rainbow Inn. We especially recommend sunset rum drinks and dinner.
    Out of Palmetto Point, try the Unique Village restaurant for lunch, dinner, or Sunday brunch.
Harbour Island Tourist Office, 242/333-2621, fax 242/333-2622.
Eleuthera Tourist Office, 242/332-2142, fax 242/332-2480.

Barclay's Bank, in Governor's Harbour, is open Monday through Friday 9:00 A.M. to 1:00 P.M.
Royal Bank of Canada, on Harbour Island, is open Monday through Friday 9:30 A.M. to 3:00 P.M.

Government medical clinics are located on Harbour Island and Spanish Wells, in Governor's Harbour and Rock Sound.

NEW DEVELOPMENTS

There is all kinds of talk about new developments and mega-resorts, but we haven't seen anything concrete in the works. In fact, Eleuthera is littered with abandoned resort and housing developments. Many of the roads leading to spectacular remote beaches were put in to reach these developments that just never happened. Breeze Away Estates is a classic example. This development is still advertising with full-page full color ads in *Island Magazine,* but the roads are overgrown, there is no sign of any activity, and none of the locals we talked to knew where this development was. Potential buyers should be cautious. Log on to our Web site for updated information at www.bahamasflyfishingguide.com.

9

New Providence and Nassau

New Providence Island is a name not many people know outside the Bahamas, yet it is the Bahamian national capital, and home to 175,000 residents, two thirds of all Bahamians. Twenty-one miles long and seven miles wide, it's one of the country's smallest inhabited islands.

Better known as the city of Nassau, the island has been the thriving hub of the Bahamas since the days of the legendary pirate Blackbeard. Its centralized location between Andros and Eleuthera, easy access to deep-water sea lanes, and its renowned harbor have made it an international transportation and banking center. Banking laws in the Bahamas rival those in Switzerland, plus there is no inheritance tax, sales tax, or income tax.

Other than to change planes en route to the Out Islands, we never spent more than a night in Nassau during the 1980s and early 1990s, and when we had to do that, the experience was unpleasant. Many of the hotels and restaurants were run-down, and the people didn't seem that happy. That all began to change in 1992, thanks in large part to the new government of Prime Minister Hubert A. Ingraham. The Ingraham administration laid out a policy to encourage foreign investment and upgrades. The policy included the Hotels Encouragement Act, which provided for significant duty exemptions and tax breaks for hotel improvements and new investments.

In the fall of 1993 we had a long layover at the domestic terminal, so we took a taxi to Cable Beach. The Crystal Palace Hotel, now the Marriott Crystal Palace, was a fun diversion from sitting around the airport. The beaches had been noticeably cleaned up, making the white sand as inviting as anywhere.

We took a public bus, or jitney, down to Bay Street. These buses cost a dollar or so, and run reliably on regular schedules. People were noticeably upbeat. The atmosphere on Bay Street was electric. Kim got into shopping in the international brand name stores. She said the duty-free prices were too good to pass up.

On the way home from the Out Islands, we decided to spend a night in Nassau at the Forte Cable Beach. The place needed some renovations, which have now been completed, but it was nice. Sitting in the beachside bar drinking Goombay Smashes we could have been somewhere on Abaco. The difference here was the choices we had for dinner.

What better way to relax, and relive the fishing events of the day?

Impulsively, we chose Graycliff, an elegant restaurant and hotel set in an old colonial mansion. The maitre d' and staff dresses in tuxedos, and jackets are preferred for men, though in the off season this is not a rule they enforce. This may sound fancy and stuffy, but it's actually relaxing and exquisite.

The Cuban cigar master who invented the Cohiba for Castro sits at a mahogany table in the polished wood-floored entry, rolling fresh tobacco into perfect cigars. Cocktails and hors d'oeuvres are served in the living room. This is also where you peruse the two-inch-thick wine list. If you want a bottle under a thousand dollars, skip the first half of the list. You place your dinner order here before moving into one of the small air-conditioned dining rooms. We could not resist ordering chocolate soufflé for desert.

The food and service was everything you would expect in one of the world's best restaurants, though Graycliff is more than just a restaurant and hotel. It is a destination all its own, one we have now made a habit of visiting on most trips through Nassau.

If you're into food, Nassau has something for every appetite. If you want down home Bahamian Johnny Cake, conch salad, steamed fish, rice and peas, no problem. If you want fast food there's pizza, McDonald's, and more. Many casual restaurants serve a varied menu, and there a number of good English-style pubs. For fine dining, Graycliff is just the beginning.

Other fine restaurants we've tried and enjoyed include Buena Vista, The Sun and . . . , Five Twins, The Bahamian Club, and the Ocean Reef Club.

For a casual evening meal overlooking the harbor and the Yacht Haven Marina, we like the Poop Deck Restaurant and Bar. Order the fresh seafood here. For delicious Bahamian food, try Mama Lyddy's Place. This restaurant does not take credit cards, which is something you should always be aware of, especially in the Out Islands. For a half dozen other good casual eateries, take a stroll through Atlantis. You will find something for any taste, from massive buffets to good tuna sandwiches.

Another turning point year for Nassau was 1995. During the celebration of the city's tercentenary, Sun International opened the Atlantis Hotel and Casino on Paradise Island. When we heard the hotel featured the world's largest outdoor aquarium we decided to check it out.

It was worth the visit. A shallow-water section is loaded with bonefish, cruising the flats just as they would off Andros. If there hadn't been so many people around we would have put our fly rods together. The deeper-water sections contain sharks, barracuda, snappers, jacks, tarpon, and countless other species of tropical fish.

It's a quick hop from New Providence to Andros . . . and to bonefish like this one.

Then there are the permit, hundreds of them. It's a mesmerizing sight. You can watch them from above, but the best view is from the tunnels where you see them at eye level through thick glass. Their eyes never stop moving, darting, and inspecting. It makes you nervous just watching them, and makes you realize why they are so hard to catch on a fly. Attracting their attention is no problem, but getting them to commit to eating is one of the toughest things in fly-fishing.

We ended up staying a night at Atlantis. Just picture a glitzy Las Vegas hotel, say the Mirage, set it down in a tropical paradise with water running through it, and you have Atlantis.

That was Atlantis then, with about a thousand rooms. In December 1998 Atlantis opened its new Royal Tower and Marina, which more than doubled room capacity, and created the most mind-boggling outdoor water theme park in the world.

We understand that some locals don't like the progress being made on New Providence, and especially on Paradise Island. In spite of the city's crowds and traffic, there are still places on the island that remain untouched and peaceful. Wanting to preserve this makes sense, but progress has dramatically improved the lives of the people on New Providence. Thousands of good-paying jobs have been created. The city is cleaner and it feels safer. Crime is certainly no worse than in any U.S. city of the same size.

The atmosphere is fun and energetic. Downtown is revitalized. Improvements at Prince George Wharf have allowed cruise ship companies to bring in more than one million visitors a year. The Straw Market is a frenzy of buying and selling that reminds us of the New York Stock Exchange.

Over a billion dollars has gone into revamping old hotel properties, turning them into competitive world-class resorts. Sandals, Breezes, Radisson, Marriott, and others have transformed Cable Beach into a mini-Riviera. With Atlantis leading the way, Paradise Island lives up to its name, and smaller elegant resorts like The Ocean Club have helped Nassau regain its past glamour.

Trendy clubs and cigar bars mingle with upscale restaurants that draw affluent travelers, while spring-breakers go wild, and cruise ship passengers shop until they drop. Chris Blackwell's Compass Point resort is a celebrity magnet, as is the exclusive gated community at Lyford Cay.

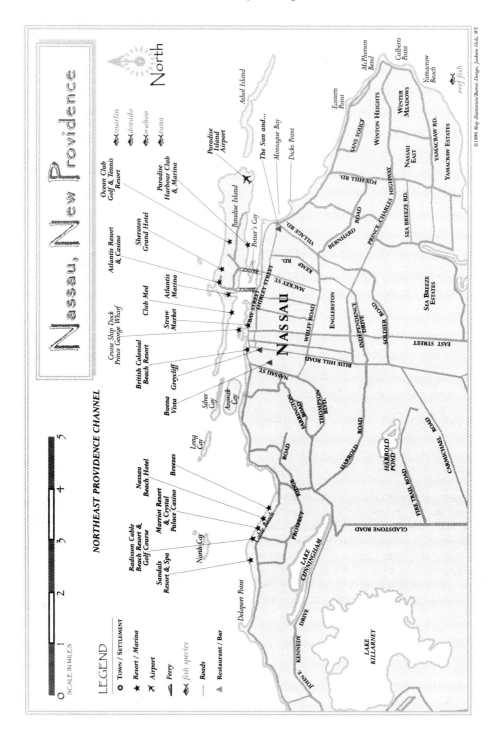

Culture is also back in force, with the Junkanoo Expo leading the way. Museums have been restored to better tell of Nassau's history, poetry readings are hip, and art fairs take place almost every week.

Outdoor enthusiasts will not be bored on New Providence. Three public golf courses are highly rated. The private Lyford Cay Club course is also well regarded, but you have to be a member, or guest of a member, or staying at the club. Most of the major resorts have tennis courts and health clubs. Water sports are the main attraction, with snorkeling and diving trips put on by a number of vendors, though there is good snorkeling that you can do on your own.

Cable Beach is wild with jet skis, parasailing, water skiing, beach volleyball, and any other type of beach activity you can think of.

While none of this is the Bahamas we crave, it is fun and exciting for many people. We're glad to see it happening because this atmosphere of rejuvenated pride and industriousness is radiating through the country, and putting smiles on the faces of a lot of people.

This renewed enthusiasm is drawing thousands of visitors, making tourism by far Nassau's leading industry. We rarely visit the Bahamas now without spending a night or two in Nassau. Many of our client couples use Nassau as a great way to compromise on a "fishing" vacation. Four nights in Nassau traded for four days of bonefishing on one of the Out Islands makes a balanced trip, though most of the anglers we know try to shift this balance in favor of the fishing.

There is good offshore and reef fishing out of Nassau with conventional gear. Experienced fly fishers with their own equipment could catch fish, too, but don't count on any help from the charter boat crews.

In the last couple of years we have put together day trips to Andros for anglers needing a bonefish fix. We arrange an early morning charter flight to Andros Town Airport. One of our best independent guides picks you up, takes you out for a day of fishing, then gets you back to the airport for the return charter to Nassau.

Nassau's International Airport is a comfortable, modern facility, and the hub of Bahamasair. Delta, Comair, American Eagle, Continental, US Airways, Air Canada, Air Jamaica, and many different charter jets fly here daily. Visitors arriving on all commercial airlines land here. Passengers clear customs, retrieve their luggage, then take a taxi to their island accommodations, or transfer over to the domestic terminal for a flight to the Out Islands.

If you are staying on Paradise Island, and not continuing on to one of the Out Islands, it makes more sense to fly into the Paradise Island Airport on Paradise Island Airlines, US Airways Express, or another charter carrier.

Ric Fogel

Stephen casting to bonefish.

If you're staying on the island, service personnel outside the international terminal will get you a taxi in orderly fashion. Zone fares are regulated by the government, so you'll know what the fare is in advance. If you're going to the domestic terminal we suggest using a porter to help with your luggage. It's a five-minute walk, and if you pack like we do, it's worth the tip money to have assistance.

The domestic terminal is basic, but there are a couple of places to get a snack, and there's a good liquor store. We often buy wine and liquor here to take with us to the Out Islands.

Bahamasair schedules rarely match up well with international flights. You will often have long layovers coming and going. You can get a taxi from the domestic terminal to Cable Beach for $12, about a ten-minute ride. We usually have the taxi drop us off at the Marriott Crystal Palace, as it is located in the center of the resort strip.

Our favorite lunch spot is Café Johnny Canoe, just east of the Marriott at the Nassau Beach Hotel. The menu offers a good variety of food, and many Bahamian specialties. Kim brings along a "beach bag" with suntan lotion, books, and swimsuits. Depending on how much time we have we might catch some rays and go for a swim.

For anglers arriving late and overnighting in Nassau, we recommend staying in a Cable Beach hotel, especially if you're getting up early the next morning for a flight to the Out Islands, and a full fishing day. These hotels are the best accommodations nearest the airport.

If you have a really long layover (at least four hours), you can go to Bay Street. Tell the driver to drop you at the British Colonial Hotel. The hotel has undergone major renovations, which were completed in June 1999. This is also a good spot to overnight, but you'll have a longer drive back to the airport. Depending on the length of your layover, you could make a dash to Paradise Island to see the Atlantis aquarium. Be advised that even with the new Paradise Island bridge, traffic jams can create an hour's drive back to the airport, even if you take the shortcut past Lake Cunningham.

We recommend making use of your taxi rides by talking with the drivers. They know everything that's going on in the city, and can make some great suggestions for things to do and places to eat. Most will offer to pick you up for the return trip to the airport. Ninety-nine percent of the time they will be where you say, right on time.

Flights returning from the Out Islands to Nassau will arrive at the domestic terminal. You will retrieve your luggage here, then trek to the international terminal. The check-in area of the international terminal is considerably farther than the arrival area, so we recommend using a porter. The porter will also get you a cart that you will need to take your luggage through customs.

After checking in with your airline, you clear U.S. Customs, then turn over your luggage, and proceed upstairs to the waiting lounge for your flight. There is a restaurant, bar, and gift shop in the lounge.

AROUND THE ISLAND

Nassau International Airport is in the northwest section of New Providence, which is a roughly oval-shaped island laid out west to east. Most visitors staying on the island, or transferring to the Out Islands, arrive here. You drive north out of the airport, then have a choice to turn right (east) toward Cable Beach and downtown, or left (west) to Love Beach, Old Fort Bay, and Lyford Cay. Most people hang a right.

The drive along West Bay Street gives you a pleasing view of the blue-green water inside the reef. Ten minutes later you hit the beginning of Cable Beach. Sandals

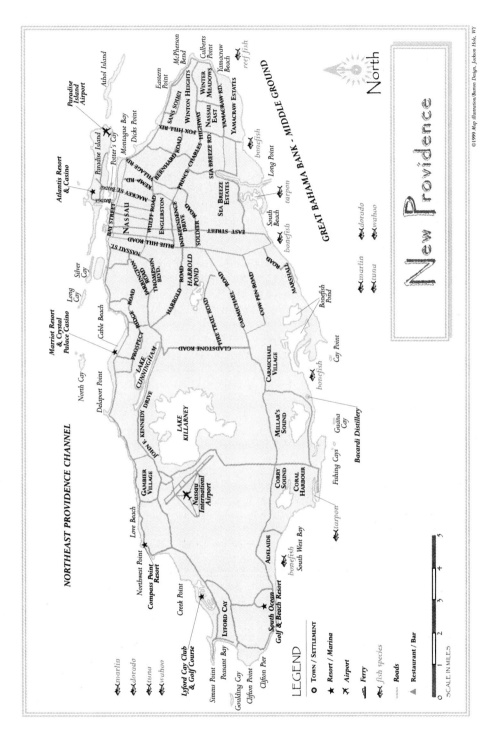

New Providence

Royal Bahamian Resort and Spa is the first major hotel, and has been opulently reno-vated since changing ownership from Le Meridien. This is an all-inclusive couples-only deluxe facility that includes an outstanding health club and spa.

Down the road a short piece is the Radisson Cable Beach Casino and Golf Re-sort. Completely renovated, the pool and beach areas are an outdoor playground. Guests receive special rates at the Cable Beach Golf Club, and tennis enthusiasts have eighteen courts to choose from. An underground walkway and mall connects to the Marriott Crystal Palace.

The Crystal Palace is one of the most garish-looking structures you'll ever see, with five gaudy towers dominating the skyline. The hotel features the second largest casino on the island, a number of good restaurants, nice pool and beach area, and a top health club.

Next is the Nassau Beach Hotel, which has undergone extensive remodeling, in-cluding much needed room improvements. Located in the middle of the action, the hotel manages to retain a low-key feeling while offering plenty of amenities.

Breezes Bahamas is next door. This SuperClub resort is an all-inclusive facility for couples and singles, and is more moderately priced than Sandals. If you want non-stop action, this is the place. If you want a quiet relaxing vacation, do not book here.

Continuing east, West Bay Street winds along the shoreline. In fifteen minutes you reach the edge of downtown, which is noticeable due to the increased traffic and McDonald's. The renovated British Colonial Beach Resort is on the northwest corner of where West Bay Street becomes Bay Street. Traffic continuing east must divert to Shirley Street, as Bay Street is one-way heading west. Driving in this area is a night-mare, so we suggest taking a taxi or a public bus, then setting out on foot.

Bay Street is the shopping mecca of the Caribbean. Prince George Wharf, the cruise ship headquarters, the Straw Market, and Rawson Square, merge in a hive of big city bedlam. A dozen blocks later traffic is still congested, but a semblance of or-der returns as you reach the new and old bridges to and from Paradise Island. The new bridge is first, and it is one-way going onto the island. The old bridge is one-way com-ing back to Nassau.

Paradise Island is its own universe that spins around the star of Atlantis. Club Med is tucked away in a twenty-one-acre compound on the southwestern side of the island. You can't miss the massive Atlantis compound if you just keep going straight after clearing the new bridge tollgate. Kim suggests driving over at night, as Atlantis is an epic sight when it's all lit up.

Atlantis is broken up into three sections: the Beach Tower, Coral Towers, and the new Royal Towers. You need to know which section of the hotel you're staying in, and check in there, or you will be walking and walking and walking to reach your room.

It's fair to say that as a beach resort, Atlantis has it all. The complex of pools, streams, water slides, lagoons, and beaches is the most amazing on the planet.

The same goes for the new marina, with full dock facilities and services for more than sixty yachts up to two hundred twenty feet in length. Full services here mean concierge and other guest services that are equal to those of the hotel.

Overshadowed by its neighbor, the Sheraton Grand Hotel has been renovated from the lobby to the enormous penthouse, which goes for $5,000 per night. This was briefly the most outrageously opulent suite on the island, but the new Atlantis Bridge Suite tops it, at $25,000 per night.

The Sheraton features nice guestrooms, a pretty beach, pool area, and a water-sports activity center that rivals those on Cable Beach.

Farther down Paradise Island Drive is the Ocean Club Golf and Tennis Resort. This is the most elegant and sophisticated hotel on the island, with manicured grounds featuring fountained courtyards and quiet gardens. When you're lounging around the peaceful pool area it's hard to believe Atlantis is a five-minute drive away. The beach offers the same remote luxurious feeling. Large guestrooms include private verandas, tasteful Caribbean furnishings, and posh marble bathrooms. If you're trying to bribe someone into going on a fishing trip, a stay here before or after should do the trick. The Ocean Club's eighteen-hole golf course and nine tennis courts complete the exclusive country club atmosphere.

The Paradise Island Airport is at the east end of the island. Flights from Florida arrive and depart daily. If you're staying at one of the resorts on the island, flying here will save you from making the long traffic-congested drive from the international airport. However, if you are continuing on to the Out Islands, you will have to drive to the domestic terminal, anyway.

For boaters cruising into New Providence from the north and northwest, the hotels of Cable Beach and the Coral World tower are obvious landmarks, but this is an extremely confusing area, and should be navigated during the day using considerable caution. As this is the entrance for cruise ships into Nassau Harbour, remember that size matters. In general, this is a very busy harbor, and all vessels are required to seek clearance with the harbor control when entering, leaving, or changing position. VHS channel 16 is the best method of communication.

Recent changes in the harbor include the new Paradise Island Bridge, west of the old bridge, and the new Atlantis marina. The marina entrance is to the north just before you reach the new bridge. In addition to all the services available at Atlantis, the marina provides complete protection from wind and tides.

After passing under both bridges and rounding the east end of Potter's Cay, you reach Nassau Yacht Haven, with full services and space for up to one hundred boats.

Across the harbor on Paradise Island is Hurricane Hole Marina. Full services are available for boaters, including a good restaurant for lunch, and walking access to a number of shops, or to the Atlantis complex.

Back on the Nassau side, the Bayshore Marina is east of Yacht Haven. One hundred fifty slips are available in this modern marina. Continuing east, the Nassau Harbour Club Hotel and Marina, and the Harbour View marina provide still more services and accommodations to boaters and vacationers.

At the eastern end of Nassau Harbour is Montagu Bay, which is sheltered by Paradise and Athol islands. Boaters cruising to and from Spanish Wells and the Exumas most often use this route. South of the bay is East Point, which is guarded by several reefs and numerous coral heads, which all produce good fishing for snappers, jacks, grouper, mackerel, and amberjack.

The south shore of New Providence is relatively undeveloped. From Port New Providence to Coral Harbour

A barracuda taken near East Point.

Brian O'Keefe

are some nice beaches, and the only flats on the island. These flats can be waded on the incoming tide, but your timing has to be just right, as the shallow areas flood quickly. Fishing a neap tide is your best bet. These flats are rarely fished, and the bonefish average five pounds. Fishing these flats is more productive from a boat, but we don't know of any flats guides living on New Providence.

Around Cay Point are more flats, but access from shore is difficult. The Bonefish Pond, aptly named, is in the lee of Cay Point, and it stretches west toward the entrance to Millars Sound. This is all good bonefish habitat with hard coral bottoms, and plentiful blue crabs, but the numbers of fish are sparse. The Bacardi distillery is nearby on the road leading to Coral Harbour.

The harbor itself is the base for the Bahamian Defense Force. The residential development is a quiet, luxury community set amidst palm trees and winding man-made canals. The canals provide sea access for the homeowners, and we have heard reports that tarpon can be found here. One angler told us he jumped six tarpon in a morning of blind fishing through the canal system.

West of Coral Harbour is the small village of Adelaide, one of the first black settlements established after the abolition of slavery. This whole South West Bay area is a quiet serene surprise. The locals tell us bonefish tail regularly throughout this area. Locals catch many of these fish on hand-line rigs with eighty-pound test and live crabs. One commercial fisherman showed us a picture of a fish that had to go fifteen pounds.

Just west of Adelaide is the South Ocean Golf and Beach Resort. This pleasant out-of-the-way resort has a colonial plantation feel, with bright comfortable rooms in the main section, and more elegant accommodations across the road on the beach. The eighteen-hole golf course is the best on the island. Tennis facilities, a dive center, two restaurants, and accompanying bars make this a complete destination.

At the west end of the island is Clifton Point, Pleasant Bay, then exclusive Lyford Cay, which is a private residential community that features a golf course, luxury guest accommodations, and a beautiful marina.

Turning the corner past Lyford you're on West Bay Street again, and a short drive from Chris Blackwell's Compass Point Resort. The small colorful facility is an Island Outpost classic, featuring Junkanoo decorations and rooms complete with fax machines and CD players. This is a great resort for those who want to be away from bustling Paradise Island and Cable Beach. Adjacent Love Beach offers some of the best snorkeling on the island.

FISHING HIGHLIGHTS

Okay, so we have to admit having never fished out of New Providence. With such great fishing in the Out Islands, and with Andros so close, it has just never made sense to wet a line here.

Several Andros guides do fish around New Providence, however. On a calm day, the trip from Fresh Creek takes less than an hour in a Maverick flats boat. Our Andros guides are in the process of training a couple of New Providence commercial fishermen to take fly fishers to the south shore flats. A trip to these flats would ideally be a half day focused on fishing the incoming tide. A full day trip could include some reef fishing, or exploring the canals for tarpon.

The unique thing about the Nassau fishery is that bonefish are not the primary species. Offshore is the draw, with the Northeast Providence Channel and the Tongue of the Ocean drop-offs minutes from the island.

Full- and half-day charter boats are available out of Nassau Harbour. Prices range from $300 for a half day to $750 and up for a full day. The major resort hotels have concierge desks that can book you a boat, or you can call the Nassau Yacht Haven directly.

White marlin and sailfish move into the Tongue of the Ocean in numbers in late March and April. Blue marlin turn up a little later, with May through July being prime.

Allison tuna are in these waters year round, with March through July the best months for fishing. From the Andros side of the Tongue we've had our best tuna fishing in May. With an average size here of about fifty pounds, these tuna can tear you up. Plus, they are ideal fly rod targets when they're crashing bait on the surface. A 10-weight rod is the minimum needed to do battle with these fireballs. Our favorite flies include Abel Anchovies, WBA Mullets, and Black Sardinas.

Dorado tend to run with the tuna, with the highest concentrations of fish occurring April through June, though October and

Brian O'Keefe

Fishing the incoming tide will yield the best results.

November can be really good, too. Average fish run about twenty pounds, but we've caught fish over fifty pounds in May on the Andros side of the Tongue. A 10-weight fly rod is the way to go. Best flies include WBA Mullets and Offshore Deceivers.

The best winter sport is for wahoo. November through April is the range, with January and February producing the highest numbers of fish. It is common to hook more than twenty fish a day during the prime months. Wahoo readily hit flies, but you need to have a good teasing partner to make this work. You also need at least 40-pound wire shock tippet.

Our favorite reef species here is amberjack. These brutes concentrate around the reefs and wrecks from March through the summer months. Fishing with conventional gear is the surest way to hook fish, but using chum will produce action on flies. Chum will also bring up everything else around the reef, including sharks, jacks, snappers, and grouper. You can't beat this kind of fishing if you want good variety and a lot of action.

While the offshore and reef fishing can be excellent off New Providence, this is not the fishing reason to travel to the Bahamas. Andros Island is a ten-minute flight away, and less than an hour by boat. Even if you're on a nonfishing vacation, Andros will tug at your fishing soul while you lie on the beach or cruise through one of the casinos. It's so close, so how can you resist?

Stephen latches into a big bone; if it makes it into the corral, his leader could be history.

OPTIONAL ACTIVITIES

Atlantis is its own center of activities. There is enough to do here for days without leaving, which is exactly as Sun International planned it. Beach and watersports aficionados can go berserk. The only drawback to sun worshippers is a winter cold front. These can come through anytime from December through February. We recommend a visit to Atlantis to see the saltwater aquarium. Plan on at least two hours, and you might as well have lunch as you wander through the massive property.

Gambling is a major draw for Nassau. The casino scene at Atlantis ranks with any Las Vegas facility. Marriott's Crystal Palace isn't shabby, either. Both hotels have sports book betting and cabaret-style shows.

Atlantis, Sandals, and the Crystal Palace have the best resort fitness clubs and spas. The Palace Spa is also open to the public, and has the most extensive exercise facilities. Massages are available in all the better hotels.

In general, the major resorts have good concierge desks where you can book any type of island activity you choose, including guided tours.

There are a number of island tours available. Many begin at downtown Parliament Square, which is the traditional center of the Bahamian government. The pastel buildings were erected in the early 1800s by Loyalists, and include the Houses of Parliament, the old Colonial Secretary's Office, and the Supreme Court.

Rawson Square, the Pompey Museum, the Junkanoo Expo, Bay Street, the Straw Market, the British Colonial Hotel, and Arawak Cay are often included in tours of this nature.

The Pompey Museum of Slavery and Emancipation was used as an auction house for slaves during the eighteenth century. Now this government-funded museum displays the history and lifestyles of African Bahamians from the slave-trading days to postemancipation. There is also a fine collection of the island's contemporary art.

The Junkanoo Museum is a celebration of the Bahamas national carnival spirit. This is a fun lively place featuring colorful, intricately designed costumes and masks. Be prepared to learn the Junkanoo dance before you leave.

The mini-tour of the Bacardi and Company rum distillery includes sampling various rum products. If you like making your own mai-tais or goombay smashes, we suggest taking home some coconut rum.

For some history about pirating days, take the tours of Fort Charlotte, built in 1789 by Lord Dunmore and named in honor of the wife of King George III. The fort features a commanding view over Nassau, and was meant to guard the western entrance of the harbor. This is a full-service fort, with moat, drawbridge, ramparts, and dungeons. Also don't miss Fort Montagu on East Bay Street, which is the oldest of the surviving forts. It overlooks the eastern entrance to the harbor and was built in 1741 in anticipation of a Spanish attack that never materialized.

A number of tours are available to nearby cays and islands. The forty-four-foot powerboat *Midnight Express* heads to the Exuma Cays for snorkeling, barbecuing, stingray and shark feeding, plus beach activities. On a calm day the water crossing is spectacular.

An excursion to nearby Rose Island is one of the best beach-oriented day trips. The long beach has plenty of room for relaxation and privacy, and you can take a fly rod along to fish for jacks and snappers along the reefs. Snorkeling, fish feeding, sea kayaking, beach volleyball, and a great lunch are featured activities.

Many diving and snorkeling trips are available to various cays, reefs, wrecks, and blue holes, and dolphin encounters are also available.

If you're interested in the conservation movement in the Bahamas, we recommend a visit to the Retreat, which is headquarters for the Bahamas National Trust. The Retreat is an eleven-acre property with beautiful gardens and an extensive collection of palm trees. You can become a member or make a donation if you wish.

LODGING AND SERVICES

FEATURED LODGES AND ACCOMMODATIONS

Atlantis Resort Casino & Marina

Paradise Island   The completion of the new Royal Towers section of the hotel now gives this resort more than 2,000 guest rooms. The Coral Towers section includes the Reef Club, which is a VIP section of luxurious rooms with private concierge service. This section also contains over 61-bedroom suites in villas facing the beach and one of the pool areas. The Beach Tower is the original section of the hotel, but it was renovated to fit in with the luxury surrounding it.

The new inner harbor marina is one of the most luxurious on the seven seas. Marina guests are entitled to full hotel privileges, which include: acres of swimming pools and water slides; snorkeling lagoons and beaches; over 30 restaurants and bars; the Entertainment Complex, with its 50,000-square-foot casino; a full-service resort spa featuring indoor/outdoor beauty treatments and a state-of-the-art workout facility; and championship golf and tennis located nearby.

Season: Year round.

Optional Activities: Indulge in all the resort amenities, or have one of the concierge desks book an outside excursion like offshore fishing, diving, golf, or island tours.

What's Included: Complete vacation packages are available including air, accommodations, and meals.

Not Included: Airfare to/from Nassau International Airport, or Paradise Island Airport, airport transfers, meals, and any optional activities you choose. It is at least a 30-minute taxi ride from Nassau International Airport to the resort, longer if there is traffic. The cost is $25.

Pricing: $$$–$$$$

Contact: Reservations and information, 800/321-3000, fax 242/363-3524. Marina: 800/ATLANTIS or 242/363-6068.

Internet: www.sunint.com/atlantis

The Ocean Club Golf and Tennis Resort

Paradise Island   If you're looking for pampered elegance and privacy just minutes from Nassau and Atlantis, this is the place for you. This 59-room world-class hotel is the best choice on New Providence for the discriminating traveler. Now operated by Sun International, the service and luxury offered here are better than ever. Dining in the Courtyard Terrace is superb and perhaps the most romantic dinner spot on the island. The adjacent golf course and tennis courts highlighted by dramatic beaches and seascapes make this location its own little paradise.

Season: Year round.

Optional Activities: You can take advantage of the amenities at Atlantis, or have the concierges book an outside excursion like offshore fishing, diving, golf, or island tours.

What's Included: Complete vacation packages are available including air, accommodations, and meals.

Not Included: Airfare to/from Nassau International Airport, or Paradise Island Airport, airport transfers, meals, and any optional activities you choose.

Pricing: $$$$

Contact: Reservations and information, 800/321-3000 or 242/363-2501, fax 242/363-2424.

Radisson Cable Beach Casino & Golf Resort

Cable Beach   This high-rise mega-resort is conveniently located only 10 minutes from the international airport on a white sand beach. The resort features 700 air-conditioned rooms, 6 restaurants, numerous bars, a huge swimming pool area, an 18-hole golf course, health club, eighteen tennis courts, racquetball, shopping, meeting rooms, and is adjacent to the Marriott Crystal Palace casino. You can walk through an underground shopping arcade right into the Crystal Palace.

Season: Year round.

Optional Activities: Golf, tennis, snorkeling, diving, offshore fishing, gambling, watersports, great dining or island tours. You might even want to relax and do nothing.

What's Included: Complete vacation packages are available including meals, accommodations, drinks, activities, golf course fees, taxes and gratuities.

Not Included: Airfare to/from Nassau International Airport, airport transfers ($12 one-way), meals, and any optional activities you choose.

Pricing: $$$

Contact: Reservations and information, 800/333-3333 or 242/327-6000, fax 242/327-6987.

British Colonial Beach Resort

Downtown, Bay Street   This old hotel has been renovated and enlarged, and is now a luxurious resort with a new marina. The Bay Street location, 20 minutes from the international airport, is in the middle of everything. You can walk out of the hotel and start shopping until your credit card melts. Many of the island's best restaurants are 5 minutes away. Over 200 air-conditioned rooms and luxury condominiums are available. Amenities include a swimming pool, beach, watersports, 3 tennis courts, a business center, and marina.

Season: Year round.

Optional Activities: Golf, tennis, snorkeling, diving, offshore fishing, gambling, watersports, great dining, shopping or island tours.

What's Included: Packages are available, though most people just book a room and then do everything else on their own.

Not Included: Airfare to/from Nassau International Airport, airport transfers, meals, and any optional activities you choose.

Pricing: $$$
Contact: Reservations and information, 242/322-3301, fax 242/322-2286.

Compass Point

Western New Providence   This Island Outpost resort is one of the most colorful in the Bahamas, literally. Painted in brilliant Junkanoo colors, the 21 cottages and cabanas are only steps from the white sand beach. Each room features island furnishings covered in handmade batik, private sundecks, coffemaker, fax machine, CD player, and an array of bathroom amenities. Some rooms include a kitchenette and VCR. Love Beach, which is great for snorkeling, is just a short walk down the sand. Additional amenities include a fine restaurant, tennis court, swimming pool, and dive shop. Blue-water fishing can be arranged. The resort is just a 5-minute taxi ride from the airport, so if you have a daytime layover this is a perfect spot for lunch.
Season: Year round.
Optional Activities: Golf, tennis, snorkeling, diving, offshore fishing, gambling, watersports, great dining, shopping, and island tours.
What's Included: Packages with meals are available. Most people book optional activities on their own.
Not Included: Airfare to/from Nassau International Airport, airport transfers, and any optional activities you choose.
Pricing: $$$–$$$$
Contact: Reservations and information, 800/688-7678 or 242/327-4500, fax 242/327-3299.

ADDITIONAL ACCOMMODATIONS

Sandals Royal Bahamian Resort & Spa

Cable Beach   Luxury all-inclusive couples retreat. Large opulent air-conditioned rooms, tons of food, rum drinks galore, and plenty of activities to work it all off. The health club and fitness center is the best on the island, and is only available to guests. Four hundred rooms, 2 swimming pool areas, private beach, 6 restaurants, a dance club, and pampering service. Two-night minimum stay.
Pricing: $$$$
Contact: Reservations and information, 800/726-3257 or 242/327-6400, fax 242/327-1894.

Breezes

Cable Beach   A SuperClubs all-inclusive resort. Families are welcome here. Four hundred air-conditioned rooms, lots of restaurants and bars, 5 swimming pools, 3 tennis courts, and a complete beach sports center.
Pricing: $$$
Contact: Reservations and information, 800/859-7873 or 242/327-5356, fax 242/327-5155.

Marriott Resort & Crystal Palace Casino

Cable Beach   Five gaudy purple and magenta towers make up this huge resort and casino, located between the Radisson and the Nassau Beach Hotel. Most of the 1,000 rooms, suites, and supersuites overlook the ocean. The supersuites are located on special Crystal Club floors, with individual concierge service. The health club features daily aerobics classes. The casino is the center of activity, with 12 surrounding restaurants and a shopping arcade. The massive pool area is on the beach, and the pool staff runs a complete water sports program. The concierge staff can arrange any activity on the island.
Pricing: $$$
Contact: Reservations and information, 800/222-7466 or 242/327-6200, fax 242/327-6308.

Nassau Beach Hotel

Cable Beach   This 400-room hotel has been partially remodeled, with additional renovations continuing. This is our favorite place to stay on Cable Beach because it's more low key than its glitzy neighbors, yet you can walk to those hotels in minutes. The swimming pool area is very nice, and adjacent to the beach. The beach bar is a great place for early evening drinks. Johnny Canoe's restaurant is a fun casual place to eat.

Pricing: $$–$$$
Contact: Reservations and information, 888/627-7282 or 242/327-7711, fax 242/327-7599.

Graycliff

This small, elegant hotel was converted from a colonial mansion, and the restaurant is our favorite in Nassau. Fourteen rooms and suites are individually furnished and include all modern conveniences. Amenities include a swimming pool, sauna, and small health club.
Pricing: $$$–$$$$
Contact: Reservations and information, 800/633-7411 or 242/322-2796, fax 242/326-6610.

South Ocean Golf & Beach Resort

Almost 300 air-conditioned rooms set in a colonial plantation-style resort. The eighteen-hole golf course is said to be the best in the Bahamas. A nice beach, 2 swimming pools, 4 tennis courts, 2 restaurants, several bars, and a complete dive shop complete the amenities. Located about 30 minutes from downtown and 10 minutes from the international airport.
Pricing: $$$
Contact: Reservations and information, 242/362-4391, fax 242/362-4810.

SERVICES

Diving and Snorkeling: A number of operations offer full services, including rental equipment and PADI certification programs. We suggest booking diving and snorkeling trips through your resort or hotel.

Out of the Radisson Hotel, Dive Dive Dive, Ltd teaches beginners in the pool, and then takes you to a variety of sites around the island. Contact: 242/362-1143.

Bahama Divers Ltd will pick you up at your hotel for PADI certification or any variety of diving options. Contact: 242/393-1466.

Diver's Haven is recommended by a number of our clients as a great overall operation for beginners through adventurous experts, plus they arrange dives to the Out Islands. They also teach beginner courses at several of the hotels. Contact: 242/393-0869.

Car Rentals: All the major agencies—Hertz, Avis, National, Dollar and others—have Nassau offices, and many have offices in the major resort hotels. We recommend booking a car rental ahead of time, though you do not need a car unless you really want to drive around the island. Traffic can be a nightmare. Taxi service and bus service is very good.

Restaurants: We've mentioned a number of good restaurants. A separate book could be written on this topic so we'll just give you our favorites here.

Graycliff is our overall favorite for a special dining experience. The atmosphere, service, food, cigars, wine and cognacs are all world class. Jackets usually required, but they sometimes make an exception.

Buena Vista and The Sun and . . . are in the same league with Graycliff, and you could make a case for them being just as good, or some would say better. Jackets required.

Johnny Canoe's is our favorite casual place to eat in the Cable Beach area, though there are so many restaurants tucked away in the hotels that you're bound to find something you like.

On Paradise Island there are many good restaurants, mostly in or around the Atlantis complex. The Bahamian Club steakhouse serves superior beef plus fresh seafood in an elegant club atmosphere. Resort evening attire required. The Five Twins provides a superior Asian dining experience in an elegant atmosphere. Jackets optional. Mama Loo's offers good Asian food with a Caribbean flair served in a tropical setting. Resort evening attire required. The Water's Edge serves a nice variety of Italian, French, Greek and Spanish cuisine. Resort evening attire for dinner.

The Courtyard Terrace at the Ocean Club is another favorite dinner spot on Paradise Island. Dine under the stars while listening to soft calypso music. This is a very romantic setting, with superb continental cuisine combined with a distinctive island touch and superior service. Jackets required. Reservations are mandatory.

Guide to Attire: Casual attire means just about anything goes, including shorts, T-shirts, jeans, sundresses, and similar apparel. Bathing suit cover-ups are required.

Resort casual attire means nice T-shirts or polo shirts, dress shorts, slacks or jeans, sundresses or skirts, and similar apparel.

Resort evening attire means polo or button-down shirts, slacks, sundresses or skirts, and similar apparel.

Jackets optional means no shorts, jeans, or T-shirts.

Jackets required means just that with no shorts, T-shirts, jeans, or tennis/athletic shoes. Most of the best restaurants are serious about this attire business, and will not let you in no matter how much you protest, or how much money you offer them.

Golf: Cable Beach Golf Club, Paradise Island Golf Club, and South Ocean Beach & Golf Resort are open to the public. You should always call ahead to reserve a tee time. You can call these clubs directly, or your hotel can make the reservations for you.

Tennis: The Nassau Cable Beach Hotel, the Radisson Grand Resort on Paradise Island, and the Atlantis resort rent their courts to the general public, otherwise you need to be a guest of the hotels with tennis facilities.

Exuma Powerboat Adventures: Full day trips to the Exuma Cays for nature walks, picnics and snorkeling. Contact: 242/327-5385.

Seaplane Safaris: Take a float plane to the Exuma Cays, including the Exuma Land and Sea Park, for hiking, beachcombing, picnicking, and snorkeling. Contact: 242/393-2522.

Shopping: Bay Street is the place. Start at the British Colonial Beach Resort and head east. You'll find just about every name brand store you can think of, plus the massive Nassau Straw Market. Don't get lost. Shops are open Monday through Saturday from 9:00 A.M. to 5:00 or 6:00 P.M. Shops are allowed to be open on Sunday, but few take advantage of this opportunity.

Additional special interest tours and activities can be arranged through your hotel. Every major hotel has a concierge desk with hundreds of brochures describing the available activities.

Banks: Nassau is a major financial capital, so a variety of banks are open Monday through Thursday 9:30 A.M. to 3:00 P.M., and until 5:00 P.M. on Friday. ATMs are available.

Princess Margaret Hospital is a major medical facility operated by the government. Doctors Hospital is privately owned. Both are on Shirley Street.

Bahamas Ministry of Tourism is located on Bay Street. You can contact the Tourism Help Line at 242/325-4357.

NEW DEVELOPMENTS

Things are hopping in Nassau. Private development of homes and luxury condos is booming across the island. The new tower and marina is now completed at Atlantis, but who knows how long Sun International will be content with this?

Two bridges now connect New Providence to Paradise Island, and constant development is going on in Nassau Harbour.

We've been talking with some people about offering half-day bonefishing trips to flats along the south shore of the island, but nothing concrete has been established. We are booking more and more people on day trips to Andros Island. Anglers take an early morning flight to Andros, are met by an independent guide, taken out for a day of bonefishing, then returned to the airport for the flight back to Nassau. For anglers with a little more time, we are arranging two days of fishing with one night accommodations at Point of View Villas. POV is also offering its own charter flights for guests staying on Andros who want to go shopping in Nassau for the day.

If these day trips to Andros are of interest, call 800/922-3474 for more information. Log on to our Web site at www.bahamasflyflishingguide.com for updated information.

10

Exuma Cays, Great Exuma, and Little Exuma

The Exuma Cays begin in the north with Beacon Cay, a little more than thirty miles southeast of Nassau. This exquisite string of cays then traverses glass clear tropical waters colored vivid blues and greens for over ninety miles to Great Exuma, Little Exuma and, finally, Hog Cay. The cays come in varying shapes and sizes, some with wavy green hills, trees, and thick vegetation, and others that are low, flat, and bare.

These cays compose the centerpiece of Exuma's claim to the title of "the sailing capital of the world." Boaters can find countless anchorages and harbors that are gorgeous, stunning, mesmerizingly beautiful—just pick your favorite adjective. Like the offshore cays of Abaco, there is a feeling here you want to keep with you always: It is peace and serenity and wonder.

That feeling is reflected in the people, though settlements are few and well spread out until you reach Great Exuma. Just over 3,600 people live on this strand of emerald islands sandwiched between the Tongue of the Ocean and Exuma Sound and fed by the Great Bahama Bank.

American Loyalists who wanted to remain true to the British king after the American Revolutionary War settled the Exumas in 1783. These people reconstructed their former way of life in the Exumas, complete with cotton plantations, farms, and slaves.

Lord John Rolle was a preeminent landowner and one of the most powerful Loyalists. He imported the first cotton seeds to the islands, and owned more than three hundred slaves. In 1835 Rolle freed his slaves and ultimately bequeathed to them more than 2,000 acres of Crown land along with his name. This land has been passed down through the generations, and we understand the land can never be sold outside the Rolle clan.

British traditions and lifestyles have remained strong through the years, with the original Club Peace & Plenty in George Town being a favorite vacation spot for the Royals. After landing at George Town Airport on Great Exuma, known locally as Moss Town, it's more than likely your taxi driver will have a British accent.

The Exumas are a breathtaking sight from the air. Flying to Long Island or Crooked Island, you are rewarded with a view of deserted coves, white sand beaches,

The view from Stocking Island, in Exuma.

flats that stretch for miles, and dark coral heads swaying beneath crystal blue water. Parachuting has crossed our minds more than once.

The locals like to say there are 365 cays, one for each day of the year. Many of our boating friends agree that there are at least that many. Diving and snorkeling doesn't get any better, and fishing is almost too easy at times.

The showcase of the cays is the Exuma National Land and Sea Park administered by the Bahamas National Trust. The park boundaries run from Wax Cay Cut in the north to Conch Cut in the south, an area about twenty-two miles long and eight miles wide. The park is home to the Bahamian iguana and mockingbird, terns, and numerous other seabirds. Many of the smaller cays only poke their sand above water at low tide.

Fishing is a way of life throughout these remote cays. People take from the sea what they need to live. On Great and Little Exuma farming and tourism combine with fishing to create the local economy. Most fruits and vegetables are brought in to these islands, and in the more remote areas supplies can often run low. Boaters should be aware of this and stock up accordingly.

George Town is the administrative center of the Exumas, and a thriving settlement with one of the best straw markets in the Out Islands. Elizabeth Harbour is a premiere anchorage and when combined with nearby Stocking Island anchorages, provides haven for up to six hundred boats during Regatta time.

Club Peace & Plenty is a tradition in George Town. This venerable waterfront hotel, which has been completely renovated, is a center of activity and the ferry headquarters for visitors going to Stocking Island. Joined by the Beach Inn and the new Bonefish Lodge, the Peace & Plenty family of accommodations and restaurants is the heart of land-based tourism to Great Exuma.

With the main highway completely resurfaced throughout Little and Great Exuma, exploring the islands by land is almost as easy as it is by water. Prime bonefish flats lie on both sides of the islands, and are accessible in many areas. There are a num-

Peace and Plenty Beach Inn on Exuma.

ber of houses for rent on secluded beaches for people who prefer to do things on their own. If you pick the right house, you can catch bonefish in your front yard, and snorkel over nearby reefs.

American Eagle flies nonstop daily from Miami to George Town. Lynx Air, Air Sunshine, and Island Express fly into George Town from Ft. Lauderdale and other Florida airports. Bahamasair has daily service from Nassau. If you have four to six people in your party, a private charter from Ft. Lauderdale or Nassau becomes economical, and is definitely more convenient.

We are not big fans of the Miami airport, so if we can avoid it, we do. We highly recommend Exuma for couples and for nonanglers, especially if you stay at one of the Peace & Plenty properties. Kim recommends flying to Nassau, then spending a night or two at Cable Beach or on Paradise Island, before heading on to George Town. This will make your trip more relaxed. Flying home in one day is no problem, as the time zones are in your favor going west.

AROUND THE ISLAND

Boaters leaving Nassau Harbour usually head for Allan's Cays and Leaf Cay as their first stop. There are several good anchorages and a variety of flats. We prefer the flats on the northwestern side of Leaf Cay. Bonefish feed here consistently on the incoming tide, plus they work their way through the cut between the cays at varying stages of the tide. Wading is fairly easy through this area, though you cannot cross the channel from Leaf Cay to Southwest Allan's Cay.

Leaf and Southwest Allan's Cays have pretty white sand beaches and nice cove areas for snorkeling. Both also have good populations of curious iguanas. If you decide to catch some rays on one of the beaches, you will draw some company.

Continuing southeast, Highbourn Cay is a popular spot for sailors. A thirty-berth marina offers fuel, water, and telephones. Our boating friends tell us you need to call ahead for reservations during popular sailing months. A nearby grocery stocks food and supplies. Rental houses are available on the cay, and the eastern beaches are right out of a fairy tale.

South of Highbourn are many small cays and rocks, then Long Cay and Norman Cay. To the west of Norman Cay is a huge sandbank that goes dry during low tides. This is an outstanding wadable flat during the last of the falling and first of the incoming tides. Bonefish move in here from the deeper surrounding water, and the visibility is very good. A Gotcha or a small Yarn Crab will catch these fish consistently.

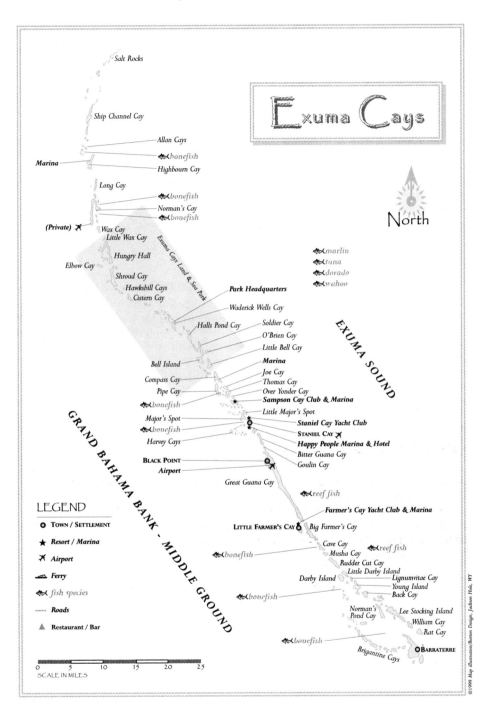

Exuma Cays

Salt Rocks

Ship Channel Cay

Allan Cays
bonefish
Marina
Highbourn Cay

Long Cay
bonefish
Norman's Cay
bonefish
(Private) Wax Cay
Little Wax Cay

Elbow Cay
Hungry Hall
Shroud Cay
Hawksbill Cays
Cistern Cay

Exuma Cays Land & Sea Park

Park Headquarters
Waderick Wells Cay
Halls Pond Cay   Soldier Cay
O'Brien Cay
Little Bell Cay
Bell Island   Marina
Joe Cay
Compass Cay   Thomas Cay
Pipe Cay   Over Yonder Cay
bonefish   Sampson Cay Club & Marina
Little Major's Spot
Major's Spot   Staniel Cay Yacht Club
bonefish   STANIEL CAY
Harvey Cays   Happy People Marina & Hotel
Bitter Guana Cay
BLACK POINT   Goulin Cay
Airport
Great Guana Cay
reef fish
Farmer's Cay Yacht Club & Marina
LITTLE FARMER'S CAY   Big Farmer's Cay
Cave Cay
bonefish   Musha Cay   reef fish
Rudder Cut Cay
Little Darby Island
Darby Island   Lignumvitae Cay
Young Island
bonefish   Back Cay
Norman's   Lee Stocking Island
Pond Cay   William Cay
Rat Cay
bonefish
Brigantine Cays   BARRATERRE

marlin
tuna
dorado
wahoo

EXUMA SOUND

North

GRAND BAHAMA BANK - MIDDLE GROUND

LEGEND
○ TOWN / SETTLEMENT
★ Resort / Marina
✈ Airport
Ferry
fish species
Roads
▲ Restaurant / Bar

0   5   10   15   20   25
SCALE IN MILES

©1999 Map illustration/Burton Design, Jackson Hole, WY

Kim fishes a flat in Exuma.

Norman's Cay is V-shaped, with the largest land mass at the southwestern edge of the inverted V. A number of private homes are located north of the private airstrip. Boaters approach the inner anchorages from both sides. The best bonefishing flats are on the Exuma Sound side, and though there are some good wading spots, a dinghy can get you into fish more consistently.

The northern boundary of the Exuma Cays Land and Sea Park begins in the center of Wax Cay Cut. To the south, Shroud Cay is a maze of mangroves and creeks that create perfect habitat for a variety of seabirds. Next is Hawksbill Cay, a deserted cay with many pristine beaches on its western shoreline. Park volunteers have cleared trails that lead to Loyalist plantation ruins.

Warderick Wells Cay is the headquarters for the park warden, and a small staff of volunteers. Several members of the Bahamian Defense Force are also stationed here to help enforce the strict park conservation laws. It is your responsibility to know these laws. Copies of the laws, trail maps, and reference books on wildlife, coral, and plants life are available at the headquarters. We suggest you call ahead on VHS channel 16 to let the warden know you are coming.

Remember that fishing, shelling, picking plants, or any type of taking of the natural resources is prohibited in the park boundaries.

Conch Cut marks the southern end of the park, with Compass Cay next in line. Prime bonefish habitat is created by a creek and mangrove swamps that split this large cay down the middle. The Compass Cay Marina can accommodate ten boats; water and electricity are available. One of our boating friends tells us a small store opened at the end of 1998. Food supplies were good at that time, but depending on demand and the supply boat schedule, this and other stores throughout the area can be depleted.

Compass Cay also features three rental houses. A couple we met on Long Island gave the houses fine marks for being air-conditioned, clean, neat, and offering nice views. This couple also told us they enjoyed miles of hiking trails and some of the best beaches they'd ever seen. They found numerous spots for good bonefishing, including the creek adjacent to the marina.

The Pipe Cay and Pipe Creek area is composed of many small islets that form miles of shallow water flats. Exploring this region in a dinghy is the way to go. You'll be able to reach many fishable and wadable flats on varying stages of the tide.

While cruising between the cays, or in and out of the many cuts, boaters trolling lures or cut bait will have a hard time keeping some variety of fish from striking. Good tidal flows rip through most cuts, creating ambush points for jacks, snappers, barracuda, and other game fish. Fishing an intermediate sinking line with short leaders and Clouser Minnow or Deceiver patterns will produce fun action, as will casting plugs and spoons on conventional tackle.

Sampson Cay is similar to Compass Cay in that its two main landmasses are divided by creeks and mangrove mazes. The Sampson Cay Club and Marina occupies an idyllic spot with a protected harbor on the southwestern side of the island. Fuel, oil, water, ice, electricity, groceries, and liquor are available. The club also rents air-conditioned cottages on the beach. The restaurant serves delicious seafood, and reservations are a must.

Many of the cays from Allan's to Staniel are private, and you may not go ashore without an invitation. It is your responsibility to know the private cays, and to respect private property.

We've talked with many people who say this area has been "discovered." A bad part of being "discovered" has meant that garbage is not an uncommon site. Imagine walking on a deserted flat, wandering ashore on a tiny cay, and seeing a pile of garbage, or several garbage bags. We can assure you that is not a pleasant sight, and one that does not breed pleasant thoughts about the inconsiderate people, and cruise ship operators, who are responsible. If you visit these cays, please have the decency to take care of your own garbage.

Speaking of "developed," Staniel Cay is the most built-up cay in the chain, but that is a relative term. The local village has a population of less than one hundred people, and you won't find any traffic jams. Golf carts, bicycles, and your own two feet are the main modes of transportation on the three-square-mile island. The 3,030-foot airstrip is adjacent to the village, while the Happy People Marina and Hotel sprawls along the waterfront. This marina, operated by Ken Rolle, can accommodate six to eight boats, and has water, ice, electricity, and telephones. The hotel features nice rooms overlooking the water, plus a new two-bedroom apartment called the Happy Suite. The adjacent restaurant serves good local fare, including cracked conch, crawfish, grouper, chicken, and pork. Reservations are necessary for dinner, and takeout lunches are available.

Two island-style grocery stores—one painted blue and the other pink—are conveniently located in the village. Both keep a decent supply of food items, though when demand is high many products can disappear until the resupply boat arrives. Berkie Rolle's Isles General Store offers convenient access for dinghies on the creek south of the village. Basic marine supplies are available, along with LP gas, some dive equipment, food, and small boat rentals. If you're looking for fresh-baked bread, you can buy it here every morning except Sunday.

Farther into the harbor, with boating access through a dredged channel, is the recently renovated Staniel Cay Yacht Club. The new dock can accommodate up to ten boats, and offers water, ice, electricity, and telephones. The club features six refurbished air-conditioned cottages and a good restaurant and bar. The cottages are distinctively decorated and include a small refrigerator, coffeemaker, and purified water. Several of the cottages have porches that overhang the water. The porches face west, making for spectacular sunset views. Package rates including a meal plan are available. The restaurant serves fresh seafood, steaks, and pork. Thirteen-foot Boston Whalers are available for rent, as are golf carts and bicycles. Guests arriving via charter flights are met at the airport and transferred to the club. Guides can be arranged for snorkeling, sightseeing, and fishing.

The beaches around Staniel Cay are idyllic and can be accessed via land or water. We recommend that land-based visitors rent a boat and do some exploring on their own. There are countless snorkeling locations, and many wadable bonefish flats. For anglers looking to do it "on their own," this is the perfect location. Fine wadable flats surround Big Majors Spot, Little Majors Spot, and other nearby cays. If you like tail-

Brian O'Keefe

This Exuma bone fell for a Crazy Charlie.

ing fish, don't miss the incoming tide when it falls early morning or late afternoon. A Blind Gotcha or a #6 Tan Yarn Crab are our favorite flies for these situations.

Fishing in the cuts, over the reefs, and offshore is also excellent. Snappers, jacks, and barracuda are abundant in all the traditional ambush points, especially when the tide is really moving. Offshore, marlin, sailfish, wahoo, dorado, and yellowfin tuna are the highlights. A yellowfin over six hundred pounds was landed recently. We recommend taking along a crane and winch for fish this size, as opposed to your fly rod.

Staniel Cay has developed a fun atmosphere over the years. For people who spend any time here, it's easy to get to know everyone. Beach cookouts, an annual bonefish tournament, and numerous regattas are just a few of the community activities that bring people together to enjoy this beautiful location.

Boaters use Big Rock Cut to access Exuma Sound. Next stop southeast of Staniel is Bitter Guana Cay, then Great Guana Cay. Black Point settlement is located on the northwest coast of Great Guana. With over three hundred residents, this is the largest settlement in the Exuma Cays, and another good spot for adventurous anglers who want to pursue bonefish on their own. The settlement has a post office, clinic, laundromat, a couple of grocery stores, a general store, several good restaurants and bars, and a new airstrip.

The Scorpio Inn and Lorene's Café both serve good Bahamian fare at reasonable prices, and freshly baked breads are a specialty. We have spoken with several anglers who have enjoyed fishing with Simon Smith and Wentzel Rolle. They stayed in one of three air-conditioned apartments that are managed by Smith's wife, Diane, and reported the rooms to be clean and comfortable, and the fishing outstanding. While seeing bonefish consistently on every visit, they never saw another angler. These anglers also rented a Boston Whaler from the Smiths and did some exploring and fishing on their own.

Off the southern tip of Great Guana Cay are Little Farmer's Cay, Big Farmer's Cay, Little Galliot Cay, and Cave Cay. This area offers more exceptional bonefishing and reef fishing. The tidal currents are strong through Farmer's Cay Cut and Galliot Cut, concentrating bait fish and therefore, game fish. Portions of the Galliot Bank go dry during low tides, making this a prime spot for wading.

The Farmer's Cay Yacht Club and Marina is at the point of the bay on the northeast side of Little Farmer's Cay. The dock juts out from the white sand beach to accommodate up to eight boats. Fuel, water, ice, electricity, telephones, and a good restaurant and bar are available here.

A small clinic is in the settlement, which can be reached on foot from the Club, or from the town dock. Ocean Cabin, operated by Terry Bain, offers private moorings in the area. The Bain operation also includes a good restaurant, a liquor store, and a rescue and towing service. If you need a local guide, someone in the family can help. Hallan Rolle and his family are also helpful guides, plus they arrange snorkeling and diving excursions. If you want guided fishing, we've heard good things about Stanley Rolle from several clients.

There are a number of deserted white sand beaches in the area that are ideal for picnicking and snorkeling. Cave Cay is especially beautiful, with dramatic cliffs and green hills, but the island is private, and visits ashore require an invitation. You can still fish the flats around the island, which provide good wading during the lower tidal stages.

Heading south toward Great Exuma, many of the cays are private property, including Rudder Cut Cay, Darby Island, and Little Darby Island. Permission is needed to go ashore, but there are wadable flats that can be accessed by small boats and dinghies.

Bock Cay, Norman's Pond Cay, Lee Stocking Island, Williams Cay, Rat Cay, and Pigeon Cay continue the chain of cays leading to Great Exuma. To the west, Bock Cat Cay, Allen Cay, and the Brigantine Cays form a smaller chain leading to Barraterre Island. Between these cays lies a mini-sound that forms prime bonefish habitat. Sand bottoms, laced with crunchy coral and patches of turtle grass, create ideal conditions for wade fishing on an incoming tide. On a calm day you can see wakes and tails in every direction on many of these flats.

Lee Stocking Island is home to the Caribbean Marine Research Center field laboratory, where scientists study marine resource management and marine food production. This is a branch project of the National Undersea Research Program administered by the National Oceanic and Atmospheric Administration (NOAA).

The settlement dock at Barraterre is located on the eastern shore. The Fisherman's Inn, operated by Norman Lloyd, is the place to hang out here. The restaurant features conch, lobster, grouper, and snapper for dinner. Make sure to call ahead for reservations on VHS channel 16. Breakfast and lunch are also served. A boat/taxi transfer can be arranged to the George Town airport.

Southwest of Barraterre is a mini-marls region that is home to thousands of bonefish. Good wadable flats lie outside the maze of mangroves. It is essential to fish this area on the very last of the falling tide, and on the low incoming tide, as the bonefish will disappear into the mangroves the rest of the time.

Boaters continuing south to Elizabeth Harbour and George Town will do best by staying outside of the inshore cays. Those looking to explore and do some fishing will find a variety of flats from Black Cay to Steventon and Roker's Point, then from Roker's Point to the Channel Cays. There are anchorages in the lee of Black Cay, about a mile north of Rollville. The Rollville settlement has a government wharf for the mail and freight boats. The coastline of Great Exuma is rugged and dramatic in this area. From land, high bluffs present spectacular ocean views over white sand beaches and emerald cays. Kermit's restaurant and tavern is located on one of these bluffs above Rollville. Lunch and dinner are served, but we suggest calling ahead to check on the menu items available. Every few weekends Kermit's features a live band with dancing outside.

The flats in this area usually extend out from the small cays, or from sandbars linked to the main island. There are also a number of bays and coves where you can find bonefish on higher stages of the tide, though the low incoming tide is best overall. Calm weather is the key to fishing success here. When the wind blows from the east you'll need to head to the other side of the island for the best fly-fishing. Reef and cut fishing in the area is good, with jacks and snappers found over the darker coral and grass bottoms.

Steventon also has a government wharf with good anchorages for boaters. The coastline is flatter from Roker's Point to the Channel Cays, but the fishing habitat remains the same. Long stretches of white sand beaches combine with lush coconut palms to create a picturesque tropical setting. There are a number of rental houses available throughout this stretch, several on their own private beaches.

The Palms at Three Sisters Beach Resort is more of a motel and restaurant than resort, but it offers land-based anglers comfortable accommodations and good food along with a prime beachfront location to fish and explore the northern part of Great Exuma. Anglers wanting to pursue this option will need to rent either a car or boat, though renting both would be best.

We have seen several major development proposals for this region over the past few years, but none have approached reality . . . as yet. These proposals have included resort complexes with golf courses, marinas, condominiums, townhouses, and custom homes. One developer raised a significant amount of seed money by selling unbuilt townhouses, and guaranteeing people lifetime memberships in the proposed resort club. The development has been canceled, and the investors lost their money. Buyer beware is definitely the motto to go by here.

Most people traveling to Exuma specifically to fly-fish arrive by air and stay on the island. The George Town airport is really in Moss Town, about a twenty-minute drive north of George Town. With a population of more than nine hundred people, George Town is the largest settlement in the southern Bahamas.

The Coconut Cove Hotel, on the northern end of the settlement, is a charming hotel that features nine distinctive air-conditioned rooms and three deluxe suites, all with ocean views. The swimming pool and bar are on the beach. The food here is excellent, and the bar comes to life during happy hour. You can choose to be on a meal plan, but the management suggests not doing this, as there are a number of good restaurants to choose from in George Town. The hotel can arrange for boat and car rentals and for fishing guides. Our suggestion to people staying here is to rent a Boston Whaler, have the hotel pack you a lunch, then take off and explore on your own. Take your fly rod, as you'll find many deserted flats interspersed between the oceanside cays.

Next door to Coconut Cove is the Peace & Plenty Beach Inn. The Beach Inn features sixteen air-conditioned guestrooms, a freshwater swimming pool, restaurant and bar, all on a small beach. A mile farther on, in the town proper, is the Club Peace & Plenty Hotel. Built on the edge of the bay, the hotel offers thirty-two air-conditioned rooms overlooking the water and the swimming pool.

The club dock is home to the P&P ferry, which shuttles guests back and forth to Stocking Island. The dock is also a

The Peace and Plenty ferry boat, docked at Stocking Island.

dinghy tie-up for boaters eating in the restaurant or drinking in the bar. Both P&P facilities serve excellent Bahamian meals. Reservations are recommended. On many weekends the club gets in the party spirit with lively local bands and dancing under the stars.

A third Peace & Plenty facility, the Bonefish Lodge, is twenty minutes south of George Town on a waterfront point facing the ferry bridge to Little Exuma. This new eight-room facility is headquarters for the bonefishing operation, though anglers also stay at the Beach Inn. The large air-conditioned rooms all have private baths and balconies with ocean views. The upstairs clubhouse is for anglers only, and contains a bar, dining area, lounge area, satellite TV, and fly-tying area. Downstairs is a beautifully crafted bar made of polished hardwood, and a large dining room that is open to the public. The grounds are landscaped with young palms, native stone and shrubs, and a sand sunbathing area. The highlight here is the saltwater pond, open to the ocean. At night the sharks have been trained to come in for a feeding worth watching.

Bob Hyde, the director of fishing for Peace & Plenty, has spent many years working with and training the guides on Exuma, and has been instrumental in establishing a guide-training program for some of the other islands as well. Bob's fishing program puts anglers on different waters that run from north of Rollville to south of Hog Cay. Most bonefishing is done on the western or leeward side of the island, where miles of wadable flats extend out from the island and cut through turquoise channels. It's easy to become distracted by the gorgeous scenery here, which is one of the reasons we recommend Peace & Plenty for couples, and for anglers traveling with nonanglers.

Guests staying at any of the three facilities can try all the restaurants on the "dine around plan." P&P operates a beach club on Stocking Island that includes a snack bar for lunch and a couple of miles of deserted beaches to explore. A full watersports program is available, including diving, snorkeling, sailing, and windsurfing. Anglers traveling to the island on the ferry might want to take a fly rod as you can catch bonefish in several bays. When the wind is down, the surf and reef fishing on the windward side is also excellent for jacks, grouper, and snappers.

Elizabeth Harbour, between Stocking Island and George Town, is one of the best anchorages in the Caribbean, and it's the headquarters for boaters exploring the southern Bahamas. Good anchorages lie off the Club P&P dock, and off Stocking Island. Several of our boating friends tell us that it's hard to secure the better spots off Stocking Island. Boaters like it so much that they drop anchor and just don't leave. We can't say that we blame them.

There are also good anchorages in Kidd Cove that are protected by Regatta Point. The government wharf is on the northern side of the point, while Exuma Docking Services operates the only marina in George Town, located just south of Kidd Cove. There is space here for thirty to fifty boats, depending on the size of craft, though many boaters become semipermanent residents, especially during the winter. Calling ahead for dock space and space at the fueling dock is a must. Use "Sugar One" as the call name on VHF channel 16.

The marina offers full services for boaters, including fuel, water, ice, electricity, laundry, showers, marine products, liquor store, restaurant, and bar. Rental cars can also be arranged. This is the most convenient location for boaters, as you can walk right into the heart of the settlement from the dock. Sam's Place is the marina restaurant, offering tasty Bahamian dishes for lunch and dinner. Exuma Docking Services also owns a new resort three miles west of town called Mount Pleasant Suites Hotel. The hotel features twenty-four air-conditioned suites with full kitchens and a new swimming pool. It's just a short walk from your suite to the white sand beach at Hooper's Bay.

Fresh produce is available across the street in a nice open-air straw market. Denzella Rolle is the woman to see here for just about anything, from fruit and vegetables to awesome conch salad, laundry service, scooter and bike rentals, or for a rundown on what's happening around the island. If you want fresh seafood, just walk on over to Fishin Good Seafood and check out the catches of the day.

George Town fronts Elizabeth Harbour, but it is also built around what locals call "the Pond," a saltwater lake connected to the harbor by a thin neck of water. The main highway bridge passes over this link, and at high tide you need to duck when going under, even in a dinghy. The Exuma Markets, next to the highway bridge, is one of the best grocery stores in the islands. Fresh produce and meats are almost always in stock, as are nonprescription medicines. As a service to boaters, and to people renting houses on the island, Exuma Markets will hold mail and faxes for you.

Minn's Watersports, a small boat dock where you can rent or buy a Boston Whaler, and have outboard motors serviced, is on the Pond. There are several stores and shops along the road that circles the Pond. You can buy items ranging from Bahamian crafts, to books, postcards, and T-shirts. Eddie's Edgewater restaurant serves breakfast, lunch, and dinner. Our boating friends tell us the seafood is excellent, and turtle steaks are a specialty. Reservations are necessary in winter.

The Two Turtles Inn has long been a favorite spot for budget-minded anglers fishing Exuma on their own. Centrally located in the settlement, the inn features fourteen air-conditioned rooms, three with kitchenettes, satellite TV, plus a laid-back restaurant and bar. You can eat inside or out, and we suggest not missing the Friday night barbecues. The Tuesday, and sometimes Monday, seafood nights are also worth a try.

Boaters and land-based visitors will find a full array of additional services available in George Town. Pay telephones are located all around the settlement, including the telephone station just south of Exuma Docking Services marina. Small groceries, liquor stores, and hardware stores usually have decent stocks of goods. The town clinic is up the hill from Club Peace & Plenty. This is one of the better Out Island clinics, with a doctor, a dentist, and nurses working regular hours. There is also a town library that features an active book swap most often used by boaters.

South of George Town the highway follows the contours of the shoreline to Rolle Town, the Peace & Plenty Bonefish Lodge, and the bridge leading to Little Exuma. The main highway running the length of the island, has been completely resurfaced and is in good condition. There are several dirt roads on the west side of the highway that lead to the leeward flats, most notably to the Airport Flat. This flat is one of the most beautiful in the Bahamas, and one of the most-fished. The white sand bottom makes wading easy, and many people wade barefoot. There is a channel between the land and the flats that you can't cross at high tide without a boat, or without swimming. While it's true that the Peace & Plenty bonefish guides try to rotate this flat (not fish it too often), anglers fishing on their own don't follow this etiquette. If you want to fish the Airport Flat just ask any taxi driver to take you. They all know the way.

Over the past couple of years the bonefish on the Airport Flat have become seriously educated. You can catch these fish by being stealthy and making longer casts, especially on the first part of the incoming tide, but plan on seeing and spooking a lot more fish than you catch. A key to fishing this area without seeing any guides is to check the tides and go early or late. Peace & Plenty guides will not show up here before 8:30 A.M. and they won't be here after 4:00 P.M.

Little Exuma brings back the feeling of being up north in the Exuma Cays. Only three settlements, the Ferry, Forbes Hill, and William's Town, occupy the twelve-mile-long and mile-wide island. Across from the tip end of Little Exuma are O'Brian's Cay, Polly Cay, and Hog Cay. Hog Cay Cut shoots between O'Brian's and Hog Cay to offer boaters a shortcut to the southern part of Long Island, or to the Jumentos Cays and Ragged Island.

A strong current rips through Hog Cay Cut with the advancing and falling tides, making for good jack, snapper, and barracuda fishing. Hog Cay itself is privately owned, and extensively farmed by the residents. White Cay is the last piece of land in the Exumas, and is surrounded by white sand beaches. This area to the south and east of Little Exuma is superb bonefish and permit habitat. There are huge wadable flats that go dry or almost dry at low tide.

Boaters continuing on from White Cay can head east for Simms settlement on Long Island. Boaters who want to fish and explore the leeward side of Little and Great Exuma turn north after passing through Hog Cay Cut. The best flats fishing starts at the northern end of Little Exuma and runs all the way back up to Barraterre.

FISHING HIGHLIGHTS

Can flats be any flatter than this?

There are two distinct ways to fish the Exumas. One is with the professional guides out of Peace & Plenty, or with the scattered independent guides. The other is to cruise and fish on your own. Either way, you'll enjoy some of the most spectacular tropical scenery and fishing in the world.

The Exuma fishery is unique to the Bahamas due to its central location and its length from north to south. The fishery is part of the Great Bahama Bank, which is a migratory area for tarpon and other game fish species. It is adjacent to the deeper waters of the Tongue of the Ocean and Exuma Sound, and is sandwiched between Andros, Eleuthera, Cat Island, and Long Island. These features combine to produce high numbers of bonefish and excellent offshore fishing.

The three main areas of this fishery are the Exuma Cays, the windward flats from Rolleville to Forbes Hill, and the leeward flats from the Little Exuma ferry bridge to Barraterre. Our favorite windward flats run from George Town to Mariah Harbour Cay. Anglers fishing on their own out of George Town can rent a small boat and explore this area with confidence by using a little common sense and a tide chart. Pack a lunch and take snorkeling gear along. White sand bottoms offer good visibility for bonefish, plus easy wading. You can also get into some great reef and cut fishing.

The leeward flats are the meat of the fishery, and the area most fished by the guides from Peace & Plenty. Just south of the Little Exuma ferry bridge is an extensive mangrove flats region. There is good protection from the wind here, plus high numbers of bonefish. Turning north you cruise out into deeper water that can be rough in bad weather, but you have to make this run to reach the Airport Flats.

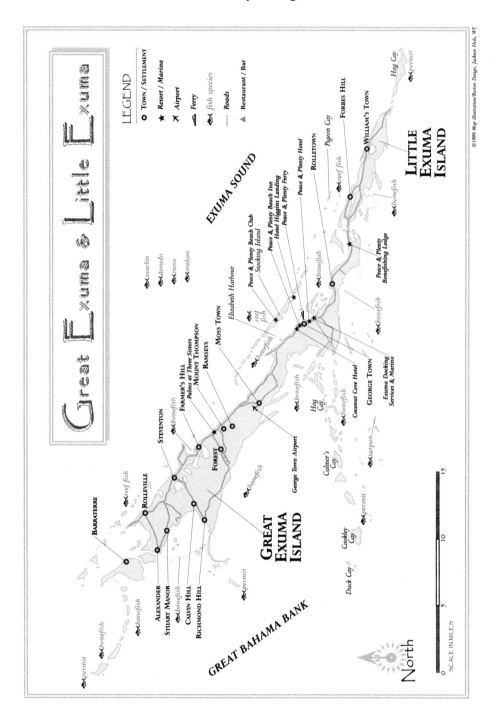

Great Exuma & Little Exuma

LEGEND

- Town / Settlement
- ★ Resort / Marina
- ✈ Airport
- Ferry
- fish species
- — Roads
- ▲ Restaurant / Bar

Between the Airport Flats and Moss Town are a chain of cays with fertile habitat for bonefish, permit, and tarpon. Local knowledge is necessary for boaters to navigate this area. Exploring in a dinghy or small boat is the way to go. Green Turtle Cay, Perpalls Cay, Hog Cay, Tommy Young's Cay, and Jew Fish Cay all support excellent flats. Green Turtle Cut is the route most often used by boaters choosing an inshore passage. Jew Fish Cut is used by the Long Island freight boats, and by boaters requiring more water.

This area has dark grass flats interspersed with white sand and coral. Mangrove bays and coves are common, providing protection and food for many smaller bonefish. Farther out to the east, Bowe Cay, Coakley Cay, and Duck Cay offer flats surrounded by deeper water that hold larger bonefish and some permit.

Continuing north to Richmond Hill and Rocky Point, anglers will find a fair selection of outside sandy flats and a varied shoreline covered with mangroves. While fishing throughout this area is good, we prefer to focus more north and south.

There are more miles of wadable flats through the Exumas than any other area of the Bahamas. Usually composed of white sand and coral, these flats are fed by countless cuts, creeks, and nearby deeper ocean water. The best time to fish these flats is on the incoming tide. Water depth is especially critical. As soon as bonefish have enough water to wriggle onto a flat they will begin to feed on shrimp and crabs. Gobies and glass minnows are a primary food source near the edges of cuts and creeks. Once water depths rise past midcalf, fish will disperse, and if mangroves are in the area, that's where they'll head.

For anglers who prefer to wade, we recommend fishing Exuma on a neap tide. This will give you more time during the day to wade your favorite flats. Be sure to check the time of day of the tides also, especially if you fish during a spring tide. On a spring tide you'll want to fish flats that are not lined with mangroves. These outside flats, or flats that extend out from various cays, will not give bonefish a place to hide. You will also find larger fish on average in these areas, plus you'll have a better chance of seeing permit.

Remember that tides are significantly different when moving from the windward to the leeward side of the island. Tides also vary two to three hours when moving from Barraterre to Little Exuma. This means anglers fishing here for a week or more will have the opportunity to fish the tides they prefer.

Since the Tropic of Cancer passes just south of George Town, weather in the region is more stable than it is in the northern Bahamas. Anglers looking to increase their chances of good weather, especially from December through February, should seriously consider fishing Exuma, Long Island, or the other islands to the south. Cold fronts often stall before reaching Exuma, as winter winds from the

Well, they aren't all trophies! Stephen with one of the world's smallest bonefish.

southeast are more common than the northeast winds that prevail on Andros, Eleuthera, Abaco, and Grand Bahama.

When bad weather does occur, the number of wade fishing options here means you'll still have a decent chance of catching fish. Clouds and wind will create difficult conditions, but the white sand bottoms will help with visibility, and wading anglers can set themselves up to cast in the direction they prefer. We usually choose to cast into the wind on a tough cloudy day. The wind will straighten out your back cast, help load your rod on the forward cast, and will carry any sounds away from the fish. This will allow you to get closer to fish, thus making shorter casts possible without spooking them.

Bonefish are by far the number one game fish species in the Exumas. Fish range two to six pounds, with three pounds being average. Because of the wading opportunities, and many well-trained guides, this is an ideal location for beginning bonefishers. To improve their skills, beginners need as many opportunities, or "shots," as possible. High numbers of fish, especially in the more remote areas, will provide these shots in conditions that are usually favorable.

We generally fish smaller and lighter flies on Exuma than we would on Andros or Grand Bahama. This strategy is very important on the wadable flats that receive the most pressure. A #6 Gotcha is one of the most popular bonefish flies now, though we remember showing a Gotcha to one of our guides years ago for the first time. The Gotcha was developed on Andros, which is where it was introduced to us. Our Exuma guide just shrugged when he first saw it, not sure if it would work. Of course, it did.

When fishing a low incoming tide we recommend eyeless flies such as a Blind Gotcha, Bonefish Special, or Horror. We also like a #6 Tan Yarn Crab, a #6 Tan/Orange Bonefish Puff, a #6 Banana Peel, and a special Marabou Puff developed by Exuma guides for extremely spooky fish. Just as important is the way you present your fly, then strip it when the time is right. We like to present the fly a good twenty feet in front of oncoming fish. It is common to see schools of six to twenty fish feeding in with the tide. Let your fly sink to the bottom, then wait for the fish to work toward it. When a fish is close, just twitch the fly with the smallest of strips, and be prepared to set the hook. Don't make too long of a strip, as the sudden movement will spook fish more often than not.

As water levels rise to knee depth a #4 Gotcha or Gold Krystal Charlie are good choices for sand bottoms. For bottoms laced with grass or coral outcroppings, try a #4 Miheve's Flats Fly. This fly is tied with a weed guard so it won't get hung up as you hop it along the bottom. As you move out toward the edges of these wadable flats the fish will be less spooky. You'll also find larger fish, and more singles and doubles. We prefer to fish these areas from a flats boat.

Fishing here for bigger bones is like anywhere else in the Bahamas: You'll find more big fish in deeper water. There are many flats dissected by deep blue creeks, and others that bump up against rugged coral cays with deep offside banks. The middle part of the incoming tide is best for these larger fish, which run seven to twelve pounds.

Exuma is one of the few places where we've consistently seen huge numbers of "laid-up" bonefish, fish that will hang together in large schools at the top of the tide. These fish are literally hanging out, milling around, just waiting for the tide to fall. We've seen this phenomenon more commonly on oceanside flats and bays on other islands, but in Exuma fish displaying this behavior can be found around a variety of cays and in mangrove bays. Usually, laid-up fish are hard to catch. You can cast and cast and cast without spooking them, but they won't eat. Throughout the Exumas, however, we've found these laid-up fish to be aggressive feeders. Why? Who knows? We've talked to a number of anglers about this, and they have reported similar observations and results.

Mudding is another bonefish behavior we've observed in the Exumas on a more consistent basis than on some of the other islands. Mudding is when a school of bonefish moves out into deeper water, usually six to ten feet in depth, and tears up the bottom in search of shrimp, crabs, and clams. Clouds of white mud bloom in otherwise clear water. These muds can stretch for hundreds of yards, making it easy to spot the school's location.

While we prefer not to fish muds, this is a good opportunity for beginning anglers to hook some fish. Tossing a #2 Gold Shiner Clouser Minnow into the leading edge of an expanding mud will usually produce repeated strikes. During bad weather and on hot days when fish have left the flats in search of cooler water, fishing the muds can provide action not available anywhere else.

We have not seen many tarpon in the Exumas, but we haven't spent much time looking. Based on the habitat, which includes the Grand Bahama Bank, and access to deep water, we have to believe that good tarpon

Stephen on a flat at Stocking Island.

fishing is available. From our conversations, it's apparent that Exuma's guides haven't spent much time looking, either.

On several occasions we've sent guides from other islands to Exuma to check out the tarpon and permit fishing options. They have reported that with some exploratory work, tarpon fishing could be respectable from April through October in several areas. We have talked with boating anglers who have seen tarpon at Pipe Creek, Darby Island, Bock Cat Cay, in the passage between Rocky Point and Richmond Hill, at Jew Fish Cay, and near the outside cays off the Airport Flat. We've also seen tarpon in this area, as have some of our clients fishing with guides from Peace & Plenty. In May and June you might want to have a tarpon rod rigged, but until the guides spend more time observing tarpon behavior, don't count on using it.

An exception to this would be fishing for tarpon in some of the blue holes. The guides do know the holes that hold tarpon, though getting them to take you will test your skills in persuasion.

Permit fishing is a step above the tarpon fishing, though getting consistent shots is not something you can count on. The outside flats and cays off the leeward side of the island lure permit out of the deeper channels throughout the year, with April through October being the best period for fishing. We have seen permit here on the backs of rays on several occasions. This is the ideal scenario, as these permit are in an eating mood. While our favorite permit flies would be Yarn Crabs, Del's Merkins, or Clouser Minnows, tossing any fly onto the back of a ray can produce a take.

We have also seen permit hanging out with laid-up bonefish around these same outer cays at high tide. For some reason, maybe competition for food, these permit are

April through October is the best period to get into permit such as this one.

more likely to eat than in most other situations. The past couple of years anglers looking for permit have spent more time to the south, from Hog Cay to White Cay and down across the sand banks to Sandy Cay. We have not fished this area, but we've talked to anglers who have had numerous shots at permit, especially along the deeper banks as the tide begins to cover the shallower flats. This is an area we look forward to exploring in the future.

Barracuda fishing is good year round over the reefs, and best on the flats from November through May. Fishing for sharks is best from April through the summer months on the flats and in the cuts and creeks. Lemons and blacktips will produce the best sport.

Reef and cut fishing is outstanding throughout the Exuma Cays, and off the windward side of Great Exuma. Jacks, grouper, and snappers are available year round. Our favorite fly-fishing method is to prospect in the cuts or over the reefs during periods of strong tidal flows. We like to use #2/0 Clouser Minnows in a variety of colors on a sinktip or full-sinking line, though fishing different types of saltwater poppers on floating lines is lots of fun for bigger horse-eye and bar jacks. For amberjack we go with larger flies such as Offshore Deceivers and Abel Anchovies in sizes #4/0 and #5/0.

Dorado, wahoo, and white marlin are the premiere offshore species during winter, though several species of tuna are available. Fishing for wahoo is great sport, and these fish are hard to beat on the dinner table, or in a fresh batch of ceviche. January and February are prime months for wahoo in the Exuma Sound, with the best areas running from Hawksbill Cay down to Darby Island.

Fishing picks up for blue marlin, sailfish, and tuna in May. By June the fishing for these species is at its best, and this is normally when most offshore tournaments take place. Sailfish are found in good concentrations in the Exuma Sound throughout the summer, as are Allison and yellowfin tuna. Conventional trolling methods will produce the most consistent results, but anglers can have luck with flies as well.

OPTIONAL ACTIVITIES

A variety of nice accommodations, good restaurants, and optional activities make Exuma an ideal choice for anglers and nonanglers to enjoy a vacation together. While boating, both sailing and motor cruising, is number one in the Exumas, diving and snorkeling are a close second. Add in sea kayaking, swimming, camping, exploring, biking, hiking, or just catching rays while reading your favorite book, and you should have enough fun and sun to stay happy.

The Exuma Dive Centre, located in George Town, is the premiere diving operation in the Exumas. It offers a variety of dives, from working over shallow reefs and coral heads teeming with fish to wall dives and blue hole adventures. A resort course is available for people looking for their first diving experience. Guided snorkeling is a great way to spend part of a day exploring the Exumas' underwater splendor, or to spear fish that can be cooked up for dinner at your hotel.

Most reef locations are near George Town, not more than a twenty-minute boat ride from the dock. The Peace & Plenty properties also feature a full watersports activity desk, including diving, snorkeling excursions, and small sailboat rentals.

The Exuma Dive Centre also rents small boats for exploring or fishing. You can even rent a push pole and test out your ability to become a guide.

Remote small hotels such as Higgins Landing on Stocking Island are the perfect choice for ecominded visitors. This resort has won several awards for its natural construction and use of solar power.

If you don't want to get away from it all, the atmosphere in George Town is festive and upbeat. The people are friendly and helpful. If you're looking for a party, you can usually find one, especially during the many regattas. In April, the National Family Island Regatta lures boaters from all over the world.

LODGING AND SERVICES

FEATURED LODGES AND ACCOMMODATIONS

Club Peace & Plenty

George Town   Peace & Plenty's centerpiece is the club, a casual 35-room Bahamian Inn featuring refurbished air-conditioned rooms with private balconies. Excellent meals are served in the dining room, and the bar is run by the famous super-friendly "Doc" Rolle. Guests can also enjoy a freshwater swimming pool, twice-weekly cocktail parties, and live calypso music and dancing on the weekends.

The Stocking Island Beach Club, with the snack-bar facility run by Doralee Roach, is one of the main attractions for P&P guests. Swim, sail, snorkel, or fish along white sand beaches and off coral reefs. If you're looking for a place to sunbathe in total privacy you'll find it on Stocking Island. The club operates daily ferry service to the island.

Season: October through July.

Suitable For: Anglers and nonanglers.

Optional Activities: The club operates a full watersports program, including diving and snorkeling options. Tennis can be arranged, as can car and boat rentals.

What's Included: Complete vacation packages are available, including airport transfers, meals, accommodations, taxes, and gratuities. If you are fishing you will stay at either the Beach Inn or Bonefish Lodge.

Not Included: Airfare to/from Exuma, optional activities.

Pricing: $$

Contact: Reservations and information, 800/525-2210 or 242/336-2551, fax 242/336-2093.

E-mail: pandp@peaceandplenty.com

Internet: www.peaceandplenty.com

Peace & Plenty Beach Inn

George Town   The inn features 16 deluxe air-conditioned rooms with tile baths, ceiling fans, and large balconies or terraces facing the beach. The airy indoor restaurant and bar are accompanied by a new covered terrace for lunches and dinners. A new pier extending into Bonefish Bay includes a waterfront Sponge Bar tended by Lawrence Saunders. Guests can also enjoy the freshwater pool and white sand beach on Bonefish Bay. A complimentary shuttle is available to the club, and guests can eat on the "dine around plan" at the Club or the Bonefish Lodge.

Season: October through July.

Suitable For: Anglers and nonanglers.

Optional Activities: The Inn participates in the club's full watersports program, including diving and snorkeling options. Tennis can be arranged, as can car and boat rentals.

What's Included: Complete bonefishing packages are available including airport transfers, meals, accommodations, guided fishing, taxes and gratuities to the lodge staff.

Not Included: Airfare to/from Exuma, alcoholic beverages, gratuities to guides, and any other optional activities.

Pricing: $$

Contact: Reservations and information, 800/525-2210 or 242/345-5555, fax 242/345-5556.

E-mail: pandp@peaceandplenty.com

Internet: www.peaceandplenty.com

Peace & Plenty Bonefish Lodge

Little Exuma Ferry Bridge   This is the headquarters for P&P's bonefishing operation, though nonanglers will be happy here, too. Eight large air-conditioned rooms feature private baths and balconies overlooking the water. An upstairs private fisherman's lounge includes a full bar, card and game room, fly-tying facilities, fishing tackle and clothing pro shop, satellite TV and video library, reading room, and sporting art gallery. Fly fishers will enjoy more than 60 miles of expansive flats surrounding the island covered with schools of 2- to 6-pound bonefish, plus larger fish cruising in pairs or alone. Guided fishing is done from skiffs and by wading, with miles of wadable flats the highlight. For the nonfisherman, the lodge participates in the club's full watersports program, including all activities on Stocking Island. Guests can also choose to eat at the club or the Beach Inn on the "dine around plan."

Season: October through June.

Suitable For: Anglers and nonanglers.

What's Included: Exuma airport pickup and return, accommodations, all meals on the dine around plan, guided fishing, hotel gratuities, and Bahamian taxes. Trips of any length are available.

Not Included: Airfare to/from Exuma, alcoholic beverages, and gratuities to guides.

Pricing: $$$

Contact: Reservations and information, 242/345-5555, fax 242/345-5556.

E-mail: ppbone@grouper.batelnet.bs

Internet: www.peaceandplenty.com

Coconut Cove Hotel

George Town   This bed-and-breakfast–style inn has spared no effort in catering to the needs of a few discerning individuals. Attention to service and details combine with a casually elegant atmosphere to create this relaxing retreat. All rooms are distinctively furnished and include queen-size beds, air-conditioning, stocked refrigerated mini-bars, ceiling fans, toiletries, bathrobes, and optional TV. The Paradise Suite features a king-size bed, extra-large bath with Jacuzzi, and a private hot tub on the beachside deck. The freshwater pool and bar are on the beach. The dining room serves breakfast, lunch, and dinner, featuring daily gourmet specialties. Special meal requests are no problem, and intimate dinners can be served in your room.

Season: November through August, closed September and October.

Suitable For: Anglers and nonanglers.

Optional Activities: Diving and snorkeling arranged with Exuma Dive Centre, boat rentals for exploring and remote picnicking, sailing, biking, swimming, flats and offshore fishing arranged with good independent fly fishing guides, including Abby McKenzie.

What's Included: Usually just accommodations and taxes, though a meal plan is available. There are no set packages. Each trip is custom designed to suit your needs. Trips of any length are available.

Not Included: Airfare to Exuma, airport transfers, alcoholic beverages, and optional activities.

Pricing: $$$

Contact: Reservations and information, 242/336-2659, fax 242/336-2658.

Hotel Higgins Landing

Stocking Island   Stocking Island, across Elizabeth Harbour from George Town, is about 4½ miles long and half a mile wide, and is lined with numerous coves and white sand beaches. Shade is provided by lush coconut palms. There are no cars or roads, and 7 full-time residents call the island home. The middle of the island is composed of a series of hurricane holes and blue water lagoons.

Hotel Higgins Landing is on a slender piece of land that stretches from the sea to one of the lagoons. It's the only hotel on Stocking Island. Excellent snorkeling is available over the reefs on the beach side, while sea kayaking and bonefishing are prime on the lagoon side in Gaviota Bay.

This ecoresort took almost four years to complete, and was constructed to be harmonious with its surroundings. The owners of Higgins Landing, Carol and Dave Higgins, want you to know that ecotourism is "not about giving up luxury." Each of 5 cottages is furnished with antiques, queen-size beds, ceiling fans, and screened windows, while large private decks present dreamlike views.

Breakfast and dinner are included in the room rate. Meals are excellent, with eggs Benedict a specialty for breakfast, and fresh seafood for dinner. Lunches are optional, and can be packed for a picnic on an even more remote cay.

Wild frangipani, orchids, red hibiscus, and other exotic plant life is labeled by management for your convenience in identification. The hotel is always peaceful, thanks to the resort's 100 percent use of photovoltaic solar electricity. All cottages are equipped with 12-volt power. There is also standard 110-volt power at several locations for guests who can't give up their hair dryers, or who need to recharge a video camera battery.

Pure great-tasting rainwater is collected from the unpolluted Bahamian skies. Supplies are ample but never wasted, as the resort has an active water-reuse program. Water from sinks and showers is used to water plants, flowers, and trees, for example.

Being an ecofriendly resort, smoking is not permitted in any building, though guests can smoke on their decks or at the beach bar.

Season: October through June.

Suitable For: Anglers and nonanglers.

Optional Activities: Bonefishing, offshore and reef fishing, diving, snorkeling, boat rentals, swimming, and relaxing.

What's Included: Accommodations, breakfast and dinner, evening hors d'oeuvres, transfers to/from George Town, use of snorkel gear, sunfish, kayaks, fishing equipment, windsurfers, paddleboats, beach chaises, and beach towels.

Not Included: Airfare to/from Exuma, airport transfers to/from George Town, 12 percent charge added for hotel taxes, resort levies and gratuities. There is no additional tipping. Incoming and outgoing phone service, including faxing, is available at the resort via wireless and cellular service. Rates are not cheap, but the resort is glad to help with your communication needs during your stay.

Pricing: $$$

Contact: Reservations and information, telephone/fax 242/336-2460.

E-mail: stockisl@batelnet.com

ADDITIONAL ACCOMMODATIONS

Two Turtles Inn

George Town   Fourteen air-conditioned rooms with ceiling fans. You can feast inside or out on some of the best Bahamian food on the island. The Flyers Bar is a local hotspot for happy hour. Special meal events are held twice a week. Snorkeling and diving and fishing guides can be arranged by the hotel. This is a popular spot due to the friendly atmosphere and economical prices, so we recommend booking well in advance.

Pricing: $$

Contact: Reservations and information, 242/336-2545 or 800/688-4752, fax 242/336-2528.

E-mail: info@twoturtlesinn.com

The Palms at Three Sisters

Mount Thompson   Twelve air-conditioned motel rooms on one of the prettiest beaches in the Exumas. The restaurant and bar serves a variety of seafood and rum drinks. Excellent snorkeling is right down the beach. Bonefishing guides can be arranged.

Pricing: $$

Contact: Reservations and information, 242/358-4040, fax 242/358-4043.

Regatta Point

George Town   Six suites and cottages, complete with kitchens, offer great views of Elizabeth Harbour and convenient walking access to town. Guests can enjoy a private beach, Sunfish sailboats, and bicycles.
Pricing: $$
Contact: Reservations and information, 242/336-2206, fax 242/336-2046.
E-mail: regattapoint@cpscaribnet.com

Mount Pleasant Suites Hotel

Hooper's Bay   Twenty-three 1-bedroom suites and 1 2-bedroom suite all with full kitchens, living room, dining area, and satellite TV. The same people who own the Exuma Docking Services own this new facility. Hooper's Bay beach is a short walk away. Reasonable rates make this property a good choice for anglers looking to explore the island on their own. You will need a rental car if you stay here.
Pricing: $$
Contact: Reservations and information, 242/336-2960, fax 242/336-2964.

Staniel Cay Yacht Club

Staniel Cay   Six air-conditioned waterfront cottages with private balconies that provide dramatic views of the ocean and the sunset. Food at the restaurant is excellent. You can rent a boat and explore on your own, or fishing guides can be arranged. Most people arrive here by boat. For flight information call Executive Air Travel at 954/224-6022, or ask the club for information.
Pricing: $$–$$$
Contact: Reservations and information, 242/355-2024 or 954/467-8920, fax 242/355-2044.

SERVICES

Fandango Air   Air charter services between Ft. Lauderdale and George Town.
Contact: 954/462-2552.

Stella Maris Charters   Air charter services between George Town and Long Island.
Contact: 954/359-8236 or 242/336-2106.

Exuma Docking Services   The only marina in George Town. Full services for boaters. Monitors VHF channel 16, call for "Sugar One." Rental cars are available. Sammy's Place restaurant, and well-stocked liquor store. You need to call ahead for slip reservations, and space at the fueling dock.
Contact: Reservations and information, 242/336-2578, fax 242/336-2023.
Hours: Monday through Saturday 7:00 A.M. to 6:00 P.M., Sunday 8:00 A.M. to 1:00 P.M.

Exuma Dive Centre   The best diving and snorkeling programs out of George Town. Resort courses are available for beginners, while advanced divers will enjoy wall and blue hole dives. Equipment is provided. They also rent small boats and motor scooters. Guided bonefishing can be arranged with the island's independent guides, and offshore boats can be chartered.
Contact: Reservations and information, 242/336-2390 or 800/874-7213, fax 242/336-2391.
E-mail: exumadive@bahamasvg.com

Exuma Fantasea   Another diving and snorkeling operation. It specializes in ecodiving, and also rents boats.
Contact: Reservations and information, 242/336-3483 or 800/760-0700.

Car Rentals: In George Town, call Thompson's Rentals at 242/336-2442, Sam Grey Enterprises at 242/336-2101. You can also rent cars through your hotel.

Restaurants: All three P&P properties have good restaurants. Our favorite is the Bonefish Lodge. Eddie's Edgewater is a must if you can make your reservations far enough in advance. The Two Turtles Inn and Coconut Cove offer a variety of tasty dishes.

Out Island Regatta: *The* yachting event of the season, held in April. If you like to party, this is the time to visit George Town. Make your reservations well in advance.

The Bank of Nova Scotia in George Town is open Monday through Friday, 9:30 A.M. to 3:00 P.M.

The George Town medical clinic is your best bet in an emergency.

Exuma Tourist Office, 242/336-2430, fax 242/336-2431.

NEW DEVELOPMENTS

We have heard about major new developments on Exuma for years, but so far none of them have materialized. With that said, we understand that the Emerald Bay complex at Ocean Bight is under construction. The resort includes a Greg Norman golf course, deluxe condominiums, a marina, and a 220-room Regent Hotel.

We also understand that The Island Club has purchased a large tract of land on the main highway five miles west of George Town. Plans call for another golf course and accompanying resort community to be built there.

The Bahamian government has agreed to fund the leasing of new jets for Bahamasair. Bahamasair is now offering jet service from Ft. Lauderdale to George Town on Thursdays and Sundays. This service should continue, though we would not be surprised to see the days change.

On a less positive note, development in the Exuma Cays has gone nuts. Most of this development is on private islands and cays, but one brilliant developer plans to build a resort in the Land and Sea Park. What fun.

Log on to our Web site at www.bahamasflyfishingguide.com for up-to-date information.

11

Cat Island

Located 130 miles southeast of Nassau, and a little more than thirty miles southeast of Eleuthera, Cat Island is forty-eight miles long and one to four miles wide. The island's name probably came from Arthur Catt, the British sea captain and notorious pirate. This boot-shaped island is one of the most beautiful and fertile Out Islands, with miles of unspoiled pink sand beaches set against tall green bluffs and rugged forest-covered hills. Just outside New Bight, Mt. Alvernia's peak reaches 206 feet, one of the highest points in the Bahamas. Atop the peak sits the Hermitage, the final home and burial site of the famous religious leader and hermit, Father Jerome.

Cat Island, like many of its neighboring islands, was once a thriving Loyalist colony. Cotton plantations established during the 1700s prospered until the abolition of slavery. Now, vine-covered mansion ruins and stone walls mingle with tropical flowers, wild grass, and sand dunes, as a reminder of the past. Many of the early settlers ended up moving back to the United States. Others stayed, with their descendants still living in the same towns. Over the past couple of years some of the original settlers' descendants began moving back to the island. Evidence of this can be seen in the elegant new homes being built on some of the prettiest beaches around the island.

Cat Islanders live by a simple day-to-day philosophy: "What nature and the

Brian O'Keefe

A commercial boat stands out at the dock.

Lord will provide." People here are known for their ingenuity at using available materials to make or build whatever they need. Musical instruments are a good example. A piece of wood, some fishing line, and a worn tin tub are combined to create the bass instrument in a "Rake 'N' Scrape" band. A conch shell is used as a horn, while an old comb covered with paper works as a harmonica. The saw is a unique instrument played throughout the Bahamas, while a goat skin stretched over a piece of rounded wood makes a great drum. Put all these instruments together and Cat Island bands produce a unique sound.

If you want to learn about the history of the Bahamas, asking longtime Cat Island residents is one of the most interesting ways. These people love to tell engrossing stories. One of their favorites is about Christopher Columbus. If you think Columbus originally landed on San Salvador, don't mention it. Cat Islanders are vehement in their belief that Columbus first landed on their island. They also believe that Bahamian music, and many Bahamian myths, were spawned from their shores. Superstition here is equal to that on Andros Island. The saying, "I'll be with you in spirit," is put into action on Cat Island. When the last of a generation dies, his or her house is left for the spirit to live in. Surviving relatives then gather stones from the site and build a new dwelling. On many parts of the island, especially up north, locals anchor spindles atop their roofs to ward off danger and evil spirits.

With the main highway from Orange Creek in the north to Hawk's Nest and Port Howe in the south now complete, driving from one end of the island to the other is a pleasurable experience. While you can make this drive in one day, you'll need two days if you want to do any exploring. There are so many small settlements that you won't average more than thirty miles an hour. And be careful of all the basketball-playing children. Hoops are set up all along the roadsides, with the pavement used as the court.

The population of Cat Island is a little over two thousand. Fishing and farming are the mainstays of the economy. Tomatoes and pineapples are the primary crops, with watermelons, bananas, and peas also exported to the other islands. Tourism is growing, and should continue to do so as more vacationers discover this splendid remote island.

Cat Island does not have as many anchorages and harbors as some of the other islands, which is one of the reasons it has remained on the quiet side of general tourism. Reefs that make anchoring difficult and dangerous until you reach the southern end of the island and Port Howe protect the wild and awe-inspiring eastern coast, called the "north shore" by locals. The beaches along this coastline are the most dramatically inviting stretches of sand in the Bahamas.

Diving and snorkeling are excellent around Cat Island, while hiking, biking, and sea kayaking are also popular. If you're looking for action, however, you'll need to look elsewhere. Cat Island is peaceful, relaxing, and soothing, an ideal place for a honeymoon or quiet family vacation.

Bahamasair flies two to three times a week from Nassau to Arthur's Town and New Bight. Air Sunshine flies from Ft. Lauderdale to New Bight, though the schedule changes frequently. Island Express also has sporadic service to New Bight from Ft. Lauderdale.

Our favorite place on Cat Island is Fernandez Bay Village. Owned and operated by Pam and Tony Armbrister, this small casually deluxe resort is on a picturesque crescent-shaped beach that's ideal for swimming and snorkeling. Good bonefishing that you can do on your own is a ten-minute bike ride away. Fernandez Bay operates its own air charter service from Nassau to New Bight on a daily basis.

Greenwood Beach Resort and Hawk's Nest Resort & Marina also offer air charter service to New Bight, and to the airstrip at Hawk's Nest settlement. The Cutlass Bay Resort offers air charter service to its private airstrip, for guests only.

AROUND THE ISLAND

Most visiting anglers and vacationers fly to Cat Island, arriving either at Arthur's Town or New Bight. Arthur's Town is the government headquarters for the north end of the island. The settlement expands out around a grass park where children play basketball and soccer. A telephone station, police station, and clinic are nearby. Several small grocery stores are well stocked when the freight boat arrives. The best place to eat is Pat Rolle's Cookie House Bakery on the north side of town. We like to eat lunch there when we drive up to Orange Creek from Fernandez Bay.

Orange Creek is the northernmost settlement on the island. The Orange Creek Inn, offering sixteen motel-style rooms, has a well-stocked store and a telephone. Tidal flow has created a long white sandbar across much of the creek mouth, part of which goes almost dry at low tide. Waves create a white-capped rip, especially during the last of the falling tide. A rough dirt road runs up the southern side of the creek, providing wading access to good bonefishing flats, but you have to fish the last of the falling or first of the incoming tide. Once the water gets up, you could become stranded if you've wandered too far to the north side of the creek.

Orange Creek is best fished and explored from a Boston Whaler or dinghy. A number of houses are for rent in this area, a couple of which include a boat and car. If you decide to rent a house here, one way or another be sure you have a car and boat or you won't have the land and water access you need to enjoy your vacation.

If you keep driving up the Orange Creek road you'll end up on a secluded white sand beach. Before you reach the beach you'll think you're lost, that the road has ended, but don't worry, just keep driving. This is a great beach for picnicking, swimming, and snorkeling when the weather is good. From here you can hike to the rugged northern point of the island. The view is worth the walk.

About fifteen miles south of Arthur's Town is Bennett's Harbour, one of the island's oldest settlements. If you're driving through during the day looking for a rental house, the mail boat dock, or access to the creek for bonefishing, you might get lost, as the narrow roads are confusing. But don't worry, you'll probably see a few local women on their way to socialize at the dock. In exchange for a ride, you'll get directions and as many interesting stories as you want to listen to.

There is a beautiful beach just north of the mouth of Bennett's Creek, where several rental houses are located. The tidal flow in and out of the creek moves at river speed. The government dock is on the northeast side of the creek. If you're looking for some incredible baked bread you can buy it here every morning. The creek winds inland for over a mile and spreads out through a maze of mangroves. Bonefishing here is decent during the lower stages of the tide, but be careful of the softer bottoms that can suck you in to your knees. This creek is best explored and fished from a small boat.

We've talked with cruising boaters who have told us that the anchorage is good in most weather conditions, but caution is still advised when entering the harbor due to the strong tidal flows. These boaters preferred to remain anchored outside the harbor over sand bottoms.

From Alligator Point to Smith's Bay the highway serpentines through one small settlement after another. There are a couple of small flats and reef areas where you can

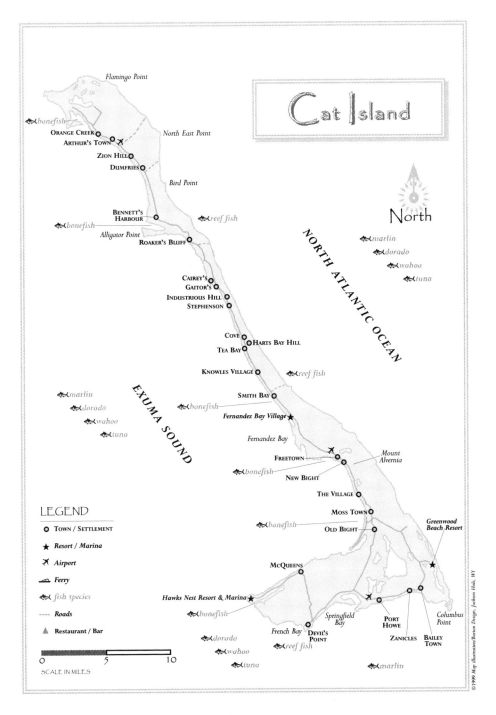

Cat Island

Flamingo Point

bonefish
ORANGE CREEK
ARTHUR'S TOWN
North East Point
ZION HILL
DUMFRIES

Bird Point

BENNETT'S HARBOUR
reef fish
bonefish
Alligator Point
ROAKER'S BLUFF

North

NORTH ATLANTIC OCEAN

marlin
dorado
wahoo
tuna

CAIREY'S
GAITOR'S
INDUSTRIOUS HILL
STEPHENSON

COVE
HARTS BAY HILL
TEA BAY

KNOWLES VILLAGE
reef fish

EXUMA SOUND

SMITH BAY
bonefish

marlin
dorado
wahoo
tuna

Fernandez Bay Village

Fernandez Bay

FREETOWN
bonefish
NEW BIGHT
Mount Alvernia

THE VILLAGE

MOSS TOWN
bonefish
OLD BIGHT

Greenwood Beach Resort

McQUEENS

Hawks Nest Resort & Marina
bonefish

Springfield Bay

PORT HOWE

Columbus Point

Hawks Nest Resort & Marina
French Bay
DEVIL'S POINT
dorado
wahoo
tuna

ZANICLES
BAILEY TOWN

reef fish

marlin

LEGEND

○ TOWN / SETTLEMENT
★ Resort / Marina
✈ Airport
⛴ Ferry
🐟 fish species
--- Roads
▲ Restaurant / Bar

0   5   10
SCALE IN MILES

© 1999 Map Illustration/Barton Design, Jackson Hole, WY

Brian O'Keefe

A bone taken near the mouth of Bennett's Creek.

catch bonefish, jacks, and snappers at low tide, but this is not an area to spend much time fishing, and there are not many beaches. The real treasure along this stretch of the island is the exquisitely beautiful north shore. There are five or six rutted dirt tracks that cut across the island from the highway to reach this magnificent area. Rental car companies will make you sign a release promising not to drive on these dirt tracks, so what you do is up to you. Hiking or biking are alternative methods to reach this must-see part of the island.

The track we most often take is just north of Smith's Bay. If you're staying at Fernandez Bay Village, you can pack a picnic lunch and ride your bikes to the north shore. Be sure to wear long pants for the bike ride, as some thorny bushes encroach on the track, and don't forget your fly rod. Once you arrive you can walk for miles along deserted pink sand beaches, at times crossing black coral outcroppings to reach the next beach. White-capped waves wash over the outer reef, while inside are many tidal pools loaded with sea life. You can walk out through these pools on hard sand and coral to reach ocean flats and coral drop-offs. We've caught some big bonefish out here, though we've never seen much in the way of numbers. The best fishing is in the cuts and along the drop-offs for jacks, snappers, and grouper. This is great sport with a floating line, long leader and big Clouser Minnow. At times you'll get a vicious take on every cast. Take plenty of flies, because the bigger jacks and grouper will often break you off on the coral.

Back on the civilized side of the island, Smith's Bay offers anchorages for boaters that can include fuel delivery. The freight boat makes regular visits to pick up produce being shipped to Nassau. To the south of the dock is a large protected flat that produces good bonefishing on the incoming tide, though these fish are spooky due to angling pressure. The flat is mostly hard sand with areas of softer mud to watch out for. The bottom is uneven in the middle, with deeper troughs that might surprise you if you're not careful. The oceanside shore and back of the bay are lined with mangroves. At high tide the bonefish disperse through the mangroves and are unreachable.

Just south of the bay is Fernandez Bay Village, one of the most idyllic Out Island resorts in the Bahamas. The resort was established in 1980 by the Armbrister family, and it specializes in personal service and a truly laid-back atmosphere. Twelve ocean-front villas and cottages are strung along a mile of sugary beach, tucked between shady casuarinas and vibrant red hibiscus. Diving, snorkeling, swimming, exploring, and fishing are the main activities, though just lying on the beach or in a hammock takes up its share of time for many visitors. Guided flats, reef, and offshore fishing can be arranged for guests of the resort. You can also rent the resort's Boston Whaler to reach flats that are only accessible by boat.

Meals are served in the open-air dining room and on the beachside terrace. Buffet dinners on the beach are outstanding, with fresh seafood, beef, salads, and fruits as specialties. Call ahead for dinner reservations if you're not staying at the resort. If you're staying in one of the villas you'll have a full kitchen that you can stock from the resort's store or from one of the markets in New Bight.

In good weather boaters can anchor off the resort and enjoy the clear aquamarine water. The creek system south of the resort can be explored by dinghy or sea kayak. This looks like perfect bonefish habitat, but we've never seen more than a couple of fish here. You can hook into some big barracuda at the creek mouth, especially on the falling tide.

South of Fernandez Bay is the New Bight airport, then the settlement itself. On the way you'll pass the Bridge Inn, a local motel with a good restaurant and bar. For a few extra bucks you can get a room with air-conditioning. Just north of the motel is a dirt road that runs along the edge of an inland lagoon that is home to bonefish, permit, and tarpon. We've caught bonefish and tarpon here, but have never seen the permit. This is a fun place to fish on a sunny day when you can see into the water. On a cloudy day you can sometimes catch fish blind casting.

New Bight has a good grocery store that is usually well stocked with frozen chicken, produce, and breakfast foods. A liquor store is next door, and you can rent a car at the service station. This is also the government headquarters for South Cat Island. Adjacent to the commissioner's office is the trail leading up to the top of Mt. Alvernia and the Hermitage.

Four miles farther south is Old Bight. Before you reach the settlement you'll come to a roundabout. Going left, or southeast, you'll head toward the Greenwood Beach Resort and Port Howe. On the southwest side of the roundabout is a narrow dirt track. You can drive onto this track to gain access to a very good bonefish flat that is best fished on a neap tide.

Continuing on past the roundabout toward Old Bight, you can take the auxiliary road along a nice stretch of beach, and in season you can stop to collect pineapples. A telephone station, laundromat, nurse-staffed clinic, and two small grocery stores are available in the settlement.

If you drive to Port Howe you'll pass a huge landlocked lake on the west side of the road. There are actually many lakes in this area, and we've been told they hold tarpon, jacks, and cubera snapper, but we haven't explored them. The turnoff to the Greenwood Beach Resort is just past the ruins of an old mansion on the left side of the road, but trust us, it's easy to miss. The resort overlooks a miles long stretch of virgin beach and the deep blue waters of the Atlantic.

Rooms at the resort are comfortable and clean and cooled with ceiling fans. The clubhouse features a restaurant, bar, and quaint library. The main attraction here is the diving and snorkeling. In fact, the resort has the island's best dive operation. Beginner snorkeling and diving courses and outings are available, while advanced divers can enjoy awesome wall diving.

If you drive past Port Howe toward Dolphin Head and Devil's Point, you'll enjoy seeing the beautiful southern coast of the island. The Cutlass Bay Club is a clothing-optional resort near Dolphin Head, while Devils' Point is a small settlement with glistening coral beaches ideal for shelling. On calm days there is good fishing from various rock outcroppings for jacks, snappers, and grouper. There are also several creeks with flats that might hold bonefish, but we've never fished them.

To reach Hawk's Nest you have to turn right off the highway before Devil's Point. This will take you back north to McQueens, which is on the leeward shore. Hawk's Nest Resort and Marina is on the southwestern tip of the island and is a prime reef and offshore fishing location. The fishing grounds between Hawk's Nest and Devil's Point are excellent, with deep ocean water pushing in close to the shoreline. As you continue south to Tarter Bank, the fishing just keeps getting better. Boaters can also take a line straight north along the bank drop-off for consistent action. Marlin, sailfish, wahoo, tuna, dorado, amberjack, kingfish, and trevally are in abundance in season.

Yes, we said trevally, though we've never seen them on the end of our line. We've only seen the pictures and talked with the guides about this amazing game fish. The guides swear these fish are trevally, and the photos look exactly like the fish we catch in Christmas Island.

The Hawk's Nest Marina and Resort offers eight slips, fuel, electricity, water, ice, a restaurant and bar, and air-conditioned guest rooms facing the Bight. You need reservations for dinner in the restaurant. The dive shop features diving and snorkeling excursions for all ability levels. A pretty beach for sunning and swimming stretches to the east of the resort. Bicycles and small boats can be rented at the marina.

Both Hawk's Nest Creek and Cove Creek have good-looking flats that should entice bonefish to feed, but we haven't talked with anyone who's given it a try. Anglers here are more interested in the offshore and reef fishing, which is some of the best in the Bahamas.

FISHING HIGHLIGHTS

The Cat Island fishing grounds are sandwiched between the Exuma Sound and the blue waters of the Atlantic Ocean. The leeward side of the island does not have the miles of sprawling wadable flats found in the Exumas and on Long Island (see the following chapter). Deeper water pushes in much closer to land here. Most of the bonefishing flats along the west coast are inside protected bays and creeks, or just outside these areas. Due to the limited number of flats, this is a delicate fishery that cannot handle much fishing pressure.

Fishing the incoming tide is best, though the last of the falling tide is also very good. Water depth and structure are the keys to setting yourself up to find the most fish. Bonefish will move into areas when water levels reach a certain point and keep moving at this depth. They like to follow shoreline structure and trough contours that run through the flats. This is really noticeable in Smith Bay, where the bonefish follow the same pattern every day. Our favorite flies include #4 Gotchas, #4–6 White Epoxy Charlies, #4 Gold Krystal Charlies, and #6 Tan Yarn Crabs. For really spooky tailing fish, go with a #6 Horror.

The east coast, or "north shore" of the island, offers some of the best wadable reef fishing anywhere. Add in the dramatically beautiful setting and this is one of the unique spots in the Bahamas. Hard sand, smooth coral, and rough jagged coral laced with irregular holes make up the bottom structure. You are completely "out there" in terms of remoteness, especially if you've walked a mile or two from where you accessed the beach, so be careful walking on the coral. A bad cut or broken ankle here would be a major problem.

Bonefish here are usually looking for crabs, and Brown or Green Yarn Crabs work well, as do Turneffe Crabs in really skinny water. When you hook up, the fish will usually try for the reef. You'll land more fish if you can keep them from going over the edge.

Stephen fighting a fish off the island's east coast.

The best time for bonefish is at the bottom of the tide, when the water is slack, though the last of the falling and first of the incoming are also good. This is also the prime time to fish for grouper. You can walk right out to the edges of the reef and cast Clouser Minnows along the drop-off. Let your fly get down, then make a jigging retrieve. We recommend using at least 30-pound mono shock tippet, or 18-pound wire. You might catch several kinds of jacks or snappers fishing this way, though these fish like a little more tidal flow. The last half of the falling tide is best for the bigger jacks, especially in the coral cuts. We like to fish baitfish imitations like WBA Sardinas and Abel Anchovies, though Saltwater Poppers work well, too. For the bigger jacks you might have to take a little pounding from the waves. Just remember to be careful.

If you're into spin fishing, take a variety of spoons and plugs. With long casts you'll be able to avoid the waves and reach the fish consistently. Carry plenty of lures as you'll definitely break off a number of fish.

The southern coast of the island produces the best boat-accessed reef fishing, and the best offshore fishing. Blue water pushes in close here, so short runs will get you into the action. Blue marlin and sailfish turn up throughout the year, though the best months are May through July; good numbers sometimes linger through the summer.

Kingfish, blackfin, bluefin, and Allison and yellowfin tuna are also at their peak during this time period, though April can be a good month for yellowfin, too. Dorado can be good through winter, but spring is usually best. The prime winter game fish is wahoo, with January and February producing the highest numbers.

Reef fishing for jacks, snappers, and grouper is good year round, with amberjack best November through May. Trevally fishing is best March through July.

Cat Island's location east of the Exuma Sound means good weather prevails throughout most of the year. Cold fronts moving down from Florida often stall before crossing the sound. It is common to be sitting on the beachside terrace at Fernandez Bay under a clear star-filled sky watching dazzling lighting storms over the Exuma Cays.

When the weather is good, the bonefishing is good. During storms the fish stay off in deeper water. As for permit, we have never seen one on the western flats. The few guides on the island report that permit rarely turn up in numbers, though the Orange Creek area is fair May through July. If you want to catch a tarpon, you'll have your best chance in the lakes at the south end of the island, or in some of the blue holes. If you're an adventurous angler looking to fish and explore on your own, you ought to explore some of these areas that have rarely been fished.

OPTIONAL ACTIVITIES

Snorkeling, diving, swimming, exploring, windsurfing, and sea kayaking are the main make-your-own-fun activities. Bring along several good books and lots of suntan lotion. Many visitors spend two to three weeks on the island. If you want to turn into a vegetable for a while, Cat Island is the place to accomplish it. If you're looking for lots of things to do, including nightlife, you need to go somewhere else.

If you want some structure, staying at one of the resorts is the best plan. At Fernandez Bay Village you can be left completely alone, or you can participate in daily activities such as snorkeling tours and evening buffet dinners. Bicycles, sea kayaks, and Boston Whalers are available to guests. Rental cars are easily arranged. We recommend getting a car for at least a day or two to explore the island. If you're into diving, Greenwood Beach Resort is the best option. If you want to be completely on your own, there are a number of houses you can rent.

Visiting the Hermitage atop Mt. Alvernia is one of the sort-of-mandatory things to do. Father Jerome retired here and spent the last twelve or so years of his life as a hermit. His final religious act was to carve the steps to the top of the mountain, which included carving the fourteen Stations of the Cross, which represent events from the Passion of Christ. Visitors begin the hike to the top next to the commissioner's office in New Bight. You will definitely get some exercise climbing to the top, but the panoramic view of the ocean on both sides of the island is spectacular. Don't forget your camera.

LODGING AND SERVICES

FEATURED LODGES AND ACCOMMODATIONS

Fernandez Bay Village

New Bight   Fernandez Bay Village rests on a beautiful crescent-shaped mile of sugary white sand beach. Twelve seaside villas and cottages are just steps away from the water. Villas are equipped with full housekeeping items, so you can cook your own meals if you choose. Fish, snorkel, explore, bike, hike, eat, drink, and dance; and if this wears you out, just kick back and relax. Dinners are served on the beachside terrace, usually in front of a blazing bonfire. Shoes are not part of the dress code. The beachfront Tiki bar is run on the honor system. Most bonefishing is done by wading. You can go out to fish for 2 hours, half a day, or a full day, whatever your pleasure. This is an ideal location for couples and families. Any length of stay is available.

Season: October through July.

Suitable For: Anglers and nonanglers.

What's Included: Packages feature accommodations with private bath, charter flight Nassau/Cat Island, and Bahamian taxes. Single rates are available.

Not Included: Airfare to/from Nassau, meals (though a meal plan is available), alcoholic beverages, guided fishing, or fishing tackle. You can book guided fishing in advance, or wait until you arrive at the resort.

Contact: Reservations and information, 954/474-4821 or 800/940-1905, fax 954/474-4864. On the island, 242/342-3043, fax 242/342-3051.
Pricing: $$–$$$
E-mail: fbv@batelnet.bs.
Internet: www.fernandezbayvillage.com

ADDITIONAL ACCOMMODATIONS

Bridge Inn

New Bight   Twelve motel rooms, some with air-conditioning. If you want AC you have to request it and pay extra. The restaurant here is very good. The inn is next to the landlocked ponds that hold bonefish, permit, and tarpon. It's a short walk to the beach.
Pricing: $$
Contact: Reservations and information, 242/342-3013, fax 242/342-3041.

Hawk's Nest Resort and Marina

Devil's Point   Located at the southwest tip of the island, this is a truly out-of-the-way resort. Ten rooms and 1 2-bedroom house are on the waterfront. The marina offers eight slips to boaters. The resort also includes a good restaurant and dive shop. Snorkeling around the point is wonderful, and a white sand beach is ideal for swimming and catching rays. This is a great location for offshore and reef fishing.
Pricing: $$–$$$
Contact: Reservations and information telephone/fax, 242/357-7257.

Greenwood Beach Resort

Port Howe   Twenty comfortable rooms are cooled by the ocean breeze and ceiling fans. The large clubhouse is the center of activity and features a nice restaurant, bar, satellite TV, and terrace overlooking the ocean and swimming pool. New management is doing a good job of running this isolated resort that specializes in diving and relaxing. Boat and car rentals can be arranged. The Cat Island Dive Center, at the resort, offers a variety of diving and snorkeling programs, and rental equipment is available. The resort operates its own air charter service from Nassau.
Pricing: $$–$$$
Contact: Reservations and information telephone/fax, 242/342-3053 or 877/228-7475.
E-mail: gbr@grouper.batelnet.bs.
Internet: www.hotelgreenwoodinn.com

Cutlass Bay Club

Cutlass Bay   This is a 300-acre, all-inclusive, couples only, clothing-optional resort. Eighteen oceanside rooms and villas with 5 secluded clothing-optional beaches. The food at this resort is exceptional. Boat and car rentals can be arranged, as can diving. You can walk to a number of prime snorkeling areas. Reef and offshore fishing is very good throughout the area.
Pricing: $$$
Contact: Reservations and information, 800/723-5688.
E-mail: cutlass-bay@the-solution.com
Internet: www.cutlass-bay.com

Orange Creek Inn

Orange Creek   Sixteen motel rooms, some with air-conditioning. If you want air-conditioning, be sure to request it.
Pricing: $–$$
Contact: Reservations and information, 242/354-4110, or 242/323-6465, fax 242/354-4042.

Sea Spray Hotel

Orange Creek   Fifteen motel rooms, some with air-conditioning. If you want air-conditioning, be sure to request it.
Pricing: $–$$
Contact: Reservations and information, 242/323-5390 or 242/354-4116.

SERVICES

Cat Island Dive Center

Port Howe   Cat Island offers some of the best diving in the Bahamas, with more than 12 miles of unlimited wall diving sites along the southern coast alone. The dive center is affiliated with PADI and PDIC and offers a complete certification course. Cat Island's southern wall begins at 50 feet and drops vertically to depths up to 6,000 feet. You can explore coral canyons and sandy valleys, and discover caves and tunnels packed with thousands of colorful fish. Just off the Greenwood Beach Resort beach are shallow reefs ranging from 15 to 40 feet that are ideal snorkeling areas.
Contact: Reservations and information, 242/342-3053.

New Bight Service Station

Car rentals are available here. If you're staying at Fernandez Bay, the hotel will drive you over to the station to pick up your car. Rates are based on the number of days you rent the car. We suggest getting a car with air-conditioning.
Contact: Reservations and information, 242/342-3014.

Bike, boat and other rentals: We suggest you make these arrangements through your hotel.

Restaurants: Not a lot of choices on the island except for the hotel and resort restaurants. Fernandez Bay is our favorite spots for delicious food and a tranquil beachfront setting.

Arthur's Town, New Bight, and Old Bight have well stocked grocery and liquor stores.

Clinics: Nurse-staffed clinics are in Arthur's Town, Smith Bay, and Old Bight.

NEW DEVELOPMENTS

We've heard that plans are underway for a new North Cat Island Marina at Orange Creek. The plan is for a sixty-slip marina inside the creek mouth. Contact developer Nick Cripps for more information at 242/354-4004.

Little San Salvador has been purchased by Holland America Line-Westours, Inc. This cruise ship company has renamed the island Half Moon Cay, and the island is now private. Boaters should be aware that anchoring in any of the island's bays or coves is prohibited. In an emergency boaters can contact the island authorities by radio for assistance, or for permission to seek shelter in bad weather. Log on to our web site at www.bahamasflyfishingguide.com for updated information.

12

Long Island

C ape Santa Maria, Long Island's northernmost landfall, is twenty-seven miles northeast of George Town, Exuma, and roughly the same distance from Devil's Point on Cat Island. From the Cape to South End, the island snakes for almost eighty miles, and is never more than four miles wide.

The island is one of stunning contrasts in geography. The west coast is composed of sandy flats, powdery-white beaches, and calm turquoise-colored bays, while the east coast consists of harsh reefs and chalk-white cliffs that plunge into often wild dark blue waters. Divided by the Tropic of Cancer, the island's terrain varies from the

Aerial view of Long Island, flats around Cape Santa Maria and Stella Maris.

dramatic limestone cliffs in the north and south, to rolling hillsides, to swampland, to stark white flatlands where salt is produced. The island is thought to be one of Columbus' early stops, probably his third, after San Salvador and Rum Cay. The Arawak Indians called the island Yuma; Columbus named it Fernandina, out of respect for his Spanish sponsor.

American Loyalists from the Carolinas settled on Long Island with their slaves in 1790. Plantations were built, and more than four thousand acres were planted with cotton. Rich soil made cotton growing more successful here than on any of the other Out Islands. With the abolition of slavery, however, the plantations failed. Today, Loyalist buildings stand in ruin, while agriculture is still a significant part of daily life.

Pothole farming is the most popular method of growing a variety of crops, from peas, squash, and corn, to bananas, pineapples, and other fruits. While many natural potholes are used, locals also blast holes in the rocky soil to create additional "fields." Along with farming, residents make a living from raising cattle, sheep, goats and pigs.

Tourism is another reason why prosperity is growing on Long Island, and why the population has grown to over five thousand permanent residents. The two major resorts, Stella Maris Resort Club and Cape Santa Maria Beach Resort, are attracting more and more visitors to this uniquely beautiful island. Fishing, diving, snorkeling, and enjoying the tropical atmosphere are the key ingredients.

More than one hundred years ago, settlers built a carriage road running the length of the island. These people understood that commerce and development required good communication and transportation routes. The island's thirty-five farming towns and settlements are situated along the road and around the harbors and anchorages. Queens Highway has been recently resurfaced to provide smooth driving from Columbus Cove to South End.

Renting a car and driving the length of the island is something we recommend.

Stella Maris Airport.

You'll have an opportunity to see many historical sights, including Loyalist and Arawak ruins, and several monuments to Christopher Columbus. You'll also be able to stop off at a number of immaculate beaches, blue holes, and deserted flats where you can wade in and start casting to tailing bonefish.

Most tourists traveling to Long Island stay at either Stella Maris Resort Club or Cape Santa Maria Beach Resort. Flying into Stella Maris airport is the way to go, as flying into Deadman's Cay airport will mean a $120 or more taxi ride to reach the resorts. Bahamasair flies most days from Nassau to Stella Maris. Island Express usually flies from Ft. Lauderdale to Stella Maris Thursday through Sunday. Stella Maris has its own charter flights from George Town, Exuma, and from Nassau.

When you arrive at Stella Maris Airport you'll find taxis waiting to take you to any destination. If you're staying at one of the resorts you won't need a car, but we recommend renting one for at least a day or two to explore the island on your own. Cars and scooters can be rented through the resorts or through Taylor's Rentals.

You will want to fly into Deadman's Cay Airport if you have booked a fly fishing package to this area, or if you are staying in the Clarence Town area. Taxis are usually waiting for every Bahamasair flight, and can take you wherever you're staying. You can rent a car in advance, or rent one after arrival. If you're not on a bonefishing package, or if you're staying around Clarence Town, you will need a car.

AROUND THE ISLAND

There are no services for boaters on the northern end of Long Island, though several good anchorages over sandy bottoms are available just north and south of the Cape Santa Maria Beach Resort. The resort itself is located on Calabash Bay, on a four-mile stretch of beach made of the softest powder white-sand that you can imagine.

Facing northwest, the resort is a sheltered paradise for people wanting a peaceful tropical vacation with good food, fishing, diving, and snorkeling. Ten colonial-style cottages feature one- and two-bedroom air-conditioned villas with over-size baths. Rattan furnishings, marble-tiled floors, and large screened porches create a feeling of casual elegance, and no room is more than sixty feet from the beach.

A new common building includes a dazzling marble and tile lobby, equipment rental center, gift shop, satellite TV room, exercise room with modern workout equipment, plus a spectacular bar and restaurant with panoramic views of Calabash Bay. Additional activities include windsurfing, sea kayaking, sailing, snorkeling, water skiing, bicycling, and hiking. This resort's beach is one of the most alluring and relaxing places we've ever been to. The resort can arrange bonefishing, reef fishing, or offshore fishing, and all equipment can be provided, including fly rods and reels.

A mile or so north of the resort is Columbus Cove, which features a monument on a windswept hilltop marking Columbus's visit. It's possible to drive here, but you'll need a four-wheel drive vehicle. If you want to hike it will take at least thirty minutes. The easiest access is by boat, but you'll want calm weather, otherwise the entrance to the cove is dangerous. You can have the resort pack you a lunch, drop you off here, then pick you up later. Don't forget your snorkeling gear and your fly rod. Bonefishing is very good at the lower tidal stages on all the flats around the cove.

The northernmost settlement of Seymour's is at the end of the Queen's Highway, though the road continues on to the bay at the southern tip of Newton Cay. You can park your car in the turnaround, then hike over the bridge and out to a gorgeous beach that offers good snorkeling. There are also bonefish along the edges of the inner bay, tarpon in the creeks, and reef fishing options at the mouth of the bay.

The well-maintained community of Seymour's, with a population of around two hundred, is on ground that's high enough to offer views of Conception Island and the southern Exuma Cays on clear days. The locals farm the higher ground around the Cape sound, and export a good portion of their crops to the other islands.

On the western side of Seymour's is Joe's Sound, a mangrove maze of creeks and small flats that merge into a gorgeous deep blue channel flanked by glistening white sand banks. Boaters line up to anchor in this protected creek, which opens to the sea at the north end of Hog Cay, and serpentines south across more flats that run into Glenton Sound. Wading anglers can gain access to the upper parts of Joe's Sound and the smaller northern creek that connects to Glenton Sound. A boat is necessary to reach the massive wadable flats farther out in Glenton Sound. While bonefish are the most plentiful gamefish in this area, there are tarpon in the creeks and channels, and permit move onto the outer flats in the summer.

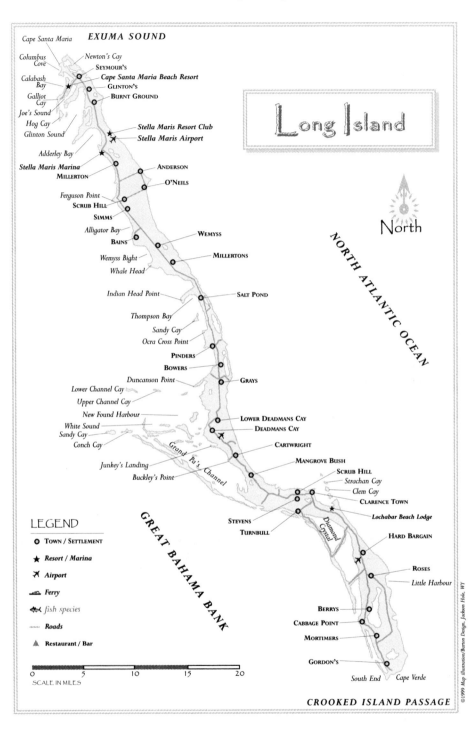

EXUMA SOUND

Cape Santa Maria
Columbus Cove
Newton's Cay
SEYMOUR'S
Calabash Bay
Cape Santa Maria Beach Resort
GLINTON'S
Galliot Cay
BURNT GROUND
Joe's Sound
Hog Cay
Glinton Sound
Stella Maris Resort Club
Stella Maris Airport
Adderley Bay
Stella Maris Marina
MILLERTON
ANDERSON
O'NEILS
Ferguson Point
SCRUB HILL
SIMMS
Alligator Bay
BAINS
WEMYSS
Wemyss Bight
MILLERTONS
Whale Head
Indian Head Point
SALT POND
Thompson Bay
Sandy Cay
Ocra Cross Point
PINDERS
BOWERS
Duncanson Point
GRAYS
Lower Channel Cay
Upper Channel Cay
New Found Harbour
White Sound
LOWER DEADMANS CAY
DEADMANS CAY
Sandy Cay
Conch Cay
CARTWRIGHT
Junkey's Landing
Grand Pa's Channel
MANGROVE BUSH
Buckley's Point
SCRUB HILL
Strachan Cay
Clem Cay
CLARENCE TOWN
STEVENS
Lochabar Beach Lodge
TURNBULL
Diamond Crystal
HARD BARGAIN
GREAT BAHAMA BANK
ROSES
Little Harbour
BERRYS
CABBAGE POINT
MORTIMERS
GORDON'S
South End
Cape Verde

Long Island

North

NORTH ATLANTIC OCEAN

CROOKED ISLAND PASSAGE

LEGEND

◎ TOWN / SETTLEMENT
★ Resort / Marina
✈ Airport
⛴ Ferry
🐟 fish species
Roads
🍴 Restaurant / Bar

0   5   10   15   20
SCALE IN MILES

©1999 Map illustration/Burton Design, Jackson Hole, WY

*The beach at Cape Santa
Maria Beach Resort.*

Other flats can be accessed by wading anglers just south of Glenton Settlement. The settlement is on the highway, and home to Barbie's Ice Cream Restaurant and Bar. As the name implies, ice cream is the ticket here, though good burgers and sandwiches are served at lunchtime. Continuing south, the highway next runs through the settlement of Burnt Ground. Mangrove swamps spread to the west of the settlement, while high bluffs run to the eastern coast.

A mini-peninsula juts out toward the southwest here, separating Glenton Sound from Adderley's Bay. The mangrove swamps and shorelines create good bonefish habitat in this area. Anglers can fish the sound or the bay on their own without a boat, though a boat will provide access to more flats. These light-bottomed flats are often glass calm, especially in the mornings and evenings. When the low incoming tide is early or late, you can cast to tailing fish in ideal conditions.

A little farther south is Stella Maris, which is composed of a marina, airstrip, and plantation-style resort complex. Boaters cruising down from the north, or east from the Exumas, will pass Dove Cay en route to the small man-made harbor and marina. Twelve slips are available for visiting boaters, and calling ahead for space is necessary. Use VHF channel 16. Full services include fuel, petroleum products, electricity, water, ice, showers, and laundromat.

The airstrip and resort are north of the marina. The resort itself sits on a hill overlooking the ruggedly beautiful eastern shore, with aquamarine water washing over dark coral reefs. The main clubhouse features an immaculate restaurant, bar, game room, satellite TV area, and gift shop. The spacious air-conditioned hotel rooms and one-bedroom cottages are situated around the clubhouse. Two-, three-, and four-bedroom beach houses, several with private pools, are also available for rent. Three freshwater swimming pools and a small beach round out the amenities.

The atmosphere at Stella Maris is laid back, but also festive, and the staff, led by owner/operators Jorg Friese and Peter Kuska, is extremely helpful and friendly. Monday nights feature the Out Island Cave Party, a lively event featuring a barbecue buffet, live band, and dancing. On Wednesday nights guests party on with special rum punches and another barbecue. On occasion these party nights are switched around and special events are added. Diving and snorkeling excursions are available every day, as is complimentary transportation to Cape Santa Maria and other beaches. All you have to do is sign up. Serious divers will want to try the wall dives off Conception Island, or one of the blue hole dives.

Stella Maris/Long Island guide Docky Smith.

Anglers staying at Stella Maris can walk over to fish Adderley Bay, or take a rod to one of the eastern snorkeling beaches and catch jacks, snappers and grouper on Clouser Minnows. The resort can arrange for bonefishing guides, or for reef and offshore fishing charters. James "Docky" Smith works for Stella Maris and is one of the best guides on the island. If you want to book Docky, you will need to do it well in advance.

Eight miles south of Stella Maris is Simms settlement, one of the oldest on the island. Neat pastel-colored houses are shaded by casuarinas and often fronted by low stone walls. A nurse-staffed clinic can be found here, along with a telephone station, several small stores, and a couple of restaurants serving Bahamian specialties. Many boaters traveling from Exuma head straight here, then on south to Salt Pond, which offers the most protected anchorages on the west coast.

Driving from Simms to Salt Pond, about ten miles, takes you past the settlement of Thompson Bay. There are several areas here where an adventurous angler could gain access to decent leeward flats, though you'd have to do some slogging through mucky mangroves. Thompson Bay itself offers fair wading right along the shoreline and easier access during the lower tidal stages.

Salt Pond is headquarters for the annual Long Island Regatta, held every May. Several stores between the main and regatta docks are well stocked with groceries, nonprescription drugs, hardwares, and household goods. The mail boat makes regular visits, and repair service is available for outboard motors.

The Thompson Bay Inn, a large yellow two-story building, is located north of Salt Pond. Proprietor, Alphonso Bowe, serves breakfast, lunch, and dinner, and the bar is a lively meeting place for friendly locals. Good quality rental cars are also available here.

If you drive through this area, be on the lookout for a couple of easy-to-miss food stands offering some of the best fresh conch salad outside of Andros. Also remember that most of the "established" restaurants are not always open for every meal, and some won't take you unless you called ahead to make a reservation. We always carry a cooler in our car with drinks, sandwiches, and snacks when exploring any of the Out Islands.

Another eight or so miles south of Salt Pond is Deadman's Cay, the largest settlement on the island, and site of the main island airport. This is a pleasant community of hardworking, friendly people. There are several good restaurants, small motels, and a couple of gas stations. Wade Smith runs a bonefishing lodge, represented by Westbank Anglers, on the bay side of the highway behind the Batelco station. Smith's guides include Sammy Knowles, and Jerry and Frank Cartwright. These guides know the area extremely well and fish out of well-maintained Rahming skiffs with Yamaha outboards. The lodge offers complete bonefishing packages including comfortable air-conditioned rooms, meals, and guided fishing, at very reasonable prices.

Stephen with guide Cecil Knowles in Deadman's Cay.

The Deadman's Cay area is actually several settlements that run together. Continuing south you'll enter Mangrove Bush. Kooters Restaurant is on the water just north of the dock where several independent guides, including Ivan Knowles and his sons, keep their boats. Kooters serves good seafood, chicken, and ribs, and you can sit out on the deck overlooking the bay while you eat or sip a cold Kalik.

A little farther on is Earlie's Tavern, run by Judy Knowles and her family. Judy's husband, Cecil, is a commercial lobster fisherman who is also a good bonefishing guide. We enjoy fishing with Cecil, who has also taken the time to teach us about the vast flats that extend north up to White Sound, Sandy Cay, and on beyond the Channel Cays. Miles and miles of protected wadable flats are only a short boat ride away. The reclaiming of salt-producing pans formed a large part of this area. After the salt company went out of business, the locals blasted holes in the dikes that maintained water levels in the salt pans. Fresh ocean water worked its magic, and now these areas are amazing bonefish flats that can be waded at any stage of the tide, as the tide rarely varies more than a foot or so from low to high.

Earlie's Tavern serves good Bahamian-style food at lunch and dinner, and their bar and outdoor dance floor are hopping on the weekends and during Regatta time. They also prepare picnic lunches to go. Judy and Cecil Knowles have put together bonefishing packages that include accommodations in rental houses or at Lochabar Beach Lodge, all meals, and guided fishing.

If you drive south toward Clarence Town, you'll see the pink-walled entrance to Turtle Cove. If you turn in here you'll have easy access to several nice beaches and Dean's Blue Hole, which has been measured to be roughly 660 feet in depth. The Stella Maris dive shop offers regular trips to explore this fascinating spot. If you decide to go don't ask the locals to tell you any of the stories attached to the blue hole. If you're superstitious, you'll never dive in any blue hole again.

Turtle Cove itself is a planned resort community, but final approval on the project was still pending during our last visit. The resort plans to feature hundreds of home sites, a hotel complex with swimming pool and restaurant, an eighteen-hole golf course, and tennis facilities.

We know of no good harbors or anchorages for boaters from Salt Pond to South End. Boaters rounding South End and heading north again will find anchorages and most services in Clarence Town.

Dean's Blue Hole near Clarence Town.

If you drive into Clarence Town you will immediately notice the two twin-spired churches. On the left side of the highway, just before town, is St. Paul's Anglican Church, with a red roof built by Father Jerome during his Anglican days. Father Jerome later converted to Catholicism and built St. Paul's Catholic Church with a blue roof, on the right side of the highway farther into the settlement and overlooking the harbor. Both churches have twin spires that can be seen by boaters approaching the harbor from miles away. Father Jerome, as you'll recall, is buried in the Hermitage tomb on the peak of Mt. Alvernia on Cat Island.

The main settlement buildings, including the commissioner's house, overlook a pretty harbor and three large cays. Our boating friends have told us they prefer the anchorage in the lee of Strachan Cay to the harbor itself. Groceries, including meat and produce, are usually in good supply, but check the mail boat schedule to see the last time supplies were delivered from Nassau. The Harbour Rest restaurant and bar is at the mail boat dock. Breakfast, lunch, and dinner are served on a somewhat regular schedule. A telephone station is near the commissioner's office, as is a nurse-staffed clinic.

A mile or so farther south is the turnoff to Lochabar Beach Lodge. The remote lodge features two large suites with full kitchens, private baths, and spacious decks overlooking a dazzling blue hole, a white sand beach, and several deserted cays. The lodge managers are happy to arrange everything from airport pickup, to grocery store trips, to guided fishing. Adventurous anglers or vacationers will enjoy the seclusion here, though you'll want to rent a car to take advantage of all the great fishing and snorkeling around the southern part of the island.

The Forest Restaurant and bar, a pastel pink building, is just south of the Lochabar Beach Lodge turnoff on the main highway. This is the best place to eat in the area, with specialties such as cracked conch, grouper, baked chicken, and bar-becued ribs. The bar serves appetizers, including chicken wings and potato skins. The pool table always seems to be in use, especially on Friday and Saturday nights. A live band also plays here a few Fridays every month, much to the delight of dancing enthusiasts.

If you continue driving south, you'll pass a good number of ruins, including what looks like an old castle on a high bluff near Dunmore. The view from here is amazing, giving you the feeling of being alone in a newly discovered place. At Hard Bargain you'll be able to continue south, or take the leeward road back up to Clarence Town. The leeward road will give you access to miles of bonefish flats, some of which are easy to reach, and others that will require walking through mucky mangrove terrain.

If you take the left fork in the road to Little Harbour, south of Hard Bargain, you'll find a picturesque bay that provides good anchorages for boaters and access to beautiful snorkeling beaches. The reef fishing is also very good, especially on calm days.

South End is the southern tip of the island. Miles of rarely fished flats sweep around to the west and back up to Mortimers. In talking with boaters and locals, and doing some exploring on our own, it's clear that good numbers of bonefish roam this southeastern edge of the Great Bahama Bank. Good numbers of permit and tarpon can also be found here.

FISHING HIGHLIGHTS

The Long Island fishery is fed by the Exuma Sound to the north, the Great Bahama Bank to the east, and the North Equatorial Current, which originates in the Canary Is-lands and eventually sweeps along the windward coast. Blue water is only a short run off Long Island's northern, eastern, and southern shores. Good numbers of blue and white marlin, sailfish, dorado, wahoo, and a variety of tuna create excellent offshore fishing opportunities in season.

The flats habitat off the western coast is home to high numbers of bonefish, plus sharks, barracuda, permit, tarpon, and some snook. Most of the flats are light-colored, composed of hard sand, variable coral, or soft white muck. Shrimp and crabs are the most common bonefish food, with white and gray sea crabs the highlight. When local guides work with spin fishermen they always use fresh sea crabs.

The northern part of the island, including Cape Santa Maria and Stella Maris, has a latitude equivalent to the fishing grounds of Great Exuma. South of Simms settle-ment, the island is below the Tropic of Cancer. This relatively southern location means that weather is more stable than in the northern Bahamas. Most cold fronts moving down from the north will stall before they reach the Deadman's Cay area. When com-bined with miles of protected leeward flats, these weather patterns mean that fly fish-ers pursuing bonefish will see favorable conditions most of the year.

Bonefish rank as the number one flats gamefish. High numbers of fish and rela-tively little fishing pressure makes Long Island a good choice for beginning fly fishers. Being able to cast to a lot of fish is the best way to improve your skills. More experi-enced anglers will have the opportunity to catch lots of fish on days when the weather is good. Fish average three to four pounds, with six- to eight-pound fish common, and fish over ten pounds possible. On the northern part of the island we prefer to fish the incoming tide, especially when wading, though the last part of the falling tide is very good as well. On the Deadman's Cay salt pan flats, wade fishing is excellent at any stage of the tide, though when you move out to White Sound, the incoming tide is best.

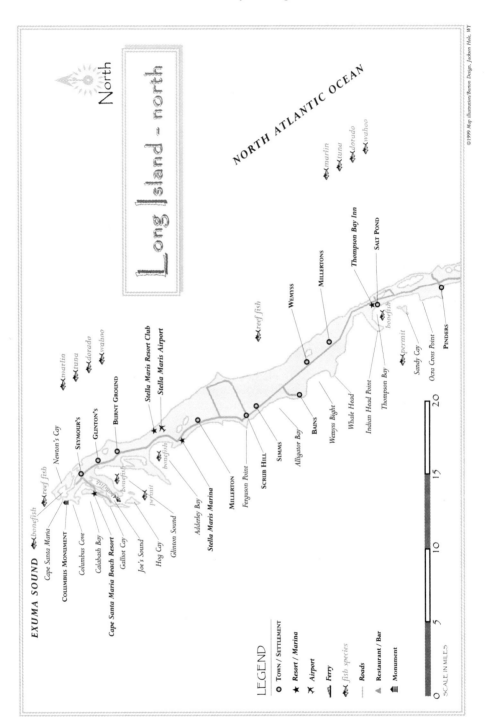

North

Long Island – north

NORTH ATLANTIC OCEAN

marlin
tuna
dorado
wahoo

EXUMA SOUND

Thompson Bay Inn
SALT POND

WEMYSS

MILLERTONS

reef fish

bonefish

permit

Sandy Cay
Oca Cross Point
PINDERS

Stella Maris Resort Club
Stella Maris Airport

BURNT GROUND

marlin
tuna
dorado
wahoo

SEYMOUR'S
GLINTON'S

Newton's Cay

reef fish

bonefish

bonefish

millhouse?
bonefish

permit

Cape Santa Maria
COLUMBUS MONUMENT
Columbus Cove
Calabash Bay
Cape Santa Maria Beach Resort
Galliot Cay
Joe's Sound
Hog Cay
Glinton Sound

Adderley Bay
Stella Maris Marina

MILLERTON
Ferguson Point
SCRUB HILL

SIMMS

Alligator Bay
BAINS

Wemyss Bight
Whale Head
Indian Head Point
Thompson Bay

LEGEND

○ TOWN / SETTLEMENT
★ Resort / Marina
✈ Airport
⛴ Ferry
🐟 fish species
— Roads
▲ Restaurant / Bar
🏛 Monument

SCALE IN MILES

0   5   10   15   20

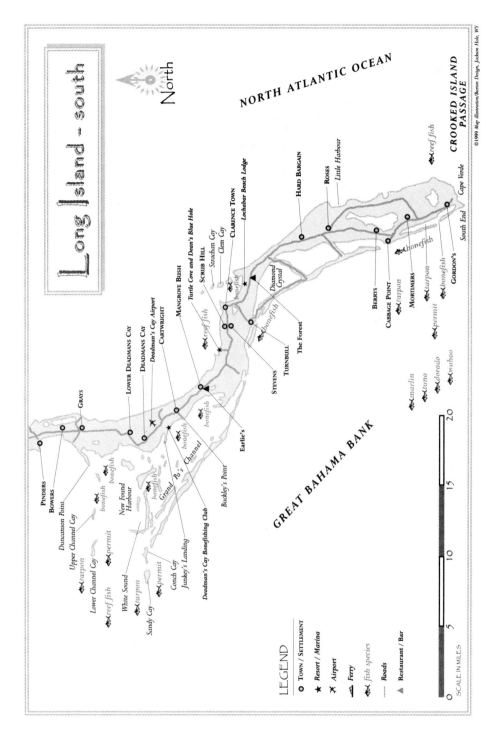

Day in and day out, bonefish will be more aggressive on the incoming tide. The length of the island means that anglers fishing on their own, and renting a car, can set up a strategy to fish an incoming tide for most of the day. This can be done by fishing both sides of the island, and by moving on the north/south axis. Tides vary at least two hours from the windward to leeward side of the island, and up to three hours from the northern to southern tips. Our favorite bonefish flies include #4–6 Gotchas, #4 Gotcha Clousers, #4–6 Gold and White Krystal Charlies, #4 White Epoxy Charlies, #4–6 Mantis Shrimp, and #6 Tan Yarn Crabs.

We recommend fishing with a guide at least part of the time. Usually, you will learn more from a guide in a day than you will on your own in a week. Guides can be arranged through professional booking agents, through the island resorts, or, in some cases, with the guides directly. You should always plan on booking in advance, especially from March through May.

Fly-fishing for permit is fair at best, though this is partly due to the fact that local guides don't understand the permit fishery. The guides have not been pushed to explore the permit options because anglers have not created a demand. Most permit fishing is done with live crabs on spinning gear, with April through July being the best time to go.

In talking with boaters and guides, we understand that the potential for permit fishing is best from Newfound Harbour to South End. Deep water meets the edge of the Great Bahama Bank throughout this area, plus there are a number of small cays and blue channels surrounded by sand banks loaded with crabs. We have just begun to explore the permit fishery, and have seen good concentrations of permit on occasion in White Sound and at Mortimers Cut. Our favorite permit flies include #4 White, Tan, and Gray Yarn Crabs, #2 Del's Merkins, and #4 Epoxy Crabs.

The tarpon story is similar to the permit story, with the best fishing grounds overlapping. The main difference is that tarpon fishing is good in many of the blue holes and landlocked lakes. We suggest hiring a guide for a day of blue hole fishing. On the flats, we've seen tarpon from Joe's Sound to South End, with the Sandy Cay and Mortimers Cut flats having the highest number of fish. A number of creeks and mangrove bays around Mortimers lure tarpon into protected feeding areas. Our favorite flies include #4/0 Shallow Water Cockroachs and Olch's Bad Crabs, and #2/0 Chartreuse/White Clousers.

Sharks and barracuda roam the flats throughout the year, but the best fishing for these species is over the reefs. In general, the reef fishing is outstanding everywhere. If you just want to catch a lot of hard-fighting game fish, take along plenty of chum and enjoy a day of reef fishing with a guide. Jacks, snappers, grouper, and mackerel will join a variety of sharks and barracuda in a feeding frenzy that will give your arms a workout.

Strip it, mon, strip it!

The offshore fishing is good most of the year, you just need to pick fishing times based on the species you want. The best months for billfish are May through July. Most billfishing is done with conventional gear. We don't know of any fly fishing savvy crews operating out of Long Island, but experienced anglers will see enough fish in the prime months to take some shots with flies. Dorado show up in March, with April through June prime. These aggressive fish hit flies with abandon. Fish average twenty to thirty pounds, with some bulls approaching seventy pounds. Yellowfin tuna in the thirty- to 150-pound range are best from April through May. Rainbow runners in the ten- to thirty-pound range are best March through May. Wahoo, our favorite blue-water fish on the table, are prime from September through November, with December a good shoulder month. Blackfin tuna turn up in good numbers in July, and run through December. These powerful fish average twenty pounds, with larger fish going over thirty.

OPTIONAL ACTIVITIES

Long Island is a great vacation choice for anglers and nonanglers. Diving and snorkeling don't get any better in terms of undersea splendor and a wide variety of options. For the best combination of fishing, diving, snorkeling, and general relaxing we recommend staying at either Cape Santa Maria Beach Resort or Stella Maris Resort.

The dive program at Stella Maris is world class. Beginning divers can learn to scuba in warm clear water without fighting currents. A resort course includes theory and practical instruction, then your first ocean dive. For advanced divers, trips to Conception Island, including overnight trips, offer pristine wall diving equal to the best locations in the world.

Other diving options include hundreds of coral heads and reef sites in the northwest lee of the island in depths of thirty to eighty-five feet, plus shark diving and diving over the wrecked freighter Comberbach. Along the northeast Atlantic coast, coral fields and reef drop-offs create an endless variety of sites. If you want to test your courage, you can dive in one of the two deepest blue holes in the world.

If you like swimming and looking at tropical fish but don't want to dive, you'll find as many snorkeling locations as you're willing to look for. Snorkeling is good around the major resorts, then along the entire length of the island from Cape Santa Maria to Little Harbour. Stella Maris offers guided snorkeling trips, plus self-guided trips that include the use of their boats to access more remote areas.

LODGING AND SERVICES

FEATURED LODGES AND ACCOMODATIONS

Stella Maris Resort Club

Stella Maris This resort sits on a green bluff overlooking the deep blue Atlantic Ocean. Deluxe air-conditioned accommodations include 20 rooms, 12 1-bedroom cottages, 7 2-bedroom cottages, and 4 houses. These accommodations range from spacious and comfortable to luxurious. Houses include full kitchens, and some have private pools. Resort amenities feature a great dining room and fun bar, satellite TV, three pools, bicycles, sailing, snorkeling, Ping-Pong, boating, waterskiing, a complete dive shop, and complimentary shuttles to area beaches. Guest activities include complimentary island excursions, boat cruises to remote beaches, and special parties several nights a week. Owner/operators Jorg Friese, Peter Kuska, and their families and staff,

Flags at Stella Maris.

all go out of their way to provide superior guest services. We highly recommend this resort for an all-around beach and sun vacation.

Season: October through July.

Suitable For: Anglers and nonanglers.

Optional Activities: The resort offers flats, reef, and offshore fishing. James "Docky" Smith is the head guide, and one of the best guides on the island. Flats skiffs are used to access the nearby flats, with wading a priority here when the tide is right. It is only a short walk to some very good flats for anglers who want to fish on their own. The Stella Maris marina offers most services for boaters. The dive shop is the best on the island, and suited to beginners or experts. The resort arranges for overnight diving excursions to Conception Island.

What's Included: As much or as little as you want. Complete bonefishing packages are available that include deluxe accommodations, meals, guided fishing, and Bahamian taxes. Custom packages can include all types of fishing, mixing flats, reefs, and/or offshore. The resort offers its own air charter service from Nassau and George Town, Exuma.

Not Included: You can book accommodations only, then choose daily activities and meals as you go. Airfare to/from Stella Maris. Taxis meet you at the Stella Maris airport for the short trip to the resort.

Pricing: $$–$$$

Contact: Reservations and information, 800/426-0466 or 242/338-2051, fax 954/359-8238 or 242/338-2052.
E-mail: smrc@stellamarisresort.com
Internet: www.stellamarisresort.com

Cape Santa Maria Beach Resort & Fishing Club

Cape Santa Maria   Looking for an intimate resort with deluxe accommodations in an isolated location on one of the world's most beautiful beaches? This is the place. Enjoy the charm and hospitality of the Bahamian people, calm waters, cooling trade winds, and a variety of abundant game fish.

The resort features 18 1- and 2-bedroom air-conditioned villas decorated in soothing tropical colors. Each large villa is adorned with ornate woodwork, a screened veranda with rattan lounge chairs, marble floors, and private baths. All rooms are within 60 feet of the idyllic white sand beach. A reverse osmosis system supplies abundant fresh water. The restaurant serves good food with a Bahamian flare and offers wonderful views of Calabash Bay. The tropical bar is a great place to sip rum drinks and watch the sunset.

Season: October through July.

Suitable For: Anglers and nonanglers.

Optional Activities: The resort offers flats, reef, and offshore fishing. Guides work out of modern flats skiffs, though wading is also a priority when the tide is right. A 26-foot Mako center console complete with outriggers is used for reef fishing. A 31-foot Bertram is fully equipped with all conventional gear for offshore fishing. The lodge can supply all the tackle for all types of trips, including fly rods and wading booties for flats fishing.

Nonfishing activities include sunbathing, snorkeling, bird watching, and boating day trips to secluded coves and caves near the lodge. Toys include a windsurfer, Hobie cat, and bicycles to explore the island.

What's Included: As much or as little as you want. Complete bonefishing packages are available that include deluxe accommodations, meals, guided fishing, and Bahamian taxes. Custom packages can include all types of fishing, mixing flats, reefs, and offshore.

Not Included: Airfare to/from Stella Maris Airport. You can book accommodations only, then choose daily activities and meals as you go. Round-trip taxi service between Stella Maris Airport and the lodge is $40 for two people.

Pricing: $$$
Contact: Reservations and information, 242/338-5273 or 800/663-7090, fax 242/338-6013.
E-mail: capesm@batelnet.bs
Internet: www.capesantamaria.com

Deadman's Cay Bonefishing Club

Deadman's Cay   Wade Smith and Samuel Knowles have put together a tremendous bonefishing package with some of the best guides on the island—Sammy Knowles, Jerry Cartwright and Frank Cartwright. The guides work out of well-maintained Rahming skiffs with center consoles and Yamaha outboards. The comfortable lodge features two-bedroom/one bath air-conditioned units with kitchenettes and a small living area. The hospitality here is top-notch. The boat dock is just a few steps from the rooms. The vast fishing areas feature some of the best wading for bonefish anywhere. While this is not a well-publicized operation, word of mouth has spread quickly, so booking well in advance is required, especially during March through June, and October and November.
Season: October through July.
Suitable For: Anglers only.
What's Included: Complete bonefishing packages are available; including accommodations, meals, guided fishing, Deadman's Cay airport transfers, and Bahamian taxes. Package prices are the lowest in the Bahamas. 7 night/6 day packages run Saturday-to-Saturday.
Not Included: Airfare to/from Deadman's Cay Airport, alcoholic beverages, and optional gratuities.
Pricing: $
Contact: Reservations and information, 800/922-3474, fax 307/733-9382. In the Bahamas, 242/337-1056.

ADDITIONAL ACCOMMODATIONS

Lochabar Beach Lodge

Clarence Town   Located 1 mile south of Clarence Town on the ocean side of the island. Open-air Bahama shutters and double screen doors bring the island right into your 600-square-foot room, which includes a kitchen and private bath. You can step from your covered deck onto a pristine beach that meanders back toward Clarence Town in one direction, and around a beautiful blue hole and natural cove in the other. If you want to bonefish on your own, there are several flats just a short walk from your room. Guided bonefishing and tarpon fishing, snorkeling, beachcombing, and other activities can be arranged. You fly into the Deadman's Cay Airport, then take a taxi to the lodge, or the managers can arrange for a rental car.
Pricing: $–$$
Contact: Reservations and information, 242/337-3123, or 800/922-3474.

Private Rental Houses

Deadman's Cay and Clarence Town   Call Judy Knowles if you want to rent a house in this area. Judy and her husband, Cecil, also put together bonefishing packages that include a private house, meals, guided fishing, and Bahamian taxes. Houses can include air-conditioning, telephones, full kitchens, and satellite TV. This is one of the most economical ways to fish the Bahamas on your own, or with a guide.
Pricing: $–$$
Contact: Reservations and information, 242/337-0329 or 242/337-1555, fax 242/337-6556. In the U.S., 800/922-3474.

SERVICES

All visitors to Long Island will be best served by making rental and activity arrangements through their hotels, or through sources listed below. There are several good restaurants on the island outside of the resorts, though some are not always open, so call ahead if you can. Also, most restaurants and bars only take cash, no credit cards, traveler's checks, or personal checks. The restaurants we especially recommend are Earlie's

Tavern in Mangrove Bush, and The Forest, a mile south of Clarence Town. The Forest proprietor, Dudley Dean, likes to fish and is a great source of fishing information throughout southern Long Island.

Diving and snorkeling gear is available for rent at the major resorts. So are bicycles, sea kayaks, small sailboats, and windsurfers. We recommend renting a car, and taking a picnic lunch along to explore the east coast of the island. Countless beaches, reefs, and outside flats offer good fishing, snorkeling, and seclusion.

Bonefishing Guides: Packages are available at Stella Maris, Cape Santa Maria, and Deadman's Cay Bonefishing. Packages are also available with anglers staying in private houses. For day trips, independent guides can be arranged through your hotel, by calling the guides directly, or by calling 800/922-3474.

Taylor's Rentals
Car and scooter rentals. You can arrange for this company to deliver your car to your hotel.
Contact: Reservations and information, 242/338-7001.

Nurse-staffed clinics are in Simms, Deadman's Cay, and Clarence Town.

The Royal Bank of Canada in Deadman's Cay and in Grays is open Monday through Thursday 9:00 A.M. to 1:00 P.M., and Friday until 5:00 P.M. The Bank of Nova Scotia in Stella Maris is open Tuesday and Thursday.

NEW DEVELOPMENTS

The bonefishing industry is gaining momentum here. We've heard lots of talk about new guides and lodges. Dudley Dean, proprietor of The Forest Restaurant and bar, is a good example. Dean has built six new motel rooms behind his restaurant, and wants to book angling packages. Judy and Cecil Knowles rent private homes to anglers now, and are talking about building a lodge of their own.

On a much larger scale, the resort development at Turtle Cove, with hundreds of home sites, a hotel, restaurant, eighteen-hole golf course, and tennis facilities, would have a major impact on southern Long Island. Resorts like this have been planned many times on other islands, without ever being completed. This resort still needs final government approvals, so we'll see what happens. Log on to our Web site at www.bahamasflyfishingguide.com for updated information.

13

Crooked and Acklins Islands

Crooked and Acklins Islands, Long Cay and Castle Island form an atoll that surrounds the fertile shallow water fishery of the Bight of Acklins. Spectacular reefs, which are dangerous to boaters, run along the northern and western edges of this triangular-shaped group. The bottom of the triangle covers forty-five miles from Portland Harbour and Pittstown Point to Castle Island. A continuous reef spans from Windsor Point off the south end of Long Cay to Salina Point off southwestern Acklins, protecting the entrance to the Bight. This island group is 225 miles southeast of Nassau and about thirty-five miles southeast of Long Island across the Crooked Island Passage.

Columbus sailed across the passage, making what historians think was his fourth Bahamian landfall at Portland Harbour. The story goes that Columbus was lured ashore by enchanting fragrances carried on the ocean breeze. Cascarilla bark was one of the herbs creating the aroma, and it remains an important export item today; it is used in certain medicines.

The islands existed in obscurity until 1783 when American Loyalists arrived with their slaves. Unlike on Long Island and Abaco, the soil here could not support the cotton-growing plantations that were built. When the cotton industry failed, the population was forced to earn a living from the sea. Sponging became the lifeblood of the island until the early 1900s, when fungus destroyed the sponging grounds. The people continued fishing, plus they eked out a living by farming the few fertile areas available. Not much has changed since then, and in most ways these islands remain as natural and beautiful as when they were first discovered.

One of the least known islands of the Bahamas, Acklins comprises the eastern and southeastern part of the atoll. The terrain is hilly and desolate, with unusual rock formations and varied plant and animal life, including an occasional swamp turtle. Along the eastern coastline treacherous reefs protect tranquil coves and stunning white sand beaches.

Spring Point, in the middle of the island, is the main settlement. The airport and government headquarters are located here. To say this island is quiet and laid-back is an understatement. Locals like to say, "You make your own sunshine." In other words, you're on your own.

Brian O'Keefe

Fishing a flat off Crooked Island. Columbus christened this island "Isabella," after his queen.

Crooked Island, together with Long Cay, forms the northern and western part of the atoll system. Columbus christened the island Isabella, after his queen, though the Arawaks called the island Samoete. Somehow, the more functionally descriptive name of Crooked Island took hold and is used today.

This remote island is lined with white sand beaches that stretch for miles to the east and south. Colonel Hill, on the northeastern end, is the main town, and the highest point on the island. The airport and government headquarters are located here. Other settlements include Cripple Hill, True Blue, French Wells, and Gun Point; all are connected by a new paved road.

Albert Town, the only village on Long Cay, is basically a ghost town. Known as Fortune Island in more prosperous times, Long Cay served as a transfer and stopover point for Spanish and British ships sailing between Europe and the Americas.

Castle Island, off the southwest tip of Acklins, was a favorite pirate retreat. A lighthouse was built on the island in 1867. Most of the island is low and sandy, with higher hills along the northern shore. A decent anchorage is available on the south side of the island in Mudian Harbour. The reef protecting the harbor is a great fishing spot for jacks, snappers, and grouper.

Both Crooked and Acklins islands have populations of about four hundred. Farming and fishing continue to be the basis for the local economies, though tourism is beginning to have an impact. The mail boat arrival from Nassau is the big weekly event. New roads run the length of both islands, and power was made available to all residents for the first time in 1998, though many houses are still not connected. Telephone service is available, though most locals don't have phones.

Bahamasair flies into Colonel Hill and Spring Point on Tuesdays and Saturdays, though the schedule could change at any time. Charter flights are available to these two airports, and to the paved strip at Pittstown Point Landing. We suggest having your insect repellent handy upon landing. If the wind is down, you will need it right away.

If you attempt anything on your own in these islands, be aware that there is no guarantee of services of any kind. Groceries and supplies may or may not be available. If you rent a car, you may or may not be able to buy gas. If you reach a telephone, it may not work. Your cellular telephone will not work here. VHF radio is still the best means of communication. Credit cards will do you no good. Same for traveler's checks. Make sure you have cash, and a nothing-bothers-me casual attitude, and you'll have no troubles, mon.

AROUND THE ISLANDS

Most visitors fly to Crooked and Acklins, with their objective being fishing or diving. Pittstown Point and Landrail Point are located on the northwestern tip of Crooked Island. Flying into Pittstown's private airstrip is the way to go, though you could fly into Colonel Hill and take a taxi ride to the resort.

Pittstown Point Landing is the only place we recommend staying on Crooked Island at this time. The resort complex, composed of twelve guest rooms, bar, restaurant, and office, overlooks Portland Harbour and the Bird Rock Lighthouse. A pristine white sand beach is just steps away. The Bahamas' first post office was located here, and its remaining walls are part of the Pittstown Point Dive Club. The lodge features an all-inclusive fishing and diving program. The fishing program offers flats, reefs, and offshore options. The best bonefishing guides on the island work for the resort. Trips to the lighthouse and to massive nearby caves can be arranged.

To the south, Landrail Point offers the best anchorage for boaters. The public wharf is where the mail boat docks. Nice beaches and groves of citrus trees flank the pretty settlement. Gibson's Lunch Room is the place for a good meal, with conch salad being a specialty. Most locals are Seventh Day Adventists, so they don't work from sundown Friday to sundown Saturday, and there is no alcohol available in the settlement. The island's only clinic, nurse-staffed, is located here.

Seven miles farther south is French Wells, which is where guides from Pittstown Point begin fishing miles of wadable flats. French Wells Harbour is fairly well protected and provides good anchorages over a sand bottom. The long creek cutting north is accessible by flats boats and dinghies only, and is home to lots of tarpon. South across the cut are Goat and Rat Cays, then Long Cay. If you continued north of French Wells on the inside you would move toward Turtle Sound, a vast mangrove-lined creek system and bonefish haven. Church Grove Landing is the entrance to the sound. The ferry to Albert Town, which usually runs on Saturdays and Wednesdays, uses the dinghy dock here. It is a two-mile walk from the landing to the Church Grove settlement, which is adjacent to Colonel Hill.

Heading east on the main road out of Pittstown Point, you'll skirt the northern part of Turtle Sound on the way to Colonel Hill and the airport. A couple of stores are pretty well stocked with necessities, including nonprescription drugs. A couple of bars serve snacks, and a telephone station is open during the week.

Continuing east, the road runs through True Blue and Browns settlements, ending at Cove Landing on the western shore of Lovely Bay. You can take a ferry across the bay to Acklins Island.

The Lovely Bay settlement is where the ferry docks on Acklins. A rough road connects to Chesters settlement, where the telephones work on occasion and a nurse-

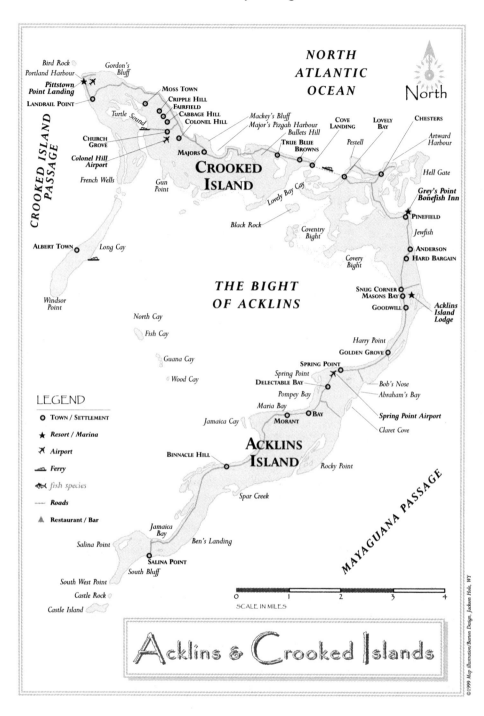

Acklins & Crooked Islands

staffed clinic operates during the week. From here it's about two miles to Atwood Harbour, one of the best anchorages in the four-island region. Heading south, the road skirts around mangrove swamps and bonefish flats to reach Pinefield Point. Grey's Point Bonefish Inn is located here on a hill overlooking Relief Bay to the west and Gordon's Bay to the east. Both bays have extensive bonefish flats. The Inn, a renovated guesthouse with three bedrooms sharing a single bath, offers all-inclusive bonefish packages for up to six anglers at a time.

If you drive south you'll pass through Hard Bargain, which is the highest point on the island. Continuing south toward Spring Point, you'll pass two bonefishing lodges. Top Choice Bonefishing Lodge is on the bight side just north of Mason's Bay settlement. The lodge, operated by Ethlyn and Felix Bain, opened in the fall of 1998, and features four air-conditioned rooms with private baths and satellite TV. Meals are served in the bar/restaurant across the street. The lodge works with three guides using Carolina and Florida skiffs, and can take six anglers.

One mile south, at the narrowest point on the island on a bluff overlooking the ocean and the Bight, is a new deluxe bonefishing lodge, Acklins Island Lodge. The lodge opened for its first full season in the fall of 1999. It features five air-conditioned rooms and a main clubhouse building with a restaurant, bar, satellite TV, and large decks. The ocean views are spectacular, and the high ground location catches cooling offshore breezes that help keep the bugs down.

Just down the hill from the lodge is Liza's OK Corral, a local restaurant that serves delicious Bahamian specialties, and packs good fishing lunches.

Spring Point is the government headquarters for the island. There is a small motel and restaurant near the airport, and a nurse-staffed clinic. The friendly locals can provide supplies and fuel, but you might have to ask around. The best means of communication is by VHF radio.

The low areas along the coastline are mosquito heaven, so make sure you are well coated with bug dope, especially when the wind is down. Continuing south the road winds around Pompey Bay, Jamaica Bay, and ends at Salina Point. There's not much going on down here, though there are wadable flats accessible from the road. On the ocean side are a number of gorgeous deserted beaches. The few residents in the area are very hospitable, and will provide supplies to boaters when available. There is a small restaurant and bar in Salina Point, and a telephone station that usually operates during the week.

FISHING HIGHLIGHTS

The Crooked and Acklins Islands fishery is one of the best and most varied in the Bahamas, and certainly one of the least fished. With its vast interior flats throughout the Bight, surrounding fertile reefs, and deep blue water minutes from shore, this atoll is similar to Andros Island.

Most of the southern shorelines of Crooked and Acklins are composed of mangrove mazes and creeks. Long Cay, which extends straight south of Crooked, and the length of Acklins, which curves back toward the west, features more defined shorelines with coral points and harder-bottomed bays. In the center is the Bight, with a grouping of small cays at the southern end. The bottom structure throughout the Bight varies from hard wadable sand, to irregular coral and grass, to softer mud areas.

This is all prime bonefish habitat, supporting amazing numbers of fish that average three pounds, with plenty of fish in the five- to eight-pound range. These fish are

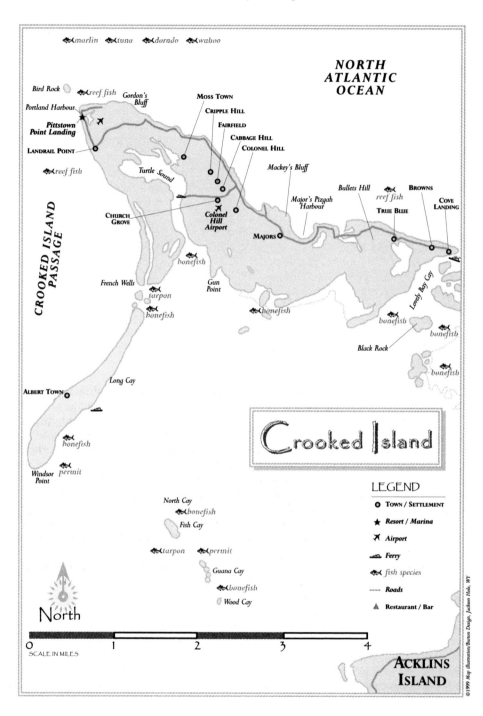

Brian O'Keefe

Amazing numbers of bonefish can be found here.

some of the most aggressive in the Bahamas, making this an ideal location for beginners. Fishing the incoming tide is best on the wadable flats, but fishing is good throughout the day at most stages of the tide. Bigger bones, ten pounds and up, are available here, too, but you'll need to spend some time looking for them instead of hooking up so many smaller fish. Our favorite flies include Gotchas, Epoxy Charlies, Bonefish Puffs, Yarn Crabs, and Clouser Minnows.

Anglers looking for permit will have a reasonable chance of getting a shot or two during a week's fishing. Some of the best permit fishing is available throughout the southern cays, from North Cay to Wood Cay. This is a pretty long boat ride, so we suggest going on a calm day. Permit also concentrate on the inside of Long Cay, around Black Rock, and around Jamaica Cay. Our favorite flies are Del's Merkins, Yarn Crabs, and Epoxy Crabs.

Tarpon move in and out of the various creeks on the tide, with French Wells, Back Creek, and the Going Through holding decent numbers of resident fish. While anglers have been catching an occasional tarpon throughout the season, the development of the tarpon and permit fishing will be up to the guides. If they choose to pursue these species on a regular basis, you might be hearing about a grand slam in the near future. Tarpon anglers should have a rod rigged with a Shallow Water Cockroach or a Red/White Sea Bunny.

The flats fishery is prime from March through July, with October and November also good. December through February can be good when the weather is decent, though these are the windier months. The far south location means cloudy cold fronts often stall before reaching the area, but the wind still likes the winter.

The inshore fishery is becoming more popular, and for good reason. Fishing is done around the reefs in water that's one hundred feet deep or less. Sharks, barracuda,

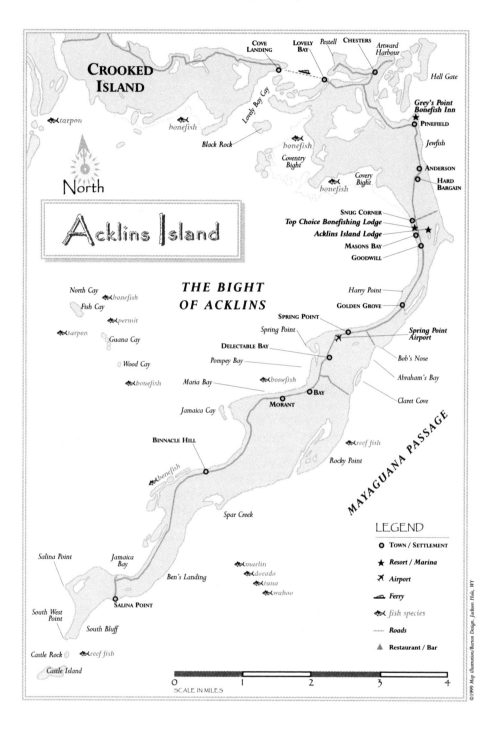

CROOKED ISLAND

Cove Landing
Lovely Bay
Pestell
Chesters
Artward Harbour
Hell Gate
tarpon
Lovely Bay Cay
honefish
Black Rock
Grey's Point Bonefish Inn
Pinefield
Jewfish
Coventry Bight
honefish
Covery Bight
Anderson
Hard Bargain
honefish

North

Acklins Island

Snug Corner
Top Choice Bonefishing Lodge
Acklins Island Lodge
Masons Bay
Goodwill

North Cay
bonefish
Fish Cay
permit
tarpon
Guana Cay
Wood Cay
bonefish

THE BIGHT OF ACKLINS

Harry Point
Golden Grove
Spring Point
Spring Point
Spring Point Airport
Delectable Bay
Pompey Bay
Maria Bay
bonefish
Bob's Nose
Abraham's Bay
Jamaica Cay
Bay
Morant
Claret Cove
Binnacle Hill
reef fish
Rocky Point
bonefish

MAYAGUANA PASSAGE

Spar Creek

Salina Point
Jamaica Bay
Ben's Landing
marlin
dorado
tuna
wahoo
South West Point
Salina Point
South Bluff
Castle Rock
reef fish
Castle Island

LEGEND

⊙ Town / Settlement
★ Resort / Marina
✈ Airport
⛴ Ferry
🐟 fish species
--- Roads
▲ Restaurant / Bar

0   1   2   3   4
SCALE IN MILES

©1999 Map illustration/Burton Design, Jackson Hole, WY

snappers, grouper, jacks, amberjack, and mackerel are the primary species. The reefs are just minutes away from Pittstown and Pinefield points, plus there is tremendous fishing around Windsor Point and Salina Point. The guides out of Pittstown are practiced in using chum (live pilchards are best) to create a feeding frenzy around their boats. If you want to catch a bunch of hard-fighting fish, this is a blast. We recommend using a 10-weight fly rod, with shock tippet matched to the species of fish you're trying to catch (though you can't be sure what you'll hook up at any given time). Sixty-pound mono shock or wire tippet will hold up against most fish. Your fly selection should include White Deceivers, Abel Anchovies, Black Sardinas, Clouser Minnows, and Saltwater Poppers in a variety of colors. The reef fishing is good year round, and if you can take the rolling, fishing is good even in bad weather.

The offshore fishery is equally impressive. Captain Robbie Gibson, out of Pittstown, is fishing areas not touched by any other sportfishing boats. Daily catches of thirty or more fish, including a variety of tuna, dorado, and wahoo approaching world-record size, are common. October through February is the best time for wahoo, king mackerel, and some tuna. April through July are prime for marlin, dorado, and yellowfin, blackfin, and skipjack tuna, with wahoo and mackerel still available. Carter Andrews, the director of fishing at Pittstown, has put together an offshore fly-fishing program to go with the already established flats and reef programs. Offshore flies depend on the species you're after, but essentials include WBA and Bluewater Mullets, Offshore Deceivers, plus Butorac and Bluewater billfish flies.

If you're looking for an incredible variety of fishing in relatively untouched waters, you should consider booking a trip to Crooked and Acklins soon.

OPTIONAL ACTIVITIES

Okay, we'll add diving and snorkeling to our mantra of "fish, drink, eat, sleep, fish, drink, eat, sleep." If you want anything beyond this, aside from lying on a beach reading a book, don't make the trip to Crooked or Acklins. The Acklins residents' saying, "Make your own sunshine" is right on the money.

Pittstown Point Landing offers an excellent diving and snorkeling program that features some of the best wall diving in the Bahamas. Snorkeling and spear fishing are sensational along the northern shore of Crooked, inside the barrier reef.

LODGING AND SERVICES

FEATURED LODGES AND ACCOMMODATIONS

Pittstown Point Landing

Crooked Island The isolated location on the northwestern tip of the island is a blend of natural beauty and convenience to the fishing grounds. The only drawback at the moment is making the run in a flats boat down to French Wells in rough weather. The resort is working on a launch site on the inside of the Bight. When they have this in place, this will be one of the best fishing operations in the Caribbean. The 12 guest rooms are large and bright, with nice furniture and big windows offering views of the Bird Rock Lighthouse. Rooms are nice and cool when the breeze is up. We've been told that air-conditioning will be installed soon. If this is important to you, check on this before you book. Also bring a good supply of insect repellent, which you will definitely need on calmer days. Ozzie's Café serves good Bahamian-style food, and the chef is good at accommodating individual dietary requirements. The beachside Tiki bar is a great spot for an apres-fishing beer or rum drink.

The best guides on the island work here, including Elton "Bone Fish Shakey" McKinney, Randy McKinney, Jeffrey Moss, and Derek Ingraham. These guys all have great attitudes, which makes them lots of fun to fish with. They are continually improving their fly-fishing skills with the help of fishing director, Carter Andrews, who is a longtime fishing guide out of Jackson Hole, Wyoming. Flats fishing is done from a variety of boats including an 18-foot Blue Runner, 17-foot Super Seas, and a 16-foot Maverick, all with 70- to 90-hp outboards to get you where you're going in a hurry.

Captain Robbie Gibson, and Carter Andrews, run the reef and offshore fishing programs. Their 36-foot Luhrs, "Thunderbird," is ideal, with a large fishing area, plenty of shade, an air-conditioned cabin and twin diesels that really move out. Additional reef fishing is done from a 26-foot center-console Boston Whaler.

The dive center runs a top-notch program for scuba and snorkeling enthusiasts. Beach barbecues are a weekly event. The resort can arrange excursions to the caves and to great shelling beaches.

It is convenient to book a charter direct to the Pittstown Point airstrip. The resort offers a first-time flyer's kit with all the necessary charts and information to assist visitors with their own aircraft.

Season: October though July.

Suitable For: Anglers and divers.

What's Included: Saturday-to-Saturday all-inclusive bonefish packages with accommodations, meals, guided fishing, and Bahamian taxes. Packages can include diving, reef, and offshore fishing also. Arrivals and departures can also be on Tuesdays, though there is no guided fishing on Saturdays.

Not Included: Airfare to/from Pittstown Point Airstrip or Colonel Hill, taxi fare from Colonel Hill, optional reef and offshore fishing, alcoholic beverages and optional gratuities.

Pricing: $$

Contact: Reservations and information, 800/752-2322 or 800/922-3474, fax 704/881-0771.

Acklins Island Lodge

Acklins Island   The lodge sits on a high bluff on the narrowest point of the island overlooking the ocean and the Bight. Five air-conditioned double rooms feature tiled floors, twin beds, ceiling fans, satellite TV, and private baths. The rooms are located in three duplexes that connect to the main clubhouse via nicely landscaped pathways. The large clubhouse includes a bar, dining room, and wide decks that provide spectacular views of the water. Good food and friendly service make this an exceptionally nice place to enjoy a week of remote fishing.

Rupert Cox is the head flats fishing guide. His crew is enthusiastic and eager to please. Guests are driven down the hill each morning to the Bight side of the island. Fishing is from Bay Skiffs with 50-hp Honda outboards. Put on your insect repellent before you leave the lodge. The lodge's hilltop location means you don't have much of a bug problem, but that changes quickly down on the shoreline. A 22-foot Glacier Bay catamaran is used for reef and offshore fishing, and to access distant flats in the Bight.

Anglers fly in on Bahamasair or private charter to Spring Point, where they are met and driven north to the lodge, about a 15-minute drive.

Season: October though July.

Suitable For: Anglers only, though accommodations are very nice.

What's Included: Saturday-to-Saturday all-inclusive bonefish packages with airport transfers, accommodations, meals, guided fishing, and Bahamian taxes. Packages can also include reef and offshore fishing. Tuesday arrivals and departures are also possible.

Not Included: Airfare to/from Spring Point, optional reef and offshore fishing, alcoholic beverages and optional gratuities.

Pricing: $$

Contact: Reservations and information, 800/922-3474.

ADDITIONAL ACCOMMODATIONS

Top Choice Bonefishing Lodge

Acklins Island   The lodge is on the bight side of the island just north of the Mason's Bay settlement. Operated by Ethlyn and Felix Bain, the lodge opened in the fall of 1998, and features 4 air-conditioned rooms with private baths, and a bar and restaurant. The lodge works with 3 guides using Carolina and Florida skiffs, and can take six anglers.

Pricing: $$

Contact: Reservations and information, 800/993-5287, fax 810/415-8577.

Grey's Point Inn

Acklins Island   Located nineteen miles north of Spring Point at Pinefield Point, the Inn is booking only 4 anglers per week. Carolina skiffs with 25-hp motors are ideal for getting into very skinny water, but not great for covering any distance, especially in rough water. The eastern flats areas from Pinefield Point to Hell's Gate are the flats fished most often. The Inn's guides can also fish the Bight out of Snug Corner. Excellent reef and blue-water fishing off the east coast is just 15 minutes from the lodge aboard an 18-foot deep-V Blue Runner.

Pricing: $$

Contact: Reservations and information, 242/344-3210.

NEW DEVELOPMENTS

Most of the action is taking place on Acklins, with talk of new bonefishing lodges reaching us weekly. Aside from the great fishing opportunities, the completion of the main road from north to south has made this development practical. The fact that power is now available across both islands hasn't hurt, either. All the new lodges we've heard about feature air-conditioning, which is something that has been missing on this atoll. We consider air-conditioning important due to the bug situation. The mosquito population is higher on these islands than we've seen anywhere else in the Bahamas.

Grey's Point owner, Newton Williamson, told us about the new lodge he's building that will replace the original inn. The new facility will feature eight air-conditioned rooms with a restaurant and bar. This lodge, near Grey's Point, is located on the eastern side of the island, facing the ocean. To fish the Bight, guides will trailer their boats fifteen minutes south to Snug Corner. Williamson plans to open sometime during the fall 1999 and spring 2000 season.

For up-to-date news on new lodge developments here, visit our Web site at www.bahamasflyfishingguide.com.

14

San Salvador, Rum Cay, and Conception Island

October 12, 1492, was the big day. Christopher Columbus made the first landfall in the New World on the island of Guanahani, which he renamed "Holy Savior," or San Salvador. There are four monuments marking the spot where Columbus first came ashore, though it is generally believed that he landed at Long Bay, about three miles south of Cockburn Town. A simple white stone cross, erected in 1956, marks the spot. A little farther south is the gaudy Olympic monument, symbolizing the transfer of the Olympic flame to the New World.

While this is the recognized spot where Columbus first landed, many scholars believe Samana Cay or Grand Turk was really the first landfall. Others have made a case for Fernandez Bay on Cat Island. Whatever the truth may be, this small island, twelve miles long and six miles wide, has earned its share of fame. Located about fifty miles southeast of Cat Island, and 108 miles southeast of Nassau, the island remains as splendid and alluring as the day Columbus arrived.

This natural beauty, and proximity to the shipping corridor through Crooked Island Passage, caused the notorious pirate George Watling to make the island his base. Watling's influence was such that the island was called Watling Island until 1925, when the name was changed back to San Salvador.

The island is also known as the "Island of Lakes," as most of the interior is composed of lakes and creeks. Many forest-covered hills dot the island, with 140-foot Mt. Kerr being the tallest. Coral reefs protect three quarters of the shoreline, which is a combination of pristine beaches and black rock.

The pace of life on the island has changed very little over the centuries. Today, Cockburn Town, on the western shore in the center of the island, is the main settlement, government headquarters, and mail boat dock. The Riding Rock Marina & Inn is located just south of the airport. Diving is the main attraction here, with some of the best reef, wreck, and wall diving in the Bahamas. North of Riding Rock Point is the luxurious Club Med-Columbus Isle, an all-inclusive resort considered to be the most spectacular in the Club Med chain.

The island's population hovers around five hundred, with fishing and tourism the economic mainstays. The remote location means you have to make a special effort to

236

travel here. Why do it? The island is considered the ultimate escape. Relax, dive, snorkel, catch some rays or some fish in an enchanting, historical, tropical paradise.

Rum Cay, about twenty-five miles southwest of San Salvador and twenty miles east of Long Island, is surrounded by coral reefs, white beaches, and forested hills that pop up around the coastline. Salt exports to Nova Scotia kept the islanders in rum until the salt flats were destroyed by two hurricanes in the early 1900s.

Port Nelson is the only settlement on the island, protected by Sumner Point on the southeast side of the island. Coconut groves shade this peaceful spot, inhabited by about fifty full-time residents. The Sumner Point Marina has several slips, fuel, electricity, water, and ice. Boating friends have told us the restaurant and bar are excellent, and the people super-friendly.

The interior of the island features a number of blue holes worth exploring. The easiest ones to reach are to the west of the road from Port Nelson to Liberty Rock and Port Boyd. We understand the road has been repaved, and a new airport is nearing completion.

Conception Island lies ten miles northwest of Rum Cay and fourteen miles northeast of Cape Santa Maria, Long Island. The island is uninhabited and protected by the Bahamas National Trust. This sanctuary is home to thousands of migratory birds and nesting green turtles. The interior of the island is composed of creeks and a huge lagoon that can go mostly dry at low tide. Several diving friends have reported seeing tailing bonefish in the southwestern creek entrance.

Diving, snorkeling, and beachcombing are the draws here, with the dive resorts on Long Island, Cat Island, and San Salvador all offering trips to these awe-inspiring waters.

Bahamasair flies from Nassau to Cockburn Town most days. New direct service on Bahamasair is available from Miami two or three days a week. Air Sunshine flies from Ft. Lauderdale direct to Cockburn Town. Riding Rock Marina & Inn operates charter flights on Saturdays.

AROUND THE ISLANDS

If you visit San Salvador you'll stay at either the Riding Rock Inn or Club Med. In either case you can rent a car or bike and tour the island. Riding Rock Inn is adjacent to the marina and just north of the settlement. Club Med is a couple of minutes north of the airport on a velvety white sand beach. Continuing north you'll pass the Northwest Arm of Great Lake on the way to Graham's Harbour. Columbus described this reef-protected anchorage at the north end of the island as big enough "to hold all the ship in Christendom." It's also a good spot for snorkeling and reef fishing.

The road turns south near Reckley Hill. The Dixon Hill Lighthouse is a mile farther on, about half way down East Beach which is protected by a continuous reef and ideal for swimming and snorkeling. The road cuts inland at Storr's Lake. Crab Cay , which you can only reach by hiking, is the site of the *Chicago Herald*'s monument to Columbus.

The road skirts across a narrow piece of land between Storr's Lake and Granny Lake before emerging along Snow Bay, only to cut inland again at the north end of Pigeon Creek. The creek is good bonefish habitat, and fishing is especially good near the mouth of the creek during the last of the falling and first of the incoming tide.

French Bay, at the southern end of the island, is a nice anchorage and a good spot for reef fishing and snorkeling. The road rounds Sandy Point and then turns north again, traversing three miles of inviting beaches that include Long Bay and Fernandez Bay before ending up back in Cockburn Town.

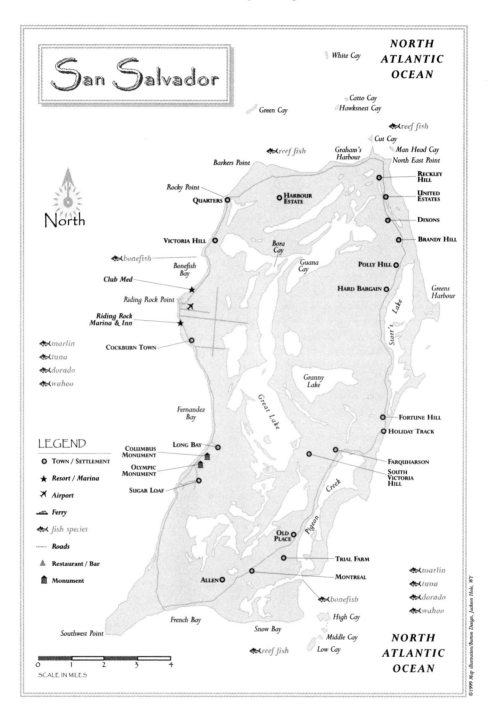

San Salvador

NORTH
ATLANTIC
OCEAN

White Cay

Catto Cay
Hawksnest Cay

Green Cay

reef fish

Cut Cay

reef fish

Graham's
Harbour

Man Head Cay
North East Point

Barkers Point

RECKLEY
HILL

Rocky Point

HARBOUR
ESTATE

UNITED
ESTATES

North

QUARTERS

DIXONS

VICTORIA HILL

Bora
Cay

BRANDY HILL

bonefish

Guana
Cay

POLLY HILL

Bonefish
Bay

Club Med

HARD BARGAIN

Greens
Harbour

Riding Rock Point

Storr's Lake

Riding Rock
Marina & Inn

marlin
tuna
dorado
wahoo

COCKBURN TOWN

Granny
Lake

Fernandez
Bay

Great Lake

FORTUNE HILL
HOLIDAY TRACK

LEGEND

COLUMBUS
MONUMENT

LONG BAY

○ TOWN / SETTLEMENT

OLYMPIC
MONUMENT

FARQUHARSON
SOUTH
VICTORIA
HILL

★ Resort / Marina

SUGAR LOAF

Creek

✈ Airport

Pigeon

Ferry

fish species

OLD
PLACE

Roads

TRIAL FARM

Restaurant / Bar

MONTREAL

Monument

ALLEN ○

bonefish

marlin
tuna
dorado
wahoo

High Cay

French Bay

Snow Bay

Middle Cay

Southwest Point

reef fish

Low Cay

NORTH
ATLANTIC
OCEAN

0   1   2   3   4
SCALE IN MILES

© 1999 Map illustration/Burton Design, Jackson Hole, WY

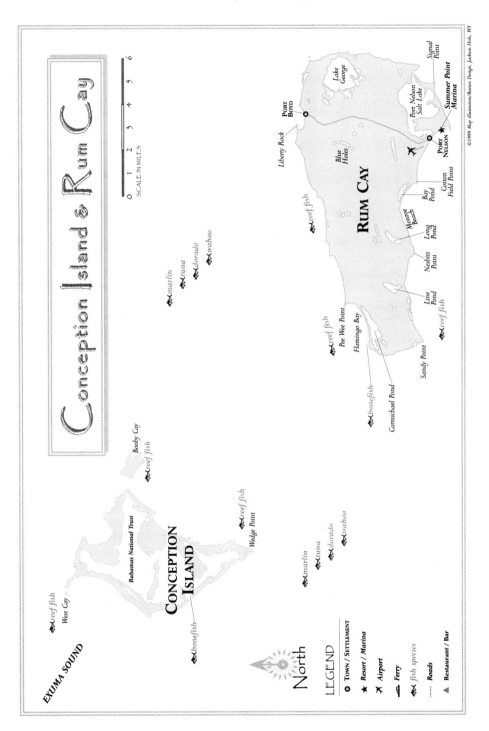

Conception Island & Rum Cay

SCALE IN MILES
0 1 2 3 4 5 6

©1999 Map Illustration/Burton Design, Jackson Hole, WY

EXUMA SOUND

West Cay
reef fish

Bahamas National Trust

CONCEPTION ISLAND

bonefish

Booby Cay
reef fish

Wedge Point
reef fish

marlin
tuna
dorado
wahoo

North

LEGEND
○ TOWN / SETTLEMENT
★ Resort / Marina
✈ Airport
⚓ Ferry
🐟 fish species
----- Roads
▲ Restaurant / Bar

Liberty Rock
reef fish

Port Boyd

Lake George

Port Nelson Salt Lake

Signal Point

Summer Point Marina

Blue Holes

RUM CAY

Port Nelson

Cotton Field Point

Bay Pond

Monroe Beach

Long Pond

Nesbitt Point

Line Pond
reef fish

Pee Wee Point
reef fish

Flamingo Bay

bonefish

Carmichael Pond

Sandy Point

marlin
tuna
dorado
wahoo

Brian O'Keefe

Bonefish in the turtle grass, near Pigeon Creek, San Salvador.

A leisurely drive around the island will take a few hours, or you can make a day outing of it. In either case, take a picnic basket and a cooler with ice and drinks.

On Rum Cay you can drive or bicycle from Port Nelson to Port Boyd and Liberty Rock, though the best exploring on this little isle is done on foot or in a small boat along the shoreline. There is good reef fishing all around the island, and a number of small flats and creeks for bonefishing. Flamingo Bay on the northwest corner of the island offers good snorkeling, sunning, and fishing in a gorgeous, isolated setting.

Conception Island has no roads. You can come ashore from small boats to do some bird watching, or to take photographs, but remember that the island is protected by the Bahamas National Trust. There is no "taking" of anything. Just look and enjoy.

FISHING HIGHLIGHTS

Offshore and reef fishing opportunities are the stars of this region, though some flats fishing for bonefish is easy to access on your own. Offshore and reef charters are available through the Riding Rock Marina on San Salvador. Charter boats from Long Island and Cat Island also fish these waters.

Wahoo are prime in January and February. Tuna, dorado, and billfish become plentiful in April and May, with excellent fishing continuing into the summer.

Reef fishing is very good year round. Water depths of twenty to eighty feet are most productive. If you use chum you'll create a boiling feeding frenzy in most areas. Toss out any sort of Clouser Minnow or Deceiver and you'll get a strike from a jack, snapper, cuda, or shark. If you want to hook up with some amberjack, fish over some of the wrecks.

You can catch bonefish on wadable flats on San Salvador just north of Club Med, and at various other spots around the island, but the Pigeon Creek area is best. Easy access is available from the main road, though you'll have to do some walking to reach the best flats at the mouth of the creek. Plan your day to fish the first of the incoming tide for the best action for tailing fish. A Gotcha or Yarn Crab will take fish consistently, but almost any bonefish fly will work, as these bones rarely have to deal with fly fishers.

We've always wanted to explore the inland lakes on San Salvador but have never had the time. We'd bet good money on these lakes holding of tarpon, cubera snapper, and jacks. The same should be true for the blue holes on Rum Cay. Someone should give it a try.

OPTIONAL ACTIVITIES

Diving, snorkeling, sailing, biking, hiking, and letting the tension drain from stress-taut muscles are the main activities. The only real vacationing option is San Salvador, unless you're cruising in your own boat, though overnight trips to Conception Island are available through Stella Maris out of Long Island. If you need things to do, stay at Club Med. The staff there has enough energy, and enough toys, to keep most people entertained twenty-four hours a day.

The diving programs out of Club Med and Riding Rock Marina are world class. Resort and certification courses are available, along with courses in underwater photography. Both facilities provide gear rentals. The Club Med facilities include a decompression chamber.

LODGING AND SERVICES

FEATURED LODGES AND ACCOMMODATIONS

Club Med

San Salvador   Friends tell us this is the most luxurious of the Club Med resorts. We haven't been to enough Club Meds to make a comparison, but this place is definitely luxurious, and located on one of the most gorgeous beaches anywhere. The 260 rooms are large and elegant, with furniture and decorations brought in from around the world. Additional room amenities include satellite TV, telephones, walk-in closets, and spacious bathrooms.

This location caters to affluent couples, and though the staff is always pushing activities, the overall feeling is pretty laid-back. Resort amenities include a complete dive center, 9 tennis courts, swimming pool, exercise room, bicycles, sailing, windsurfing, massages, beauty salon, and 3 restaurants. Car rentals are available. You can walk to some good bonefishing flats to the northeast.

Season: October through July.

Suitable For: Anglers and nonanglers.

What's Included: All-inclusive packages are the Club Med way, though they do tack on some extras here and there.

Not Included: Airfare to/from Cockburn Town, taxi transfers, optional reef and offshore fishing.

Pricing: $$$

Contact: Reservations and information, 800/258-2633 or 242/331-2000, fax 242/331-2222.

Riding Rock Marina & Inn

San Salvador   People primarily travel here to dive, though offshore and reef fishing are also specialties. Forty air-conditioned motel-style rooms face either the swimming pool or the ocean. Two villas are also available for rent. We suggest the deluxe rooms facing the ocean. Amenities include telephones, satellite TV, an okay tennis court, and a good restaurant/bar. A meal plan is available. Guanahani Dive Limited runs the diving program. Car and bicycle rentals are available. The expanded marina offers 7 slips plus fuel, electricity, water, ice, and laundromat.

Season: October through July.

Suitable For: Anglers and divers.

What's Included: Dive packages including accommodations and meals are available. Complimentary airport transfers.

Not Included: Airfare to/from Cockburn Town, optional reef and offshore fishing, alcoholic beverages, and optional gratuities.

Pricing: $$

Contact: Reservations and information, 800/272-1492 or 954/359-8353, fax 954/359-8254.

NEW DEVELOPMENTS

None that we know of. Log on to our Web site at www.bahamasflyfishingguide.com for up-to-date information.

15

Mayaguana, Great Inagua, Little Inagua, and Ragged Islands

O f all the Out Islands, these are the most *out,* as well as the least developed and visited. Located 350 miles southeast of Nassau, and fifty miles across the Mayaguana Passage from Acklins Island, Mayaguana is the eastern-most Bahamian island. Twenty-four miles long and as much as six miles wide, the island features forests of lignum vitae and other hardwoods, ideal soil for farming, plus miles of stunning beaches and rich coral reefs.

Mayaguana, which is the original native name, was uninhabited until 1812, when people from the nearby Turks Islands began to settle here. The main settlements and best anchorages are at Abraham's Bay, Betsy Bay, and Pirates Well. These settlements, which retain an authentic Bahamian appearance and mood, just received electricity and telephone services in 1997 and 1998. The population of around three hundred makes their living by farming and fishing. The weekly mail boat visits always create a stir among the locals, as do visits by boaters. The friendly people often greet visitors coming ashore with hugs, and offers of food and drink.

Deep blue water surrounds most of the island, creating a phenomenal fishery for both commercial and sportfishing interests. Conch is abundant on the flats, and in other shallow-water areas. If you want to learn about the pirate days, many of the locals can tell you stories of battles between the buccaneers and treasure-laden Spanish galleons.

Mayaguana's airstrip is the residual of a U.S. missile tracking station used in the early days of space exploration. Bahamasair flies in a couple of times a week, while private aircraft use the strip on a daily basis. Some of the base buildings have been renovated for storage use by ERGB, the acronym for Environmental Research Group Bahamas, Ltd. This company has built a Euro-style villa north of Abraham's Bay and has plans for a sixty-room luxury hotel.

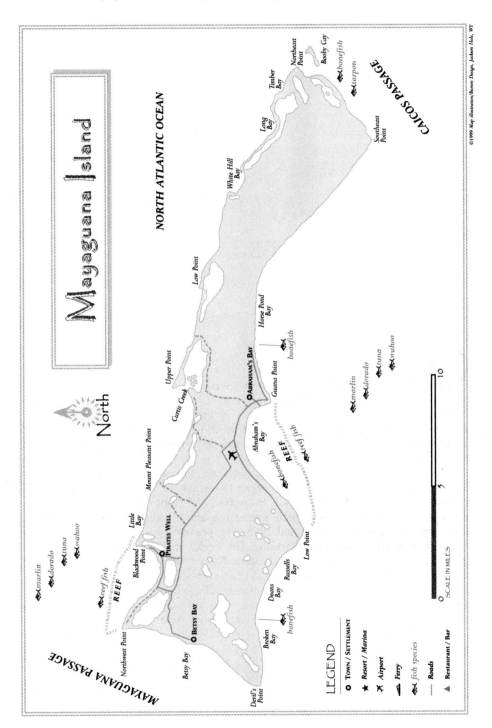

Mayaguana Island

NORTH ATLANTIC OCEAN

North

CAICOS PASSAGE

MAYAGUANA PASSAGE

Northeast Point

Booby Cay

bonefish

tarpon

Southeast Point

Timber Bay

Long Bay

White Hill Bay

Low Point

Horse Pond Bay

bonefish

tuna

wahoo

dorado

marlin

Upper Point

Curtis Creek

ABRAHAM'S BAY

Guana Point

Abraham's Bay

REEF

reef fish

bonefish

Mount Pleasant Point

Little Bay

PIRATES WELL

Blackwood Point

REEF

reef fish

wahoo

tuna

dorado

marlin

Northwest Point

BETSY BAY

Betsy Bay

Deans Bay

Broken Bay

bonefish

Russells Bay

Low Point

Devil's Point

LEGEND

○ TOWN / SETTLEMENT

★ Resort / Marina

✈ Airport

⚓ Ferry

fish species

Roads

▲ Restaurant / Bar

SCALE IN MILES

0 5 10

© 1999 Map Illustration/Burton Design, Jackson Hole, WY

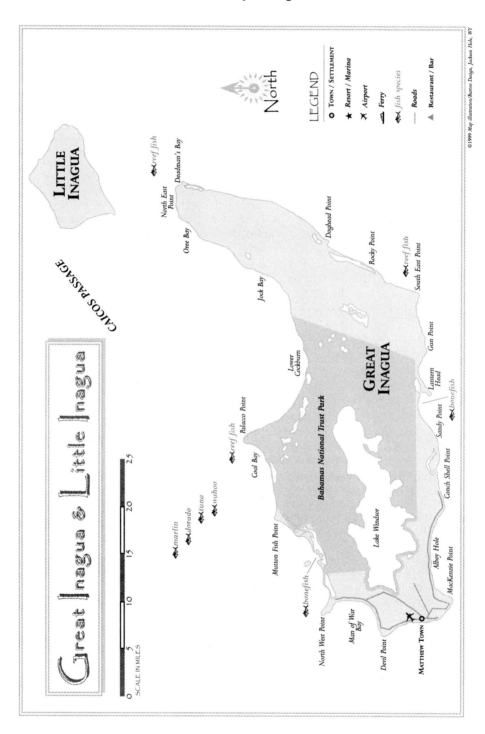

Great Inagua & Little Inagua

LITTLE INAGUA

CAICOS PASSAGE

SCALE IN MILES
0   5   10   15   20   25

Deadman's Bay
cref fish
North East Point
Oree Bay
Doghead Point
Jock Bay
Rocky Point
cref fish
South East Point
Lower Cockburn
Gun Point
GREAT INAGUA
Lantern Head
Bahamas National Trust Park
bonefish
Sandy Point
Palacco Point
cref fish
Coal Bay
Conch Shell Point
Lake Windsor
martin
dorado
tuna
wahoo
Mutton Fish Point
bonefish
Alboy Hole
MacKenzie Point
North West Point
Man of War Bay
Devil Point
MATTHEW TOWN

North

LEGEND
○ TOWN / SETTLEMENT
★ Resort / Marina
✈ Airport
⚓ Ferry
🐟 fish species
— Roads
▲ Restaurant / Bar

©1999 Map illustration/Burton Design, Jackson Hole, WY

Activities at any resort on this island would include excellent diving, snorkeling, and shelling, plus superb untouched reef and offshore fishing. There are some good bonefishing flats along the southern shoreline and off the eastern end of the island. The eastern flats also hold good numbers of tarpon and permit.

Great Inagua is eighty to eighty-five miles south of Acklins and Mayaguana, and fifty miles east of Cuba. At forty-five miles long and twenty-five miles wide, it is the third-largest Bahamian island. Inagua is an anagram for the iguana, a common island resident. Together with uninhabited Little Inagua, the islands are simply referred to as the Inaguas.

The lure here is the Bahamas National Trust Park and wildlife sanctuary, administered by the Bahamas National Trust. The 287-acre park, which includes Lake Windsor, is home to the world's largest population of West Indian flamingos. These birds number close to sixty thousand now, after having approached extinction. Other birds include the endangered Bahama parrot and white-crowned pigeon, plus thousands of egrets, herons, cormorants, owls, pelicans, hummingbirds, and ducks. There are also populations of wild boar and wild donkeys.

Most of the coastline is sheltered by reefs that make life difficult for boaters, while creating sensational dive sites. We've heard rumors that Great Inagua Tours may open a diving operation, but for now tourism doesn't contribute much to the local economy. There are no reef or offshore sportfishing operations that we know of, though Great Inagua Tours arranges for snook and tarpon fishing in the inland lakes. There are also several bonefish flats around the island that anglers can fish on their own, and we have talked with commercial fishermen who tell us there are good numbers of tarpon around Lantern Head.

Salt is the commodity on Inagua, with a high percentage of the island's thousand residents working for the Morton Salt Company. The main settlement is Matthew Town, on the southwestern coast. The town is made up of a few restaurants, motels, and grocery and liquor stores, along with the usual array of varied residential dwellings. Services include a post office, customs office, commissioner's office, bank, and clinic. The mail boat arrives at the government wharf once a week. There are no good services or anchorages for boaters. The airport, serviced three times a week by Bahamasair, is a mile north of town.

The Morton Salt Company produces about a million pounds of salt a year at this location, and more when worldwide demand increases. Inagua's environment is ideal for salt production. The weather is unusually hot and dry, the terrain harsh and for the most part flat. There are more cacti on Inagua than anywhere else in the Bahamas, basically because the salt-soaked soil makes it impossible for other plants to survive. The most striking features of the island are the miles of crusty salt beds and sparkling white mountains of brine you can't miss when flying into the airport.

Little Inagua is five miles to the north off the eastern tip of Great Inagua. It covers thirty square miles and is uninhabited except for herds of wild donkeys and goats, and a variety of bird life, including a rare species of heron.

The Ragged Island chain extends for ninety miles from Ragged Island in the south to the Jumentos Cays in the north. These islands form the southeastern end of the Great Bahama Bank, with most of the islands and cays being uninhabited.

It's only about twenty miles from the Jumentos Cays to Little Exuma, and to Sandy Cay on Long Island, yet this is another universe. Rough windy weather is common in the winter, though during spring and summer calm seas create ideal conditions for boating, fishing, and diving. Excellent reef and offshore fishing is available along the entire chain, while there are flats interspersed throughout many of the smaller cays.

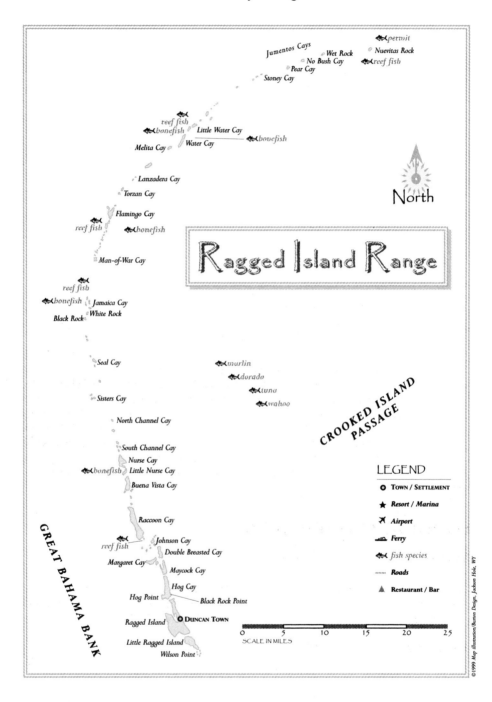

The flats at Water Cays can offer surprisingly good bonefishing.

Ragged Island is about four miles long and not very wide. Duncan Town is the only settlement. Less than one hundred residents try to make a living from fishing and some farming. We've heard, however, that improvements are in the works. A new police station is being built and the town is hooked up with electricity and telephones. A grocery store has decent provisions, and there are a couple of places to eat, drink, and shoot pool. Bahamasair usually services the Duncan Town airstrip twice a week.

To the north, Ragged Island Harbour is located between Duncan Town and Hog Cay. The mail boat calls here weekly, and some services are available to boaters, but don't count on anything in particular. The harbor authorities monitor VHF channel 16.

Continuing north, boaters will have good fishing off the reefs and in a number of cuts. You'll see more flats starting around Jamaica Cay. Flamingo Cay is relatively high and covered with vegetation. A boating acquaintance told us about beautiful beaches here, and some good fishing for bonefish, and for jacks off the reef. The same person told us about even better bonefishing around the Water Cays and Stony Cay. We've heard rumors that a group of adventurous anglers are thinking of opening a bonefish lodge somewhere in the chain.

LODGING AND SERVICES

Mayaguana

Even though telephone service is theoretically available, not many residents have it. VHF channel 16 is used by most people for day-to-day communications, which means you'll have to get within 50 miles or so of the island to see what's going on.

Mayaguana Inn Guest House

Abraham's Bay   Comfortable rooms and good meals.
Pricing: $
Contact: Reservations and information, 242/339-3065.

Camelot House

Abraham's Bay   Comfortable rooms and good meals.
Pricing: $
Contact: VHF channel 16.

There are several other guesthouses that are just rooms in people's houses. Restaurants are the same, with food often cooked in someone's home kitchen. People here consider this "the way it is," and they're happy to have you for a meal or a drink.

There is also a police station, commissioner's office, and telephone station, plus two small grocery stores that carry some provisions.

GREAT INAGUA

Matthew Town

This is the only settlement on the island. The commissioner's office and police and telephone stations are located here, along with a station for the Bahamas Defense Force. The U.S. Coast Guard keeps a helicopter at the airstrip to monitor potential drug traffic.

Crystal Beach View Hotel

This is the largest hotel in the settlement. Rooms are okay, and some have air-conditioning. You can watch satellite TV in the lobby, and the restaurant serves breakfast, lunch, and dinner.
Pricing: $
Contact: Reservations and information, 242/339-1550, fax 242/339-1660.

Main House

Operated by the Morton Salt Company, the 5 rooms are large, clean, and air-conditioned. There are telephones in the rooms, and satellite TV. Take some ear plugs as the hotel is right across from the settlement power plant.
Pricing: $
Contact: Reservations and information, 242/339-1267, fax 242/339-1265.

Walkine's Guest House

Five comfortable rooms with air-conditioning, 2 rooms share a bath, 3 have private baths. Meals are served in nearby Topps Restaurant.
Pricing: $
Contact: Reservations and information, 242/339-1612.

Great Inagua Tours

Run by Larry and Marianne Ingraham, this operation does it all in terms of tours, sightseeing, and island information for tourists. Rental houses are also available. The Ingraham's specialty is ecotourism based on bird watching and wildlife viewing. The company rents cars, bikes, and Larry arranges bonefish, tarpon, and snook fishing trips.
Contact: Reservations and information, 242/339-1862, fax 242/339-1204.

Flamingo and turtle tours (in the Union Creek Turtle Reserve) can also be arranged in advance with the Bahamas National Trust in Nassau, or by calling warden Henry Nixon at 242/339-1616.

NEW DEVELOPMENTS

We've heard most about potential fishing and tourism-related development on Mayaguana and Ragged Island, though we have no idea when anything might really happen. Our bet is that the fishing off Mayaguana is too good to remain untapped for long. Visit our Web site at www.bahamasflyfishingguide.com for up-to-date information.